Environment and Employment: A Reconciliation

Mounting evidence suggests that GDP growth is damaging the natural environment and unlikely to be ecologically sustainable in the long run. At the same time, an annual GDP growth rate of around 3 per cent is regarded as the minimum necessary to prevent unemployment from escalating. Clearly, a trade-off exists between environmental goals and employment goals, yet this trade-off has been largely ignored or denied.

This book aims to resolve the environment–employment dilemma by suggesting ways and means to achieve low rates of unemployment, or preferably full employment, in the context of a low-growth or steady-state economy. In search of a solution to this dilemma, this book seeks to answer the following questions:

- What existing paradigms offer a possible foundation for further investigation into issues dealing with both the environment and employment?
- What specific initiatives can be implemented to deal with unemployment given that any potential solution must be consistent with responsible macroeconomic policy?
- To what extent can ecological tax reform provide a solution to the environment–employment dilemma?
- Under what circumstances is it clear that certain forms of employment generation are antithetic to the goal of ecological sustainability?
- How can more favourable employment-generating opportunities be exploited in ways that lower unemployment or achieve full employment without the need for ecologically destructive GDP growth?

This book will no doubt stimulate a broader discussion on the issue, and it may just begin a process that leads to the eventual emergence of a viable policy strategy to generate a sustainable, full-employment future. This book will be of interest to decision-makers, civil servants, researchers, and NGO employees as well as students of environmental and ecological economics and issues related to employment and unemployment.

Philip Lawn is a Senior Lecturer in ecological economics at Flinders University, Australia. His work includes six books, numerous book chapters, and nearly 50 journal articles. His more recent book, co-edited with Matthew Clarke, focuses on sustainable welfare in the Asia-Pacific region.

Routledge Studies in Ecological Economics

Sustainability Networks
Cognitive tools for expert collaboration in social-ecological systems
Janne Hukkinen

Drivers of Environmental Change in Uplands
Aletta Bonn, Tim Allot, Klaus Hubaceck and Jon Stewart

Resilience, Reciprocity and Ecological Economics
Northwest coast sustainability
Ronald L. Trosper

Environment and Employment
A reconciliation
Philip Lawn

Environment and Employment:
A Reconciliation

Edited by

Philip Lawn

Routledge
Taylor & Francis Group

LONDON AND NEW YORK

First published 2009
by Routledge
2 Park Square, Milton Park, Abingdon, Oxon, OX14 4RN

Simultaneously published in the USA and Canada
by Routledge
270 Madison Avenue, New York, NY 10016

Routledge is an imprint of the Taylor & Francis Group, an informa business

Typeset in Times New Roman by Prepress Projects Ltd, Perth, UK
Printed and bound in Great Britain by TJI Digital, Padstow, Cornwall

British Library Cataloguing in Publication Data
A catalogue record for this book is available from the British Library

Library of Congress Cataloging in Publication Data
Environment and employment: a reconciliation/[edited by] Philip Lawn.
p. cm.
1. Environmental economics. 2. Gross domestic product. I. Lawn, Philip A.
HC79.E5E5685 2009
331.1—dc22
2008044654

ISBN10: 0-415-44879-4 (hbk)
ISBN10: 0-203-87919-8 (ebk)

ISBN13: 978-0-415-44879-6 (hbk)
ISBN13: 978-0-203-87919-1 (ebk)

Contents

PART II

Post-Keynesian economics and the environment 95

PART III

Guaranteed employment versus guaranteed income 161

Figures

Tables

Contributors

Paul Christensen, Department of Economics, Hofstra University, New York, USA.

Nancy Golubiewski, New Zealand Centre for Ecological Economics, Massey University, Palmerston North, New Zealand.

Friedrich Hinterberger, Sustainable Europe Research Institute, Vienna, Austria.

Richard Holt, Economics Department, Southern Oregon University, Oregon, USA.

Nigel Jollands, International Energy Agency, Paris, France.

Philip Lawn, Faculty of Social Sciences, Flinders University, Adelaide, Australia.

Michael A. Lewis, School of Social Welfare at Stony Brook, State University of New York, USA.

Garry McDonald, Market Economics Ltd, Takapuna, New Zealand.

Antonio Manresa, Department of Economic Theory, University of Barcelona, Spain.

Andrew Mearman, University of the West of England, Bristol, UK.

William Mitchell, Centre of Full Employment and Equity, University of Newcastle, Australia.

Ines Omann, University of Graz and Sustainable Europe Research Institute, Graz, Austria.

Gideon Rosenbluth, University of British Columbia, Vancouver, Canada.

Ferran Sancho, Department of Economics, Universitat Autonoma de Barcelona, Barcelona, Spain.

Andrea Stocker, University of Graz and Sustainable Europe Research Institute, Graz, Austria.

Pavlina R. Tcherneva, Levy Economics Institute, Bard College, New York, USA.

Peter Victor, Faculty of Environmental Sciences, York University, Toronto, Canada.

Martin Watts, Centre of Full Employment and Equity, University of Newcastle, Australia.

Karl Widerquist, Lecturer in Politics, University of Reading, UK.

Acknowledgments

I would like to acknowledge the support of Flinders University and the cooperation and assistance of the contributors; in particular, the willingness of contributors to meet deadlines and respond quickly and diligently to feedback. Thanks should also be extended to Robert Langham (Routledge) for being so patient during the extended time it took me to prepare the manuscript.

The editor and publisher would like to thank the copyright holders who have kindly given their permission to use variations of the following copyright material:

Chapter 4: This chapter is a slight variation of Christensen, P. (2005), 'Recovering and extending classical and Marshallian foundations for Post-Keynesian environmental economics', *International Journal of Environment, Workplace and Employment*, 1 (2), 155–173 (Inderscience Publishers).

Chapter 12: This chapter is a slight variation of Hinterberger, F., Omann, I. and Stocker, A. (2002), 'Employment and environment in a sustainable Europe', *Empirica*, 29, 113–130 (Springer).

Chapter 13: This chapter is a slight variation of Victor, P. and Rosenbluth, G. (2007), 'Managing without growth', *Ecological Economics*, 61 (2/3), 492–504 (Elsevier Limited).

Part I

An introduction to environment and employment

1 Why focus on the connection between the environment and employment?

Philip Lawn

Introduction

The growth of real Gross Domestic Product (GDP) is a policy goal pursued by almost every national government.[1] In view of rising environmental concerns, most national governments have begun to focus on how a range of economic and social goals can be realised without undermining the ecosphere's capacity to sustain the economic activity that is central to their achievement – a condition often referred to as 'sustainable development'. Because the growth of real GDP remains a prime policy objective, it is abundantly clear that two presumptions are being made with respect to sustainable development: (a) the accomplishment of most economic and social goals requires the continued growth of real GDP; and (b) the continued growth of real GDP need not threaten the capacity of the natural environment to sustain the higher output levels deemed necessary to achieve most economic and social goals.

In direct contrast to this position, there are a number of commentators who, because of alleged biophysical limits to growth, take particular umbrage with presumption (b). They have consequently urged for the growth of economic systems to be curtailed to satisfy the condition of ecological sustainability (Georgescu-Roegen, 1971; Meadows *et al.*, 1972; Ehrlich *et al.*, 1980; Goodland and Ledec, 1987; Ehrlich and Ehrlich, 1990; Daly, 1991, 1996, 2008; Gowdy, 1994; Lawn, 2000, 2007; Lawn and Clarke, 2008). Indeed, some of these commentators have argued that all but impoverished nations should immediately commence a rapid transition towards a steady-state economy (Daly, 1991; Lawn and Clarke, 2008).[2] A relatively new group of economists – labelled 'ecological economists' – also hold this view but believe there is a more pressing reason why nations should make this transition.[3] They argue that growth becomes economically undesirable well before it becomes ecologically unsustainable.[4] Given this, they insist that achieving sustainable development will require economic systems to be stabilised at a physical scale much smaller than their maximum sustainable scale (Max-Neef, 1995; Daly, 1996; Lawn, 2007). Ecological economists have therefore called for an immediate cessation to the high-growth policies being widely adopted by the governments of industrialised nations.

There is little doubt that if the approach being advocated by ecological econo-mists were adopted it would severely limit any immediate rises in the real GDP of wealthy nations and eventually preclude the growth of real GDP altogether. In the process, it would also lead to the emergence of a major policy dilemma. It is widely recognised that unemployment is an instrumental factor behind many social maladies and the rise in income disparities within nations (Theodossiou, 1998; Harding and Richardson, 1998; Burgess and Mitchell, 1999). Given the existing institutional arrangements in most countries and projected increases in population, a growth rate of around 2 to 3 per cent is generally regarded as the minimum required to prevent unemployment from escalating. With this in mind, the following question arises: how can low rates of unemployment, or preferably full employment, be achieved in a low-growth or steady-state economy? Ecologi-cal economists have been largely silent on this issue. Their failure to adequately respond to this question has significantly harmed their cause. But ecological economists are not alone in their failure to deal with the environment–employ-ment dilemma. Whereas many ecological economists are guilty of ignoring the employment implications of their environmental position on growth, economists of other persuasions, as Part II of this book will testify, have paid little attention to the environmental implications of GDP growth. Worse still, many economists (and non-economists) have failed to deal appropriately with both environmental and employment concerns.

This book attempts to deal with the many issues that arise when seeking an answer to the above question. Although few of the chapters deal with this ques-tion directly, they all provide valuable insight into one of more of the following issues that must be considered when reconciling any potential conflict between environmental and employment goals. They include:

- What existing paradigms offer a possible foundation or worthy starting points for further investigation into issues dealing with both the environment and employment?
- Within the context of a sustainable economy, what specific initiatives can be implemented to deal with unemployment given that any potential solution must be consistent with macroeconomic realities and responsible macroeconomic policy?
- To what extent can ecological tax reform (ETR) – a recently conceived policy initiative involving tax impositions on resource depletion/pollution and tax cuts on labour/income – provide a solution to the environment–employment dilemma?
- Under what circumstances is it clear that certain forms of employment generation are antithetic to the goal of ecological sustainability?
- How can more favourable employment-generating opportunities be exploited in ways that lower unemployment or achieve full employment without the need for ecologically destructive GDP growth?

Of course, for this book to have any contributive value, it needs to be established that a potential conflict exists between the goals of ecological sustainability and full employment. In addition, it must be shown that unemployment is a social scourge of such proportions that its continuance cannot be morally justified – thereby rendering the full employment objective a moral imperative. Much of the remainder of this chapter is devoted to the second of these requirements. The first requirement is dealt with in Chapter 2.

For two main reasons, it was felt that an entire chapter (Chapter 2) should be devoted to demonstrating why there is a potential conflict between the goals of ecological sustainability and full employment. Firstly, many commentators do not believe that any such conflict exists because: (a) they regard the continuous expansion of economic systems as both desirable and ecologically unsustainable; or (b) where ecological limits are recognised, they overestimate the capacity of a sustainable economy to generate sufficient jobs to achieve full employment. With respect to (b), many observers overlook the physical basis of many employment-creating forms of economic activity – a fact not only revealed in Chapter 2, but also empirically supported by Jollands *et al.* in Chapter 11. By doing so, these observers overestimate the extent to which employment levels can be increased simply by altering the mix of jobs within a sustainable economy (e.g., by transferring labour from manufacturing to service-sector jobs).

Secondly, demonstrating the economic undesirability of, and ecological limits to, the continuous physical expansion of economic systems demands a detailed explanation of relevant theoretical principles and supporting empirical evidence. May I say that the need to elucidate the 'limits to growth' position does not arise because of past failures on the part of the scientific community to adequately explain this position. Many before me have successfully demonstrated the vacuity of the 'sustainable growth' position even if they have been less effective in transfusing this knowledge and understanding to the general public. However, given the mainstream position on growth – i.e., that continuous growth is ecologically sustainable – the 'limits to growth' position warrants reiteration which, to do adequately, requires a thorough debunking of many pro-growth arguments.

Coverage of the book

In order to demonstrate why there is a potential conflict between the goals of ecological sustainability and full employment, Chapter 2 begins with a brief overview of three alternative views of the relationship between economy, society, and the natural environment. From this, a coevolutionary world-view is adopted to show that the throughput of matter–energy needed to fuel the economic process must increase over time should a nation continue to grow its economy. With this in mind, six sustainability precepts are established as a means of demonstrating that an ever-increasing rate of throughput and, therefore, a continuously expanding economy, is ecologically unsustainable. Also explained is how the growth of an economic system will eventually become 'uneconomic' and that a so-called economic limit to growth is likely to precede the ecological limit.

Evidence is then provided to show that most wealthy nations have surpassed their economic limit to growth and that the economies of most of the world's nations have grown beyond their biophysical carrying capacity. The evidence is subsequently used to indicate that the majority of the world's nations, should they aspire to achieve sustainable development, are already severely constrained in their capacity to increase real output levels to lower unemployment, let alone to attain full employment.

Following a thorough debunking of three major pro-growth arguments designed to subvert the limits to growth position, Chapter 2 continues by demonstrating that the world's richest countries appear to be engaged in an undesirable trade-off between employment and environmental goals with the countries impacting least on the ecosphere paying a significant price in terms of a high unemployment rate. It is because of this trade-off that it is suggested that the attainment of the twin goals of ecological sustainability and full employment will require much more than an increase in efficiency and a transfer of employment from the dirty sectors to the green sectors of the economy.

As for the remainder of the book, Part II includes three chapters on how Post-Keynesian economics has previously dealt with environmental considerations and what it potentially offers as the basis for future examination of the environment–employment dilemma. Post-Keynesian economics constitutes a useful starting point given that it is a school of thought that has focused a great deal of its attention on the causes of unemployment. As such, it has already established much of the foundation required to deal with one half of the environment–employment dilemma.

In the first of these three chapters, Chapter 3, Mearman goes straight to the heart of the issue by drawing upon data obtained from a questionnaire distributed to a number of leading Post-Keynesian researchers and eminent Post-Keynesian sympathisers. Also utilised by Mearman is data gathered from interviews with two renowned Post-Keynesian economists and an audit of prominent Post-Keynesian and heterodox journals. The central aim of the interviews and questionnaire was to determine: (a) whether the leaders in the field believe that Post-Keynesian economists have neglected environmental concerns; (b) if so, why this is the case; and (c) how Post-Keynesian economists might, in future, make a greater contribution to the resolution of environmental problems. The audit of the relevant journals was conducted to ascertain the extent to which Post-Keynesians have been publishing articles on environmental matters over the 1999–2007 period.

As expected by Mearman, the data reveals that Post-Keynesians have had relatively little to say about the environment – a consequence of Post-Keynesians exhausting most of their time attacking the prevailing economic orthodoxy on major macroeconomic policy issues, such as unemployment and growing income disparities. Mearman stresses the need for Post-Keynesians to embrace environmental concerns if only because the success of any form of economic analysis requires ecological factors to be incorporated into the economic model being employed. However, Mearman believes that the pluralism which characterises Post-Keynesianism places it in an ideal position to incorporate complexity theory, notions of 'open systems', and the more holistic approaches being adopted by ecological economists. Indeed, Mearman believes that progress in these areas could well emerge from within the school of Post-Keynesian economics itself. Thus, rather than acting as a hindrance, Post-Keynesianism could well serve as an effective catalyst for future investigation into the environment–employment dilemma.

In Chapter 4, Christensen reveals some of the reasons why Post-Keynesians have paid insufficient attention to the environment. Echoing some of the conclusions made by Mearman, Christensen points to the Post-Keynesian preoccupation with demand-side problems, which has led many Post-Keynesians to assume that the growth of real GDP is both automatically desirable and ecologically sustainable. As a means of demonstration, Christensen explains how production theories used by Post-Keynesians to identify the major causes of unemployment invariably ignore the physical basis of economic activity as well as the interdependencies that exist between the environment and economy.

Nevertheless, when Christensen asks if this oversight is fatal for Post-Keynesian economics, he answers in the negative – largely because the methodological approaches required to tackle environmental concerns already constitute an important part of the Post-Keynesian expertise. But Christensen qualifies his assertion by pointing out that this Post-Keynesian expertise must be extended to include ecological thinking. According to Christensen, this can best be achieved by drawing upon the classical economic tradition and by exploring possible links with ecological economists.

Not unlike Christensen, Holt (Chapter 5) compares the fundamental principles of Post-Keynesian and neoclassical economics and outlines how both schools of thought relate to the concept of sustainable development. Holt argues that the current methodological approach of neoclassical economics is ill-equipped to deal with the many economic and social complexities associated with achieving sustainable development goals. On the other hand, Holt shows that Post-Keynesian economics provides a theoretical framework considerably more amenable to the sustainability concept than its neoclassical counterpart. Holt therefore argues that Post-Keynesian economics has much to offer the sustainable development debate, including the means to reconcile the goals of ecological sustainability and full employment.

The three chapters in Part III advance the book beyond Post-Keynesianism to a debate on whether the social problems of poverty and unemployment can best be ameliorated through the institution of (a) a universally guaranteed income, (b) a guaranteed employment programme, or (c) a mixture of both. Although the degree to which the environmental concerns expressed in each chapter varies considerably, they all serve a useful function for the following reason. Irrespective of how employment and poverty issues are framed or contextualised, the potential solutions to these social ailments must be consistent with macroeconomic realities and social attitudes towards work and government welfare support. In other words, as important as it is for all potential poverty/unemployment solutions to be consistent with the principles of ecological sustainability, macroeconomic and social factors inescapably emerge as important considerations when assessing the efficacy of guaranteed income and guaranteed employment programmes.

In the first of the three chapters in Part III, Widerquist and Lewis (Chapter 6) argue that poverty alleviation requires a comprehensive programme that takes all forms of poverty into account. Following a summary of the five major causes of poverty, Widerquist and Lewis consider how well a guaranteed employment programme is likely to address the poverty issue. After outlining what they consider to be four major weaknesses of such a programme, Widerquist and Lewis reveal their support for a Basic Income Guarantee. Effectively a form of income insurance, Widerquist and Lewis view the Basic Income Guarantee as the most efficient and comprehensive means of attacking poverty as well as the social problems associated with unemployment.

In addition, Widerquist and Lewis believe that the Basic Income Guarantee can be employed as part of an environmental strategy to help reduce the human costs of environmental policies. For example, some of the environmental policies being widely advocated involve tax imposts to deter certain forms of environmentally destructive behaviour (see Part IV). Often these policies lead, initially at least, to significant increases in the prices of basic goods and services. Widerquist and Lewis argue that a Basic Income Guarantee can lessen the impact of environmental taxes on the poor while also serving as a way of redistributing resource scarcity rents. Although Widerquist and Lewis recognise its potential to adversely affect work incentives, they believe this can be averted by ensuring there are enough meaningful jobs on offer to encourage people to remain in the workforce – thus rewarding the work ethic, not enforcing it.

In Chapter 7, Tcherneva evaluates the economic and environmental viability of Basic Income and Job Guarantee schemes – the former similar to the Basic Income Guarantee advocated by Widerquist and Lewis in Chapter 6; the latter an example of a guaranteed employment programme. Although the Basic Income and Job Guarantee schemes rest on a similar conviction regarding poverty-alleviation programmes, Tcherneva sets out to expose the key differences between the two proposals. To do this, Tcherneva explores the macroeconomic viability of each programme and follows it with a close examination of their respective environmental merits.

What Tcherneva discovers is that a Basic Income Guarantee is likely to be inflationary. In addition, because the Basic Income Guarantee 'freely' guarantees a minimum standard of living, it has the potential to induce a mass exodus of workers from the labour force. Both are likely to result in a number of perverse macroeconomic effects – namely, the inability of a central government to achieve budget neutrality; a decline in national output; and the erosion of the Basic Income Guarantee's purchasing power. On the other hand, Tcherneva believes that an appropriately designed Job Guarantee can eliminate unemployment and its associated poverty whilst simultaneously preventing inflation. Furthermore, because spending on the Job Guarantee varies according to the level of private sector activity, Tcherneva believes it can serve as a powerful automatic stabiliser of the business cycle.

From an environmental perspective, Tcherneva argues that the Basic Income Guarantee is of potential value in the sense that it is likely to cause output levels to fall. However, more directly, Tcherneva believes that any genuine environmental improvements from a Basic Income Guarantee are likely to stem from the tax mechanisms proposed to finance it (e.g., depletion/pollution taxes). Because tax mechanisms of this type can be used to finance alternative poverty-alleviation programmes, Tcherneva stresses that the implementation of a Basic Income Guarantee is not necessary to generate tax-induced environmental benefits.

As for the Job Guarantee, Tcherneva explains how it can be designed to generate jobs to support and rehabilitate the environment. Giving reasons, Tcherneva eventually argues for a poverty-alleviation programme that incorporates a guaranteed source of income for elderly, disabled, and incapacitated citizens, plus a guaranteed source of meaningful work opportunities for those people genuinely capable of making a useful contribution to society.

In Chapter 8, Mitchell and Watts delve much deeper into the macroeconomic consequences of the Basic Income Guarantee and Job Guarantee schemes. After pointing out that the Basic Income Guarantee is largely motivated by a belief that full employment is unattainable, Mitchell and Watts explain how its proponents have inappropriately constructed the problem of income insecurity and have also failed to come to grips with the full range of options available to a currency-issuing government to achieve and maintain full employment.

Mitchell and Watts begin their explanation by examining the implications of modern money on public finance and argue that a Basic Income Guarantee would trigger an unstable macroeconomic dynamic consistent with the indiscriminate 'pump-priming' policies of the past. On the other hand, Mitchell and Watts believe that a Job Guarantee would: (a) not only ensure full employment, but eliminate income insecurity; (b) maintain price stability by paying Job Guarantee workers a minimum living wage; (c) promote macroeconomic stability by ironing out the boom–bust cycle; and (d) be entirely consistent with contemporary social attitudes towards work and government welfare support. Mitchell and Watts also reveal how a Job Guarantee scheme could entail jobs in environmentally enhancing activities that, because of their public goods nature, would not be undertaken by the private sector. Finally, Mitchell and Watts explain why a Job Guarantee would be equally viable in developing countries where income insecurity arising from high rates of unemployment is particularly prevalent.

Part IV of the book focuses on a new policy initiative currently being promoted to resolve the environment–employment dilemma. Referred to as ecological tax reform (ETR), this policy initiative involves a revenue-neutral mix of tax impositions on both resource depletion and pollution and tax cuts on labour and income (Daly, 1996; O'Riordan, 1997; Roodman, 1998; Hoerner and Bosquet, 2001). The aim of the tax impositions is to discourage environmentally destructive behaviour and to promote the development and uptake of resource-saving technology. Conversely, the tax cuts on labour and income are designed to facilitate the substitution towards labour – thereby increasing employment levels – and to encourage greater value-adding in production. Should ETR be successful, its advocates argue that it generates a double dividend in the form of low unemployment and ecological sustainability.

In the first of the two chapters in Part IV, Manresa and Sancho (Chapter 9) consider whether ETR, if applied in Spain, would generate a double dividend to the Spanish economy. Using a computable general equilibrium model with CO_2 emissions serving as a proxy for environmental performance, Manresa and Sancho undertake a number of simulation exercises based on different tax rates and varying degrees of labour market flexibility. Manresa and Sancho reveal that a double dividend for Spain is feasible given a standard set of model characteristics and the implementation of commonly recommended ETR policy measures. However, Manresa and Sancho demonstrate that the success of tax policies aimed specifically at reducing CO_2 emissions and improving labour utilisation diminishes as labour market flexibility increases. Moreover, as labour markets exceed a certain degree of flexibility, ETR policies prove to be counterproductive in terms of reducing CO_2 emissions. In view of this latter result, Manresa and Sancho conclude that, in the Spanish context at least, revenue-neutral ETR policies are a valuable but insufficient means of achieving the double dividend.

In Chapter 10, Lawn examines the outcome of ETR policies implemented since 1990 in Sweden, Denmark, the Netherlands, and Finland. To a large degree, Lawn emerges with a similar conclusion to that of Manresa and Sancho although it is drawn from a vastly different perspective. In Lawn's case, empirical evidence is provided to support the ecological economic position that conventional ETR measures – namely, depletion/pollution taxes and reduced tax rates on income and labour – are unlikely to deliver the double dividend of ecological sustainability and low unemployment. The reason for this, according to ecological economists, is that conventional ETR measures, although capable of improving resource use efficiency and increasing the attractiveness of employing labour, cannot guarantee ecological sustainability. In addition, ETR measures are likely to fall well short of achieving full employment.

Using CO_2 emissions as a proxy for environmental stress and a GDP/CO_2 emissions ratio as an indicator of efficiency, Lawn shows that the implementation of conventional ETR measures has led to greater efficiency and lower CO_2 emissions in each of the case-study countries, but only in the short term. Following initial positive adjustments, efficiency advances began to slow within three to four years of the tax changes. Moreover, as a consequence of the scale effect of increasing economic activity, CO_2 emissions eventually began to rise. As for the employment implications, ETR measures had some positive impact but rarely resulted in any large reductions in the unemployment rate.

Overall, Lawn argues that the empirical evidence supports the doubts expressed by ecological economists with respect to conventional ETR measures. Having said this, Lawn argues that ETR should still be enthusiastically embraced by policy-makers but, to ensure ecological sustainability, should incorporate 'cap-and-trade' systems in the form of tradeable resource use and pollution permits. Since an ETR package cannot be relied upon to achieve full employment, Lawn also believes that the tax cuts on income and labour should be supplemented by some of the additional measures outlined in Part III of the book – in particular, the Job Guarantee.

Part V includes three chapters which, in one way or another, examine how healthy employment levels can be maintained without the need for ecologically destructive forms of economic activity. In the first of these chapters, Jollands *et al.* (Chapter 11) examine the dilemma that confronts policy-makers in the Greater Christchurch area as they attempt to grapple with the need to create employment opportunities in the face of impending resource constraints. To conduct their examination, Jollands *et al.* determine the impact that the employment structure of the Greater Christchurch area is having on the city's ecosystem service requirements. Following a calculation of the ecosystem service requirements of each sector of the Greater Christchurch economy, Jollands *et al.* rank each sector in terms of their total land, energy, and waste intensities. What the ranking process reveals is that many of the potential employment growth sectors, as identified by the architects of the Greater Christchurch Urban Development Strategy, rank poorly in terms of their ecosystem service intensities. Should the planned development strategy be pursued, Jollands *et al.* argue that the growth of the employment-generating sectors is likely to place significant future demands on ecosystems services. Jollands *et al.* therefore stress the need for policy-makers to consider these additional resource demands if Greater Christchurch is to remain an 'ecologically viable' city.

In Chapter 12, Hinterberger *et al.* develop a method to determine whether European nations are satisfying the sustainable development criteria outlined in Article 2 of the EU Treaty. To simplify matters, Hinterberger *et al.* reduce the sustainable development criteria to the following two performance indicators: (a) *social sustainability* as measured by either rising employment levels or a declining unemployment rate; and (b) *environmental sustainability* as measured by a falling rate of resource throughput and declining CO_2 emissions. The two performance indicators are then applied to Germany and Austria.

In the German case, a disaggregated econometric model is used to provide insights into possible trade-offs between economic, social, and environmental variables resulting from hypothesised policy measures (e.g., eco-taxes, investment subsidies, increased research expenditure, and work-sharing arrangements). The simulation results presented by Hinterberger *et al.* suggest that Germany's development path is likely to become ecologically unsustainable by 2015 unless novel policy measures are introduced to prevent the rise in material inputs and CO_2 emissions. As for the condition of social sustainability, Hinterberger *et al.* reveal that the growth rate of the average product of labour is likely to remain less than the growth rate of real GDP over the 2000–2020 study period, thus leading to a steep decline in the unemployment rate by 2020.

The Austrian employment results, which are based on data obtained for the periods 1970–1980 and 1980–1990, reveal a sharp rise in labour productivity. This has led to two positive social outcomes: (a) an increase in the total number of people employed; and (b) fewer hours worked per employee – the latter suggesting that productivity advances have afforded Austrian workers the opportunity to enjoy more leisure time. In terms of environmental sustainability, Hinterberger *et al.* provide empirical evidence at both the macroeconomic and sectoral levels. Disconcertingly, Hinterberger *et al.* show that Austria failed to satisfy the minimum sustainability condition at the macro level. In addition, the sustainability condition was satisfied in just 4 of the 93 sectors of the Austrian economy. Given the results of the two studies, Hinterberger *et al.* urge policy-makers in both Germany and Austria – and across Europe generally – to develop strategies that closely follow economic, social, and environmental goals in mutually supportive ways.

In the final chapter in Part V (Chapter 13), Victor and Rosenbluth explore whether it is possible for Canada to reduce its unemployment rate to historically low levels, eliminate poverty, maintain a fiscal balance, and meet its Kyoto Protocol obligations without reliance on GDP growth. To assist them, Victor and Rosenbluth employ a dynamic simulation model of the Canadian economy – LOWGROW – which they build using a dynamic systems-modelling language.

Following an explanation of the model and the assumptions embodied within it, Victor and Rosenbluth present the results of a number of no-growth scenarios. In each case, Canada fails to meet what would generally be regarded as a range of desirable economic, social, and environmental objectives. Victor and Rosenbluth then present the likely outcome of a low-growth and eventual no-growth scenario phased in over a 10-year period beginning in 2007. Incorporating a stabilisation budget option, an appropriate redistribution of income, implementation of a specific Kyoto strategy, active labour management policies, and altered personal and corporate tax rates, Victor and Rosenbluth demonstrate that Canada can meet a number of employment, poverty alleviation, and environmental targets without having to continuously grow the economy. But to achieve such an outcome, Victor and Rosenbluth argue that Canada would need to depart significantly from the policy status quo. Victor and Rosenbluth therefore conclude their chapter by sketching some of the required policies, including: (a) the installation of more comprehensive redistribution mechanisms; (b) policies to redirect the consumption of positional goods to the provision of public goods; (c) greater investment in efficiency-increasing infrastructure; (d) reforms to better convert productivity gains into increased leisure (reduced working hours); (e) reductions in the rate of population growth; and (f) quantitative limits on the rate of resource throughput to protect the environment.

To conclude the book, Lawn (Chapter 14) draws upon the views expressed throughout the book to develop a potential strategy to reconcile the goals of ecological sustainability and full employment. Following a reiteration of what is required to achieve these two critical goals, a number of environmental and employment policy options are outlined and discussed. Having done this, the relative merits of four macro policy approaches examined at various stages in the book are assessed: (1) the NAIRU or 'non-accelerating inflation rate of unemployment' approach to macroeconomic policy setting; (2) the Basic Income Guarantee; (3) the Job Guarantee (employer of last resort); and (4) ecological tax reform.

By extracting the desirable aspects from three of these policy approaches, a strategy is put forward as a means to resolving the goals of ecological sustainability and full employment in a manner consistent with the broader goal of sustainable development. At no stage is it suggested that the proposed strategy is the only one capable of reconciling the environment–employment dilemma. Furthermore, it is also stressed that the necessary policies may have to be phased in over time given political realities and the structural inertia of economic systems. However, the concluding message is clear – whatever form the eventual strategy takes, it must be consistent with biophysical and macroeconomic realities. Anything less is certain to fail.

The moral imperative of full employment

Even if there is friction between the ecological sustainability and full employment goals, the conflict is of no relevance if the full employment objective is inconsequential. For the remainder of this chapter, my aim is to demonstrate that unemployment is unacceptably costly and, more importantly, that the full employment objective is a moral imperative. That is, far from being a minor social ailment, unemployment imposes enormous costs on society at large, and the failure to provide sufficient access to meaningful employment reduces the capacity of many individuals to satisfy the full spectrum of their human needs.

Before it is possible to argue that full employment is a moral imperative, it is first necessary to know what constitutes full employment itself. In conventional terms, full employment is said to occur when the official unemployment rate equals what is widely referred to as the 'natural unemployment rate' (Norris, 1989). By this, economists mean an unemployment rate that occurs as a consequence of the natural movement of people between jobs and the impossibility of perfectly matching the location and skills of the unemployed with those of the jobs being offered by the private sector.

An important feature of the natural rate hypothesis is the implicit assumption that the acceptance of paid work by someone who seeks it equates to being fully employed.[5] Mitchell and Muysken (2008) are highly critical of this assumption since they argue that full employment is conditional upon people working the number of hours they desire. Hence, if some people desire full-time employment but can find only casual jobs entailing a limited number of work hours, it is grossly misleading to regard them as fully employed. They are, in effect, underemployed – the implications of which can be almost as injurious as being unemployed. In all, full employment is best defined as a situation in which the economy is able to generate sufficient paid work to eradicate all forms of unemployment, except frictional unemployment, as well as eliminate underemployment.[6]

The cost of unemployment and underemployment

From an economic perspective, the direct cost of unemployment and underemployment is usually measured in terms of the income that would otherwise be generated if the labour force were fully employed. There are other costs that need to be borne in mind but, for now, we shall consider the extent of this particular cost and whether it ought to be disregarded. To do this, it is worth recognising that the various microeconomic reforms implemented in Australia during the 1990s were essentially motivated by a desire to minimise economic inefficiencies that were costing Australia $22 billion per annum in income losses, or approximately $1,250 per Australian (Industry Commission, 1992; Burgess and Mitchell, 1998). It is also worth recognising that similar reforms were introduced throughout most of the industrialised world for the very same reason (European Commission, 1997; OECD, 1999, 2000, 2002a, 2002b).

By the 1990s, a 'fight inflation first' strategy had replaced a number of macroeconomic policy targets that were previously regarded as policy absolutes, including the full employment objective. Yet as Burgess and Mitchell (1998) have stressed, the losses from microeconomic inefficiencies were dwarfed by the annual income losses arising from unemployment and underemployment, which were estimated at $57 billion or $3,100 per Australian in the early 1990s (Mitchell and Watts, 1997).[7] One might therefore facetiously suggest that greater economic gains could have been made during the 1990s if the Australian government had opted to eliminate unemployment rather than pursue a microeconomic reform agenda, particularly given that many of the microeconomic reform measures initially contributed to a higher unemployment rate.[8]

Some observers would argue that the net benefits of microeconomic reform have only begun to emerge in recent years, as evidenced by Australia's official unemployment rate falling in 2008 to its lowest level in 35 years. Yet it is because of the prevalence of underemployment that the 'effective' unemployment rate in Australia is still around 8 per cent of the labour force – close to double the official rate (CofFEE, 2007). Given the importance of underemployment, it is not surprising that the Centre of Full Employment and Equity estimated that the combined income losses in Australia from unemployment and underemployment in 2003 was in the order of $44 billion (CofFEE, 2003). In real terms, this amounted to a cost at least as large as the inefficiency losses that existed prior to the implementation of the microeconomic reform measures. Thus, by overlooking the full employment goal over the past 20–30 years, policy-makers can be accused of being unduly selective when resorting to income losses as a policy-justifying factor. Some would go further and claim that the relegation of the full employment objective is an example of policy hypocrisy that has been driven more by ideological conviction than by economic logic (Mitchell and Muysken, 2008).

Adding to the cost of forgone income are the indirect costs of unemployment and underemployment. Many studies have revealed a clear link between unemployment/underemployment and the prevalence of family breakdown, substance abuse, alienation, discrimination, psychological disorders, suicide, and criminal activity (Fryer, 1992, 1995; Feather, 1997; Sen, 1997; Theodossiou, 1998; Harvey, 2000; Watts and Mitchell, 2000; Biddle, 2001; Layard, 2005). Of course, governments do not passively ignore these maladies and have in place programmes to limit their current impact and future side-effects. However, it is because the various expenditures on these programmes are defensive or rehabilitative in nature that they represent costs, not benefits, even though they contribute to a nation's real GDP (Leipert, 1986). What is particularly alarming is that the total expenditure on defensive and rehabilitative measures currently constitutes around 10 per cent of real GDP in most countries. In addition, this cost is increasing in both absolute and relative terms (Lawn, 2008a, 2008b; Lawn and Clarke, 2008; Clarke and Shaw, 2008; Nguyet Hong *et al.* 2008; Chhinh and Lawn, 2008).

It is true that not all defensive and rehabilitative expenditures can be attributed to the negative side-effects of unemployment and underemployment. However, enough of them can to suggest that the indirect cost of unemployment and underemployment is at least as large as the direct cost. Altogether, the total economic cost of unemployment and underemployment is more than sufficient to warrant an ameliorative response to the unemployment issue.

The right to paid employment

Although economic factors would appear to justify reinstatement of the full employment objective, a more compelling case for full employment can be made by demonstrating that access to paid employment is a fundamental human right. This naturally leads to the question: what is a right? In a general sense, a right can be regarded as an inherent claim to a condition or state predicated on what is required for an individual to be fully human. Unquestionably, it is impossible for someone to be fully human if their *needs* are not being entirely satisfied. Given this, it would seem necessary to examine the concept of human needs very closely and determine the extent to which paid employment constitutes a pre-condition to their fulfilment, or at least constitutes an essential part thereof.

One well-known conceptualisation of human needs is Maslow's (1954) needs hierarchy. Maslow's hierarchical approach is underpinned by a rigorous psychological theory of human motivation where human needs are classified into five distinct categories. Beginning with lower-order needs and ascending through to higher-order needs, the five categories of need are (see Figure 1.1):

1 Basic *physiological* needs – i.e., one's basic need for food, clothing, and shelter.
2 *Safety* needs – i.e., the need for physical and mental security; freedom from fear, anxiety, and chaos; and the need for stability, dependency, and protection.
3 The need for *belongingness and love* – i.e., the need for affectionate relationships with people in general; the hunger for human contact and intimacy; a sense of place and value in one's family or peer group; and the need to avoid the pangs of loneliness, ostracism, rejection, and rootlessness.
4 *Self-esteem* needs – i.e., the desire for strength, achievement, adequacy, mastery, and competence; the need for independence and freedom; and the desire for recognition, attention, importance, dignity, and appreciation.
5 The need for *self-actualisation* – i.e., the desire for self-fulfilment; in other words, the desire to become fully actualised in what one is capable of becoming.

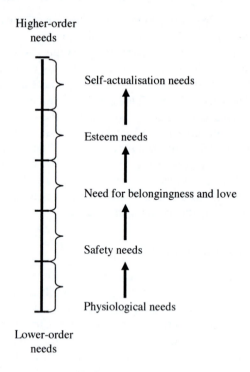

Higher-order
needs

Self-actualisation needs

Esteem needs

Need for belongingness and love

Safety needs

Physiological needs

Lower-order
needs

Figure 1.1 Maslow's needs hierarchy (1954).

In the context of Maslow's hierarchical framework, human effort is initially devoted to the satisfaction of basic physiological needs. Once satisfied, the greater part of one's attention moves to the next tier of human needs. Assuming that each tier of human needs is satisfied following its emergence, the process culminates with the need for self-actualisation, which, according to Maslow, is the most creative and rewarding phase of the human development process. To ultimately experience what it is to be fully human, emerging higher-order needs must be satisfied along with basic physiological needs – a state of human well-being previously referred to by Weisskopf (1973) as a healthy existential balance. Sen (1992) has elsewhere described this state of well-being as fulfilling one's capabilities.

I should point out that the dominant need of any given individual is always shifting (Maslow, 1970). A person devoting their attention to self-actualisation needs will eventually become hungry and be forced to shift their attention to eating. Nevertheless, there is a fundamental difference between someone who must sporadically focus on lower-order needs and a person who is forced, through circumstances, to remain permanently focused on their basic needs. The former will be someone readily able to fulfil the daily emergence of lower-order needs (e.g., hunger, thirst, and affection); the latter will be someone whose daily life involves a constant struggle to fulfil basic needs, many of which may continue to go unsatisfied.

Basic physiological needs

Where, then, does paid employment fit within Maslow's spectrum of human needs? If we begin with basic physiological needs, there is little doubt that, in a market economy at least, paid employment is often the sole means to an income level sufficient enough to access basic goods and services (Mitchell and Muysken, 2008). Must this be the case? As we shall see in Chapter 6, it is possible to satisfy the basic needs of all citizens by granting each individual an unconditional form of income (i.e., a Basic Income Guarantee). In this sense, it is conceivable to have a system in place where the satisfaction of basic needs is not dependent upon paid employment.

Having said this, a number of observers believe that a Basic Income Guarantee would be economically destructive given that the smooth functioning of a market economy depends in part upon a major portion of the nation's income being allocated according to one's contribution to the social product (Chapters 7 and 8). Should this be the case, access to paid employment is likely to be the only economically viable means of guaranteeing an income sufficient enough to meet an individual's basic needs.[9]

Safety needs

It is because of the close association between income and work that unemployment denies many people a reliable source of income. A number of undesirable consequences typically follow in the wake of this. To begin with, unemployed people invariably become reliant upon family transfers or past savings to supplement their meagre welfare payments. This consequently erodes their wealth and/or that of other family members (Burgess and Mitchell, 1998). Secondly, the unemployed are often forced to accept sub-standard jobs and precarious employment conditions. In many instances, people seeking full-time employment are compelled to work under casual employment arrangements, thereby: (a) denying them access to paid annual leave and sickness benefits; (b) rendering them vulnerable to immediate termination; and (c) forcing them to endure week-to-week fluctuations in work hours (Mitchell and Muysken, 2008). Finally, the lack of a reliable source of income can lead to family breakdown and ostracism that can eventually result in the loss of human relations and family life.

Altogether, the unreliable source of income typically associated with unemployment makes it difficult for the unemployed to enjoy the stability required to minimise the onset of anxiety, stress, and a loss of control over one's life and destiny. All of these have been shown to be major causes of depression and stress-related illnesses. This suggests that the ability to access paid employment is essential to ensure the adequate satisfaction of an individual's safety needs.

In saying this, the fulfilment of safety needs does not require everyone to be engaged in paid work. A stay-at-home parent whose partner possesses a well-paid job can comfortably enjoy the stability and security needed to fulfil their safety needs. However, being in this position still requires the partner to have unfettered access to paid employment. Overall, it is difficult to imagine a set of circumstances where the widespread satisfaction of safety needs is not conditional upon paid employment being available to all who seek it.

The need for belonging and love

Apart from diminishing one's ability to access basic goods and services, one of the worst features of unemployment is that it denies unemployed people the opportunity to participate fully in a market economy. It is a consequence of this that unemployment is a major source of alienation and social exclusion that, according to Burgess and Mitchell (1998), constitutes a violation of the basic concept of citizenship. Indeed, Burgess and Mitchell believe that the failure to ensure employment for anyone who seeks it is on a par with denying someone the right of free speech or the right to vote.

Although this last point is debatable, what is less arguable is the fact that the ostracism, alienation, and stigmatism associated with unemployment greatly reduce one's capacity to meaningfully and purposefully engage with fellow citizens. As a consequence, unemployment diminishes one's sense of place and value in society. When this is considered together with the propensity of unemployment to increase the probability of family and relationship breakdown, paid employment can be considered an essential means to satisfying one's need for belongingness and love.

Self-esteem needs

Almost every negative aspect of unemployment so far mentioned has the potential to diminish an individual's capacity to satisfy self-esteem needs. For example, the exclusion associated with unemployment leaves an unemployed person devoid of the status normally attached to work, and a lack of economic participation reduces one's capacity to contribute to the social product – the latter of which is often the barometer of worth in a market economy. Other examples include the sense of reduced personal value that arises from: (a) being ostracised and socially stigmatised; (b) earning a much lower income than wage- and salary-earning peers; (c) experiencing a decline in previously acquired human capital skills, which reduces one's adequacy, mastery, and competence; and (d) suffering motivational loss as a consequence of prolonged alienation and disillusionment.

Not unlike the needs lower down in Maslow's hierarchical framework, paid work is not necessarily required to satisfy one's self-esteem needs. The desire for achievement, competence, and recognition can be fulfilled through child rearing, voluntary work, and recreational pursuits. But, again, this is possible only if the person in question has access to a stock of wealth or an income source that, in the latter case, is dependent upon a relationship of sorts with a person engaged in paid employment.[10] Hence, access to paid work is once more necessary to guarantee the satisfaction of self-esteem needs.

The need for self-actualisation

To become fully actualised in what one is capable of becoming, it is necessary for one's opportunities for personal advancement to remain open. Unfortunately, unemployment, by eroding human capital and reducing one's capacity to engage in a market economy, significantly impedes one's ability to realise their full development potential. What's more, the lack of structure and purpose that accompanies unemployment makes it difficult for unemployed people and their dependents to establish a development pathway to successfully advance through life. It is for these reasons that Sen (1997) believes unemployment is an instrumental factor behind the lack of freedom many people confront when choosing between various combinations of functionings. This lack of freedom consequently reduces their capacity to experience a rich and meaningful life.

It would not be unreasonable to believe that the importance of paid employment is far greater with respect to self-actualisation needs than it is for any other tier of human needs. As previously suggested, lower-order needs could conceivably be met through a direct and unconditional provision of basic goods and services, despite how economically destabilising this might be. But it is doubtful whether the universal fulfilment of self-actualisation needs could ever be possible without a guaranteed access to paid employment, particularly given that it is only through the agency of work that some people are able to fully utilise and exploit their natural talents and abilities.

Concluding comments

Either directly or indirectly, unemployment prevents the full spectrum of human needs of everyone in society from being adequately satisfied. As a consequence, unemployment results in at least some people being unable to experience what it is to be fully human. For this reason, access to paid employment should be regarded as a fundamental human right (Burgess and Mitchell, 1998; Mitchell and Muysken, 2008).

Unbeknown to many, the right to paid employment is already codified at the international level. Article 23 of the 1948 Universal Declaration of Human Rights clearly recognises the link between full employment and human rights. Regrettably, however, full employment is generally not codified in legislation at the national level. But if access to paid employment is a fundamental human right, it follows that national governments have a moral obligation to rectify this situation and, more importantly, to act upon their moral responsibilities accordingly – namely, by introducing a permanent full employment policy.

Of course, should governments take up this moral responsibility, the challenge becomes one of achieving and maintaining full employment in a manner consistent with the goal of ecological sustainability. This, in my view, is the major dilemma that governments must successfully overcome to achieve a comprehensive and genuine form of sustainable development. By the end of this book, I hope that a clearer image will have emerged of what can and must be done to resolve one of the greatest policy dilemmas of our time.

Notes

1. Real GDP is measured using constant prices – that is, by using the prices of goods and services as they were in a particular year, often referred to as the base year. Hence, if 2006 is the base year, the real GDP of every year is calculated in terms of the prices of goods and services in 2006. This differs from nominal GDP, which is based on the prices of goods and services during the year in which they were produced. Hence, the nominal GDP of 2004 would be based on the prices of goods and services in 2004; the nominal GDP of 2005 on the price level in 2005; and so on. Because the calculation of real GDP involves constant prices, real GDP constitutes an approximate index of a nation's physical production level. That is, if real GDP in 2005 is higher than the real GDP of 2004, it effectively implies that a nation has produced more goods and services in 2005 than in 2004. The same cannot be implied by observing changes in nominal GDP because variations in the nominal value of GDP include price changes as well as physical output changes.
2. A steady-state economy is an economy that does not physically grow but qualitatively improves over time in terms of the content of the physical goods of which it is composed, the means by which the goods are produced and maintained, and the purpose for which the goods are intended.
3. For a description of what ecological economics involves, see Lawn (2002).
4. The logic behind the economic and ecological limits to growth is explained in great detail in Chapter 2.
5. If the natural rate concept were not based on this implicit assumption, underemployment would also be included in final measures of the natural rate of unemployment. Underemployment is not included in these measures.
6. Frictional unemployment is unemployment arising from people: (a) moving between jobs; or (b) entering/re-entering the labour market and, because of imperfect information, must spend time searching for an appropriate form of work. For the individuals involved, frictional unemployment is usually a short-term phenomenon.
7. This cost includes the impact of hidden unemployment. Hidden unemployment refers to people who, despite wanting to work, refrain from participating in the labour market because of the small probability of gaining the form of work and number of work hours they desire.
8. This in no way means that policy-makers should abandon attempts to eliminate microeconomic inefficiencies. It merely serves to highlight that, from a pure cost perspective, the benefits of eradicating unemployment should at least be considered on a par with the benefits accruing from an improvement in the efficiency of resource allocation.
9. In saying this, I am excluding pensioners and people physically and mentally unable to work.
10. Not everyone in society can rely entirely on a stock of stored wealth to finance the satisfaction of self-esteem needs. Once more, I am excluding pensioners and people unable to work.

References

Biddle, D. (2001), 'Youth unemployment and government policy in Australia', in W. Mitchell and E. Carlson (eds), *Unemployment: The Tip of the Iceberg*, Centre of Applied and Economic Research, Sydney: University of New South Wales Press, pp. 117–134.

Burgess, J. and Mitchell, W. (1998), 'Employment, unemployment, and the right to work', *Australian Journal of Human Rights*, 4 (2), 76–94.

Burgess, J. and Mitchell, W. (1999), 'Unemployment, Human Rights, and a Full Employment Policy in Australia', Centre of Full Employment and Equity Working Paper 99-03, University of Newcastle.

Centre of Full Employment and Equity (CofFEE) (2003), 'CofFEE Labour Market Indicators (CLMI), August 2003', http://e1.newcastle.edu.au/coffee/pubs/CLMI/2003/CLMI_August_2003.pdf.

Centre of Full Employment and Equity (CofFEE) (2007), 'CofFEE Labour Market Indicators (CLMI), November 2007', http://e1.newcastle.edu.au/coffee/pubs/CLMI/2007/CLMI1_total_Nov_2007.pdf.

Chhinh, N. and Lawn, P. (2008), 'The Sustainable Net Domestic Product of Cambodia, 1988–2004', *International Journal of Environment, Workplace and Employment*, 3 (2), 154–174.

Clarke, M. and Shaw, J. (2008) 'Genuine progress in Thailand: a systems-analysis approach', in P. Lawn and M. Clarke (eds), *Sustainable Welfare in the Asia-Pacific: Studies Using the Genuine Progress Indicator*, Edward Elgar, Cheltenham, UK, pp. 260–298.

Daly, H. (1991), *Steady-State Economics: Second Edition with New Essays*, Washington, DC: Island Press.

Daly, H. (1996), *Beyond Growth*, Boston: Beacon Press.

Daly, H. (2008), *Ecological Economics and Sustainable Development: Selected Essays of Herman Daly*, Cheltenham, UK: Edward Elgar.

Ehrlich, P., Ehrlich, A. and Holdren, J. (1980) 'Availability, entropy, and the laws of thermodynamics', in H. Daly (ed.), *Economics, Ecology, and Ethics: Essays Toward a Steady-State Economy*, San Francisco: W. H. Freeman, pp. 44–48.

Ehrlich, P. and Ehrlich, A. (1990), *The Population Explosion*, New York: Simon & Schuster.

European Commission (1997), *Competition Law in the European Communities – Volume IIB Explanation of the Rules Applicable to State Aid*, Brussels: EC.

Feather, N. (1997), 'Economic deprivation and the psychological impact of unemployment', *Australian Psychologist*, 32 (1), pp. 37–45.

Fryer, D. (1992), 'Psychological or material deprivation: why does unemployment have mental health consequences?', in E. McLaughlin (ed.), *Understanding Unemployment*, London: Routledge, pp. 103–125.

Fryer, D. (1995), 'Labour market disadvantage, deprivation, and mental health: benefit agency?', *The Psychologist*, June: 265–272.

Georgescu-Roegen, N. (1971), *The Entropy Law and the Economic Process*, Cambridge, MA: Harvard University Press.

Goodland, R. and Ledec, G. (1987), 'Neoclassical economics and the principles of sustainable development', *Ecological Modelling*, 38, 19–46.

Gowdy, J. (1994), 'The social context of natural capital: the social limits to sustainable development', *International Journal of Social Economics*, 21 (8), 43–55.

Harding, A. and Richardson, S. (1998), 'Unemployment and income distribution', in G. Debelle and J. Borland (eds), *Unemployment and the Labour Market*, Sydney: Reserve Bank of Australia, pp. 139–164.

Harvey, P. (2000), 'Combating joblessness: an analysis of the principle strategies that have influenced the development of American employment and social welfare law during the 20th century', *Berkeley Journal of Employment and Labor Law*, 21 (2), 677–758.

Hoerner, J. and Bosquet, B. (2001), *Environmental Tax Reform: The European Experience*, Washington, DC: Centre for a Sustainable Economy.

Industry Commission (1992), *Annual Report 1991–92*, Canberra: AGPS.

Lawn, P. (2000), *Toward Sustainable Development: An Ecological Economics Approach*, Boca Raton: Lewis Publishers.

Lawn, P. (2002), 'Grounding the ecological economics paradigm with ten core principles', *International Journal of Agricultural Resources, Governance, and Ecology*, 2 (1), 1–21.

Lawn, P. (2007), *Frontier Issues in Ecological Economics*, Cheltenham, UK: Edward Elgar.

Lawn, P. (2008a), 'Genuine progress in Australia: time to rethink the growth objective', in P. Lawn and M. Clarke (eds), *Sustainable Welfare in the Asia-Pacific: Studies Using the Genuine Progress Indicator*, Cheltenham, UK: Edward Elgar, pp. 91–125.

Lawn, P. (2008b), 'Genuine progress in India: some further growth needed in the immediate future but population stabilisation needed immediately', in P. Lawn and M. Clarke (eds), *Sustainable Welfare in the Asia-Pacific: Studies Using the Genuine Progress Indicator*, Cheltenham, UK: Edward Elgar, pp. 191–227.

Lawn, P. and Clarke, M. (eds) (2008), *Sustainable Welfare in the Asia-Pacific: Studies Using the Genuine Progress Indicator*, Cheltenham, UK: Edward Elgar.

Layard, R. (2005), *Happiness: Lessons from a New Science*, London: Penguin.

Leipert, C. (1986), 'From gross to adjusted national product', in P. Ekins (ed.), *The Living Economy: A New Economics in the Making*, London: Routledge & Kegan Paul, pp. 132–139.

Maslow, A. (1954), *Motivation and Personality*, New York: Harper & Row.

Maslow, A. (1970), *The Farther Reaches of the Human Mind*, New York: Viking Press.

Max-Neef, M. (1995), 'Economic growth and quality of life', *Ecological Economics*, 15 (2), 115–118.

Meadows, D. H., Meadows, D. L., Randers, J., and Behrens, W., III (eds) (1972), *The Limits to Growth*, New York: Universe Books.

Mitchell, W. and Muysken, J. (2008), *Full Employment Abandoned: Shifting Sands and Policy Failures*, Cheltenham, UK: Edward Elgar.

Mitchell, W. and Watts, M. (1997), 'The path to full employment', *Australian Economic Review*, 30, 436–444.

Nguyet Hong, V. X., Clarke, M. and Lawn, P. (2008), 'Genuine progress in Vietnam: the impact of the Doi Moi reforms', in P. Lawn and M. Clarke (eds), *Sustainable Welfare in the Asia-Pacific: Studies Using the Genuine Progress Indicator*, Cheltenham, UK: Edward Elgar.

Norris, K. (1989), *The Economics of Australian Labour Markets*, second edition, Melbourne: Longman Chesire.

OECD (1999), *The Role of Competition Policy in Regulatory Reform in the United States*, Paris: OECD.

OECD (2000), 'Recent Labour-Market Performance and Structural Reforms', *OECD Economic Outlook 67*, Paris: OECD, pp. 215–224.

OECD (2002a), *The Role of Competition Policy in Regulatory Reform in Canada*, Paris: OECD.

OECD (2002b), *The Role of Competition Policy in Regulatory Reform in the United Kingdom*, Paris: OECD.

O'Riordan, T. (ed.) (1997), *Ecotaxation*, London: Earthscan.

Roodman, D. (1998), *The Natural Wealth of Nations: Harnessing the Market for the Environment*, Washington, DC: World Resources Institute.

Sen, A. (1992), *Inequality Reexamined*, Oxford: Oxford University Press.

Sen, A. (1997), 'Inequality, unemployment, and contemporary Europe', *International Labour Review*, 136 (2), 155–171.

Theodossiou, I. (1998), 'The effects of low-pay and unemployment on psychological well-being: a logistic regression approach', *Journal of Health Economics*, 17 (1), 85–104.

Watts, M. and Mitchell, W. (2000), 'The costs of unemployment', *Economic and Labour Relations Review*, 11 (2), 180–197.

Weisskopf, W. (1973), 'Economic growth versus existential balance', in H. Daly (ed.), *Towards a Steady-State Economy*, San Francisco: W. H. Freeman, pp. 240–251.

2 The potential conflict between ecological sustainability and full employment

Philip Lawn

Introduction

As previously indicated, the aim of this chapter is to demonstrate that a conflict currently exists between the goals of ecological sustainability and full employment. To achieve this aim, two conditions need to be established. Firstly, it must be shown that the continued growth in real GDP – and of the economy generally[1] – is both economically undesirable and ecologically unsustainable. Once this condition has been established, it follows that any nation which has reached or surpassed its limits to growth will be greatly constrained in its capacity to increase employment levels to the extent required to reach and maintain full employment. Secondly, since there are some observers who recognise limits to growth but believe that full employment can be comfortably achieved by altering the mix of jobs within a sustainable economy, it needs to be demonstrated that these observers overestimate the capacity of a sustainable economy to generate enough jobs to achieve full employment.

I should point out that achieving full employment in a sustainable economy will undoubtedly require a shift in the type of work undertaken and a change in the industries in which most people are employed. In this sense, the latter observers are not so much incorrect for what they say is needed to avoid a jobs–environment trade-off. Where they are mistaken is that they exaggerate the ease with which employment growth in environmentally benign industries can offset the loss of jobs in environmentally destructive industries. This has led to notions that ecological sustainability can be readily achieved by establishing a 'green' core of unemployed workers together with an 'environmental' industry whose purpose it is to ameliorate environmental damage or foster improved environmental management. It has also led to the view that most nations, should they begin the transition to a sustainable economy, are already well positioned to undergo the restructuring of employment necessary to lower unemployment, thus demanding little or no drastic employment policies on the part of governments. On the contrary, evidence revealed later in this chapter will show that most nations are poorly placed to prevent net job losses. Achieving both ecological sustainability and full employment will therefore require the implementation of policy measures that go well beyond the facilitation of increased efficiency and a shift in jobs from a declining dirty sector to a growing green sector.

Economic and ecological limits to growth

Alternative world-views

The task of demonstrating that continued growth in real GDP is economically undesirable and ecologically unsustainable begins with a brief consideration of three alternative views of the relationship between economy, society, and the natural environment. The first of these world-views can be loosely described as the *mainstream* world-view. As Figure 2.1 shows, this view of the world regards the three major spheres as essentially independent systems. Moreover, the links between these systems are considered tenuous in the sense that any undesirable exchange from one system to another can be readily overcome through within-system action. Because of implied independency, the achievement of sustainable development – which might best be described as 'continuous qualitative improvement' or 'ongoing human betterment' – requires a nation to make various trade-offs. Hence, if a nation undertakes a particular course of action which benefits the environment (e.g., creates a national park to protect an ecologically significant forest), it is likely to come at the expense of the economy and/or society (e.g., forgone income and lost jobs). Societies are therefore constantly compelled to strike an appropriate balance between the need to preserve the environment and the need to satisfy the conditions required for a healthy economy.

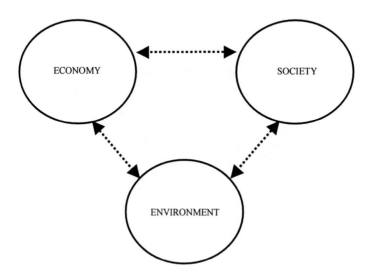

Figure 2.1 Mainstream view of the world.

Adherents to the mainstream world-view also entertain the idea that economic, social, and ecological sustainability can exist as separate and independent forms of sustainability. In other words, economic and social sustainability are possible without the need for ecological sustainability, albeit the simultaneous achievement of all three forms of sustainability is a preferable outcome. In recent times, this has led to the mainstream support for 'triple-bottom-line' accounting.[2]

Above all, the mainstream world-view regards the continuous growth of the economy as both desirable (makes people better off) and ecologically sustainable (can continue indefinitely). As such, the growth of real GDP is not just consistent with achieving sustainable development, it constitutes a sustainable development prerequisite.

The second major world-view is what many commentators, following the release of the Brundtland Report in 1987 (WCED, 1987), refer to as the *Brundtland* view of the world. Once again, the three major spheres are considered largely independent of each other (Figure 2.2). On this occasion, there is greater recognition of the critical exchange of matter, energy, and information between the various systems and the potential for intersystem feedback to impact either positively or negatively on the health of the receiving system (WCED, 1987: 5). Although the Brundtland world-view is more holistic than the conventional position, it continues to entertain the idea that economic, social, and ecological sustainability can exist as independent forms of sustainability and that, from time to time, trade-offs have to be made between the environment and economy. Continued growth of the economy is still regarded as desirable and ecologically sustainable provided there is consistent improvement in the 'quality' of the growth taking place (WCED,

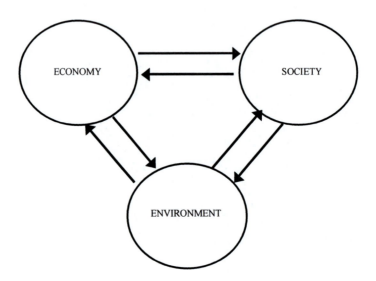

Figure 2.2 Brundtland view of the world.

1987: 52–54). In all, the Brundtland world-view recognises the existence of potential limits to growth but remains open to the possibility that these limits can be overcome through better economic and environmental management (i.e., growth becomes infeasible only following poor management and inappropriate policy implementation) (WCED, 1987: 8).

The third and final view of the world is the *coevolutionary* world-view and is represented by Figure 2.3. For the remainder of this chapter, the coevolutionary world-view is assumed to be the best representation of concrete reality. Unlike the previous two world-views, the coevolutionary position regards the three major spheres as interdependent systems whereby the economy exists as a sub-system of society and society exists as a sub-system of the ecosphere. Given the ineluctable exchange of matter, energy, and information between the various systems, all three major spheres and the constituent sub-systems contained within them collectively evolve. In other words, they coevolve. Coevolution occurs when the feedback between the various systems initiates an interdependent and reciprocal process of systemic change (Norgaard, 1985).[3] In the process, incessant intersystem exchange not only shapes the evolution of a particular system through time, but each system constantly affects the evolution of all other systems (Norgaard, 1984, 1988).[4]

More self-evidently, the coevolutionary world-view dictates that the economy cannot outgrow society and society itself cannot outgrow what is undeniably a finite, non-growing ecosphere. As such, the coevolutionary world-view recognises ecological limits to growth. In addition, the coevolutionary world-view suggests

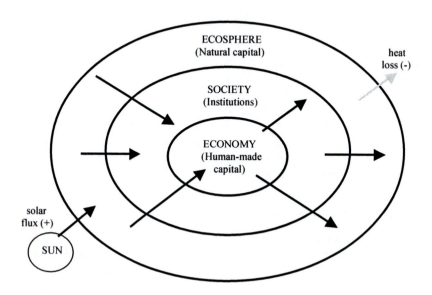

Figure 2.3 Coevolutionary view of the world.

that the growth of the economy may become economically undesirable (i.e., reduce human well-being) before becoming ecologically unsustainable. I will have more to say about this soon.

Lastly, the coevolutionary world-view refuses to entertain the concept of economic, social, and ecological sustainability as separate forms of sustainability. Ecological sustainability is instead considered the sustainability 'bottom line'. Should human endeavour not be ecologically sustainable, it follows that it cannot be socially or economically sustainable. Of course, many observers belonging to the Brundtland world-view would point out that social and economic disintegration often leads to ecologically unsustainable practices. As a direct consequence, social and economic stability is often a key factor underpinning the achievement of ecological sustainability. There is no denying this. However, there is a fundamental difference between the unsustainability of society and economy that may or may not lead to the unsustainability of the ecosphere and the unsustainability of the ecosphere which categorically rules out the sustainability of society and economy. Whereas we clearly need to be mindful of the health of our social and economic systems given that social and economic instability is detrimental to human well-being and can ultimately put the longevity of the ecosphere at risk, we must forever be mindful of the health of the ecosphere given that ecological unsustainability renders everything else unsustainable – including what might appear to be a stable society and economy.

Given the preference in this chapter for the coevolutionary world-view, one is ultimately compelled to consider the following two critical questions:

- How big can the economy grow before it is no longer ecologically sustainable?
- How big can the economy grow before human well-being begins to decline?

Unbeknown to many people, the answers to these questions are not the same. This is because the first question relates to a physical scale of the economy that ought to be categorically avoided whereas the second question relates to a scale that we would be better off avoiding even if the long-term consequences of reaching it are not ecologically catastrophic. As we shall see, the desirable physical scale of the economy (the answer to the second question) is likely to be considerably smaller than the economy's maximum sustainable scale (the answer to the first question). Importantly, this suggests that an 'economic' limit to growth may precede an 'ecological' limit to growth.

Production, consumption, and resource throughput

Before we can answer the two questions above, it is first necessary to outline a number of additional key concepts. In view of the fact that ecological sustainability is essentially the sustainability 'bottom line', we shall ignore the role of social institutions for the moment and reduce our analysis to the physical relationship between the economy and the ecosphere. This simplified relationship, which is depicted in Figure 2.4, assumes that the physical scale of the economy is repre-

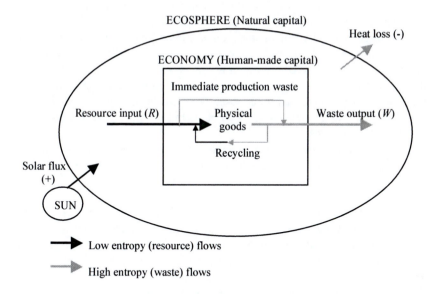

Figure 2.4 Simplified physical relationship between the economy and the ecosphere.

sented by the quantity of physical goods located within the economy itself. There are basically three categories of goods that make up the entire stock of all goods: (a) producer goods (plant, machinery, and equipment); (b) infrastructural goods (roads, bridges, ports, hospitals, schools, etc.); and (c) consumer goods (both durable and non-durable household goods). In the Irving Fisher (1906) sense, the total stock of all goods will henceforth be referred to as the stock of human-made capital.

Because the stock of human-made capital is either directly consumed (e.g., consumer non-durables) or worn out through use (e.g., producer goods, infrastructural goods, and consumer durables), retired goods must be continuously replaced if only to keep the total stock of human-made capital intact. Since replacement requires ongoing production, the mere replacement of consumed and depreciated goods requires the continuous input of resources (R). At the same time, the consumption and depreciation of goods results in the continuous generation of wastes (W). The input of resources and the output of wastes can best be described as the *throughput* of matter–energy that is constantly required to fuel the economic process.

Throughput in a steady-state economy

We shall now consider the throughput of matter–energy in relation to a steady-state economy. A steady-state economy is one composed of a non-growing stock of human-made capital.[5] In a steady-state economy, the quantity of consumed and worn out goods must equal the quantity of new goods produced since only then can the total stock of human-made capital remain physically intact over time. Like all economies, the steady-state economy is subject to the first law of thermodynamics (the law of conservation of matter–energy). Since this law dictates that no matter or energy can be created or destroyed during the economic process, the matter–energy embodied in the resources used for production must be quantitatively equal to the matter–energy embodied in the waste that is subsequently generated (i.e., $R = W$).

Having said this, the rate of throughput required to keep the stock of human-made capital intact can be reduced by one or more of the following technological advances:

- an increase in the technical efficiency of production (E), where E is measured as the ratio of the matter–energy embodied in new goods produced (Y) to the matter–energy embodied in the resources used in their production (R) – i.e., $E = Y/R$;[6]
- an increase in the rate of materials recycling;
- an increase in the durability of human-made capital;
- an increase in the operational efficiency of human-made capital (i.e., a reduction in the energy required to operate individual items).

The first of the above advances reduces the rate of throughput for an obvious reason – if more goods can be produced from a given input of resources, it follows that the same quantity of goods can be produced from fewer resources. An increase in the rate of materials recycling can have a similar beneficial impact. How? Some portion of the retired stock of physical goods will contain materials that can be reused through recycling. In many instances, an increase in the reuse rate of waste materials will reduce the demand for virgin materials. I say 'in many instances' because it should always be remembered that the recycling of materials is not energy free. Indeed, the more degraded is the material being recycled, the greater is the quantity of energy that must be expended to avail waste materials again for production purposes. Hence, whether recycling contributes to a reduction in the overall rate of throughput depends on whether the virgin resource inputs saved through recycling exceed the virgin resources expended to drive the recycling process.

The third advancement – an increase in the durability of human-made capital – reduces the quantity of goods requiring replacement at a given point in time. Because this reduces the rate of production, it lessens the need for resource inputs. Finally, goods have no operational value unless powered by an energy source. Clearly, when less energy is required to operate human-made capital, fewer resources are expended.

Owing to the fact that $R = W$ in a steady-state economy, the quantity of waste output (W) exiting the economy is largely determined by the quantity of resources entering it (R). Since the four technological advances outlined above have the potential to reduce the quantity of resource inputs needed to maintain a given physical stock of human-made capital, they also have the capacity to reduce the quantity of waste associated with operating a steady-state economy.

It should be noted, however, that the negative ecological consequences of waste output are not necessarily diminished by reducing the quantity of waste being generated by the economic process. Even in small doses, the generation and subsequent release of hazardous wastes can have devastating ecological effects. As such, the qualitative dimension of waste output always remains a critical sustainability factor.

Another key sustainability consideration concerns the constraints imposed on technological progress by a number of immutable physical laws. Of the technological advances so far discussed, all four are subject to severe limits. For example, the first and second laws of thermodynamics ensure that the technical efficiency of production can never reach 100 per cent (i.e., E must be less than a value of one). These same laws also preclude the 100 per cent recycling of matter and the recycling of energy altogether. The second law of thermodynamics – the Entropy Law – prevents anything from being eternally durable and ensures at least some quantity of energy must always be expended to operate and enjoy the service-yielding qualities of human-made capital.

From a steady-state perspective, the limits imposed on technological progress render it impossible for humankind to continuously reduce the throughput required to keep the stock of human-made capital intact. As we shall soon see, technological limits are not a major cause for concern unless society aims to perpetually increase the physical scale of the economic sub-system.

Throughput in a physically growing economy

Unlike the steady-state scenario, for an economic system to grow (i.e., for the accumulation of human-made capital to take place), the quantity of new goods produced must exceed the quantity of consumed and worn out goods. Despite the first law of thermodynamics, the surplus of new goods over retired goods is possible if only because matter–energy can remain 'frozen' in durable goods for extended periods of time. Because more goods are produced than consumed in a growing economy, the matter–energy embodied in the resources used for production must, at a point in time, be quantitatively greater than the matter–energy embodied in the wastes being returned to the ecosphere (i.e., $R > W$).[7]

Having said this, both R and W can decline while the economy is still physically growing. For this to occur, the rate of technological progress must be sufficient for the percentage increase in the rate of resource use efficiency to exceed the percentage increase in the quantity of new goods produced (i.e., $dE/E > dY/Y$). This is technically possible, but can only occur for a short period of time. Why? To begin with, it has already been pointed out that E must be less than a value of one. As a consequence, increases in technical efficiency are subject to diminishing returns. This means that dE/E must inevitably diminish over time and eventually approximate a value of zero. Next, if the economy is growing exponentially, *dY/Y* must eventually surpass *dE/E*. Clearly, a declining rate of throughput in the presence of a growing economy is a temporary phenomenon. As such, we can safely conclude that a continuously growing economy must eventually require an increasing rate of throughput.

Increasing throughput and ecological sustainability

To consider what an increasing rate of throughput implies in terms of ecological sustainability, let us now consider the role played by the ecosphere as the host system of the economy. The ecosphere essentially provides three *non-substitutable* functions. They are:

1   a source of low entropy resources;[8]
2   a sink to assimilate high entropy wastes;
3   a provider of critical life-support services.

The ecosphere's source function

In terms of the first major function of the ecosphere, low-entropy resources can be sourced from two categories of natural capital. The first category is renewable natural capital (N_R) and includes such resources as timber, fish stocks, water, etc. Being renewable, these resources can be sustainably exploited provided the quantity extracted (R_R) does not exceed the quantity made available through natural regeneration or replenishment $(r.N_R)$. I say 'natural' regeneration because the productivity of many renewable resources is often boosted by non-renewable resource inputs (e.g., inorganic fertilisers). Where this is the case, the sustainable rate of extraction is confined to the rate at which the resources would regenerate either without the application of non-renewable additives or where the productivity of the resources has been assisted by the sustainable input of other renewable resources. Overall, the following can be considered our first sustainability precept.

> Sustainability precept no. 1: To sustainably exploit renewable natural capital, the quantity of renewable resources extracted must not exceed the quantity of renewable resources made available through natural regeneration or replenishment; that is:

$$R_R \leq r.N_R \tag{2.1}$$

The second category of natural capital – non-renewable natural capital (N_{NR}) – consists of resources such as oil, gas, coal, copper, iron, etc. (R_{NR}). Being incapable of renewal,[9] this category of resources cannot be exploited in a sustainable manner. Having said this, it is possible to make available a certain flow of non-renewable resources and subsequently sustain an equivalent flow of additional renewable resources. To do this, two things are required. In the first instance, some of the proceeds from non-renewable resource depletion activities must be reinvested to cultivate renewable resource replacements (i.e., increase N_R) and/or increase the regeneration rate of the existing stock of renewable resources (i.e., increase r). Secondly, the rate at which the non-renewable resources are extracted must be no greater than the regeneration rate of the renewable resources eventually cultivated and/or no greater than the additional renewable resource flow generated by augmenting the productivity of existing renewable resources.

Extracting non-renewable resources at the rate at which an additional renewable resource flow becomes available is a delicate exercise. Fortunately, a useful formula has been devised which can assist the transition process (El Serafy, 1989). A variation of the formula is given below:

$$R_{NR}/R_{NR} = \frac{1}{(1+r)^{n+1}} \tag{2.2}$$

where:

- R_{NR} = the quantity of an extracted non-renewable resource available each year for production purposes (note: R_{NR} also equals the quantity of resources that are eventually harvested from the cultivated renewable resource asset);
- R_{NR} = the total quantity extracted each year of the non-renewable resource;
- r = the natural regeneration rate of the cultivated renewable resource asset;
- n = the number of years over which the non-renewable resource is fully exhausted.

Provided R_{NR}, r and n are known, it is possible to calculate R_{NR} by rearranging equation (2.2) as follows:

$$R_{NR} = R_{NR}\left[1 - \frac{1}{(1+r)^{n+1}}\right] \tag{2.3}$$

Once R_{NR} is calculated, the quantity of the extracted non-renewable resource that needs to be invested to establish the renewable resource asset (R_{INV}) is:

$$R_{INV} = R_{NR} - R_{NR} \tag{2.4}$$

To simplistically illustrate the transition process, consider a hypothetical situation in which a non-renewable resource consists of 1,000 units of low entropy matter–energy (i.e., N_{NR} = 1,000); the resource is scheduled to be fully exhausted over nine years (i.e., n = 9); there are 10 extractions in total (i.e., $R_{NR} = N_{NR}/10 =$ 100);[10] and the regeneration rate of the renewable resource is 5 per cent (i.e., $r =$ 0.05). Using equations (2.3) and (2.4), one obtains the following values: $R_{NR} =$ 38.61 and R_{INV} = 61.39. The actual process of exhaustion, resource availability, and investment is represented by Table 2.1.

Table 2.1 Conversion of a non-renewable resource into sustainable flow of renewable resources

Time	N_{NR}	R_{NR}	R_{NR}	R_{INV}	N_R	r	$N_R(1 + r)$	R_R	$R = R_{NR} + R_R$
0	1,000	100	38.61	0	0	0.05	0	0	38.61
1	900	100	38.61	61.39	61.39	0.05	64.46	0	38.61
2	800	100	38.61	61.39	125.85	0.05	132.14	0	38.61
3	700	100	38.61	61.39	193.54	0.05	203.21	0	38.61
4	600	100	38.61	61.39	264.60	0.05	277.83	0	38.61
5	500	100	38.61	61.39	339.23	0.05	356.19	0	38.61
6	400	100	38.61	61.39	417.58	0.05	438.46	0	38.61
7	300	100	38.61	61.39	499.85	0.05	524.84	0	38.61
8	200	100	38.61	61.39	586.23	0.05	615.54	0	38.61
9	100	100	38.61	61.39	676.94	0.05	710.78	0	38.61
10	0	0	0	61.39	772.17	0.05	772.17	38.61	38.61

Table 2.1 shows the non-renewable resource (N_{NR}) diminishing at the rate of 100 units of low-entropy matter–energy per year for nine years. The fourth column (R_{NR}) indicates that 38.61 units of low-entropy matter–energy are available each year for production purposes. The remaining 61.39 units (R_{INV}) must be annually invested to build up the renewable resource which grows over the nine-year period at the rate of 5 per cent per year. By the end of the ninth year (beginning of the tenth year), 772.17 units of renewable matter–energy have been cultivated. It is now possible, on a permanent basis, to provide a flow of 38.61 units of low entropy matter–energy for production purposes – an amount exactly equal to the quantity made available for production purposes during the depletion phase of the non-renewable resource (note: 38.61 = 772.17 × 0.05). In effect, the stock of resource-providing natural capital has been kept intact.[11] We are now in a position to posit our second sustainability precept.

> Sustainability precept no. 2: In order to keep the combined stock of resource-providing natural capital intact, non-renewable resources should be exploited at a rate no faster than renewable resource substitutes can be created and/or an additional renewable resource flow can be generated by augmenting the productivity of existing renewable resources.

Before we move onto the ecosphere's sink function, two important caveats need to be made. It is highly likely that the deliberate cultivation of additional renewable resources will be taking place in most countries. The same can also be said for improved resource management, which is likely to lead to further increases in the productivity of renewable natural capital. As important as these developments are in terms of the above precept, there are a number of things worth bearing in mind. Firstly, there are limits to how much renewable natural capital can be cultivated at any point in time and over time. Secondly, it is not possible to continuously increase the productivity of renewable natural capital (i.e., the regeneration rate of renewable resources cannot be augmented indefinitely). Although these two limits do not necessary restrict how much non-renewable natural capital can be exploited over time, if we wish to adhere to precept no. 2 these limits will undoubtedly constrain the rate at which non-renewable natural capital can be exploited at a single point in time. Hence, the discretion over the scheduled rate of exhaustion of a non-renewable resource will be restricted by the maximum amount of renewable natural capital that can be cultivated in each investment period. If, in the hypothetical scenario depicted in Table 2.1, it is not possible to cultivate 61.39 units of additional renewable matter–energy per year, it will be necessary to lengthen the exhaustion schedule beyond nine years. This will subsequently reduce the amount of non-renewable matter–energy available for production purposes in each year during the depletion phase.[12]

Thirdly, although there is likely to be further cultivation of renewable resources and advances in the productivity of renewable natural capital, these gains must be contrasted against any clearance of native vegetation – which often occurs for agricultural and urban expansion purposes – and the possible over-harvesting of some existing renewable resources. Hence, even if the liquidators of non-renewable resources are adequately cultivating renewable resource substitutes or an agent is performing the function on their behalf, the process can be undermined by imprudent forms of renewable resource management elsewhere within the system.

Finally, human activities can unwittingly upset the coevolutionary balance between the economy, society, and ecosphere, which can lead to the destruction of renewable natural capital and a decline in its natural regeneration rate. This imbalance need not arise simply from humankind's resource extraction activities. As we shall soon see, it can also be the product of an excessive rate of waste generation and the degradation of critical ecosystems. A good example of this is the substantial and growing emission of carbon dioxide (CO_2) and the detrimental impact that global climate change is likely to have on most of the world's resource systems (see Stern, 2007; IPCC, 2007).[13] In all, the benefits of adhering to precept no. 2 can be fully realised only if there is no diminution of the existing stock of renewable natural capital.

The second major caveat relates to the fact that renewable resource substitutes do not currently exist for some non-renewable resources (e.g., copper). We cannot, therefore, apply precept no. 2 to these resources. One might argue that the relatively rapid depletion of these resources is justifiable provided we satisfy the first two sustainability precepts. I beg to differ. Given that many of these non-substitutable resources have very useful properties, this would be an intergenerationally unjust course of action. A much fairer strategy would involve the cautious depletion of these resources and concerted attempts to overcome any long-run reliance upon them well short of their eventual depletion. In view of this requirement, the following becomes our third sustainability precept.

Sustainability precept no. 3: Where a substitute for a non-renewable resource does not exist, the availability of the resource should be spread across as many generations as possible. Any long-run reliance on the resource prior to its eventual depletion must be overcome.

The ecosphere's sink function

The second major function of the ecosphere relates to its capacity to assimilate high-entropy waste materials and transform them into useful, low-entropy, material resources. The ecosphere is able to perform this function – in effect, a natural recycling process – through the agency of biogeochemical processes driven by the free importation of solar energy. Because the ecosphere's waste assimilative capacity (A) has developed slowly over eons of evolution, its capacity to metabolise a growing quantity of high-entropy wastes (W) is severely limited. In addition, while it may be possible for humankind to augment the ecosphere's waste assimilative capacity, this is a very slow process subject to severe limits (Norgaard, 1984). Compounding these difficulties is the fact that a major portion of the ecosphere's waste-absorbing capacity exists in the form of the world's photosynthetic biomass and much of this has already been greatly reduced by logging, natural vegetation clearance, and wetland dredging.

If we assume that measures have been instituted to immediately cease the decline in a nation's waste-absorbing biomass, the condition required to fully preserve the ecosphere's conversion of high-entropy waste materials into usable resources is not unlike the condition applicable to the preservation of renewable resources. That is, the quantity of wastes being generated by the economic process must remain within the ecosphere's waste assimilative capacity. Indeed, the need to remain within the ecosphere's waste assimilative capacity is doubly important given that an excessive rate of waste generation can upset the coevolutionary balance of the global system which can impair the critical life-support services provided by the ecosphere. This brings to bear our fourth sustainability precept.

> Sustainability precept no. 4: To help maintain critical life-support services and to preserve the ecosphere's capacity to recycle high entropy waste materials, the quantity of waste generated by the economic process must not exceed the ecosphere's waste assimilative capacity. That is:

$$W \leq A \tag{2.5}$$

It was mentioned earlier that the deleterious ecological consequences of waste output are not confined to the quantity of waste being generated by the economic process. Mounting evidence indicates that the production and use of particular forms of industrial and agricultural substances have led to the widespread destruction of biological species. In some instances, this has resulted in severe ecological degradation and a subsequent decline in various ecosystem services (Marco, 1987). Critically, many of these substances persist in the natural environment for long periods of time and, since they are easily absorbed in fatty tissues, have the propensity to bioaccumulate in the natural environment (Crathorne *et al.*, 1996).

What is particularly alarming about many toxic substances is that their long-term impacts are largely unknown, although there is clear evidence that continued human exposure can lead to the development of tumours, cancers, leukaemias, and other chronic ailments. Exposure to toxic elements has also been linked to infertility and escalating birth defects (Pimentel *et al.*, 2007). Despite the fact that many toxic compounds are difficult to destroy or safely dispose of (Davies and Doon, 1987), illegal dumping is a common practice (IMPEL, 2005), and a large proportion of toxic compounds are inadequately stored (FAO, 2001), the global production of a variety of toxic compounds continues to increase.

Such is the concern over the growing generation and long-term impact of toxic pollutants, the following recommendation was made in a report published by the Food and Agriculture Organization (FAO) of the United Nations (FAO, 2001):

> The identification, neutralization, and safe disposal of obsolete stocks of pesticides and other chemicals, especially polychlorinated biphenyl (PCB), must be urgently facilitated, particularly in developing countries and countries with economies in transition. As well, future stockpiling of other obsolete pesticides and chemicals must be prevented. With respect to the final disposition of chemicals, the IFCS [Intergovernmental Forum on Chemical Safety] and IOMC [Inter-Organization Programme for the Sound Management of Chemicals] should promote the use of less polluting and safer technologies.

In view of this recommended course of action and the unknown impacts of many toxic pollutants, the following can be regarded as our fifth sustainability precept:

> Sustainability precept no. 5: The generation of particular forms of hazardous waste – i.e., those which pose a major long-term threat to a healthy ecosphere – should be limited and, in some cases, prohibited altogether. At the international level, there is an urgent need to co-ordinate the safe storage and disposal of toxic pollutants.

The ecosphere's life-support function

The ecosphere's third major function comprises the myriad of life-support services provided either directly or indirectly by critical ecosystems and other key biophysical systems. The ability of the ecosphere to support life exists because, as a far-from-thermodynamic-equilibrium system characterised by a range of biogeochemical clocks and essential feedback mechanisms, it has developed the self-organisational capacity to regulate the temperature and composition of the Earth's surface and atmosphere.[14] Unfortunately, there has been a growing tendency for human beings to take for granted the conditions needed to support life – a consequence of technological optimism and the growing detachment most people have from the vagaries of the natural world. In particular, two false beliefs have emerged. The first is a widely held belief that the Earth's current unique ability to support life was preordained. This is not so since, as Blum (1962) has previously explained, had the Earth been a little smaller, or a little hotter, or had any one of an infinite number of past events occurred only marginally differently, the evolution of living organisms on Earth might never have eventuated.

Secondly, it is widely believed that organic evolution is confined to living organisms responding to exogenously determined environmental factors. It is now transparently clear that 'fitness' is a byproduct of the coevolutionary relationship that exists between the ecosphere and its constituent species. Indeed, the ecosphere is as uniquely suited to existing species as are the latter to the ambient characteristics of the ecosphere. Hence, according to Blum (1962: 61), it is 'impossible to treat the environment as a separable aspect of the problem of organic evolution; it becomes an integral part thereof.' Unequivocally, just as current environmental conditions were not preordained, neither are the environmental conditions of the future. They will always be influenced by the evolution of constituent species and, in particular, the actions of recalcitrant species.

An awareness of the above brings to bear a critical point. Whereas human intervention can never ensure that the Earth remains eternally fit for human habitability, humankind does have the capacity to bring about a premature change in its prevailing comfortable state. Many people believe that global climate change constitutes an impending sign of a radical change in the planet's comfortable conditions. Conversely, there are some observers who argue that events such as climate change are of no great concern because they are little more than symptoms of a benign coevolutionary adjustment brought on by the eccentricities of humankind. That is, any malady caused by human activity will be short-lived because whatever may threaten the human habitability of the planet will induce the evolution of a new and more comfortable environmental state. For such observers, humankind is potentially immune from the consequences of its own actions.

Nothing, however, could be further from the truth. The quasi-immortality of the ecosphere prevails only because of the informal association that exists between the global system and its constituent species. But quasi-immortality in no way extends to any particular species. Historical evidence indicates a tendency for the global system to correct ecological imbalances in ways that are invariably unpleasant for incumbent species. Hence, although the Earth has revealed itself to be immune to the emergence of wayward species (e.g., oxygen-bearers in the past), individual species – including human beings – are in no way immune from the consequences of their own collective folly.

What, then, constitutes the special feature of the ecosphere that bestows it with the unique capacity to support life? Is it the sheer quantity of natural capital existing within it or is it some particular aspect of natural capital? Lovelock leaves us in no doubt by emphasising that a minimum number and complexity of species is required to establish, develop, and maintain the Earth's biogeochemical clocks and essential feedback mechanisms. To wit:

> The presence of a sufficient array of living organisms on a planet is needed for the regulation of the environment. Where there is incomplete occupation, the ineluctable forces of physical or chemical evolution soon render it uninhabitable.

> (Lovelock, 1988: 63)

It is, therefore, a combination of the convoluted interactions and interdependencies between the various species, the diversity of species, and the complexity of ecological systems – in all, the *biodiversity* present in natural capital – that underpins its life-supporting function. That is not to say that the quantity of natural capital is unimportant. It is important if only because the biodiversity needed to maintain the Earth's habitable status requires a full, not partial, occupation by living organisms. But the quantity of natural capital, itself, should never be equated with biodiversity.

If the sheer magnitude of natural capital is an inadequate indication of the effectiveness with which it can foreseeably support life, what is the minimum level of biodiversity needed to maintain the ecosphere's life-support function? Unfortunately, this is not known, although there is general agreement that some semblance of a biodiversity threshold does exist. What we do know about biodiversity is that, in the same way as biodiversity begets greater biodiversity, diminutions beget further diminutions.[15] It is also known that the present rate of species extinction is far exceeding the rate of speciation – indeed, so much so that biodiversity has, on any relevant time-scale, become a non-renewable resource (Daily and Ehrlich, 1992).

Given that a rise in the global rate of extinction will unquestionably increase the vulnerability of human beings to their own extinction, a sensible risk-averse strategy would be to rigidly adhere to a biodiversity 'line in the sand'. Ehrlich (1993) provides a hint to where this line should be drawn by pointing out that humankind knows enough about the value of biodiversity to operate on the principle that 'all reductions in biodiversity should be avoided because of the potential threats to ecosystem functioning and its life-support role'. As a corollary of Ehrlich's dictum, humankind should draw a line at the currently existing level of biodiversity. Conscious efforts should thus be made to preserve remnant vegetation and critical ecosystems.[16] Furthermore, humankind needs to avoid the exploitation of areas largely unaffected by past human endeavours. This places us in a position to posit a sixth sustainability precept.

Sustainability precept no. 6: To maintain the ecosphere's life-support services, native vegetation and critical ecosystems must be preserved, rehabilitated, and/or restored. In addition, the future exploitation of natural capital should be confined to areas already significantly modified by previous human activities.

Increasing throughput and the six sustainability precepts

Let us recapitulate for a moment. We have meticulously considered the non-substitutable role of the ecosphere and listed a number of sustainability precepts which must be satisfied to ensure maintenance of the ecosphere's three critical functions. We are now in a position to determine what an increasing rate of throughput implies in terms of ecological sustainability.

Clearly, if renewable resources constitute a stable proportion of the total rate of resource use, it follows that any steady increase in resource throughput must lead to an increase in the input of renewable resources. This must eventually result in the violation of precept no. 1 (i.e., $R_R > r.N_R$). As for precept no. 2, it has already been explained that there is a limit to the amount of renewable resources that can be cultivated to offset the depletion of non-renewable resources as well as a limit to humankind's capacity to augment the productivity of existing renewable resources. Should the rate of non-renewable resource input increase over time, precept no. 2 must also eventually be violated.

Sustainability precept no. 3 involves a different set of circumstances in the sense that it can be violated regardless of whether or not the rate of throughput is increasing. Any physical scale of the economic subsystem is potentially unsustainable in the long run if: (a) a particular non-renewable resource is critical to the operation and maintenance of the economy at hand; (b) prior to the inevitable exhaustion of the non-renewable resource, a renewable resource substitute has not been discovered; and (c) reliance upon the non-renewable resource has not been overcome. Having said this, so long as the remaining sustainability precepts continue to be satisfied, it is possible to sustain the economy at the physical scale that prevailed at the time of the resource's exhaustion. What will undeniably differ is the range of goods that can be produced in the future. The new mix of goods may be such that the economy is unable to function at a previous level of performance.[17] For example, the lack of a particular resource may preclude the manufacture of goods which are critical to the smooth operation of a modern, complex economy (e.g., goods in the transport and communications sectors). Even so, this would not rule out the possibility of sustaining the same physical magnitude of human-made capital – albeit a stock that would be of inferior quality – by shifting to other resource types used in the manufacture of less critical goods. Nevertheless, such a situation should be avoided since the quality of human-made capital is likely to become an increasingly important development factor in the context of a sustainable economy.

It was pointed out earlier that, despite the first and second laws of thermodynamics, matter–energy can remain locked up in durable goods for extended periods of time (i.e., until durable goods wholly depreciate). Although this can delay the discharge of waste matter–energy back into the ecosphere, eventually the quantity of matter–energy exiting the economy as high-entropy wastes must equal the quantity of matter–energy that has entered the economy as low-entropy resources. With this in mind, if the rate of throughput increases over time, the quantity of wastes being generated by the economic process must also rise. It therefore follows that an increasing rate of throughput must inevitably lead to the violation of precept no. 4 (i.e., $W > A$).

Precept no. 5 is not unlike precept no. 3 in that it can be violated irrespective of the rate of throughput. That is, if an excessive generation of hazardous substances is the inevitable byproduct of producing goods of critical economic importance, an economy of any particular scale is potentially unsustainable in the long run. Once again, violation of precept no. 5 will not necessarily rule out the ability to sustain an economy of a similar or larger physical scale, which can potentially be achieved by substituting towards goods involving the generation of more benign forms of waste. What it will rule out is an economy consisting of the goods associated with the generation of certain intractable and hazardous substances. Not unlike the circumstances applicable to precept no. 3, this could greatly reduce the overall quality of human-made capital that can be sustained.

Because there are limits to rises in the productivity of natural capital, an increasing rate of throughput will require more and more natural capital to be exploited over time. This must inevitably lead to encroachment upon and a subsequent decline of both the number and integrity of critical ecosystems and the low-impacted areas still capable of providing valuable life-support services. Without question, an increasing rate of throughput must eventually result in the violation of precept no. 6.

Interestingly, even if the rate of throughput is non-increasing but the economy is physically growing (i.e., $dE/E > dY/Y$), precept no. 6 can still be violated. The ecosphere is, after all, a non-growing system, and a physically expanding subsystem of the ecosphere must eventually spill over into the domain of critical ecosystems unless there is an offsetting increase in the concentration of goods and human beings within the economy. However, the ability to increase these concentration levels is limited – one hectare of land can only accommodate so many goods and persons. Moreover, a society will almost certainly wish to remain well short of a particular concentration limit given that undesirability of extreme population densities.

In conclusion, it is transparently clear that an increase in the rate of throughput over time – the inevitable consequence of a continuously growing economy – must lead to the eventual violation of all six sustainability precepts. Put simply, the continued physical expansion of the economic subsystem is ecologically unsustainable. What's more, from a long-run perspective, the physical growth of the economy becomes unsustainable as soon as any one of sustainability precepts nos 1, 2, 4, and 6 is violated.[18] Which of these sustainability precepts is likely to be violated first (or has been violated first) is a moot point and a question to which we may never find a precise answer. However, one thing is certain. In the event that precept no. 4 is the first to be violated, it will be the ecosphere's waste assimilative capacity that imposes the limit on the rate at which low-entropy resources can sustainably enter the economy for production purposes – and this applies equally to renewable resources, such as solar energy (note: waste heat is also a form of pollution). Clearly, in such circumstances, it would be waste-related limits that would determine the maximum sustainable scale of an economic system, not the quantity of low-entropy resources available for use.[19]

Increasing throughput and the economic desirability of growth

We have so far ascertained that there is an ecological limit to growth. But, given the first question raised by the coevolutionary world-view, what is this limit? That is, how big can the economy get before it becomes unsustainable in the long run, and have the economies of most nations exceeded this limit? We shall leave these questions for the moment since it is equally if not more important to determine whether it is economically desirable to keep expanding economic systems up to their maximum sustainable scale.

As an economy physically grows, it generates additional benefits predominantly in the form of the 'utility' or 'psychic income' arising from the increased availability of consumer goods (Fisher, 1906). In keeping with Chapter 1, the employment of extra labour to produce more goods can, up to a point, also provide an important flow of additional benefits. Indeed, it is not difficult to envisage a wide range of additional economic and non-economic benefits emerging as a consequence of a physically expanding economy.

At the same time, a growing economy also leads to a number of additional costs which fall into the economic, social, or environmental cost categories. The costs belonging to the two former categories are somewhat different from the costs of the latter category in that they are generally experienced as a form of 'psychic disutility' or 'psychic outgo' (e.g., the costs of commuting, crime, and family breakdown).[20] If we subtract the psychic outgo against the psychic benefits of the economic process we arrive at what might be deemed the *net psychic income* of economic activity.

For the following reasons, net psychic income effectively constitutes the *uncancelled benefit* of economic activity (Daly, 1979). Why? Imagine tracing the economic process from its original source – natural capital – to its final psychic conclusion. Every intermediate transaction involves the cancelling out of a receipt and expenditure of the same magnitude (i.e., the seller receives what the buyer pays). Once a physical good is in the possession of the final consumer, there is no further exchange and, hence, no further cancelling out of transactions. Apart from the good itself, what remains at the end of the process is the uncancelled exchange value of the psychic income that the ultimate consumer expects to gain from the good plus any psychic disbenefits and other costs associated with the good's production. Note, therefore, that if the costs are subtracted from the good's final selling price, the difference approximates the 'use value' added to low-entropy matter–energy during the production process. Presumably the difference is positive, otherwise the economic process is a pointless exercise.

If we go in the opposite direction and trace the economic process from its psychic conclusion back to its original source, all transactions again cancel out. However, what remains on this occasion is the unpaid contribution of nature or, more definitively, the uncancelled exchange value of any natural capital services sacrificed in obtaining the throughput of matter–energy necessary to fuel the economic process – in effect, the costs belonging to the environmental cost category.[21] Thus, using the same logic applied to net psychic income, lost natural capital services can be regarded as the *uncancelled cost* of economic activity (Daly, 1979; Lawn and Sanders, 1999).

Consider, now, Figure 2.5, in which we shall ignore efficiency-increasing technological progress for the moment and assume that all technological advances are of the throughput-increasing kind. Throughput-increasing technological progress enables a nation to augment the rate of throughput which, as a consequence, allows it to physically expand its economy – albeit one that may not be sustainable in the long run. In Figure 2.5, the physical expansion of the economy is represented by a rightward movement along the horizontal axis. Additionally, the uncancelled benefits (net psychic income) and uncancelled costs (lost natural capital services) are respectively represented by the UB and UC curves.

In keeping with the principle of diminishing marginal benefits, we can expect the uncancelled benefits associated with a physically growing economy to increase at a diminishing rate. Conversely, on account of the principle of increasing marginal costs, we can expect the uncancelled costs to rise at an increasing rate. The shapes of the UB and UC curves in Figure 2.5 reflect these two standard economic principles. Moreover, the UC curve – which is directly related to the prevailing rate of throughput – becomes vertical once the economy reaches the maximum sustainable scale of S_S (i.e., the largest physical scale of the economy consistent with the satisfaction of all six sustainability precepts).[22] As Figure 2.5 shows, the growth of the economy up to a physical scale of S_S is ecologically sustainable. Although the growth of the economy beyond a scale of S_S is still technically feasible for a short period of time (i.e., by drawing down stocks of natural capital), it is ecologically unsustainable in the long run.

From an economic perspective, matters change considerably. The economic welfare generated by a growing economy is measured in terms of the vertical distance between the UB and UC curves. Figure 2.5 indicates that the growth of the economy up to a physical scale of S_* increases a nation's economic welfare. As such, it constitutes a form of 'economic' growth. However, growth beyond S_* reduces economic welfare. That is, growth beyond what might be termed the *optimal macroeconomic scale* (i.e., the scale at which sustainable economic welfare is maximised) effectively becomes 'uneconomic' growth and clearly ought to be avoided. The critical point here is that growth beyond the optimal scale becomes economically undesirable despite the fact that the physical expansion of the economy between S_* and S_S is ecologically sustainable. In all, Figure 2.5

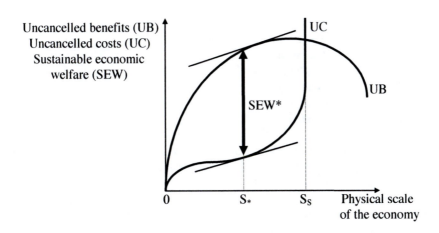

Figure 2.5 The sustainable economic welfare generated by a growing economy.

demonstrates that an economic limit to growth precedes an inevitable ecological limit to growth.

Efficiency-increasing technological progress and beneficial institutional reform

The previous analysis was somewhat over-simplified in that we ignored the possibility of efficiency-increasing technological progress. Technological advances of the efficiency-increasing kind result in an upward shift of the UB curve or a downward/rightward shift of the UC curve. Institutional reform can also generate similar outcomes. To explain how, we can arrange the uncancelled benefits and costs to arrive at a benefit–cost ratio referred to by Daly (1996) as a measure of 'ecological economic efficiency' (EEE):

$$\text{EEE} = \frac{Uncancelled\ benefits}{Uncancelled\ costs} = \frac{Net\ psychic\ income}{Lost\ natural\ capital\ services} \tag{2.6}$$

For a given physical scale of the economy, an increase in the EEE ratio indicates an improvement in the efficiency with which natural capital and the low entropy resources it provides are transformed into benefit-yielding human-made capital. A multitude of factors can be shown to contribute to an increase in the EEE ratio. To demonstrate how, the EEE ratio can be decomposed to reveal the following four eco-efficiency ratios:

$$\begin{array}{ccccc} & \text{Ratio 1} & \text{Ratio 2} & \text{Ratio 3} & \text{Ratio 4} \\ \text{EEE} = \dfrac{\text{NPY}}{\text{LNCS}} = \dfrac{\text{NPY}}{\text{HMK}} & \times & \dfrac{\text{HMK}}{\text{RT}} & \times & \dfrac{\text{RT}}{\text{NK}} & \times & \dfrac{\text{NK}}{\text{LNCS}} \end{array} \tag{2.7}$$

where:

- EEE = ecological economic efficiency
- NPY = net psychic income
- LNCS = lost natural capital services
- HMK = human-made capital
- RT = resource throughput
- NK = natural capital.

The order in which the four eco-efficiency ratios are presented in equation (2.7) is in keeping with the nature of the economic process – that is, net psychic income is enjoyed as a consequence of the creation and maintenance of human-made capital (Ratio 1); the maintenance of human-made capital requires the continued throughput of matter–energy (Ratio 2); the throughput of matter–energy is made possible thanks to the three instrumental services provided by natural capital (Ratio 3); and, in exploiting natural capital, the three instrumental services provided by natural capital are, to some degree, sacrificed (Ratio 4). Each eco-efficiency ratio represents a different form of efficiency pertaining to a particular sub-problem contained within the larger problem of achieving sustainable development. The four eco-efficiency ratios will now, along with the implications they have for the UB and UC curves, be individually explained and discussed.

Shifts of the uncancelled benefits (UB) curve

Ratio 1 is a measure of the *service efficiency* of human-made capital. It increases whenever a given amount of human-made capital yields a higher level of net psychic income. An increase in Ratio 1 causes the UB curve to shift upwards (see Figure 2.6). This can be achieved by improving the technical design of newly produced goods or by advancing the means by which human beings organise themselves in the course of producing and maintaining the stock of human-made capital (thereby reducing such things as the disutility of labour, the cost of commuting, and the cost of unemployment). A beneficial shift in the UB curve can also be achieved by redistributing income from the low marginal service or psychic income uses of the rich to the higher marginal service uses of the poor (Robinson, 1962).[23]

Figure 2.6 illustrates what happens to sustainable economic welfare when the UB curve shifts upwards. Because an increase in Ratio 1 augments the net psychic income yielded by a given amount of human-made capital, the UB curve shifts

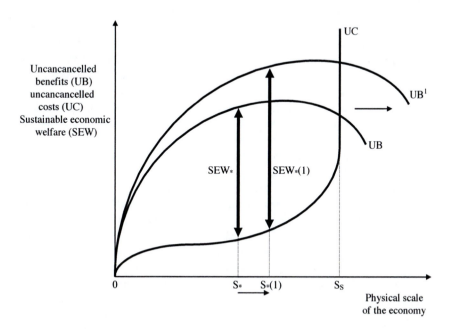

Figure 2.6   A change in sustainable economic welfare brought about by an increase in the service efficiency of human-made capital (Ratio 1).

up to UB_1. The UC curve does not move since the natural capital services lost as a consequence of creating and maintaining a given stock of human-made capital remain unchanged. For this reason, the maximum sustainable scale remains at S_S. However, sustainable economic welfare is no longer maximised at the prevailing scale of S_*. In the circumstances depicted in Figure 2.6, it is now economically desirable to expand the economy to the new optimal scale of $S_*(1)$ where sustainable economic welfare equals $SEW_*(1)$.[24]

Shifts of the uncancelled costs (UC) curve

Shifts of the UC curve arise in response to changes in Ratios 2, 3, and 4. Ratio 2 is a measure of the *maintenance efficiency* of human-made capital. It increases whenever a given physical magnitude of human-made capital can be maintained by a lower rate of resource throughput. This can be achieved by means of any one of the following advances outlined earlier in the chapter: (a) an increase in the technical efficiency of production; (b) increased rates of material recycling; (c) greater product durability; (d) improved operational efficiency. An increase in Ratio 2 causes the UC curve to shift downwards and to the right by enabling any given scale of the economy to be sustained by a reduced rate of resource throughput. This lessens the quantity of natural capital that needs to be exploited and, in doing so, results in the loss of fewer natural capital services.

Ratio 3 is a measure of the *growth efficiency* or productivity of natural capital. This form of efficiency is increased whenever a given amount of natural capital can sustainably yield more low-entropy resources and/or assimilate a greater quantity of high-entropy waste. Better management of natural resource systems and the preservation of critical ecosystems can lead to a more productive stock of natural capital. An increase in Ratio 3 leads to a downward and rightward shift of the UC curve because a more productive stock of natural capital reduces the quantity of natural capital that must be exploited to obtain the throughput of matter–energy needed to sustain the economy at a given physical scale. This allows an economy of a particular scale to be sustained at the expense of fewer natural capital services.

Ratio 4 is a measure of the *exploitative efficiency* of natural capital. An increase in Ratio 4 occurs whenever the natural capital services lost from directly exploiting a given quantity of natural capital declines. Once again, this allows an economy of a particular physical scale to be sustained at the expense of fewer natural capital services. Increases in Ratio 4 can be obtained through the development and execution of more ecologically sensitive extractive techniques, such as the use of underground rather than open-cut mining practices.

Figure 2.7 illustrates what happens to sustainable economic welfare when there is a beneficial shift of the UC curve. Because an increase in Ratios 2, 3, and 4 reduces the uncancelled cost of maintaining an economy at a given physical scale, the UC curve shifts down and out to UC_1. However, the UB curve remains stationary since any increases in Ratios 2, 3, and 4 do not augment the net psychic income generated by a given stock of human-made capital. Prior to the shift of the

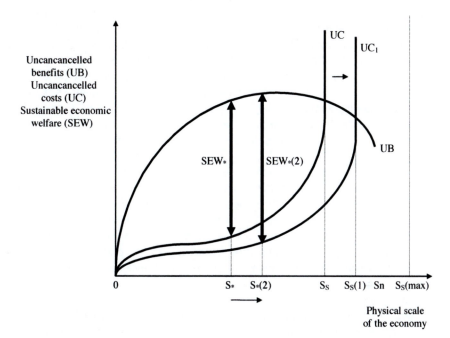

Figure 2.7 A change in sustainable economic welfare brought about by increases in the maintenance efficiency of human-made capital (Ratio 2), and the growth and exploitative efficiencies of natural capital (Ratios 3 and 4).

UC curve, sustainable economic welfare is maximised by operating the economy at a physical scale of S_*. Upon increases in Ratios 2, 3, and 4, it becomes economically desirable to expand the economy to the new optimal scale of $S_*(2)$ where sustainable economic welfare increases to $SEW_*(2)$.

Unlike the UB curve, a shift in the UC curve presents us with two maximum sustainable scales of the economy to consider. The first involves the largest physical scale of the economy that can be sustained given current levels of human know-how – what might be deemed the *prevailing* maximum sustainable scale. Given the potential to increase Ratios 2, 3, and 4, the prevailing maximum expands in accordance with shifts in the UC curve. Hence, as depicted in Figure 2.7, the shift in the UC curve from UC to UC_1 leads to an increase in the prevailing maximum from S_S to $S_S(1)$.

The second maximum sustainable scale is denoted by the dotted line at the physical scale of $S_S(max)$. This dotted line represents the largest physical scale of the economy that a nation can sustain given: (a) the efficiency, recycling, and durability limits imposed by the first and second laws of thermodynamics; (b) the limits imposed by the restriction on how much renewable natural capital can be cultivated on a finite, non-growing planet; (c) humankind's inability to continuously increase the productivity of renewable natural capital; and (d) the limited waste assimilative capacity of the ecosphere. In effect, S_s(max) represents the *ultimate* ecological limit to the growth of an economic system.[25] As such, S_s(max) constitutes the limit to which a nation can shift the UC curve to the right.

From a sustainability perspective, it is logical to ask whether a nation should be concerned if the economy exceeds the maximum sustainable scale pertaining to current levels of human know-how when it is considerably smaller than the ultimate ecological limit. After all, if technological progress can shift the prevailing maximum scale to the ultimate maximum, would this not render an economic scale of Sn in Figure 2.7 potentially sustainable? There are two good reasons to believe not.

Firstly, in a coevolutionary world, the scale of the ultimate maximum depends entirely upon a nation continuing to satisfy the six sustainability precepts. This is because their violation results in the progressive degradation of natural capital and a consequent reduction in the sustainable rate of resource throughput. Should the economy remain larger than the prevailing maximum scale, the ultimate maximum of S_s(max) will diminish over time. Indeed, the prevailing maximum sustainable scale will also diminish in size, thereby indicating it is possible for a steady-state economy in excess of the prevailing maximum scale to become increasingly unsustainable.

Secondly, if a nation is in a position such as Sn > S_s(1) in Figure 2.7, the only way it can grow its economy and again operate within the prevailing maximum scale is to increase the rate of technical efficiency (*dE/E*) faster than it physically expands the economy (i.e., by shifting the UC curve to the right faster than the economy moves rightwards along the horizontal axis). Given that *dE/E* is subject to diminishing returns, this is unlikely to be feasible.

Clearly, for a nation in this situation to again operate sustainably it would almost certainly be forced to decrease the physical scale of its economy. Having returned to a sustainable scale, its capacity to safely expand the economy once more would depend upon the economy remaining within the confines of the prevailing maximum scale. In all, the fact that an ultimate limit exists at a scale much larger than the prevailing maximum offers little if any relief for a growth-obsessed nation that happens to be violating at least one of the six sustainability precepts.

The steady-state imperative – the need to focus on qualitative improvement, not the physical growth of the economy

We have seen that the ecological limit to growth will ultimately restrict a nation's capacity to beneficially shift the UC curve. What about the UB curve? Is there a constraint on its upward adjustment? This is a more complex issue because service, as a psychic magnitude, is not subject to the same physical laws as human-made capital.[26] Yet there are at least two aspects worth considering. Firstly, there is a probable limit on humankind's physiological capacity to experience service (i.e., a point of satiation exists for everyone). Indeed, economists have implicitly recognised this limit with their reference to a consumer 'bliss point'.[27]

Secondly, Weisskopf (1973) has argued that the additional benefits generated by an improving stock of human-made capital are subject to diminishing returns. The basis for Weisskopf's reasoning is that each new quality-related breakthrough becomes increasingly difficult and time-expensive to accomplish once the human capacity to experience consumption-related utility nears its saturation point. Consequently, even if the service-yielding qualities of human-made capital can be augmented indefinitely, its achievement would reduce the time available for individuals to satisfy high-order needs. Given this, a point must be reached at which the marginal benefits of a better form of consumption are exceeded by the marginal costs of forgone non-economic pursuits. It is at this point that the net psychic income yielded by a given quantity of human-made capital reaches an asymptotic limit. It is also at this point where upward shifts of the UB curve effectively become unobtainable.

There are, however, good reasons to believe that the potential to positively shift the UB curve is far from exhausted. This aside, it is because of fast-approaching ecological and economic limits to growth (i.e., impending limits to the beneficial shifts of the UC curve) that achieving sustainable development will undeniably require all nations to make the transition to a steady-state economy – preferably somewhere near their optimal scale. Given this steady-state imperative, it is clear that the goal of physically expanding the economy (growth) must eventually give way to an emphasis on qualitative improvement (development). This means that a nation must focus on qualitatively advancing the stock of human-made capital; on ensuring the stock of wealth is more equitably distributed; on minimising the rate of resource throughput; and on reorganising the production process to both increase job satisfaction and reduce any associated social costs. Provided these advances can be made, the need to move towards a steady-state economy should not be a cause for concern. Indeed, unlike the impact of growing the economy beyond its ecological and economic limits, there is no reason why an appropriately managed steady-state economy cannot deliver increasing levels of sustainable economic welfare for many years to come.[28]

Empirical evidence concerning the ecological limits to growth

Returning now to the first of the two questions raised by the coevolutionary world-view, there is little agreement on how to determine whether the economies of the world's nations have exceeded their ecological limits (i.e., their maximum sustainable scale). A number of indicators have been devised to resolve this matter and each has its supporters and detractors. Some of these indicators will now be discussed.

Human Appropriation of Net Primary Production

The Human Appropriation of Net Primary Production (HANPP) is an aggregate indicator designed to measure the product of photosynthesis appropriated by humankind for its own purposes (Vitousek *et al.*, 1986). Because the Earth's net primary production constitutes the basic food source for everything not capable of photosynthesis, the HANPP reflects the extent to which human activities alter the availability of trophic energy flows in ecosystems (Haberl *et al.*, 2007). It has therefore been argued that the HANPP is a useful means of measuring the scale of human activities relative to the supporting ecosphere.

As early as 1986, it was estimated that humankind's appropriation of the planet's net primary production (terrestrial and aquatic) was around 25 per cent (Vitousek *et al.*, 1986). If we assume that it is possible for humankind to sustainably appropriate 100 per cent of the world's total net product – which implies zero energy for non-human species – Vitousek *et al.*'s results suggest that the global economy of 1986 was effectively limited to two doublings in scale. Should the global economy continue to grow at an average annual rate of 2.5 per cent, it is conceivable that it will reach its ultimate ecological limit by around 2045.[29]

In reality, some of the Earth's total net product must be made available to allow life-supporting ecosystems to thrive. Hence, a human appropriation rate of 100 per cent is a mere arithmetic possibility. To genuinely achieve ecological sustainability, the renowned biologist Edward Wilson has argued that at least 50 per cent of the planet must be set aside to maintain the necessary level of ecosystem functioning (Wilson, 2002). If this is true, the ultimate ecological limit to growth – the point beyond which critical ecosystems begin to collapse across much of the globe – will be reached as early as 2015.

It has been widely recognised that the HANPP estimates made by Vitousek *et al.* are subject to large uncertainties (Common and Sagl, 2005; Haberl *et al.*, 2007). This is because the indicator includes both intermediate uses of the products of photosynthesis and the loss of potential primary productivity from land use conversion. Although there is little controversy about the inclusion of these two factors, the calculations pertaining to them involve assumptions which, if varied, have the potential to significantly alter the overall HANPP estimates (Haberl *et al.*, 2007).

Environmental Sustainability Index

The Environmental Sustainability Index (ESI) is a composite indicator composed of 76 individual variables (Yale Center for Environmental Law and Policy *et al.*, 2005). The aim of the ESI is to capture the following five components of ecological sustainability: (a) the state of environmental systems; (b) stresses on environmental systems; (c) human vulnerability to environmental change; (d) social and institutional capacities to cope with environmental change; and (e) global stewardship.

According to the results published in the 2005 ESI Report, four of the top five ranked ESI performers were the Scandinavian countries of Finland, Norway, Sweden, and Iceland (Yale Center for Environmental Law and Policy *et al.*, 2005). Also featuring high in the ESI rankings were the low-population, settler countries of Canada, Australia, and New Zealand; some small European countries

(Switzerland, Austria, Latvia, and Croatia); and a number of South American nations (Uruguay, Guyana, Argentina, Brazil, and Peru).

There are a number of debatable issues pertaining to the weighting of the variables used in the ESI's construction. Although the devisers of the ESI have done their best to address them, the index has been heavily criticised (e.g., Jesinghaus, 2001). One of the ESI's shortcomings is that the inclusion of institutional parameters – which constitute 60 per cent of the final index value – bias the ESI in favour of the world's wealthy nations. Virtually all of the wealthy nations have been responsible for most of the ecological damage that has occurred over the past century and, because of their high consumption levels, continue to place the greatest stress on the ecosphere. Furthermore, although these countries have greater capacity to deal with environmental challenges than poorer nations, capacity itself does not guarantee resilience, particularly when ecological sustainability involves limits that no amount of human-made capital or human ingenuity can overcome.

A good example of this bias can be seen by comparing Switzerland and Angola. As at 2005, Switzerland was ranked seventh of 146 nations with an ESI of 63.7. Angola, with an ESI of 42.9, was ranked 123rd. Owing to a much lower rate of resource consumption and minimal conversion rate of ecosystems into agricultural land, Angola outscored Switzerland in terms of the state of, and stress on, its environmental systems (components (a) and (b) of the ESI). However, Switzerland achieved a higher ESI score essentially because of its advanced institutional, political, and economic capacity to deal with environmental challenges.

Not for one moment am I suggesting that a nation's capacity to deal with environmental challenges is unimportant or that Angola is well positioned to achieve ecological sustainability. However, it seems reasonable to ask why a nation with an entirely modified natural environment, such as Switzerland, should be ranked so much higher than a country with superior ecological health simply because it has a greater capacity to deal with future environmental problems? We wouldn't consider a person with high blood pressure to be healthier than someone with normal blood pressure just because they are financially more able to afford ameliorative medication and a membership fee at the local fitness centre. Yet in terms of the relative sustainability performances of nations, something equivalent to this is implied by the ESI rankings.

Material Flow Accounting

Material Flow Accounting (MFA) involves the use of input–output matrices to measure the throughput of materials used in the economic process (Perman *et al.*, 2003). Based on the materials-balance principle (first law of thermodynamics), MFA aims to calculate the environmental pressure being exerted by economic activity at both the aggregate and sectoral levels (Ayres and Kneese, 1969; Leontief, 1970; Victor, 1972; Perrings, 1987).

MFA statistics have long been published by a variety of organisations. The most comprehensive international coverage of MFA indicators is regularly released by the Sustainable Europe Research Institute (SERI). Calculated for the 1980–2005 period, these MFA indicators reveal that most of the world's wealthy nations have increased their material throughput flows over the study period (www.material-flows.net/mfa). Exceptions were Germany, the UK, the Netherlands, and Canada. The worst offenders were Norway, Portugal, New Zealand, Spain, Australia, Denmark, Sweden, and the USA.

One of the shortcomings of MFA indicators is that no measuring stick exists against which the material flows of a nation can be assessed to determine if they are sustainable in the long run. This makes it difficult to ascertain whether a nation's economy has exceeded the physical scale of S_S depicted in Figure 2.5. Another unfortunate weakness of MFA indicators pertains to the set of simultaneous equations employed to mathematically represent the economic process. These equations embody fixed coefficients which preclude the modelling of behavioural changes and the impact of factor substitution as relative prices vary over time (Perman *et al.*, 2003). Consequently, a time series of MFA indicators can often falsely reflect the changing environmental stress levels applicable to different sectors of the economy. Many observers have therefore argued that the input–output models used to generate MFA indicators are only useful for short-term modelling purposes. Since ecological sustainability analyses involve extended time-frames, this severely limits the value of MFA indicators.

Genuine Savings

Genuine Savings (GS) is an economic indicator first developed by Pearce and Atkinson (1993) that was predicated on earlier work by Hicks (1946), Hartwick (1977), Solow (1986), and Victor (1991). The aim of the GS indicator is to measure the impact of economic activity on a nation's stock of income-generating capital. This is achieved by subtracting the depletion of natural resource stocks, pollution damages, and the depreciation of producer goods from gross investment in all forms of capital (Pearce and Atkinson, 1993; Hamilton, 1994; Pearce *et al.*, 1996; Dietz and Neumayer, 2006). So long as the value of GS is non-negative, it is assumed that a nation has maintained the productive capacity of its economy and is operating on a sustainable basis.

GS measurements on over 150 countries for the 1976–2000 period reveal that the worst-performing nations were those in North Africa and the Middle East (World Bank, 2004). Although some countries in the Caribbean and Latin America had a negative GS in the mid-1980s, virtually all the nations of East Asia, South Asia, and the OECD maintained a positive GS over the entire study period. As a whole, the GS of the global economy also remained in positive territory between 1976 and 2000.

Since the GS indicator first emerged, a number of deficiencies have come to light. Firstly, it has been demonstrated that a positive GS value reflects, at best, a necessary but insufficient condition for achieving sustainability (Asheim, 1994; Pezzey and Withagen, 1998). Secondly, Dietz and Neumayer (2006) have shown that exogenous shocks are inadequately accommodated by the models used to generate GS values. Finally, GS models assume perfect substitutability between human-made capital and natural capital; in particular, the ability of human-made capital to replicate the services provided by critical ecosystems (Lawn, 2007a). In all, these weaknesses cast serious doubts over the efficacy of using GS measures as indicators of the long-term sustainability of national economies.

Ecological footprint versus biocapacity

One of the more recently publicised biophysical indicators is the measure of a nation's ecological footprint (EF) (Wackernagel *et al.*, 1999). A country's EF constitutes the area of land *required* to generate the renewable resources needed to sustain economic activity at its current level and to absorb the resultant wastes (Wackernagel and Rees, 1996). The explicit emphasis on renewable resources in the calculation of the EF arises because of the inevitable exhaustion of non-renewable resources. To determine if a nation's economy has exceeded its maximum sustainable scale, the EF is compared to its biocapacity. A nation's biocapacity is indicated by the quantity of land *available* to generate an ongoing supply of renewable resources and to absorb the wastes it generates. Ecological unsustainability (ecological deficit) occurs if a nation's EF exceeds its biocapacity.

Table 2.2 reveals that, in 2003, 80 of 140 surveyed nations had ecological footprints in excess of their biocapacities (Global Footprint Network, 2006). Some observers have suggested that ecological deficits need not present a problem given that countries with ecological surpluses can aid deficit countries by exporting their surplus resources. As much as the trade in resources can assist some individual countries, it needs to be recognised that the impact of an ecological deficit is not always confined to a resource shortfall on the part of the debtor country. In many cases it will include the loss of critical ecosystem services that no importation of resources can overcome.

Furthermore, even if the trade in resources could overcome the ecological deficits of some nations, Table 2.2 shows that the global EF has already exceeded the planet's biocapacity by an amount equal to 0.5 hectares per person. Indeed, had 2003 global consumption levels been fuelled exclusively by renewable resources, Table 2.2 reveals that it would have required an area of land equivalent to 1.25 Earths (Global Footprint Network, 2006).[30] Since this situation cannot continue indefinitely, it follows that the ecological surpluses enjoyed by some nations are insufficient to finance the combined ecological deficits of the remainder.

A major weakness of the EF is its use of land area as a numeraire for sustainability. There is little doubt that, if a nation were compelled to generate its entire resource flow in the form of renewable resources, land area and fertility would constitute critical limiting factors. However, there are other factors that can also potentially impinge on a nation's renewable resource flow (e.g., climate and water availability) (Patterson, 2006). Australia is a good example. According to Table 2.2, Australia had a per capita ecological surplus in 2003 of 5.9 hectares. In what is a country beset with water shortages at the best of times, recent droughts have significantly reduced water allocations to irrigators in the Murray–Darling Basin. This has severely reduced agricultural output from what is normally regarded as

Table 2.2 Ecological footprint (EF) and biocapacity (2003)

	Ecological footprint (gha per person)	Bio-capacity (gha per person)	Ecological deficit (–) or suplus (+) (gha per person)		Ecological footprint (gha per person)	Bio-capacity (gha per person)	Ecological deficit (–) or suplus (+) (gha per person)		Ecological footprint (gha per person)	Bio-capacity (gha per person)	Ecological deficit (–) or suplus (+) (gha per person)
World	2.2	1.8	–0.5								
Africa											
Algeria	1.6	0.7	–0.9	Gabon	1.4	19.2	17.8	Namibia	1.1	4.4	3.3
Angola	1.0	3.4	2.4	Gambia	1.4	0.8	–0.5	Niger	1.1	1.5	0.4
Benin	0.8	0.9	0.1	Ghana	1.0	1.3	0.3	Nigeria	1.2	0.9	–0.2
Botswana	1.6	4.5	3.0	Guinea	0.9	2.8	1.8	Rwanda	0.7	0.5	–0.1
Burkina Faso	1.0	1.0	0.0	Guinea-Bissau	0.7	2.9	2.2	Senegal	1.2	0.9	–0.3
Burundi	0.7	0.6	–0.1	Kenya	0.8	0.7	–0.2	Sierra Leone	0.7	1.1	0.4
Cameroon	0.8	1.3	0.4	Lesotho	0.8	1.1	0.3	Somalia	0.4	0.7	0.3
Cent. Afr Rep.	0.9	3.7	2.8	Liberia	0.7	3.1	2.4	South Africa	2.3	2.0	–0.3
Chad	1.0	2.5	1.5	Libya	3.4	1.0	–2.4	Sudan	1.0	1.8	0.8
Congo	0.6	7.8	7.2	Madagascar	0.7	2.9	2.2	Swaziland	1.1	1.1	–0.1
Côte d'Ivoire	0.7	2.0	1.2	Malawi	0.6	0.5	–0.1	Tanzania	0.7	1.3	0.6
Dem. Rep. Congo	0.6	1.5	0.9	Mali	0.8	1.3	0.5	Tunisia	1.5	0.8	–0.8
Egypt	1.4	0.5	–0.9	Mauritania	1.3	5.8	4.5	Uganda	1.1	0.8	–0.2
Eritrea	0.7	0.5	–0.2	Morocco	0.9	0.8	–0.1	Zambia	0.6	3.4	2.8
Ethiopia	0.8	0.5	–0.3	Mozambique	0.6	2.1	1.4	Zimbabwe	0.9	0.8	–0.1

Table 2.2 (Continued) Ecological footprint (EF) and biocapacity (2003)

	Ecological footprint (gha per person)	Bio-capacity (gha per person)	Ecological deficit (−) or suplus (+) (gha per person)		Ecological footprint (gha per person)	Bio-capacity (gha per person)	Ecological deficit (−) or suplus (+) (gha per person)		Ecological footprint (gha per person)	Bio-capacity (gha per person)	Ecological deficit (−) or suplus (+) (gha per person)
Asia–Pacific											
Australia	6.6	12.4	5.9	Korea DPRP	1.4	0.7	−0.8	New Zealand	5.9	14.9	9.0
Bangladesh	0.5	0.3	−0.2	Korea Republic	4.1	0.5	−3.5	Pakistan	0.6	0.3	−0.3
Cambodia	0.7	0.9	0.1	Laos	0.9	1.3	0.4	Papua NG	2.4	2.1	−0.3
China	1.6	0.8	−0.9	Malaysia	2.2	3.7	1.5	Philippines	1.1	0.6	−0.5
India	0.8	0.4	−0.4	Mongolia	3.1	11.8	8.7	Sri Lanka	1.0	0.4	−0.6
Indonesia	1.1	1.0	0.0	Myanmar	0.9	1.3	0.4	Thailand	1.4	1.0	−0.4
Japan	4.4	0.7	−3.6	Nepal	0.7	0.5	−0.2	Vietnam	0.9	0.8	−0.1
Latin America											
Argentina	2.3	5.9	3.6	Dominican Rep.	1.6	0.8	−0.8	Mexico	2.6	1.7	−0.9
Bolivia	1.3	15.0	13.7	Ecuador	1.5	2.2	0.7	Nicaragua	1.2	3.5	2.4
Brazil	2.1	9.9	7.8	El Salvador	1.4	0.6	−0.8	Panama	1.9	2.5	0.6
Chile	2.3	5.4	3.0	Guatemala	1.3	1.3	0.0	Paraguay	1.6	5.6	4.0
Colombia	1.3	3.6	2.3	Haiti	0.6	0.3	−0.3	Peru	0.9	3.8	3.0
Costa Rica	2.0	1.5	−0.5	Honduras	1.3	1.8	0.5	Uruguay	1.9	8.0	6.1
Cuba	1.5	0.9	−0.7	Jamaica	1.7	0.5	−1.3	Venezuela	2.2	2.4	0.2
North America											
Canada	7.6	14.5	6.9	USA	9.6	4.7	−4.8				

Table 2.2 (Continued)   Ecological footprint (EF) and biocapacity (2003)

	Ecological footprint (gha per person)	Bio-capacity (gha per person)	Ecological deficit (−) or suplus (+) (gha per person)		Ecological footprint (gha per person)	Bio-capacity (gha per person)	Ecological deficit (−) or suplus (+) (gha per person)		Ecological footprint (gha per person)	Bio-capacity (gha per person)	Ecological deficit (−) or suplus (+) (gha per person)
M-E & Cent Asia											
Afghanistan	0.1	0.3	0.2	Israel	4.6	0.4	−4.2	Syria	1.7	0.8	−0.9
Armenia	1.1	0.6	−0.5	Jordan	1.8	0.3	−1.5	Turkey	2.1	1.4	−0.7
Azerbaijan	1.7	1.2	−0.5	Kazakhstan	4.0	4.1	0.1	Turkmenistan	3.5	3.6	0.1
Georgia	0.8	1.2	0.5	Kuwait	7.3	0.3	−7.0	UAE	11.9	0.8	−11.0
Iran	2.4	0.8	−1.6	Lebanon	2.9	0.3	−2.6	Uzbekistan	1.8	0.8	−1.1
Iraq	0.9	0.0	−0.8	Saudi Arabia	4.6	1.0	−3.7	Yemen	0.8	0.4	−0.5
EU25											
Austria	4.9	3.4	−1.5	Germany	4.5	1.7	−2.8	Netherlands	4.4	0.8	−3.6
Belg and L/bourg	5.6	1.2	−4.4	Greece	5.0	1.4	−3.6	Poland	3.3	1.8	−1.4
Czech Rep.	4.9	2.6	−2.3	Hungary	3.5	2.0	−1.5	Portugal	4.2	1.6	−2.6
Denmark	5.8	3.5	−2.2	Ireland	5.0	4.8	−0.2	Slovakia	3.2	2.8	−0.5
Estonia	6.5	5.7	−0.7	Italy	4.2	1.0	−3.1	Spain	5.4	1.7	−3.6
Finland	7.6	12.0	4.4	Latvia	2.6	6.6	4.0	Sweden	6.1	9.6	3.5
France	5.6	3.0	−2.6	Lithuania	4.4	4.2	−0.2	UK	5.6	1.6	−4.0
Rest of Europe											
Albania	1.4	0.9	−0.5	Croatia	2.9	2.6	−0.3	Russia	4.4	6.9	2.5
Belarus	3.3	3.2	−0.1	Macedonia	2.3	0.9	−1.4	Serbia and Mont.	2.3	0.8	−1.5
Bosnia Herzeg.	2.3	1.7	−0.6	Norway	5.8	6.8	0.9	Switzerland	5.1	1.5	−3.6
Bulgaria	3.1	2.1	−1.0	Romania	2.4	2.3	−0.1	Ukraine	3.2	1.7	−1.5

Source: Global Footprint Network (2006).
Note: Totals may not add up because of rounding.
gha denotes global hectares.

Australia's 'bread basket'. Should the severity and frequency of droughts increase in future years, as many climatologists predict, Australia's biocapacity could decline significantly even if the area of land available for renewable resource generation remains unchanged (note: the arable land area can also diminish on account of urban sprawl).

Because factors other than land area can restrict the flow of renewable resources, the calculations involved in EF analyses almost certainly overestimate a nation's biocapacity (underestimate ecological deficits). As such, the EF can be regarded as a very conservative indicator, which is all the more concerning given the EF estimates revealed in Table 2.2.[31] I should point out that, following the work of Lenzen and Murray (2001), a number of improvements have recently been made to EF estimates to better account for additional limiting factors.

Despite its shortcomings, it would seem that the EF is the best of the sustainability indicators outlined above. The ESI includes social variables which flatter wealthy, high resource-consuming countries; there are considerable uncertainties surrounding HANNP measures; MFA estimates are not amenable to time-series comparisons; and the GS indicator overlooks the non-substitutability of natural capital assets, including critical ecosystems. Three things appear to work in favour of the EF. Firstly, it is a very conservative form of analysis. Secondly, it incorporates a sustainability measuring stick in so far as it permits comparisons between 'actual consumption levels' (ecological footprint) and 'maximum sustainable consumption levels' (biocapacity). Finally, a measure of a nation's EF includes the renewable resources that must eventually be generated to replace the non-renewable resources currently being exhausted. This is a significant advance over the HANNP, perhaps the most legitimate rival indicator.

Assuming that the EF is the best available sustainability indicator, it would seem that many countries – i.e., those with ecological deficits – are operating their economies beyond the maximum sustainable scale. In other words, they are operating beyond a scale of S_S. Whether some countries are operating beyond $S_S(max)$ is difficult to say because technological and institutional advances can, for some time, reduce the ecological footprint associated with current levels of consumption in the same way as they can beneficially shift the UC curve. But this will be difficult to achieve if the population and per capita consumption levels of deficit countries continue to rise. I might also add that increases in these two variables would also make it increasingly difficult for countries to maintain ecological surpluses.

It goes without saying that the global economy has already grown beyond its maximum sustainable scale. Alarmingly, in view of global population projections and forecast increases in the per capita consumption levels of China and India, it is unlikely that the global economy will return to a sustainable status in the immediate future. In fact, it is likely to take nothing short of the world's wealthy nations moving rapidly to a steady-state economy and the world's poorer nations doing the same over the next two to three decades to bring the global economy into line with the Earth's maximum carrying capacity.

Empirical evidence concerning the economic limits to growth

To recall, the second question raised by the coevolutionary world-view related to the economic limits to growth – namely, how big can a nation's economy get before its sustainable economic welfare begins to decline? Figure 2.5 showed that sustainable economic welfare is measured by the difference between the benefits and costs of economic activity. Fortunately, an indicator has recently been developed which incorporates around 20 benefit and cost categories of the economic, social, and environmental variety. Known as the Genuine Progress Indicator (GPI), this indicator subtracts the costs from the benefits to obtain a macroeconomic estimate of sustainable economic welfare.[32]

GPI studies have been predominantly conducted on wealthy, industrialised nations. A recent study of seven countries in the Asia-Pacific region has boosted the number of GPI calculations of poorer nations (Lawn and Clarke, 2008a). The results of the Asia-Pacific study are very illuminating and I shall refer to the significance of them soon. For now, consider Figure 2.8, which reveals the results of GPI studies conducted on six wealthy nations in the 1990s.

In each of the country panels, the trend change in the GPI is contrasted against real GDP by setting both indicators at an index of value of 100 for the first year of the study period.[33] Figure 2.8 shows, in all six cases, that the GPI initially rises in unison with real GDP. A point is then reached where the GPI decreases or plateaus, although the timing of this turning point differs for each country. What does not alter significantly upon close examination of the data is that the rise in the GPI ceases once a nation's per capita GDP reaches Int$15,000 to Int$20,000.[34] Although real GDP is not strictly an indicator of the physical scale of a nation's economy, the decline in the GPI within this per capita GDP range suggests that all six countries have surpassed their optimal scale (i.e., S_* depicted in Figure 2.5).[35] In other words, they all appear to have exceeded their economic limit to growth. Crucially, the GPI results of other wealthy nations reveal a similar pattern (see Diefenbacher, 1994; Moffatt and Wilson, 1994; Rosenberg and Oegema, 1995; Jackson and Stymne, 1996; Jackson *et al.*, 1997; Stockhammer *et al.*, 1997; Guenno and Tiezzi, 1998; Lawn and Sanders, 1999; Forgie *et al.*, 2008; Makino, 2008).[36]

The uniform trend displayed in Figure 2.8 was first recognised in the mid-1990s. It led Max-Neef (1995) to put forward a 'threshold hypothesis' – namely, when a nation's per capita GDP exceeds a critical threshold level, one can expect its per capita economic welfare to either plateau or decline. As disconcerting as this hypothesis first appeared for countries already at the threshold point, it nonetheless offered comfort to the world's poorer nations. That is, because the per capita GDP of poor nations is much lower than the threshold range of Int$15,000–Int$20,000, a positive relationship should prevail for some time between the growth of their economies and the economic welfare it generates. Distressingly, this may not eventuate. Recent studies on China and Thailand indicate that the per capita GPI of both countries is already falling – China's per capita GPI peaking in 2002; Thailand's peaking in 2001 (Wen *et al.*, 2008; Clarke *et al.*, 2008). Yet these declines took place when the per capita GDP for China and Thailand was just

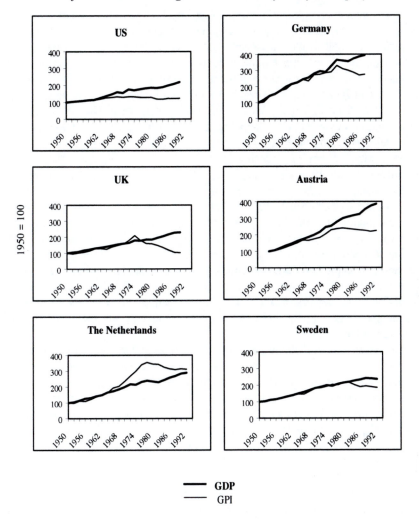

Figure 2.8 The GPI and GDP for the USA and a range of European countries. Source: Jackson and Stymne (1996).

$Int4,926 and $Int7,373 respectively (Lawn and Clarke, 2008b). Unsurprisingly, the per capita GPI of China and Thailand peaked well short of the value currently being enjoyed by wealthy nations.

I might add that the environmental costs in India and Vietnam – the other two poor countries included in the Asia-Pacific study – are escalating to such an extent that it may not be long before they also experience a downturn in their per capita GPI (Lawn, 2008; Nguyet Hong *et al.*, 2008). As it is, the rate at which the per capita GPI of these two countries is rising is considerably lower than the rate of increase in their per capita GDP.

In an endeavour to examine the relationship between growth and economic welfare in the Asia-Pacific region, the annual per capita GPI values of the seven countries included in the Asia-Pacific study were plotted by Lawn and Clarke (2008b) against their corresponding per capita GDP values. Figure 2.9 is the result of this comparison.[37] It reveals that the three wealthy countries – Australia, New Zealand, and Japan – have all reached a threshold level of per capita GDP.[38] It is also clear from Figure 2.9 that China and Thailand have likewise reached a threshold point of sorts. Alarmingly, it appears that the later a nation experiences an initial expansion phase of its economy, the lower is its per capita GDP when its per capita GPI begins to decline.[39] This is no better exemplified than by the tunnelling of each country's per capita GPI–GDP curve below that of their growth predecessor.

Lawn and Clarke (2008b) believe that the phenomenon revealed in Figure 2.9 can be explained by: (a) the migration of manufacturing operations to countries with low wages and feeble environmental regulations; and (b) growth late-comers having to contend with GDP expansion in a world full of human beings and human-made capital, yet one with much less natural capital and many fewer eco-systems. Whereas the second factor increases the marginal cost of an increment of GDP growth, the first factor results in poor nations having to bear a dispro-portionately large share of the social and environmental costs associated with an expanding global economy.

It is because of the above factors that Lawn and Clarke (2008b) have gone beyond Max-Neef (1995) to propose a new *contracting threshold hypothesis*. The hypothesis is essentially this: as the economies of the world collectively expand in a globalised economic environment, there is a contraction over time in the threshold level of per capita GDP. Thus, growth late-comers face the prospect of being unable to attain the level of economic welfare enjoyed by the early-movers.

Despite this hypothesis, Lawn and Clarke still believe it is possible for poor nations to experience higher levels of economic welfare. However, they argue that progress will occur only if an extension can be made to the threshold point at which the per capita GPI of the world's poor countries begins to decline. This, according to Lawn and Clarke (2008b), will necessitate dramatic policy changes on the part of the world's poorer countries. Just as importantly, it will require rich nations to cease growing their economies in order to provide the 'ecological space' that poor nations need to enjoy a phase of welfare-increasing growth.[40]

This, of course, implies that some of the responsibility for the fate of poor nations lies with the industrialised world. This may well be the case. But it would be wrong to believe that a plea for rich countries to reduce their per capita GDP would require them to make an unacceptable sacrifice. With the per capita GPIs of the industrialised world in decline, a valid economic reason already exists as to why rich countries would benefit from an immediate transition to a steady-state economy.

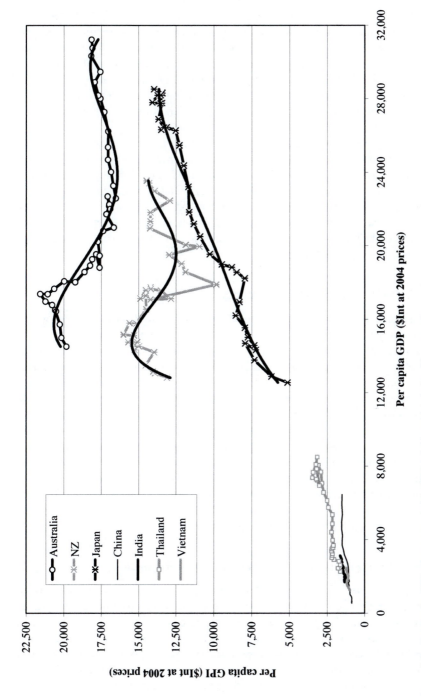

Figure 2.9 Per capita GPI versus per capita GDP of selected Asia-Pacific countries.

Concluding comments

In this major section of the chapter it has been demonstrated that there is an ecological and economic limit to the physical growth of economic systems and that the latter limit precedes the former. It has also been shown that most countries have exceeded their maximum sustainable scale and that the majority of the world's rich countries have long surpassed their optimal scale/economic limit to growth. Unfortunately, a number of poor nations have also reached a welfare threshold point which, in contradistinction to rich countries, has taken place at very low per capita GDP levels.

Because the lower threshold point confronting the world's poor nations is in large part due to the increased marginal cost of growing an economy in a 'full' world, it has been argued that rich countries should cease growing their economies to allow poor nations to enjoy a period of beneficial growth. But having to abandon the growth objective does not mean the end of progress. To the contrary, it has been shown that a well-managed steady-state economy offers a viable means – indeed, the only viable means – of increasing a nation's sustainable economic welfare long into the future.

Debunking pro-growth arguments

The arguments of the type just outlined should be enough to convince pro-growth advocates that the continued physical growth of economic systems is neither ecologically sustainable nor economically desirable. Their failure to accept them is invariably the result of denial or the promotion of pro-growth arguments that appear to offer an 'escape hatch' through which the limits to growth can be indefinitely avoided. The three most common pro-growth responses are: (a) human-made capital can adequately substitute for the decline in natural capital; (b) although the rate of environmental degradation rises early on in a nation's development process, it later falls because a richer society places greater value on environmental goods and possesses the means by which environmental damage can be ameliorated; and (c) resource use intensities and environmental degradation can be reduced by shifting the focus of economic activity away from the manufacturing of goods to the delivery of services. My aim in this major section is to debunk each of these pro-growth arguments.

Human-made capital is not a substitute for natural capital

Many advocates of the pro-growth position argue that an expanding and/or qualitatively improving stock of human-made capital can substitute for the gradual decline in natural capital. The basis for this position is the strong belief that human-made capital can offset any fall in natural resource stocks sufficiently to preserve an economy's long-run productive capacity. The immediate problem with this line of argument is that it concentrates on whether human-made capital can overcome the dwindling source function of natural capital but it ignores the implications associated with its inability to replicate the ecosphere's sink and life-support services. Given the significance of this oversight, one could stop right here and reject any notion that human-made capital and natural capital are close substitutes. But it is worth delving into the false logic behind the standard substitutability position if only to quash it completely.

In the early 1970s, a unique approach to resolving the substitution issue was adopted by Nordhaus and Tobin (1972). What Nordhaus and Tobin did was employ a production function supposedly representing the production possibilities of the US economy to estimate the elasticity of substitution between human-made capital (producer goods) and natural resource inputs. Nordhaus and Tobin opted for this approach on the widespread understanding that, if the elasticity of substitution between any two inputs has a value of at least one, it is safe to assume that an increase in one input is enough to overcome the loss of productive capacity caused by a decline in the other.[41] This type of approach had been extensively used in the 1960s to ascertain the substitution possibilities between labour and capital (e.g., Arrow *et al.*, 1961). The approach had not, up this point, been applied to natural resources.

Following a number of simulation exercises, Nordhaus and Tobin emerged with a value of two for the elasticity of substitution between human-made capital and natural capital over the 1909–1958 period. Nordhaus and Tobin therefore concluded that the accumulation of human-made capital had been more than enough to prevent the decline in resource stocks from reducing the productive capacity of the US economy. They also argued that this trend was likely to continue well into the future. Implicit support for the Nordhaus and Tobin study soon came from Solow (1974) during the delivery of his Robert T. Ely Lecture at the 1974 American Economics Association meeting. During the lecture, Solow referred to the apparent ease with which human-made capital could substitute for natural capital. Solow also spelt out how resource rents could be invested to ensure a sustainable consumption stream over time. A similar 'sustainability prescription' was put forward by Stiglitz (1974) in a paper dealing with the optimal depletion rate of exhaustible resources. The Solow/Stiglitz sustainability prescription was later developed by Hartwick in the form of an elegant mathematical rule for reinvesting natural resource rents (Hartwick, 1977, 1978).

Just as the empirical evidence appeared to support the substitutability position, a major shortcoming was revealed by Daly and Georgescu-Roegen in 1979. Both correctly pointed out that since production is a physical transformation process, a production function must obey the first and second laws of thermodynamics (Daly, 1979; Georgescu-Roegen, 1979).[42] What they subsequently noticed was that all the work undertaken on the substitutability issue had involved the use of neoclassical production functions (e.g., Berndt and Wood, 1975; Atkinson and Halvorsen, 1976; Griffin and Gregory, 1976; Fuss, 1977; Halvorsen and Ford, 1978). The problem with neoclassical production functions is that they violate the first and second laws of thermodynamics. That is, they are formulated in such a way as to mathematically permit a range of physically infeasible substitution possibilities. As a consequence, neoclassical production functions can generate a false if not implausible value for the elasticity of substitution.

Despite the revelation of this major shortcoming, studies based on neoclassical production functions continued. This led to renewed criticism of the neoclassical approach in the mid-1990s, which culminated in an entire issue of *Ecological Economics* being dedicated to the debate in 1997 (volume 22, number 3, 1997). As a result of this special issue, most ecological economists were left in no doubt that human-made capital could not continue to offset the loss of productive capacity caused by a diminution of natural resource stocks. However, in view of some of the work which followed, it was clear that many observers remained unconvinced of the anti-substitution arguments.

In an attempt to resolve the matter further, Lawn (2004) set out to determine the range of elasticity of substitution values derivable from a production function obeying the first and second laws of thermodynamics. Upon the manipulation of one such production function – a Bergstrom production function (Ayres and Miller, 1980) – Lawn discovered that the elasticity of substitution between human-made capital and natural resources is always less than one.[43] Hence, contrary to the results generated from the use of neoclassical production functions, Lawn showed that the decline in natural resource stocks must eventually result in a gradual reduction in an economy's productive capacity.

In many ways, Lawn's results merely substantiated the obvious – low-entropy resources provided by natural capital constitute the *material cause* of production whereas human-made capital (producer goods), along with labour, serve as agents in the transformation of the incoming resource flow into final goods. That is, human-made capital and labour constitute the *efficient cause* of production and cannot, as such, substitute for the material cause of production (Daly, 1996). For example, the same quantity of wooden furniture cannot be produced from half the necessary timber and double the required carpenters and tools. Nor, upon the collapse of a fishery, can the same quantity of fish be harvested by a larger fishing fleet.

Compounding this weakness is the fact that human-made capital is itself the product of the physical transformation of natural resources. This leaves the advocates of the substitutability position having to explain how more human-made capital can be accumulated to offset the decline in natural capital when the latter must exist in greater quantities to increase the stock of the former! As Daly (1996) emphasises, this is a defining condition of complementarity, not substitutability.

Of course, the above criticism relates to whether larger quantities of human-made capital can maintain the productive capacity of a nation's economy. There are alternative claims that it is not the accumulation of human-made capital per se that matters, but the resource-saving technology embodied within it. In other words, if advances in human-made capital can increase the technical efficiency of production, a non-growing stock of human-made capital should be capable of reducing the low entropy resources needed to produce a given quantity of output.

There are two main problems with this argument. Firstly, reducing the resources needed for production purposes is not an example of human-made capital 'taking the place of natural capital, which is what is required for human-made capital to constitute a genuine substitute. Secondly, technological progress can maintain the productive capacity of the economy only under very restrictive conditions. Indeed, it can do so only if the percentage increase in technical efficiency (dE/E) is at least as large as the percentage decrease in resource input (dR/R). Because the technical efficiency of production is subject to thermodynamic limits (i.e., $E < 1$), a given output level is likely to be sustainable only if the decline in resource input, over time, is small.[44] Large decreases in resource input would almost certainly be insurmountable.

In the long run, however, the ability to sustain an economy's productive capacity is further restricted. This is because dE/E must eventually approach zero, which means it will become impossible to secure any major resource savings through technological progress. Once this point in time arrives, sustaining a given output level will effectively require a minimum inflow of resources that, in turn, will require the presence of a minimum quantity of resource-providing natural capital.

In sum, should the stock of natural capital diminish over time, neither technological progress nor the accumulation of human-made capital have the capacity to indefinitely maintain the productive capacity of an economic system. When considered alongside the inability of human-made capital to replicate the ecosphere's sink and life-support services, it is clear that human-made capital cannot be regarded as a substitute for natural capital.

Being richer does not mean being greener and cleaner

For some time, it has been claimed that the rate of environmental degradation within a country is likely to rise but later fall as its citizens gets richer (i.e., as a nation's per capita GDP increases). The reasoning behind this claim is twofold. Firstly, early on in a nation's development, the desire for increased levels of consumption is much stronger than concerns about environmental protection. Hence, initially, the economic activity that contributes to the rise in a nation's per capita GDP also contributes to a rising rate of environmental degradation. Secondly, as a country continues to get richer, its citizens place greater importance on environmental goods and are thus willing to forgo additional levels of consumption to enjoy the benefits of a more amenable local environment. At the same time, a rich nation acquires more of the pollution-abatement and ameliorative technology that is needed to prevent and undo environmental damage. As a consequence, a point is reached at which a rise in a nation's per capita GDP leads to a general improvement in environmental quality.

Until the early 1990s, there was very little in the way of evidence to support this claim. A breakthrough then emerged with the release of the *1992 World Development Report* (IBRD, 1992). Revealed in the report was an inverted U-shaped or concave relationship between per capita GDP and pollution levels. Although the empirical analysis was confined to a small number of pollutants, it was enough to convince many observers that a concave relationship also exists between per capita GDP and the overall quality of the environment – the exact relationship between GDP growth and the environment that had long been hypothesised (see Figure 2.10). The curve representing this relationship soon became known as the 'Environmental Kuznets Curve' (EKC) after it was recognised that it resembled a similar relationship between per capita GDP and income inequality first revealed in the mid-1950s by Simon Kuznets (1955).

The policy message of the EKC hypothesis was significant. It suggested that all nations should be unconcerned about the environmental impact of a growing economy because, as real GDP rises, environmental quality eventually and increasingly improves. More than this, it implied that the solution to environmental degradation is the continued growth of a nation's real GDP, not its curtailment.

A number of observers were quick to criticise the EKC hypothesis. At no stage did they doubt the strong demand that rich countries have for environmental quality or their capacity to reduce their environmental impact per unit of economic activity. However, they categorically rejected the idea that a broad conclusion regarding GDP growth and overall environmental quality could be extrapolated from an empirical relationship between per capita GDP and a limited range of pollutants (Arrow *et al.*, 1995; Kaufmann and Cleveland, 1995; Stern *et al.*, 1996).

The rejection of the EKC hypothesis has been largely based on two major factors. The first is the belief that rich nations have significantly reduced their generation of certain pollutants by offloading 'dirty' production onto poorer countries (e.g., Daly, 1996; Suri and Chapman, 1998). Hence it has been argued that the apparent disparity in pollution performances has principally been the result of a compositional shift in national output that has allowed rich nations to benefit at the expense of low-income countries.[45] This stands in stark contrast to the EKC thesis, which claims that improvements in environmental performance are domestically driven and generated.

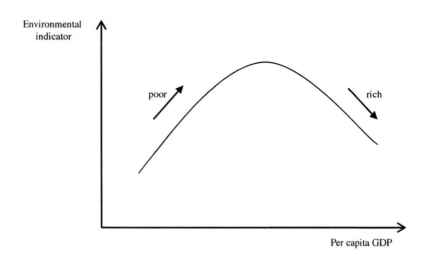

Figure 2.10 Environmental Kuznets Curve (EKC). Source: Adapted from IBRD (1992).

The second weakness concerns the fact that the empirical analysis upon which the EKC hypothesis is based is limited to a small number of 'avoidable' pollutants. Furthermore, it would appear that national regulations aimed at restricting the generation of these pollutants have had little impact on the domestic output levels of rich countries and, because of international trade, even less of an impact on the range of goods that rich countries consume. EKC critics have therefore argued that the EKC hypothesis cannot be substantiated until an examination is made of the relationship between per capita GDP and either: (a) a broad, biophysical indicator of environmental stress; or (b) an unavoidable, large-scale resource input (Arrow *et al.*, 1995; Ayres, 1995; Costanza, 1995; Rothman, 1998).

It was with this recommendation in mind that Lawn (2007b) recently extended a theoretical model first developed by Munasinghe (1999) to determine the likely relationship between per capita GDP and the overall rate of environmental degradation. By taking account of the first and second laws of thermodynamics and some basic ecological principles, Lawn showed that the relationship would, at best, be represented by an N-shaped curve. That is, even though an opportunity is likely to arise for a nation to briefly reduce its rate of environmental degradation as its per capita GDP increases, the rate of degradation must eventually rise and do so indefinitely.[46]

Crucially, even when Lawn allowed for the offloading of dirty production onto poor countries, rich nations could do little more than defer the eventual rise in environmental degradation. Compositional changes in output would not allow rich countries to indefinitely delay the degradational impact of increasing levels of economic activity.

In what follows, empirical support will now be given to Lawn's theoretical findings. In order to do this, it will be assumed that a nation's total energy consumption is an adequate indicator of environmental stress. This assumption is based on the fact that: (a) the aggregate environmental impact of a nation's economic activity is closely tied to its total throughput of material and energy resources; (b) energy use is the driving force behind all economic activity; and (c) the activities associated with energy consumption (i.e., acquisition, use, and byproducts) are responsible for many of the world's pressing environmental concerns.

Consider Figure 2.11, which illustrates the relationship between the per capita GDP and per capita energy consumption of 12 countries over the 1980–2005 period. These countries have been selected to ensure an even spread of high-income, middle-income, and low-income nations from different parts of the world. Figure 2.11 shows that the per capita energy consumption of all four low-income countries (China, India, Thailand, and Indonesia) rose sharply over the study period. In direct contrast, there was a much lower rate of increase in the per capita energy consumption of the four high-income nations (USA, UK, France, and Japan). As for the middle-income countries (Portugal, Greece, Mexico, and Chile), their per capita energy consumption increased at a rate somewhere between the rates experienced by the low-income and high-income countries.

Although Figure 2.11 reveals an apparent improvement in environmental performance as nations get richer, there is no sign of the concave relationship

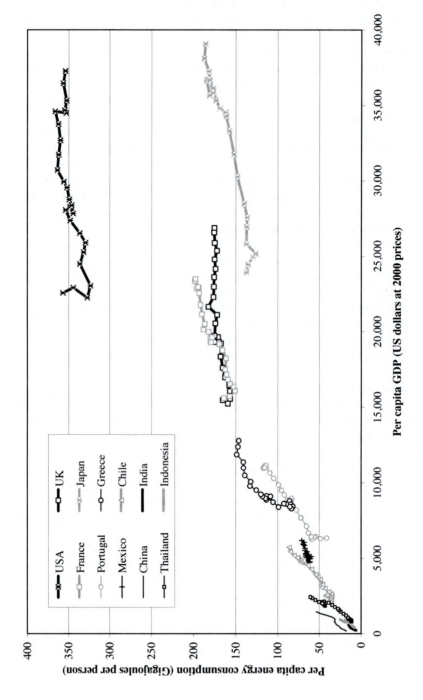

Figure 2.11 Per capita GDP and per capita energy consumption, 1980–2005.

claimed by EKC advocates. Making matters worse is the fact that Figure 2.11 understates the levels of environmental stress. The reason for this is that Figure 2.11 is based on a nation's per capita energy consumption – an approach that must be undertaken to permit a comparison between the selected countries. It is, however, *total* energy consumption which better represents a nation's impact on the natural environment. Given that the population of all 12 countries rose during the 1980–2005 period, the rise in environmental stress levels was much greater than that depicted in Figure 2.11.

As enlightening as a comparison of selected countries can be, the conclusions drawn can always be considered dubious given the non-random nature of the selection process. In order to provide stronger support for Lawn's theoretical findings, the average per capita GDP and average per capita energy consumption of 118 countries (1980–2005) are presented in Figure 2.12.[47] In each of the panels, a different regression line has been added. The results of all three regressions are provided in Table 2.3.

Table 2.3 reveals that the quadratic function and the third-degree polynomial fit the data equally well (R^2 values of 0.6715 and 0.6734 respectively) and slightly better than the linear function ($R^2 = 0.6471$). Despite the strong fit of the quadratic regression line (Panel 2.12b), there are three good reasons to doubt the existence of a concave relationship between per capita GDP and per capita energy consumption. To begin with, the maximum point of the quadratic regression line occurs at a per capita GDP of US$33,394. Only six of the 118 countries exceeded this per capita GDP level during the study period (Luxembourg, Switzerland, the USA, Norway, Iceland, and Japan). Although the per capita energy consumption of the USA and Switzerland remained quite steady beyond this point, it rose slightly in Iceland and very strongly in Luxembourg, Norway, and Japan. In neither instance was there a downward trend in per capita energy consumption. It would therefore be misleading to conclude that a concave relationship between per capita GDP and per capita energy consumption will unequivocally emerge as countries move well beyond the US$33,394 level.

Secondly, the third-degree polynomial (Panel 2.12c) has no maximum point but an upward-turning inflection point at a per capita GDP of US$25,926. Close examination of the data reveals that the per capita energy consumption of all but one of the eleven countries that surpassed the $25,926 mark was steady or increasing. In fact, the rise in per capita energy consumption was more prominent amongst the group of countries located well beyond the inflection point than it was amongst the group that had only recently exceeded it.

Thirdly, consider the regression results in Table 2.4, which were obtained by dividing the 118 countries into three separate income categories.[48] In each case, an exponential regression line best fitted the data (see Figure 2.13). Although the exponential growth rate of the high-income group was lower than the middle-income and low-income groups, and the regression line for the high-income group (Panel 2.13c) was a comparatively weak fit ($R^2 = 0.237$), these results clearly refute the notion that high-income countries have been reducing their environmental impact while getting richer.[49] Moreover, they point to the third-degree polynomial as be-

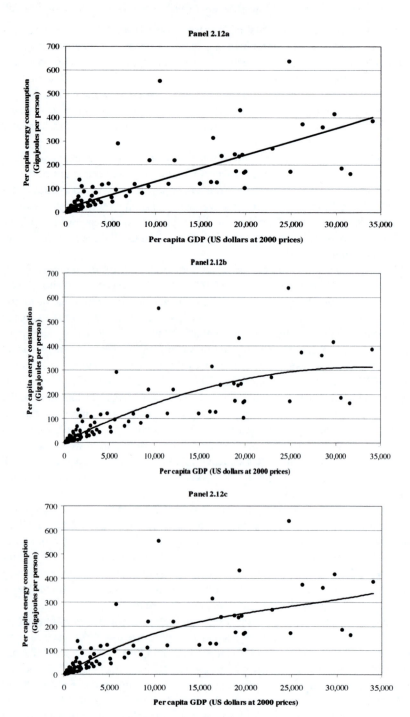

Figure 2.12 Average per capita GDP versus average per capita energy consumption, 1980–2005 (118 countries).

Table 2.3 Average per capita GDP versus average per capita energy consumption, 1980–2005 (118 countries)

Function type	Fitted equation	R^2	Turning/ inflection point
Linear *t*-statistics (Panel 2.12a)	$y = 0.0113x + 16.972$ (14.586) (2.115)	0.6471	
Quadratic *t*-statistics (Panel 2.12b)	$y = -3 \times 10^{-7}x^2 + 0.0185x + 4.5413$ (2.919) (7.163) (0.512)	0.6715	\$US33,394 per capita (maximum point)
Cubic *t*-statistics (Panel 2.12c)	$y = 9 \times 10^{-12}x^3 - 7 \times 10^{-7}x^2 + 0.0228x + 0.0406$ (0.000) (1.372) (3.912) (0.003)	0.6734	\$US25,926 per capita (inflection point)

Data sources: WRI (http://earthtrends.wri.org/searchable_db/index.php?theme=5) and EIA (www.eia.doe.gov/iea).

Notes
y denotes per capita energy consumption
x denotes per capita GDP

Table 2.4 Average per capita GDP versus average per capita energy consumption, 1980–2005

Income group	Fitted exponential equation	R^2
Low-income countries *t*-statistics (Panel 2.13a)	$y = 1.2961 exp(3.1 \times 10^{-3})$ (5.231) (8.137)	0.5888
Middle-income countries *t*-statistics (Panel 2.13b)	$y = 18.573 exp(3.0 \times 10^{-4})$ (4.728) (4.380)	0.3354
High-income countries *t*-statistics (Panel 2.13c)	$y = 105.55 exp(3.5 \times 10^{-5})$ (4.108) (2.952)	0.2370

Data sources: WRI (http://earthtrends.wri.org/searchable_db/index.php?theme=5) and EIA (www.eia.doe.gov/iea).

Notes
y denotes per capita energy consumption
x denotes per capita GDP

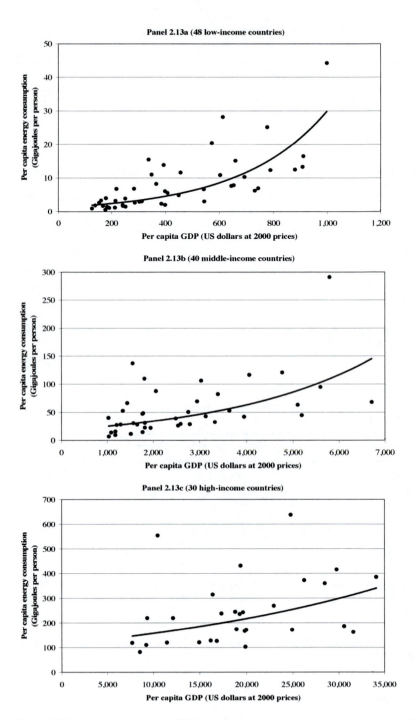

Figure 2.13 Average per capita GDP versus average per capita energy consumption, 1980–2005 (low-income, middle-income, and high-income countries).

ing the best indicator of what is likely to happen to per capita energy consumption as nations strive to increase their per capita GDP.

Overall, there is no indication of a fully developed concave relationship between per capita GDP and per capita energy consumption/environmental degradation. Given this, the EKC hypothesis has no empirical support. On the other hand, the empirical evidence appears to endorse Lawn's conclusion that a nation's environmental impact will inevitably intensify as it endeavours to increase its per capita GDP – again, a further reason why all countries must eventually make the transition to a steady-state economy.

Shifting towards 'services' does not reduce a nation's environmental impact

Believing that service industries are not as resource-intensive or pollutive as the remaining sectors of the economy, growth advocates frequently argue that the environmental impact of economic activity can be reduced by shifting economic activity away from agriculture and manufacturing to the provision and delivery of services. Indeed, by increasing services as a proportion of total output, growth advocates believe that nations can augment their real GDP without having to place greater demands on the natural environment. In doing so, growth advocates argue that all nations can successfully achieve sustainable GDP growth.

Not unlike the EKC hypothesis, this so-called 'dematerialisation' argument can be criticised from a theoretical and empirical perspective. Let us consider the theoretical shortcoming first. The belief that services are largely material- and energy-free stems from the historical use of the term 'goods and services' to categorise different forms of economic activity. Prior to the twentieth century, many people were deprived of the basic necessities of life. Consequently, any additional consumption undertaken by the general public was considered a desirable or good outcome. Over time, the desirability of basic forms of consumption led many to generically refer to all consumption items as 'goods'. Later, as nations got richer, there was a growing willingness of people to pay for the benefits directly generated by the employment of physical goods as capital. This residual activity was soon regarded as a service and all such activities as services. Hence, the term 'goods and services' emerged as a means of differentiating between the two major forms of economic activity.

Although the term is still widely used today, there is a general tendency to divide economic activity into the following three industry sectors: (a) the primary sector – which includes the agricultural and resource-extractive industries; (b) the secondary sector – which includes the resource-processing and manufacturing industries; and (c) the tertiary sector – which includes the various service industries (e.g., education, health, life-style, administrative, legal, and financial industries). There is, of course, a good reason for categorising economic activity in this way. It enables analysts to better identify the industrial, compositional, and employment trends within the economy, which can assist policy-makers to make better policy decisions. Nevertheless, it is wrong to believe that the three major sectors are independent of each other, which is what growth advocates implicitly do when they apply the dematerialisation strategy to support their pro-growth argument. Much of the output of the secondary sector constitutes an input into the tertiary or services sector, and almost all the output of the primary sector constitutes an input into the secondary sector.[50] In this sense, the matter–energy used to produce the capital goods required for the service sector to function is an indirect input into the service sector itself.

Repeatedly, promoters of the dematerialisation strategy ignore this indirect expenditure of matter–energy except to include it as an end-of-line input into the secondary sector. By doing so, they completely overlook the physical foundation of the service sector or, at best, underestimate the extent of the resource inputs involved in service sector activities. By how much? According to at least two embodied energy studies (Costanza, 1980; Ayres and Ayres, 1999), the ratio of output to combined direct and indirect inputs in the service sector is much the same as it is in the secondary sector. Given this, the belief that a nation's environmental impact can be reduced by shifting economic activity towards services is a fallacy.

Some readers may feel that I am being inconsistent here. After all, I argued earlier in the chapter that the goal of physically expanding the economy must eventually give way to qualitative improvement whereby, among other things, the latter can be achieved by increasing the service-yielding qualities of human-made capital (i.e., increasing Ratio 1 in equation (2.7)). There is, however, a fundamental difference between the notion of shifting towards a category of economic activity that exists at the end of the economic 'food chain' and undertaking measures to increase the per unit service of human-made capital. The latter involves qualitative improvement that can be secured at any stage of the economic process, whereas the former is likely to have no bearing on the rate of qualitative improvement and very little impact on the rate of resource throughput and its ultimate environmental impact.

I have already mentioned how embodied energy studies cast serious doubts over the legitimacy of the dematerialisation argument. In order to analyse the issue further, it would seem useful to compare, at the national level, the change in total energy consumption with the change in the service sector contribution towards GDP. Should the dematerialisation argument carry any weight, the correlation between these two variables should be negative. That is, when services as a proportion of total output increase, total energy consumption should fall. Restricting the analysis to the 1980–2002 period and the same 12 countries used in the EKC assessment, Figure 2.14 shows that the service sector contribution towards GDP rose over the study period in all countries except Chile, Thailand, and Indonesia. While the service sector contribution rose steadily in France, Japan, Portugal, Greece, China, and India, the contribution fluctuated considerably in the USA, UK, and Mexico.

Apart from a few brief instances in which the correlation between the service sector contribution towards GDP and total energy consumption was negative (e.g., the early 1980s and mid-1980s in the USA and UK), the correlation between the two indicators was predominantly a positive one. In fact, all nine countries which experienced an overall rise in the service sector contribution towards GDP

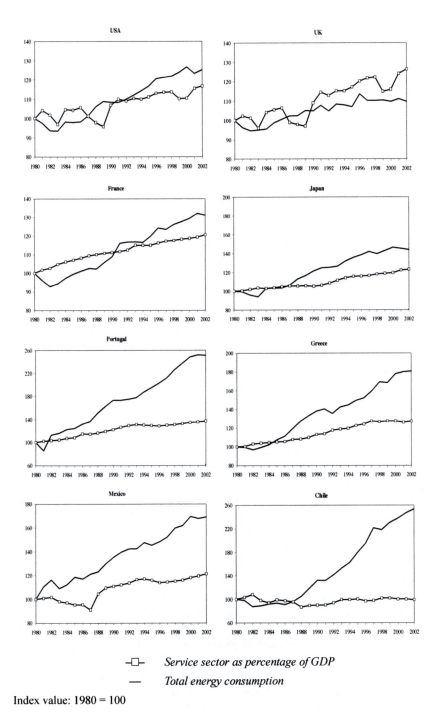

Service sector as percentage of GDP

Total energy consumption

Index value: 1980 = 100

Figure 2.14 Service sector percentage of GDP versus total energy consumption, 1980–2002.

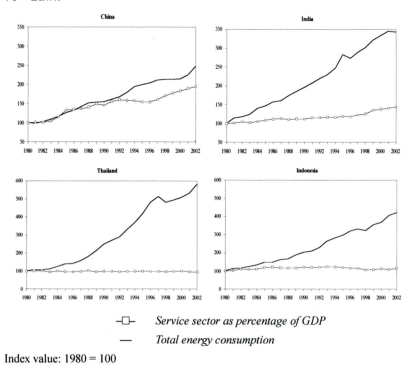

-□-   *Service sector as percentage of GDP*

—   *Total energy consumption*

Index value: 1980 = 100

Figure 2.14 (Continued)   Service sector percentage of GDP versus total energy consumption, 1980–2002.

also experienced an increase in total energy consumption. From this simple analysis alone, there is no indication that a shift towards services reduces a nation's environmental impact.

A more in-depth understanding of the dematerialisation issue can be gained from Figure 2.15, which presents the average percentage contribution of the service sector towards GDP and the average per capita energy consumption of 98 countries over the 1980–2002 period.[51] Not unlike Figure 2.12, a different regression line has been added to each of the panels. The regression results are summarised in Table 2.5.

As can be seen from Figure 2.15, the regression line in each panel is upward sloping. This indicates a general increase in per capita energy consumption as countries shift their economic activity towards services, not the converse as claimed by the dematerialisation advocates. To make matters worse, Table 2.5 reveals that the exponential function (Panel 2.15c) best fits the data ($R^2 = 0.389$). Thus, if anything, augmenting the contribution made by services towards GDP causes per capita energy consumption to rise at an increasing rate!

Of course, the increase in per capita energy consumption may have more to do with the fact that: (a) the service sector constitutes a larger proportion of real GDP in countries with a high per capita GDP; and (b) countries with a high per

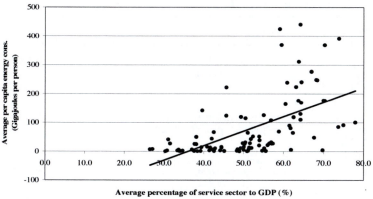

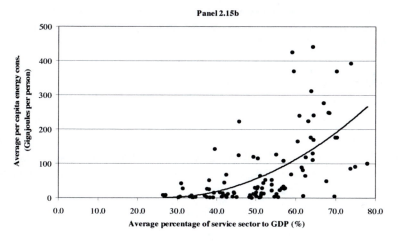

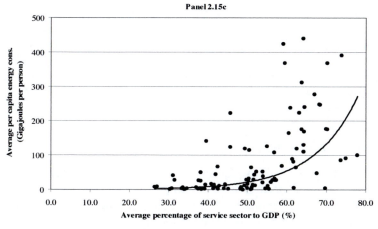

Figure 2.15   Average percentage of service sector to GDP versus average per capita energy consumption, 1980–2002 (98 countries).

Table 2.5   Tertiary (services) sector versus average per capita energy consumption, 1980–2002 (98 countries)

Function type	Fitted equation	R^2
Linear *t*-statistics (Panel 2.15a)	$y = 5.0132x - 180.2$ (6.860) (4.659)	0.3289
Quadratic *t*-statistics (Panel 2.15b)	$y = 0.1012x^2 - 5.404x + 73.237$ (1.901) (0.978) (0.529)	0.3535
Exponential *t*-statistics (Panel 2.15c)	$y = 0.2488exp(0.090)$ (1.648) (7.834)	0.3890

Data sources: WRI (http://earthtrends.wri.org/searchable_db/index.php?theme=5) and EIA (www.eia.doe.gov/iea).

Notes
y denotes per capita energy consumption
x denotes tertiary (services) sector as percentage of GDP

capita GDP have the largest per capita consumption of energy. In other words, per capita energy consumption may have little at all to do with the service sector contribution towards real GDP. Although this is probably true, it only reinforces the point being made – namely, shifting towards services does not reduce a nation's environmental impact.

Concluding comments

It is clear from this section that the three major pro-growth arguments designed to discredit the 'limits to growth' assertion have no theoretical or empirical support. To the contrary, the empirical evidence indicates that a nation's environmental impact rises as its real GDP increases over time. This can only imply one thing – regardless of capital substitution, technological progress, and the shift in economic activity towards the services sector, an economy that continues to grow is one that is destined to exceed its maximum sustainable scale.

The current sustainability–employment trade-off

Whether by design or accident, the structure of virtually every economic system is such that employment levels are strongly linked to a nation's total output or real GDP. Given the existence of economic and ecological limits to growth and the evidence revealed in this chapter, it follows that all nations, should they wish to operate sustainably, are significantly constrained in their capacity to use GDP growth as a means to increase employment levels. Moreover, all countries face the prospect of having to deal with a sustainability–employment trade-off unless they can implement well-targeted policy measures to facilitate employment growth without the need for real output growth.[52]

Many people, of course, many people would disagree with this last sentence. Growth advocates refute the existence of a sustainability–employment trade-off on the basis that ecological sustainability and growth are compatible. I would like to think that any notion of sustainable growth has been thoroughly dispelled in this chapter. But there are many advocates of a low-growth or steady-state economy who also believe that a sustainability–employment trade-off does not exist. The basis for their position is that the proliferation of environmental regulation in wealthy nations has led to investment in cleaner and more efficient forms of production, which has resulted in at least one new 'green' job being created for every 'brown' job lost. In other words, environmental regulation has not led to net job losses but has induced a shift in the types of jobs being performed across the economy as well as sectoral changes in employment levels as clean industries displace dirty industries (Goodstein, 2008).

Exactly what evidence is there to endorse this argument? Supporters believe that the rise in environmental regulations in the 1970s and 1980s and the decline in the official unemployment rate in most wealthy countries since the early 1990s is proof that there has been a simultaneous trend towards ecological sustainability and lower unemployment. After all, if a sustainability–employment trade-off exists, there ought to have been a widespread rise in the unemployment rate.

Although I acknowledge that the unemployment rate in most wealthy nations has fallen over the past decade (1998–2008) and there has been a shift in employment towards cleaner industries, there is a major weakness with this 'no trade-off' argument. The shortcoming exists in the form of the false assumption that all wealthy countries have moved closer to achieving ecological sustainability simply because there has been an increase in environmental regulation over the past 35 years. On the contrary, the total energy consumption and ecological footprint of almost every country has increased over the same period, thus suggesting that the world's economies either are approaching their maximum sustainable scale or have grown beyond it (Global Footprint Network, 2006).[53]

Because almost every nation would appear to be moving away from the goal of ecological sustainability, the sustainability–employment trade-off is unfolding in an unexpected manner. Instead of jobs being sacrificed to achieve environmental goals, it appears that long-term sustainability goals are being sacrificed to achieve more desirable employment goals – albeit the latter goal does not extend as far as achieving full employment. In other words, it is the environment that is being sacrificed for the sake of saving jobs, not vice versa.[54] By falsely believing that nations are moving closer to the sustainability goal, supporters of the 'no trade-off' position are, in effect, overestimating the capacity of a *sustainable* economy – not a typical, contemporary economy – to generate enough jobs to lower unemployment and to ultimately achieve full employment.

To support my argument of a jobs-biased trade-off between sustainability and employment, consider Figure 2.16. In each panel, the per capita energy consump-

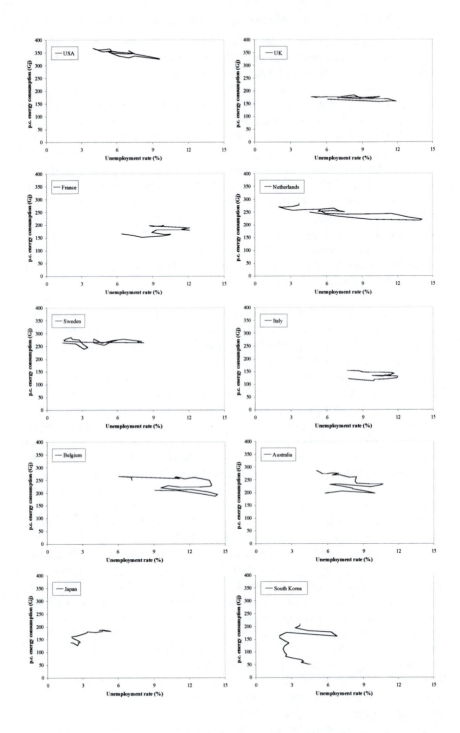

Figure 2.16 Per capita energy consumption and unemployment rate (selected high-income countries), 1980–2005.

tion of a selected high-income nation has been plotted against its unemployment rate. It is reasonable to assume that the curves in each panel would be positively sloped if there has been a simultaneous trend towards ecological sustainability and lower unemployment (i.e., no sustainability–employment trade-off). Figure 2.16 shows that no such general trend occurred. Admittedly, Japan had a positively sloped curve, but it moved up the curve, thus indicating that Japan experienced a rise in both unemployment and per capita energy consumption at various stages during the study period. The curves for the USA, the UK, and Sweden are somewhat different from the remaining countries in that they reveal an almost constant trade-off between per capita energy consumption and unemployment throughout the study period (i.e., a trade-off within much the same unemployment and energy consumption range).

As for France, the Netherlands, Italy, Belgium, Australia, and South Korea, each country experienced a rise in per capita energy consumption when the unemployment rate declined but little if any change in per capita energy consumption when the unemployment rate increased. That is, the increase in per capita energy consumption that accompanied the decline in their unemployment rate was rarely reversed during spells when unemployment returned to somewhere near its former rate. For this reason, the curves of this group of nations gradually ratcheted upwards over the study period. Hence these countries not only experienced a trade-off between per capita energy consumption and unemployment, but the trade-off progressively occurred at a higher per capita rate of energy consumption.

To further support the existence of a sustainability–employment trade-off, the average unemployment rate and average per capita energy consumption of 26 high-income countries (1980–2005) are presented in Figure 2.17.[55] Once again, a different regression line has been added to each panel. The regression results are summarised in Table 2.6.

Figure 2.17 reveals that all three regression lines are downward sloping with the third-degree polynomial (Panel 2.17c) best fitting the data ($R^2 = 0.1347$). Although neither regression line constitutes a very strong fit, there is enough evidence to suggest that high-income countries with low unemployment rates were more likely to possess a higher per capita rate of energy consumption. There is certainly no indication of the converse. It is therefore quite conceivable that the high-income nations most active in trying to curb their energy consumption paid a significant price in terms of a high rate of unemployment. If so, this evidence reveals how important the implementation of appropriate policies is likely to be in achieving the twin goals of ecological sustainability and full employment.

Concluding remarks

In this chapter, a coevolutionary world-view has been adopted to outline the following key points, all of which lead to the conclusion that a potential conflict is likely to exist between the twin goals of ecological sustainability and full employment. Firstly, the throughput of matter–energy constantly required to fuel the economic process must increase over time should a nation continue to grow its economy. Secondly, as the rate of throughput increases, each of the six sus-

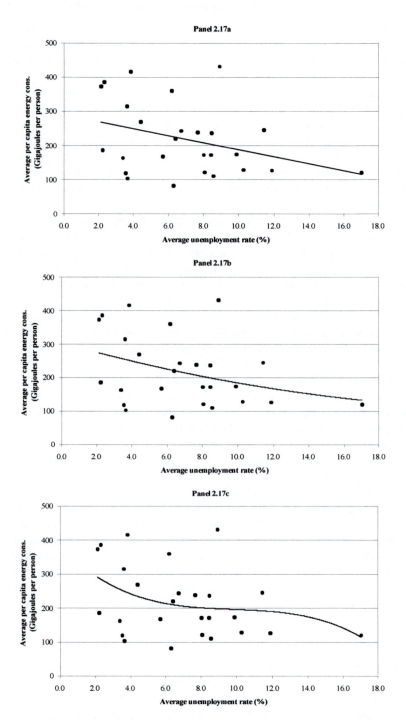

Figure 2.17 Average unemployment rate versus per capita energy consumption, 1980–2005 (26 high-income countries).

Table 2.6   Average unemployment rate versus average per capita energy consumption, 1980–2005 (26 high-income countries)

Function type	Fitted equation	R^2	Turning/ inflection point
Linear *t*-statistics (Panel 2.17a)	$y = -10.159x + 288.19$ (1.811) (6.627)	0.1182	
Quadratic *t*-statistics (Panel 2.17b)	$y = 0.2721x^2 - 14.656x + 303$ (0.243) (0.749) (3.980)	0.1203	26.9% u/e rate (minimum point)
Cubic *t*-statistics (Panel 2.17c)	$y = -0.175x^3 + 5.155x^2 - 52.569x + 380.47$ (0.549) (0.571) (0.472) (2.366)	0.1347	9.8% u/e rate (downward inflection point)

Data sources: EIA (www.eia.doe.gov/iea) and ILO (2008).

Notes
y denotes per capita energy consumption
x denotes unemployment rate

tainability precepts outlined in this chapter must eventually be violated. In short, continuing growth is ecologically unsustainable.

Thirdly, prior to reaching ecological limits, a nation will encounter an economic limit to growth, which, as explained, is a point beyond which the additional costs of growth rise faster than the additional benefits. Disconcertingly, almost all wealthy countries and some relatively poor countries appear to have exceeded their economic limit to growth and many nations have already surpassed their ecological carrying capacity – indeed, enough for the global economy as a whole to be in ecological deficit.

Fourthly, since employment levels are closely tied to real GDP, the economic and ecological limits to growth are likely to significantly restrict a nation's ability to operate sustainably and achieve full employment. As it is, the empirical evidence suggests that the world's richest countries are engaging in an undesirable trade-off between employment and environmental goals with the countries impacting least on the ecosphere paying a hefty price in terms of a high unemployment rate.

Despite the employment constraints imposed by the economic and ecological limits to growth, there is no reason why a nation should be compelled to make a sustainability–employment trade-off. But achieving the twin goals of ecological sustainability and full employment will not be an easy task and will require much more than increased efficiency and a shift in employment from a shrinking dirty sector to a burgeoning green sector. It will also demand the implementation of policies and a range of institutional modifications which, apart from imposing throughput constraints on the economy, also encourage greater value-adding in production, overcome labour market distortions, ration work better across the entire labour force, and sever the link between employment levels and real GDP. In their own way, and not always in concurrence with each other, the remaining chapters explain and outline how some of these changes can be introduced to meet one of humankind's most critical challenges – namely, how to reconcile environmental and employment goals in order to achieve the broader goal of sustainable development.

Notes

1   It is conventionally believed that the growth of real GDP and the growth of the economy are the same thing. That is, if real GDP has grown by 5 per cent, the economy has also increased by 5 per cent. This is not true. Real GDP effectively measures the quantity of physical goods produced over a year by domestically located factors of production. In a roundabout way, it measures what is physically added to the economy. Real GDP is therefore equivalent to the number of births of a particular species. If real GDP rises by 5 per cent, it approximately amounts to a 5 per cent increase in the 'births' of new goods. Given that the quantity of new goods produced (births) is likely to be proportionately less than the existing stock of all goods (existing population), it is more than likely that the rise in the total population of all goods will be something far less than 5 per cent. Once we also take into account the number of 'deaths' of goods – namely, the recently produced non-durable goods that are directly consumed or perish, and the number of existing durable goods that have fully depreciated (worn out) – the net change to the total stock of goods can either be positive or negative. In other words, even if real GDP rises by 5 per cent, the economy, as measured by the total stock of all goods, can actually shrink if deaths (consumption/depreciation) exceed births (production). Only under an extraordinary set of circumstances, the likes of which has probably never occurred in relation to an economy of any nation, would a 5 per cent increase in real GDP amount to a 5 per cent increase in the scale of an economic system (see Lawn, 2007c).
2   Triple-bottom-line accounting involves the publishing of reports which reveal not just the financial (economic) performance of a corporation, but also its social and environmental performance.
3   For a more detailed explanation of coevolution, see Norgaard (1994).
4   Having said this, the degree of influence depends on the association between two or more particular systems. For example, the degree of coevolutionary influence is likely to be greater between an ecosystem and a neighbouring economic system than the influence between the same economic system and a distant ecosystem elsewhere. However, a far-away ecosystem can still influence the evolution of an economic system if it is a critical system, such as the rainforests of the Amazon Basin.
5   There will naturally be some minor fluctuations either side of the steady physical quantity of goods, but the average quantity will effectively remain unchanged.
6   This is sometimes referred to as a 'second law' efficiency measure since it is derived on the basis of the second law of thermodynamics (the Entropy Law) (Ayres, 1978).
7   Because of the first law of thermodynamics, the quantity of matter–energy entering the economy as low-entropy resources must ultimately equal the quantity of matter–energy exiting the economy as high-entropy wastes. As explained, the eventual exiting of some wastes can be delayed through the creation of durable goods whereby waste matter–energy is released over the time as the goods depreciate. Overall, however, if the input of resources increases over time, the output of wastes must also increase.
8   To understand what is meant by low entropy and high entropy matter–energy, the importance of the first and second laws of thermodynamics needs to be explained. The first law of thermodynamics is the *law of conservation of energy and matter*. It

declares that energy and matter can never be created or destroyed. The second law is the *Entropy Law*. It declares that, whenever energy is used in physical transformation processes, the amount of usable or 'available' energy always declines. Whereas the first law ensures the maintenance of a given quantity of energy and matter, the Entropy Law determines that which is usable. This is critical since, from a physical viewpoint, it is not the total quantity of matter–energy that is of primary concern, but the amount that exists in a readily available form.

The best way to illustrate the relevance of these two laws is to provide a simple example. Consider a piece of coal. When it is burned, the matter–energy embodied within the coal is transformed into heat and ash. Whereas the first law ensures that the total amount of matter–energy in the heat and ashes equals that previously embodied in the piece of coal, the second law ensures that the usable quantity of matter–energy does not. In other words, the dispersed heat and ashes can no longer be used in a way similar to the original piece of coal. To make matters worse, any attempt to reconcentrate the dispersed matter–energy, which requires the input of additional energy, results in more usable energy being expended than that reconcentrated. Hence, all physical transformation processes involve an irrevocable loss of available energy or what is sometimes referred to as a 'net entropy deficit'. This enables one to understand the term *low entropy* and to distinguish it from *high entropy*. Low entropy refers to a highly ordered physical structure embodying energy and matter in a readily available form. Conversely, high entropy refers to a highly disordered and degraded physical structure embodying energy and matter that is, by itself, in an unusable or unavailable form. By definition, the matter–energy used in economic processes can be considered a low-entropy resource whereas unusable by-products can be considered as high-entropy wastes.

9   In reality, some of these resources are renewable (e.g., oil and coal). However, the time-frame over which they can be renewed is entirely policy-irrelevant.

10 There are ten extractions over nine years because the initial extraction is effectively undertaken at time zero. By the end of the first year, there is another extraction of non-renewable resources. Thus, after one year, two extractions have taken place.

11 In doing so, one satisfies the condition of 'strong sustainability' (see Lawn, 2007b).

12 As a means of illustration, if 50 units per year is the maximum quantity of renewable matter–energy cultivatable from an investment of the non-renewable resource in question, the sustainable exhaustion schedule increases to 19 years (20 extractions) and the annual amount of non-renewable matter–energy available for production purposes falls from 38.61 to 31.16 units of low-entropy matter–energy.

13 Although it is possible for climate change to have positive impacts on some resource systems, it is expected that the impact will be detrimental in the aggregate.

14 It is the self-organisational capacity of the Earth to maintain the conditions fit for life that has led Lovelock to develop his 'Gaian hypothesis' – an hypothesis based on the notion that the Earth, or Gaia, behaves like an immense quasi-organism. See Lovelock (1988).

15 It has been estimated that for every one plant species lost, approximately 15 animal species will follow. See Norton (1986: 117).

16 Of course, the mere preservation or 'locking up' of large and small ecosystems will not, by itself, ensure biodiversity maintenance. Given the interdependent relationships between systems of all types, individual ecosystems are not entirely self-supporting (Lovelock, 1988). Their continued existence and the well-being of the biodiversity they contain are conditional upon the exchanges of matter and energy with and between neighbouring and far distant systems. This applies to systems of all kinds, whether they be relatively pristine, moderately disturbed, or totally refined. Above all else, maintaining biodiversity requires the exploitation of natural capital to be conducted on the principle of respecting the holistic integrity of geographical land and water resource units.

17   The economy is unlikely to consist of the same quality of human-made capital because, if it were achievable, it would have made sense to have abandoned the use of
the non-renewable resource and forgone the type of goods that its use makes possible.
That is, reliance upon the resource would have already been overcome and sustainability precept no. 3 would not have been violated in the first instance.

18   Even when one of more of the sustainability precepts is being violated, it is possible
to continue growing the economy if only because a nation can, for a limited time,
eat away at its natural capital stocks. But it cannot keep doing this indefinitely. One
might ask whether humankind could not, at this point, begin exploiting other parts of
the solar system for natural resources. Perhaps, through advances in space travel, we
could, but the decline in natural capital on Earth would almost certainly reduce the
ecosphere's life-support services below the critical levels needed to maintain a planet
fit for human habitation (and habitation for most earthly creatures).

19   The limits imposed by the ecosphere's waste assimilative capacity on the rate of
resource use are best exemplified by the fact that most of humankind's pressing environmental concerns now appear to exist on the waste side of the sustainability coin.
Whereas much of the focus of early sustainability studies was on the scarcity of low-
entropy resources (e.g., Barnett and Morse, 1963; Meadows *et al.*, 1972; Nordhaus
and Tobin, 1972; Solow, 1974), the attention has more recently turned to the problems
caused largely by the excessive generation of waste, such as climate change, ozone
depletion, ecosystem destruction, and biodiversity loss (e.g., IPCC, 2007; Stern,
2007). Does this mean that the sink and life-support services are the limiting factors?
Again, this is difficult to ascertain because humankind is heavily dependent upon the
use of non-renewable resources and many nations may have violated sustainability
precept no. 2 some time ago.

20   There is no doubt that some environmental costs also involve a form of disutility.
For example, pollution has serious health implications and can reduce the aesthetic
qualities of the natural environment. However, health costs are invariably regarded as
economic or social costs, whereas the erosion of the ecosphere's source, sink, and life-
support functions is related more to the impact they have on humankind's capacity to
sustain the economic process.

21   There are two things worthy of note here. Firstly, uncancelled costs are often un-
dervalued because many natural capital values escape market valuation. Secondly,
uncancelled costs should reflect the higher of two classes of opportunity costs. The
first is the cost of transforming an extracted unit of low-entropy resource into physical
goods in terms of alternative goods forgone. For example, if an extracted unit of
low-entropy resource X is used to produce good A, it cannot be used to produce goods
B, C, or D, etc. The second class of opportunity cost involves any reduced capacity
of natural capital to provide a future flow of low-entropy resources that is required
to produce physical goods in the future. For example, if the extraction of a unit of
low-entropy resource X reduces the capacity of natural capital to provide a continuous
flow of a unit of X over time, a unit of X will be unavailable to produce goods of any
type in the future. Once weighed up, it is the larger of these two classes of opportunity
costs that should be used to value the uncancelled costs of the economic process.

22   It should be pointed out that the maximum sustainable scale of S_s is not a precise
point. Coevolutionary feedback between the various systems leads to a fluctuation in
the maximum sustainable scale over time. Just how much the maximum sustainable
scale is likely to fluctuate and in what general direction it is likely to move depends on
any efficiency-increasing technological progress that might take place and the nature
and extent of the economic activity that humankind conducts.

23   This having been said, there is a limit on the capacity for income redistribution to
increase Ratio 1 because, at some point, an excessive approach is likely to adversely
dilute the incentive structure built into a market-based economy.

24   I should point out that the new optimal scale need not necessarily be physically larger

as a consequence of shifting the UB curve upwards. This will depend upon the nature of the UB and UC curves and, in particular, the extent to which the shape of the UB curve alters following its upwards shift.

25 Perhaps another way of describing the difference between the prevailing and ultimate maximum sustainable scales is to say that the former, like the latter, is defined by (a) to (d) plus whatever humankind's technological capacities happen to be within these limits. Thus, as humankind's technological capacities increase over time, the disparity between the prevailing and ultimate maximum sustainable scales diminishes. Should the two eventually equate, humankind will have effectively reached the limits defined by (a) to (d) but obviously will never be able to overcome them.

26 Since human-made capital is required to experience service, the service enjoyed by a nation's citizens always has a physical foundation.

27 A bliss point is reached when the marginal utility of consuming any additional good is negative. In these circumstances, the consumption of more goods reduces a person's total utility.

28 For more on the welfare-increasing institutions of an appropriately managed steady-state economy, see Daly (1991) and Lawn (2007b).

29 Gross World Product (GWP) increased at an average rate of 3 per cent per annum between 1986 and 2005. An annual growth rate of 3 per cent results in a doubling in scale every 24 years.

30 You might ask how this is possible if there is only one Earth? It is possible only because non-renewable resources constitute a major portion of all resource use at present and, as previously mentioned, resource limits can be exceeded in the short run by liquidating natural capital stocks.

31 Other criticisms of the EF include: (a) not all land is of the same productive capacity; and (b) spatial boundaries play a key role in EF calculations and the assumptions made in relation to this variable are unavoidably arbitrary (Patterson, 2006). Although the devisers of the EF have used yield factors to overcome the shortcomings associated with (a) (see Wackernagel and Rees, 1996), some observers believe the adjustments are insufficiently comprehensive.

32 The GPI was originally labelled an Index of Sustainable Economic Welfare (Daly and Cobb, 1989). To view a list of the items typically used in the calculation of the GPI, see Lawn (2007b).

33 In each case, the study period begins in 1950, except for Austria, which begins in 1955.

34 These figures are based on international dollars (Int$) at 2004 prices. An international dollar is a fictitious monetary unit which represents the same purchasing power that a nation's currency has over its GDP as a US dollar has over the GDP of the United States. Two people living in different countries with the same international dollar-valued income would, from their income alone, be able to purchase an equivalent quantity of goods or services within their own country.

35 Real GDP more closely reflects the physical rate of resource throughput than it does the physical scale of an economic system (see Lawn, 2007c).

36 Although the per capita GPI of some wealthy countries has recovered slightly since the early 1990s, in every case it has failed to come close to reaching its earlier peak value.

37 A line of best fit was superimposed over the curves of Australia, New Zealand, and Japan but not for China, India, Thailand, and Vietnam owing to the shortness of their length and their close proximity.

38 Figure 2.9 suggests that Japan avoided the threshold point for a considerably longer time than Australia and New Zealand. According to Lawn and Clarke (2008b), this can be attributed to two main factors – the most important being that Japan relies heavily upon the importation of raw materials, which enables it to offload many environmental costs onto other countries. This is evidenced by the fall in Japan's

environmental costs from ¥30,293 billion in 1970 to ¥12,377 billion in 2003 (Makino, 2008).

39 It also brings forth the possibility that the poorer countries in the Asia-Pacific region (and throughout the world generally) may never attain the per capita GPI levels currently enjoyed by wealthy nations.

40 Of course, to increase economic welfare, this period of growth will need to be as green, efficient, and equitable as possible. See Lawn and Clarke (2008b) on the types of policies required in the world's poorer nations.

41 The value of the elasticity of substitution can range between zero and infinity. A zero value implies perfect complementarity whereas a value of infinity implies perfect substitutability. A value between zero and one indicates that no amount of additional human-made capital can offset the decline in natural capital enough to sustain real output in the long run.

42 This is no different from a mathematical equation describing an aircraft's flight possibilities having to obey the law of gravity.

43 In fact, the elasticity of substitution can be greater than one, but only in circumstances where the ratio of human-made capital to natural resource inputs is less than approximately 10^{-8}. These cases are entirely irrelevant because the ratios are so small they involve an abundance of natural capital and little if any human-made capital. This is exactly opposite to the circumstances which make the substitutability issue relevant in the first place.

44 I say contemporary circumstances because most of the significant resource-saving forms of technology have already been discovered and applied (Ayres, 1978).

45 Evidence of this has already been revealed in terms of the steep rise in the environmental costs of poorer Asia-Pacific nations and the lower threshold point at which their per capita GPIs have begun to decline (Figure 2.9).

46 The reasons for the inevitable rise in environmental degradation are the same which prevent a nation from continuously shifting the UC curve (see Figure 2.7).

47 Because of data restrictions and inconsistencies, most former Eastern-bloc countries have been excluded.

48 The three income groups were based on the World Resources Institute categorisation of income groups (http://wri.earthtrends.org).

49 The ecological footprint of most high-income countries has also risen over the 1980–2005 period (Global Footprint Network, 2006).

50 The remaining output of the manufacturing sector is simply consumed or used as household capital to generate services in the home (e.g., cooking, cleaning, and gardening). It should also be pointed out that almost all the output of the primary sector constitutes an input into the secondary sector.

51 The number of countries used in the study fell from 118 to 98 because of a lack of national data on the service sector contribution towards GDP.

52 A number of these potential policies are outlined in future chapters.

53 There are two main reasons why countries are continuing to move along an unsustainable path despite the recent increase in environmental regulations: (a) environmental regulations have been insufficient to prevent the violation of the six sustainability precepts outlined earlier in the chapter; and (b) the efficiency gains induced by the regulations have been overwhelmed by the rise in real GDP (i.e., $dY/Y > dE/E$).

54 Given the widespread abandonment of the full employment objective, some would argue that it is not healthy employment levels that are being protected, but a healthy growth rate of real GDP. It is merely fortunate that the growth in real GDP has been sufficient in recent times to lower the unemployment rate.

55 This analysis is confined to high-income countries in order to facilitate a more realistic comparison.

References

Arrow, K., Chenery, H., Minhaus, B., and Solow, R. (1961), 'Capital–labor substitution and economic efficiency', *Review of Economics and Statistics*, 18 (3), 225–250.

Arrow, K., Bolin, B., Costanza, R., Dasgupta, P., Folke, C., Holling, S., Jansson, B.-O., Levin, S., Maler, K.-G., Perrings, C., and Pimentel, D. (1995), 'Economic growth, carrying capacity, and the environment', *Science*, 268, 520–521.

Asheim, G. (1994), 'Net national product as an indicator of sustainability', *Scandinavian Journal of Economics*, 96, 257–265.

Atkinson, S. and Halvorsen, R. (1976), 'Inter-fuel substitution in steam electric power generation', *Journal of Political Economy*, 84, 959–978.

Ayres, R. (1978), *Resources, Environment and Economics*, New York: John Wiley & Sons.

Ayres, R. (1995), 'Economic growth: politically necessary but not environmentally friendly', *Ecological Economics*, 15 (2), 97–99.

Ayres, R. and Ayres, L. (1999), *Accounting for Resources*, Northampton, MA: Edward Elgar.

Ayres, R. and Kneese, A. (1969), 'Production, consumption, and externalities', *American Economic Review*, 59 (3), 282–297.

Ayres, R. and Miller, S. (1980), 'The role of technological change', *Journal of Environmental Economics and Management*, 7, 353–371.

Barnett, H. and Morse, C. (1963), *Scarcity and Growth: The Economics of Natural Resource Availability*, Baltimore, MD: Johns Hopkins University Press.

Berndt, E. and Wood, W. (1975), 'Technology, prices, and the derived demand for energy', *Review of Economic Statistics*, 57, 259–268.

Blum, H. (1962), *Time's Arrow and Evolution*, 3rd edn, Princeton, NJ: Harper Torchbook.

Clarke, M., Shaw, J., and Lawn, P. (2008), 'Genuine progress in Thailand: a systems-analysis approach', in P. Lawn and M. Clarke (eds), *Genuine Progress in the Asia-Pacific: Studies Using the Genuine Progress Indicator*, Cheltenham, UK: Edward Elgar, pp. 260–298.

Common, M. and Sagl, S. (2005), *Ecological Economics: An Introduction*, Cambridge: Cambridge University Press.

Costanza, R. (1980), 'Embodied energy and economic valuation', *Science*, 210, 1219–1224.

Costanza, R. (1995), 'Economic growth, carrying capacity, and the environment', *Ecological Economics*, 15 (2), 89–90.

Crathorne, B., Dobbs, A., and Rees, Y. (1996), 'Chemical pollution of the aquatic environment by priority pollutants and its control', in R. Harrison (ed.), *Pollution: Causes, Effects, and Control*, 3rd edn, Cambridge: Royal Society of Chemistry.

Daily, G. and Ehrlich, P. (1992), 'Population, sustainability, and Earth's carrying capacity', *BioScience*, 42 (10), 761–771.

Daly, H. (1979), 'Entropy, growth, and the political economy of scarcity', in V. K. Smith (ed.), *Scarcity and Growth Reconsidered*, Baltimore, MD: Johns Hopkins University Press, pp. 67–94.

Daly, H. (1991), *Steady-State Economics: Second Edition with New Essays*, Washington, DC: Island Press.

Daly, H. (1996), *Beyond Growth: The Economics of Sustainable Development*, Boston: Beacon Press.

Daly, H. and Cobb, J. (1989), *For the Common Good: Redirecting the Economy Toward Community, the Environment, and a Sustainable Future*, Boston: Beacon Press.

Davies, J. and Doon, R. (1987), 'Human health effects of pesticides', in G. Marco, R. Hollingworth, and W. Durham (eds), *Silent Spring Revisited*, Washington, DC: American Chemical Society.

Diefenbacher, H. (1994), 'The index of sustainable economic welfare in Germany', in C. Cobb and J. Cobb (eds), *The Green National Product*, New York: UPA.

Dietz, S. and Neumayer, E. (2006), 'A critical appraisal of Genuine Savings as an indicator of sustainability', in P. Lawn (ed.), *Sustainable Development Indicators in Ecological Economics*, Cheltenham, UK: Edward Elgar, pp. 117–135.

El Serafy, S. (1989), 'The proper calculation of income from depletable natural resources', in Y. Ahmad, S. El Serafy, and E. Lutz (eds), *Environmental Accounting for Sustainable Development*, Washington, DC: World Bank, pp. 10–18.

Fisher, I. (1906), *Nature of Capital and Income*, New York: A. M. Kelly.

Food and Agriculture Organization of the United Nations (FAO) (2001), *Baseline Study on the Problem of Obsolete Pesticide Stocks*, Rome: FAO.

Forgie, V., McDonald, G., Zhang, Y., Patterson, M., and Hardy, D. (2008), 'Calculating the New Zealand Genuine Progress Indicator', in P. Lawn and M. Clarke (eds), *Genuine Progress in the Asia-Pacific: Studies Using the Genuine Progress Indicator*, Cheltenham, UK: Edward Elgar, pp. 126–152.

Fuss, M. (1977), 'The demand for energy in Canadian manufacturing: an example of the estimation of production structures with many inputs', *Journal of Econometrics*, 5, 89–116.

Georgescu-Roegen, N. (1979), 'Comments on the papers by Daly and Stiglitz', in V. K. Smith (ed.), *Scarcity and Growth Reconsidered*, Baltimore, MD: Johns Hopkins University Press, pp. 95–105.

Global Footprint Network (2006), '2006 National Footprint Accounts', www.footprintnetwork.org.

Goodstein, E. (2008), *Economics and the Environment*, 5th edn, Hoboken, NJ: John Wiley & Sons.

Griffin, J. and Gregory, P. (1976), 'An intercountry translog model of energy substitution responses', *American Economic Review*, 66, 845–857.

Guenno, G. and Tiezzi, S. (1998), *An Index of Sustainable Economic Welfare for Italy*, Working Paper 5/98, Fondazione Eni Enrico Mattei, Milan.

Haberl, H., Erb, K.-H., and Krausmann, K. (2007), 'Human appropriation of net primary production', *Internet Encyclopaedia of Ecological Economics*, International Society for Ecological Economics, www.ecoeco.org/publica/encyc.htm.

Halvorsen, R. and Ford, J. (1978), 'Substitution among energy, capital, and labour inputs in US manufacturing', in R. Pindyck (ed.), *Advances in the Economics of Energy and Resources*, Volume 1, Greenwich, CT: JAI Press.

Hamilton, K. (1994), 'Green adjustments to GDP', *Resources Policy*, 20 (3), 155–168.

Hartwick, J. (1977), 'Intergenerational equity and the investing of rents from exhaustible resources', *American Economic Review*, 65, 972–974.

Hartwick, J. (1978), 'Substitution among exhaustible resources and intergenerational equity', *Review of Economic Studies*, 45, 347–354.

Hicks, J. (1946), *Value and Capital*, 2nd edn, London: Clarendon.

IMPEL (2005), *The Illegal Shipment of Waste among IMPEL Member States*, Project Report, University College, London.

International Bank for Reconstruction and Development (IBRD) (1992), *World Development Report 1992: Development and the Environment*, Oxford: Oxford University Press.

International Labour Organization (ILO) (2008), *Yearbook of Labour Statistics, 2008*, Geneva: ILO.

International Panel on Climate Change (IPCC) (2007), *IPCC Fourth Assessment Report: Climate Change 2007*, Geneva: World Meteorological Organisation.

Jackson, T. and Stymne, S. (1996), *Sustainable Economic Welfare in Sweden: A Pilot Index 1950–1992*, Stockholm: Stockholm Environment Institute.

Jackson, T., Laing, F., MacGillivray, A. Marks, N., Ralls, J., and Styme, S. (1997), *An Index of Sustainable Economic Welfare for the UK, 1950–1996*, Guildford: University of Surrey Centre for Environmental Strategy.

Jesinghaus, J. (2001), *The World Economic Forum's Environmental Sustainability Index: Strong and Weak Points*, Ispra: European Commission Joint Research Centre.

Kaufmann, R. and Cleveland, C. (1995), 'Measuring sustainability – an interdisciplinary approach to an interdisciplinary concept', *Ecological Economics*, 15 (2), 109–112.

Kuznets, S. (1955), 'Economic growth and income inequality', *American Economic Review*, 49, 1–28.

Lawn, P. (2004), 'How important is natural capital in sustaining real output? Revisiting the natural capital/human-made capital substitutability debate', *International Journal of Global Environmental Issues*, 3 (4), 418–435.

Lawn, P. (2007a), 'A stock-take of green national accounting initiatives', *Social Indicators Research*, 80, 427–460.

Lawn, P. (2007b), *Frontier Issues in Ecological Economics*, Cheltenham, UK: Edward Elgar.

Lawn, P. (2007c), 'What value is Gross Domestic Product as a macroeconomic indicator of national income, well-being, and environmental stress?', *International Journal of Ecological Economics and Statistics*, 8, 22–43.

Lawn, P. (2008), 'Genuine progress in India: some further growth needed in the immediate future but population stabilisation needed immediately', in P. Lawn and M. Clarke (eds), *Genuine Progress in the Asia-Pacific: Studies Using the Genuine Progress Indicator*, Cheltenham, UK: Edward Elgar, pp. 191–227.

Lawn, P. and Clarke, M. (eds) (2008a), *Genuine Progress in the Asia-Pacific: Studies Using the Genuine Progress Indicator*, Cheltenham, UK: Edward Elgar.

Lawn, P. and Clarke, M (2008b), 'Genuine progress across the Asia-Pacific region: comparisons, trends, and policy implications', in P. Lawn and M. Clarke (eds), *Sustainable Welfare in the Asia-Pacific: Studies Using the Genuine Progress Indicator*, Cheltenham, UK: Edward Elgar.

Lawn, P. and Sanders, R. (1999), 'Has Australia surpassed its optimal macroeconomic scale? finding out with the aid of benefit and cost accounts and a sustainable net benefit index', *Ecological Economics*, 28 (2), 213–229.

Lenzen, M. and Murray, S. (2001), 'A modified ecological footprint method and its application to Australia', *Ecological Economics*, 37 (2), 229–255.

Leontief, W. (1970), 'Environmental repercussions and the environmental structure: an input–output approach', *Review of Economic Statistics*, 52, 262–277.

Lovelock, J. (1988), *Ages of Gaia: A Biography of Our Living Planet*, New York: Norton & Co.

Makino, M. (2008), 'Genuine Progress in Japan and the need for an open economy GPI', in P. Lawn and M. Clarke (eds), *Genuine Progress in the Asia-Pacific: Studies Using the Genuine Progress Indicator*, Cheltenham, UK: Edward Elgar, pp. 153–190.

Marco, G. (1987), 'A Summary of Silent Spring', in G. Marco, R. Hollingworth, and W. Durham (eds), *Silent Spring Revisited*, Washington, DC: American Chemical Society, pp. xvii–xviii.

Max-Neef, M. (1995), 'Economic growth and quality of life', *Ecological Economics*, 15 (2), 115–118.

Meadows, D. H., Meadows, D. L., Randers, J., and Behrens, W., III (eds), *The Limits to Growth*, New York: Universe Books.

Moffat, I. and Wilson, M. (1994), 'An index of sustainable economic welfare for Scotland, 1980–1991', *International Journal of Sustainable Development and World Ecology*, 1, 264–291.

Munasinghe, M. (1999), 'Is environmental degradation an inevitable consequence of economic growth?: Tunneling through the environmental Kuznets curve', *Ecological Economics*, 29 (1), 89–109.

Nordhaus, W. and Tobin, J. (1972), 'Is economic growth obsolete?', in *Economic Growth: The National Bureau of Economic Research, Fiftieth Anniversary Colloquium*, New York: Columbia University Press.

Nguyet Hong, V. X., Clarke, M., and Lawn, P. (2008), 'Genuine progress in Vietnam: the impact of the Doi Moi reforms', in P. Lawn and M. Clarke (eds), *Genuine Progress in the Asia-Pacific: Studies Using the Genuine Progress Indicator*, Cheltenham, UK: Edward Elgar, pp. 299–330.

Norgaard, R. (1984), 'Coevolutionary development potential', *Land Economics*, 60, 160–173.

Norgaard, R. (1985), 'Environmental economics: an evolutionary critique and a plea for pluralism', *Journal of Environmental Economics and Management*, 12, 382–394.

Norgaard, R. (1988), 'Sustainable development: a co-evolutionary view', *Futures*, December 1988, 606–620.

Norgaard, R. (1994), *Development Betrayed: The End of Progress and a Coevolutionary Revisioning of the Future*, New York: Routledge.

Norton, B. (1986), 'On the inherent danger of undervaluing species', in B. Norton (ed.), *The Preservation of Species*, Princeton, NJ: Princeton University Press, pp. 110–137.

Patterson, M. (2006), 'Selecting headline indicators for tracking progress to sustainability in a nation', in P. Lawn (ed.), *Sustainable Development Indicators in Ecological Economics*, Cheltenham, UK: Edward Elgar, pp. 421–448.

Pearce, D. and Atkinson, G. (1993), 'Capital theory and the measurement of sustainable development: an indicator of weak sustainability, *Ecological Economics*, 8, 103–108.

Pearce, D., Hamilton, K., and Atkinson, G. (1996), 'Measuring sustainable development: progress on indicators', *Environment and Development Economics*, 1 (1), 85–101.

Perman, R., Ma, Y., McGilvray, J., and Common, M. (2003), *Natural Resource and Environmental Economics*, 3rd edn, Harlow: Pearson.

Perrings, C. (1987), *Economy and Environment: A Theoretical Essay on the Interdependence of Economic and Environmental Systems*, Cambridge: Cambridge University Press.

Pezzey, J. and Withagen, C. (1998), 'The rise, fall, and sustainability of capital-resource economies', *Scandinavian Journal of Economics*, 100, 513–527.

Pimentel, D., Cooperstein, S., Randell, H., Filiberto, D., Sorrentino, S., Kaye, B., Nicklin, C., Yagi, J., Brian, J., O'Hern, J., Habas, A., and Weinstein, C. (2007), 'Ecology of increasing diseases: population growth and environmental degradation', *Human Ecology*, 35 (6), 653–668.

Robinson, J. (1962), *Economic Philosophy*, London: C. A. Watts & Co.

Rosenberg, K. and Oegema, T. (1995), *A Pilot ISEW for The Netherlands 1950–1992*, Amsterdam: Instituut voor Milieu- en Systeemanalyse.

Rothman, D. (1998), 'Environmental Kuznets curves – real progress or passing the buck? A case for consumption-based approaches', *Ecological Economics*, 25 (2), 177–194.

Solow, R. (1974), 'The economics of resources or the resources of economics', *American Economic Review*, 64, 1–14.

Solow, R. (1986), 'On the intergenerational allocation of resources', *Scandinavian Journal of Economics*, 88 (1), 141–149.

Stern, N. (2006), *The Economics of Climate Change: The Stern Review*, London: HM Treasury.

Stern, N. (2007), *Stern Review on the Economics of Climate Change*, Cambridge University Press, Cambridge.

Stern, D., Common, M., and Barbier, E. (1996), 'Economic growth and environmental degradation: the environmental Kuznets curve and sustainable development', *World Development*, 41, 1151–1160.

Stiglitz, J. (1974), 'Growth with exhaustible natural resources: efficient and optimal growth paths', *Review of Economic Studies*, Symposium on the Economics of Exhaustible Resources, pp. 123–138.

Stockhammer, E., Hochreiter, H., Obermayr, B., and Steiner, K. (1997), 'The index of sustainable economic welfare (ISEW) as an alternative to GDP in measuring economic welfare: the results of the Australian (revised) ISEW calculation 1955–1992', *Ecological Economics*, 21, 19–34.

Suri, V. and Chapman, D. (1998), 'Economic growth, trade, and energy – real progress or passing the buck?: A case for consumption-based approaches', *Ecological Economics*, 25 (2), 177–194.

Victor, P. (1972), *Pollution: Economy and Environment*, London: Allen & Unwin.

Victor, P. (1991), 'Indicators of sustainable development: some lessons from capital theory', *Ecological Economics*, 4, 191–213.

Vitousek, P., Ehrlich, P., Ehrlich, A., and Matson, P. (1986), 'Human appropriation of the products of photosynthesis', *BioScience*, 36, 368–373.

Wackernagel, M. and Rees, W. (1996), *Our Ecological Footprint: Reducing Human Impact on the Earth*, Gabriola Island: New Society Publishers.

Wackernagel, M., Onisto, L., Bello, P., Callejas Linares, A., Susana Lopez Falfan, S., Mendez Garcia, J., Suarez Guerrero, A. I., and Suarez Guerrero, M. G. (1999), 'National natural capital accounting with the ecological footprint concept', *Ecological Economics*, 29 (3), 375–390.

Weisskopf, W. (1973), 'Economic growth versus existential balance', in H. Daly (ed.), *Towards a Steady State Economy*, San Francisco: W. H. Freeman, pp. 240–251.

Wen, Z., Yang, Y., and Lawn, P. (2008), 'From GDP to GPI: quantifying thirty-five years of development in China', in P. Lawn and M. Clarke (eds), *Genuine Progress in the Asia-Pacific: Studies Using the Genuine Progress Indicator*, Cheltenham, UK: Edward Elgar, pp. 228–259.

Wilson, E. O. (2002), *The Future of Life*, New York: Alfred A. Knopf.

World Bank (2004), 'Adjusted net savings data', http://lnwb18.worldbank.org/ESSD/essdext.nsf/44ByDocName/GreenAccountingWealthEstimates.

World Commission on Environment and Development (WCED) (1987), *Our Common Future*, Oxford: Oxford University Press.

Yale Center for Environmental Law and Policy, Center for International Earth Science Information Network, and World Economic Forum (2005), *2005 Environmental Sustainability Index*, New Haven, CT: YCELP.

Part II

Post-Keynesian economics and the environment

3 Why have Post-Keynesians (perhaps) inadequately dealt with issues related to the environment?

Andrew Mearman

Introduction[1]

The central aim of this chapter is to investigate why it is the case that, in spite of the crucial nature of the issue and their claims to relevance on policy matters, Post-Keynesians have had relatively little to say on the economics of the environment. The chapter makes use of questionnaire and interview data collected from a number of leading Post-Keynesian economists. The data suggests that there are many reasons why Post-Keynesians have had little to say on the environment. The main reasons are: (a) Post-Keynesians have adopted a strategic focus on criticising key areas on orthodox economic theory; (b) their social history has reinforced and entrenched their initial foci; (c) they have used static tools ill-equipped for analysing the environment; and (d) they have focused more on growth and full employment.

The chapter proceeds as follows. The next section establishes the premise that Post-Keynesianism has had little to say about the environment. The third section discusses the method by which data was collected for this study. The fourth section examines factors that are significant in explaining the relatively low level of work done by Post-Keynesians on the environment. The fifth section explores factors regarded as insignificantly explanatory, and the final section presents a summary and conclusions.

Post-Keynesianism and the environment

There are several ways to establish the premise that the school of economic thought known as Post-Keynesianism has had little to say on the economics of the environment, relative to mainstream economics, to its own body of work, to other heterodox schools, and to the extent of political and social debate on the environment. This chapter, building on Mearman (2005a), utilises various measures: a survey of published Post-Keynesian literature on the environment; an audit of heterodox journals for articles on the environment; and a survey of leading Post-Keynesian economists.

Recent years have seen something of an increase in interest in the environment by Post-Keynesians. This volume is an example, as is Holt *et al.* (forthcoming).

Both show a wide range of authors working in and around Post-Keynesianism who have engaged with the environment, as well as links between that tradition and ecological economics. A 2005 symposium on Post-Keynesian economics and the environment is another example (Mearman, 2005a, 2005b; Christensen, 2005; Courvisanos, 2005; Holt, 2005). All four of the constituent papers were critical of the neoclassical approach, in particular its treatment of the environment; but all are optimistic about the future and about the capacity of Post-Keynesianism to advance an ecologically responsible economic framework. In addition, the work by Holt on sustainability – for instance, Chapter 5 of this volume – is evidence of a growing interest. Holt (2005) refers particularly to developments in complexity theory pursued by Post-Keynesians, such as Rosser (1999), as an approach which incorporates non-linear dynamics, systems theory, and an evolutionary perspective. It also allows economics to move beyond the Newtonian physics and associated tools in which it is currently trapped and has the 'scientific rigour' that economists tend to demand. Mearman (forthcoming) discusses how recent developments in Post-Keynesian methodology (building on older ideas), such as developments on uncertainty, ontology, and pluralism, may suggest a distinctive Post-Keynesian approach to the environment. Forstater (2004, 2006) and Tcherneva (Chapter 7 of this volume) have addressed the question of employment and the environment. Marangos and Williams (2005) have examined the economic effects of drought.

However, the growing interest in the environment by Post-Keynesians is not (yet) necessarily reflected in the output on the environment in Post-Keynesian journals. The cited works, above, are exceptions. Table 3.1 shows the proportion of articles with significant environmental content on the environment from journals that are popular publication destinations amongst Post-Keynesians for 1999–2007.[3] As Table 3.1 shows, the proportion of issues of the *Journal of Post-Keynesian Economics* (*JPKE*) containing environmental articles was only 14.7 per cent. Of course, environmental issues are only one of many competing to be published. However, arguably, this figure overstates the amount of environmental work done by Post-Keynesians. An alternative measure would be the proportion of the total number of articles published which had significant environmental content. That figure is in fact much lower, at only 1.5 per cent of all articles published being on environmental questions. Often, of course, the policy of the journal's editor is significant in determining content. In the case of the *JPKE*, its editor, Paul Davidson, is both a writer on environmental issues (see above) and a promoter of environmental enquiry. Indeed, Davidson's (2002) statement of purpose for the *JPKE* stresses the importance of ecological and natural resource issues and makes an explicit call for environmental work to be published in the journal.

Moreover, for other favourite journals of Post-Keynesians, the numbers are similar. The *Cambridge Journal of Economics* (*CJE*) has a somewhat higher proportion, but compared with, say, the institutionalist *Journal of Economic Issues* (*JEI*) its figure is relatively low. Table 3.1 splits the sample period into two, showing the state of play before and after the investigations conducted by Mearman (2005a). The table shows that, in some cases, the proportion of articles and issues

Table 3.1 Incidence of environmental articles by journal, 1999–2007, by (a) proportion of total articles and (b) proportion of issues containing environmental articles[2]

Journal	Articles 1999–2004 (%)	Issues 1999–2004 (%)	Articles 2004–2007 (%)	Issues 2004–2007 (%)	Articles 1999–2007 (%)	Issues 1999–2007 (%)
JPKE	2.0	19.0	0.8	8.3	1.5	14.7
RRPE	1.6	10.0	1.1	7.7	1.4	9.1
JEI	6.8	52.4	7.6	76.9	7.1	61.8
CJE	3.4	19.4	3.3	28.6	3.3	23.1
RSE	2.4	14.3	3.3	15.4	2.8	14.7
AER	4.2	53.8	1.3	25.0	3.0	42.9
C&C	8.8	29.4	0.0	0.0	5.7	18.5
Average	4.2	28.3	2.5	23.1	3.5	26.4
Weighted average	4.4	28.7	2.7	24.2	3.7	27.0

containing articles on the environment in journals targeted by Post-Keynesians has fallen. The picture is mixed; the *CJE* scores have increased. Moreover, the overall decrease is not restricted to Post-Keynesians; the scores for the Marxist *Capital and Class* (*C&C*) fell to zero. This may suggest that heterodox economists are also becoming less interested in the environment, or it may suggest that journals such as *Ecological Economics* are becoming more effective. Evidence for that perspective is given by the fall-off in the publication rate in the mainstream *American Economic Review (AER)*.

Although the current picture is mixed, it does suggest a relative dearth of work historically done by Post-Keynesians on the environment. That is not to say that there has been no Post-Keynesian work on the environment. Paul Davidson is a leading Post-Keynesian who has seriously addressed the environment in his work. Davidson was the Post-Keynesian whose work was cited most often by respondents to the questionnaire discussed below. Davidson produced a considerable body of work in the 1960s on the oil industry and on the valuation of leisure-related ecology (see Mearman, 2004a, for a full inventory).

Going back further in Post-Keynesian economics, there are isolated patches of concern for the environment. Kahn (1935) provides perhaps the earliest example of Post-Keynesian concern for the environment in a paper which responds to Pigou (1932) on the question of 'ideal' output. However, amongst the early Post-Keynesians, based in Cambridge, this was an isolated example. Kaldor had really nothing to say on the environment, and Robinson's first significant published comment came in her Richard T. Ely lecture to the American Economic Association in 1971 (Robinson, 1972). Other claims of Post-Keynesian work on the environment partly depend on which economists are counted in the Post-Keynesian category. The work of Galbraith (1958, in particular) on pollution, Boulding (*passim*), and Georgescu-Roegen (*passim*), who applied systems and physical theories to economics, may all qualify.

Similarly, more recently, there are others, writing in what might be called a Post-Keynesian tradition, who have published elsewhere. John Gowdy, for example, has published extensively on ecological issues, particularly in *Ecological Economics* (e.g., Gowdy and Mayumi, 2001). Clive Spash has also published in *Ecological Economics* (e.g., Spash, 2000) and extensively in non-economic journals, particularly *Environmental Values*. Moreover, there are other Post-Keynesian-like economists who have published in books or have written their own books on the ecology (e.g., Vercelli, 1998; Jespersen, 2004).

However, Winnett's (2003) survey of Post-Keynesian environmental economics is particularly instructive. Although he offers several useful suggestions for future Post-Keynesian contributions on the environment,[4] Winnett's piece is most illuminating in this context for its almost complete failure to cite existing Post-Keynesian works. This indicates very strongly that there is no current, distinctive Post-Keynesian approach to the environment. Further evidence that Post-Keynesians have had relatively little to say on ecological issues is Table 3 of Kennet and Heinemann (2006), from which Post-Keynesianism is absent.

Data collection and questionnaire design

The previous section presented the results of a literature review and an audit of recent editions of heterodox journals. The conclusion drawn was that Post-Keynesians have had relatively little to say on the environment. A third data source was to ask leading Post-Keynesian authors and eminent sympathisers. The data was collected by two methods: interview and questionnaire. Two interviews were carried out, one in person over approximately one hour; the other electronically. The purposes of the interviews were to collect data and to clarify some of the key issues in the compilation of the questionnaire.[5] The interviews were semi-structured in that they comprised three main questions: (a) has Post-Keynesianism had little to say about the environment?; (b) why has it had little to say?; and (c) how might it make more of a contribution? On the basis of these questions, further issues were explored and points clarified. The interviews informed the construction of the questionnaire.

The questionnaire was distributed to 21 economists in the UK, North America, and Australia. All are leading Post-Keynesians or economists sympathetic to the Post-Keynesian project. Twelve of them are full professors. All have published extensively, mainly in heterodox journals. Fifteen had written books on Post-Keynesian economics. All are/were members of journal editorial boards and at least five are/were editors of prominent journals. In all, 13 responses were received; a response rate of 61.9 per cent, which would usually be considered good for postal or electronic questionnaires. The profile of the sample indicates that the respondents are well qualified to comment on the current state of Post-Keynesian economics. Clearly, the sample is not technically random; but neither is it obviously biased towards specific answers to the questions set. However, in light of the sampling method employed, and of the sample size, inferences made about the population of heterodox economists must be made with more than usual caution. Nonetheless, the data are evidential regarding various hypotheses about Post-Keynesianism and the environment.

The questionnaire can be found in Appendix 3.1. As its preamble states, the questionnaire comprised a mixture of closed and open questions. Closed and open questions have different advantages and disadvantages (see, for example, Oppenheim, 1966; Wilson and McClean, 1994; Coolican, 1999). Closed questions are advantageous because they allow definite answers, they permit the questioner to control the information flow, they facilitate quantification and thereby ease presentation, and they are easier to compare between respondents or groups of respondents. However, closed questions are also quite restrictive; they allow only prescribed answers and prevent the respondents from expanding upon an argument or clarifying their answer. The quantification requirement of closed questions also suppresses different motivations for the same response from different respondents. Open questions offer different advantages and counteract the disadvantages of closed questions. Open questions are less suggestive and offer the respondent freedom and spontaneity of response to the questions; thus, they enable subtleties to be explored. Open questions also allow a depth of feeling and a level of knowledge on a question to be expressed. The questionnaire attempted to exploit the advantages of both closed and open questions. The mixture of closed and open questions was attained in two ways: first, a mixture of closed and open questions were asked; second, the questionnaire allowed the respondent to write comments to explain their answers to the closed questions.

In all, there were five main questions. Question 4 was broken down into eight sub-questions. For Question 1 and for all parts of Question 4, the questions were closed with the option to comment. In each case, a Likert scale was used to ascertain the extent to which the respondent agreed with the proposition put to them. Likert scales are advantageous because they are relatively simple yet achieve relatively precise information, they achieve better unidimensionality (that the same thing is being measured each time), they are reliable, and they eliminate the need for investigator judgment of responses (Oppenheim, 1966: 133–141). In collation, a score of 1 to 5 was used to quantify the Likert scale: 1 signified that the respondent strongly disagreed with the proposition; 5 signified strong agreement. Questions 2, 3, and 5 are open questions. For the analysis of the open questions and comments, key words were noted. Moreover, the comments provide an excellent source for quotations to be inserted into the text below. This has the advantage that the respondent's original meaning can be preserved and also removes the need for cumbersome coding and quantitative analysis of the responses.

Survey results: why have Post-Keynesians said little on the environment?

The results from the questionnaires are summarised in Table 3.2.

The first point to note is that the survey results support the claim made above that Post-Keynesians have said relatively little on the environment. This, of course, was an implicit assumption of this chapter. As the descriptive statistics show, there was a range of views on this question – some of which are undoubtedly relevant to the answers to Question 4. Moreover, many interesting issues are suggested by these particular results. For example, responses elicited several definitions of Post-Keynesianism. However, this issue is beyond the scope of this chapter. Instead, the chapter focuses on the responses to Question 4, pertaining to the reasons why Post-Keynesians have said so little on the environment.

The questionnaire content was based on prior expectations and explanations (partly from the interviews) of why Post-Keynesians have been relatively inactive on the environment. However, based on the questionnaire and on further consideration, it seems that some of those factors might be less important than previously thought. Similarly, other factors previously considered insignificant or ignored have emerged as important. Thus, the chapter will present factors as significant and insignificant. Bearing in mind Ziliak and McCloskey's (2004) concerns, significance here is not reduced to statistical significance; factors are considered significant if they seem to explain the level of output of Post-Keynesians on the environment.

Table 3.2 Average scores of questionnaire responses (in each case 5 = strongly agree) (n = 13)

	Mean	Mode	Median
Q1: Post-Keynesians have had little to say on the environment	3.92	4, 5	4
Q4a: focus on growth → neglect of environment	3.5	2, 4	4
Q4b: environmental economics is a new subject → neglect of environment	2.42	1, 4	2
Q4c: environmental economics less important → neglect of environment	2.58	3	3
Q4d: focus on fighting neoclassicism → neglect of environment	4.08	4	4
Q4e: Post-Keynesians do not value natural resources → neglect of environment	3.25	4	4
Q4f: no theory of value → neglect of environment	2.08	1	1.5
Q4g: leading Post-Keynesians are older → neglect of environment	1.75	1, 2	2
Q4h: other heterodox schools have dealt with the environment → neglect of environment	2.08	1, 2	2

Significant factors

The main aim of the questionnaire was to ascertain the reasons for the relatively low volume of Post-Keynesian environmental economics. It did so in two separate stages. The first stage was to ask for reasons in an open question (Question 3). The questionnaire asked the respondent to attempt this question before moving on to Question 4, which contained possible answers to Question 3. The reason for this was to try to attain a first reaction from the respondent, unconditioned by the (implicit) explanations contained in Question 4. Perhaps unsurprisingly, many of the answers given to the open question anticipate the possibilities in Question 4; however, the answers also provide much greater detail than was provided in response to Question 4.

The most common response (five) to Question 3 was that Post-Keynesians are more interested in 'macroeconomic' concerns, such as money, than microeconomics. This echoes King (2002), who defines and discussed Post-Keynesianism in terms of macroeconomics, consciously ignoring any microeconomic developments (cf. Lee, 1998; Downward, 1999). This is significant because, as one respondent (Marc Lavoie) remarked, 'environmental questions could also be studied from a macro angle.' Indeed, viewed from a 'systems' perspective, environmental questions are primarily about the system and its sustainability. Admittedly, none of those who responded in terms of a macro focus professed to be, or would be classified as, environmental economists. Nor had they written on the subject. It is possible that their responses were conditioned by the mainstream classification of environmental economics as a branch of microeconomics.

The last point is also significant because it suggests that a Post-Keynesian response was conditioned by the prevailing orthodoxy. This observation is connected to several other comments from respondents. One respondent argued that a reason for the dearth of Post-Keynesian environmental economics is that Post-Keynesians are trapped in neoclassical tools; one example given was the concept of user cost, 'the sacrifice which [the entrepreneur] incurs by employing the equipment instead of leaving it idle' (Keynes, 1936: 23). User cost has been advanced, for instance, by Paul Davidson (2002), as being potentially significant in Post-Keynesian economic analysis of the environment. However, user cost was described as 'static' and 'Marshallian' by the respondent. The subsequent argument was that Post-Keynesians needed to adopt and develop dynamic frameworks, such as systems and complexity theory, which the respondent describes as being currently 'on the fringes' of Post-Keynesianism. In diametric opposition to that respondent, two respondents (incidentally, those who argued that Post-Keynesians has much to say on the environment) argued that Post-Keynesians used concepts (such as non-ergodicity and, interestingly, user costs) which were anathema to the mainstream, hence leading to the rejection of those Post-Keynesians.

The open responses to Question 3 are also illuminating because they point to several strands of explanation for the relatively low output of Post-Keynesian work on the environment. Obviously, all of them can be considered 'historical' because the development of Post-Keynesianism is an historical artefact as well as being an ongoing process. However, the historical can be broken down into related categories: the intellectual, the social (academic community), and the political (the wider context of the intellectual and social factors). Given this, the chapter draws on works such as Lee (2000), Tymoigne and Lee (2003), and particularly King's (2002) history of Post-Keynesianism, all of which have helped to create an institutional history of Post-Keynesianism, which, unlike in other traditions, was missing.

Tiryakian (1977) portrays schools of thought as being organised around a leader, with converts, interpreters, students, and auxiliaries. King's (2002) analysis borrows from Tiryakian but, as King notes, it is not simple to fit Post-Keynesianism into this description – perhaps, it might be added, because Post-Keynesianism has more than one charismatic leader – but it does hold some resonance. If, as many respondents suggested, Keynes's *General Theory* had little to say directly about the environment – his concept of user cost, though applicable to the environment, did not refer directly to it – it is unsurprising that his students and followers would not pay much attention to it. The same can be said for other leaders, such as Kalecki and Sraffa. Moreover, as Keynes and Kalecki were concerned more with macroeconomics, money (particularly in Keynes' case), growth, and unemployment, it would again be expected that their followers would share these interests.

As Tymoigne and Lee (2003) argue, King's early chapters show that Post-Keynesianism emerged out of alternative interpretations of the *General Theory* rather than merely a critique of orthodox economics. Geoff Harcourt's questionnaire response makes the same point. To be clear, this is not to suggest that Post-Keynesianism is merely a negative programme, as has been suggested. In the initial period, leading economists who might now be called Post-Keynesians, such as Joan Robinson, Townshend, Kahn, and Kaldor were busy trying to understand the *General Theory* whilst wrestling with their own intellectual backgrounds. Many of them, particularly Robinson, initially remained trapped in pre-Keynesian ideas, which coexisted somewhat uneasily with their more radical interpretations of Keynes's work. Thus, much of the early work retained the ambiguity that many regard as pervading the *General Theory*. At the same time, Robinson and Kaldor, in particular, were attempting to assimilate Kalecki's ideas with their own. The next stage of Post-Keynesianism, according to King, was to attempt, via Harrod's work, to meld Keynes' short period insights into a long-run framework.

What this meant for the theoretical content of Post-Keynesianism was that it was concerned primarily with issues of (un)employment, growth, capital accumulation, business cycles, class, income distribution, money (King, 2002: ch. 8; Tymoigne and Lee, 2003), and government policy. Post-Keynesians were engaged in an attempt to advance the case for this alternative approach by developing new theories and also by attacking the old orthodoxy. In some cases, this process of critique led them into other areas, such as methodological issues. Significant questions were raised against the concepts of the long run and equilibrium (Robinson, in particular).

This potted history of early Post-Keynesianism is well known. The crucial question is how this history affected the development (or lack) of environmental positions. Clearly, the birth and development of a new approach expends considerable energy and left little time for what might have been considered minority concerns. Moreover, the overriding concern of early Post-Keynesianism was employment and its achievement via growth, the distribution of which was also crucial. Furthermore, when that energy is concentrated in a few institutions, because Post-Keynesianism was then and remains a minority view, it is difficult to organise resources to fight the orthodoxy on all fronts. As Lavoie responded:

> There is a limited amount of Post-Keynesian economists out there, and a lot of them devote their time and energy to history of economic thought; plus a lot of them have to teach neoclassical economics, or learn more neoclassical stuff in order to criticise it; so once you have taken out those that are concerned with macro policy issues, there isn't that much left for theory or environmental economics!

There seems to be no direct evidence that this focus on growth contributed to a neglect of environmental issues; perhaps this just did not occur to the early Post-Keynesians.

Thus, even though the leading contemporary orthodox economist, Pigou, was a main target for the early Cambridge Keynesians, only Kahn (1935) addressed Pigou's welfare economics and therefore environmental concerns. The rest of the group, and their descendants, focused on the core issues of growth, distribution, money, and capital. Question 4d asked if an approach to environmental economics had failed to develop because Post-Keynesians had devoted their resources to fighting neoclassical economics. As can be seen from Table 3.2, this question elicited a mean response of 4.08, and a mode and median response of 4, indicating consistent agreement with the proposition. Moreover (see Table A3.1), the correlation was strong between the answer to 4d and the answer to Question 1, suggesting that respondents disagreed with the proposition in 4d because they rejected its premise.[6] John King responded that the fighting of Post-Keynesians against the neoclassicals was 'the key' factor in explaining why Post-Keynesians had not developed environmental literature.

However, it is also possible that the way in which Post-Keynesians were fighting neoclassicism might have been crucial. This claim is supported by the questionnaire data. As was mentioned above, one respondent criticised the nature of the tools developed by Post-Keynesians and claimed that this might explain the underdevelopment of a Post-Keynesian environmental economics. Another wrote: 'P[ost]K[eynesians] tend to "fall" into the "deductive science" of deducing proofs rather than constructing solutions in their efforts to fight [neoclassical economics]. This is changing and thus [is creating] room for P[ost]K[eynesian] environmentalism.' This response is highly significant in two ways. First, it suggests a critique of a particular approach to Post-Keynesianism that advocates the adoption of neoclassical tools, and perhaps premises, in order to attack the orthodoxy. Second, it points to developments in Post-Keynesian methodology that eschew deductive modelling.

On the first point, it is the position of, for example, Paul Davidson, that the orthodoxy needs to be attacked on its own ground. For many, this position is based on the belief that Keynes adopted the same rhetorical strategy. As a result, the Marshallian microeconomics of Keynes's work is left intact. In terms of environmental issues, this methodological position encourages the adoption of orthodox concepts, but seen through a Post-Keynesian lens. Given this, Davidson's approach to the environment is consistent with this general project. For example, King (2002: 118) claims that Davidson 'remained a Marshallian rather than a Kaleckian on matters of microeconomic theory and method.' Consequently, much of Davidson's environmental analysis, particularly his earliest work, looks very orthodox, using marginalist terminology, utility, etc. Davidson implies that a Post-Keynesian approach employs non-ergodicity (and is therefore anathema to neoclassical treatments – which is one reason for its lack of development of environmental literature); however, this literature is currently underdeveloped.

Davidson's position seems to be that the embryonic Keynesian framework, incorporating concepts such as user costs, should be developed and that this would be a way forward for Post-Keynesians interested in the environment (see Davidson, 2002). However, one respondent (also see above) suggested that Davidson's attempts had not been very satisfactory; and was one explanation for why a Post-Keynesian literature had not developed. This claim raises the possibility that Post-Keynesian environmental analysis was stunted by lack of previous success. As noted above, Davidson's work has been criticised as being overly Marshallian and trapped inside neoclassical microeconomic concepts. One respondent cites user cost as an inadequate static Marshallian tool. Indeed, Jerry Courvisanos argues that 'using static (Marshallian) tools, environmental issues are poorly handle[d] (economic rents, user costs, cost–benefit analysis).' It is also possible that valuation by Davidson's methods (see below) was seen as too neoclassical and therefore unattractive given the prevailing goal of Post-Keynesians to develop alternatives to the mainstream. This is not to overly criticise Davidson, who is a rare example of a Post-Keynesian who has engaged the environment; however, it must be acknowledged that many heterodox economists argue for a complete break from the orthodoxy, and would thus find Davidson's approach unattractive.

More encouragingly, Courvisanos notes that the tools, such as complexity theory, necessary for environmental analysis have not made their way far enough into Post-Keynesianism yet, but are gaining momentum. According to King's (2002) history, the last great developmental change in Post-Keynesianism was the focus on methodology. King traces this back to the rediscovery in the late 1980s of Keynes's work on uncertainty (Carabelli, 1988; O'Donnell, 1989; Davis, 1989); but this is not strictly correct. For example, Dow's (1985) work is contemporary but distinct from the analysis of Keynes' philosophy. However, Dow quickly developed along these lines. Davidson's (*passim*) attack on ergodicity can be interpreted as a methodological argument. Moreover, although Davidson professed to extend Keynes's theoretical analysis, his own work does not draw on Keynes's philosophical writings explicitly. Rather, he draws on Keynes's treatments of, say, uncertainty, in the *General Theory* and in Keynes (1937). Chick's

(1983) analysis of Keynes shows methodological awareness. However, King is correct to argue that the major impetus for the new methodological focus was the renewed interest in Keynes's philosophy and methodology. An early example of this was Lawson and Pesaran (1985). Interestingly, this work is an early example of Lawson's concern with philosophy, which was emerging at the time but was not fully evident until later (although see Lawson, 1985). Only then did several works follow that drew on Keynes' own philosophy.

What impact, if any, did this methodological turn have on Post-Keynesianism's approach to the environment? If the previous inactivity can be explained by stretched resources, as above, the effect of the new turn would have been once again to squeeze out environmental issues. The methodological turn exhibited similar patterns to previous phases of Post-Keynesianism; it was the chance to both advance a new alternative and also attack the underlying neoclassical methodology based on prediction, falsification, and formalism. This focus again militates against Post-Keynesians doing environmental work. On the other hand, one of the key concepts of the recent methodological literature has been 'open systems'. This is a concept embraced by Dow (1996), Chick (2003), Lawson (*passim*), Downward (1999), Lee (2002), and others writing on Post-Keynesian methodology. Clearly, the term 'open systems' should imply systems theory, and thereby a route into the ecological way of thinking; however, this is not directly manifest in the same way that it is in other heterodox perspectives (e.g., Eberle and Hayden, 1991; cf. Dow, 1996). Indeed, Mearman (2004b) has argued that the term 'open systems' has been underdeveloped. However, there is an impetus towards developing Post-Keynesian methodology and therefore a distinctive Post-Keynesian approach, which could then be applied to the study of the environment. Mearman (forthcoming) argues that Post-Keynesian methodological developments on ontology, uncertainty, and pluralism may contribute to a more vigorous Post-Keynesianism of the environment.

The questionnaire (Question 4a) asked if a Post-Keynesian focus on growth and employment was responsible for its apparent neglect of the environment. A possible tension between growth and the environment may be a feature of Post-Keynesians. Keynes (1936: ch. 16) famously intimated that people should be paid to dig holes in the ground rather than sit idle. Of course, in ecological terms, this could be harmful, if only for the damage done to topsoil. The employment versus environment question is also informed by the common argument that there is an inherent conflict between growth and/or employment, and the environment. Such an argument is found in Malthus, who argued that population growth (associated in classical economics with wages exceeding subsistence and therefore growth) would outstrip agricultural production and lead to mass starvation. This basic argument has been restated in more sophisticated form by ecological economists, who stress the environmental 'limits to growth' (Meadows *et al.*, 1972, 1992). The environmental limits exist in terms of, for example, the carrying capacity of the earth, its ability to absorb waste ('sink' capacity), including pollution, the pressure of growth on existing resources or resources which can be renewed, and the thermodynamic effects of energy use. Moreover, given this, within Post-Keynesianism, at least since Kaldor, manufacturing is seen as the engine for growth. Given that, in general, manufacturing relies on thermodynamically inefficient and apparently scarce fossil fuels, and appears to be generally degrading of the environment, the conflict between Post-Keynesian macroeconomic concerns and environmental issues seems strong.

The questionnaire responses agreed somewhat with the hypothesis that a focus on growth led to the neglect of the environment. The average response was 3.5 – i.e., mild agreement. Within these responses, the view was expressed that Post-Keynesians had implicitly taken the view that the environment was secondary to the overriding goal of growth. Lavoie responded thus: 'It may also be that P[ost] K[eynesian] authors consider that poverty and unemployment arise from a lack of effective demand, and they fear that an overly amount of attention devoted to environmental issues may slow down the economy even more?' Mark Setterfield agrees:

> The focus of P[ost]K[eynesian]E[conomics] is on the notion that demand is the fundamental constraint on aggregate economic activity, and this just does not lead as immediately or obviously to a concern with environmental matters (e.g., problems associated with exhaustible resources, or limits on growth due to problems of environmental sustainability) as a supply side focus might.

Stephen Dunn suggests that Galbraith is an example of a Post-Keynesian who accepted that growth was in conflict with the environment. However, Geoff Harcourt responds, with some justification, that the early Post-Keynesians (Kalecki and those at Cambridge) 'were concerned mostly with other[,] what to them were/ are then more pressing and immediate issues.' As noted above, some of these issues were internal to economics – e.g., the establishment of a theoretical alternative. Also, of course, they were concerned with specific real-world problems, such as large-scale unemployment, war, reconstruction, growth, and the economic policies needed to deal with these issues.

Are these questionnaire responses on growth implicitly accepting the neoclassical growth–environment trade-off, as well as accepting a mainstream stereotype of Post-Keynesians as focusing too heavily on growth? A number of respondents question the trade-off, for a variety of reasons. Lavoie supports the view that Post-Keynesians might be guilty of accepting the trade-off. He notes:

> P[ost]K[eynesian] economists have already to face left-wing thinkers who believe that low-paid jobs in the service industry (to provide services to the sick and the elders), rather than the Providence State, is the way of the future to remedy unemployment and poverty, given the limited resources of Government. These 'social or solidarity' economists or sociologists believe that raising minimum wages is bad for the poor because they will lose their jobs. So environmentalists who oppose economic growth are looked at with some suspicion.

Two respondents claimed that questions of exhaustible resources, limits to growth, and environmental sustainability are not immediately in the ambit of Post-Keynesians, who have more of a demand-side focus. Setterfield argues, therefore, that Post-Keynesians have simply missed the issue; they are not explicitly taking a position on the trade-off. However, he also argues that:

> Analysing the causes of growth isn't the same as being a hyper-expansionist and always advocating more growth. Indeed, P[ost]K[eynesian] interest in the causes of growth might have led to an interest in the consequences of growth which could in turn have developed into a more systematic interest in environmental matters. Some might even think it strange that this hasn't happened.[7]

Are there solutions to the employment/environment conundrum? Recent work by Post-Keynesians (for example, Tcherneva, Chapter 7 of this volume; Forstater, 2004, 2006) has taken into account the ecological dimension in their employment policy proposals. It has long been recognised that services are more labour-intensive and therefore more employment-generating than manufacturing, even though its growth potential is lower. Furthermore, work on dematerialisation suggests ways in which employment growth and economic growth can be achieved whilst placing reduced strains on ecosystems. Indeed, mainstream writers such as Quah (1997, *et passim*) argue that this process is already happening, in that an increasing share of GDP of developed countries comes not only from services, but specifically from IT-related, knowledge (and implicitly creative) activities. However, such notions are challenged. Huws (1999), in a wide-ranging critique, argues that in fact dematerialisation is a myth; 'weightless' activities in one place still require weighty others in other places. In effect, dematerialisation in advanced economies takes advantage of material consumption in developing countries. In ecological terms, that means that the external effects of consumption are felt in other countries. Post-Keynesians must contribute to this debate if they are to resolve their apparent tension between employment and the environment.

Up to this point, intellectual history has been emphasised; however, it is clear that social factors are inextricably connected to intellectual history. Obviously, the presence of Keynes at Cambridge and his working relationship with Kahn, Robinson, Kaldor, *et al.*, helped disseminate his ideas. Above, we saw that earlier Post-Keynesians (and hence the current 'older generation' of Post-Keynesians) did not address the environment, at least in their published work. As Dunn states, the 'interesting point is that younger ones have been less [concerned with the environment even than older Post-Keynesians].' Survey responses elicited various reasons why younger Post-Keynesians have not addressed the environment. Three different arguments can be made to explain this fact. First, Frederic Lee and Davidson, for example, felt that one main reason for the lack of environmental work by young Post-Keynesians was that the constraints facing young Post-Keynesians in general are so great. Davidson claimed that the reason Post-Keynesians have not been successful in publishing environmental work is that, like all Post-

Keynesian work, it goes against core neoclassical assumptions, such as ergodicity. However, this does not explain why Post-Keynesians have not published on the environment in their own journals using their own framework. One respondent talks of younger economists being 'strong-armed' into neoclassical economics. This explains why there are low numbers of Post-Keynesians relative to the mainstream; however, again, it does not really explain why the Post-Keynesians who do exist have not pursued an environmental route. This respondent's and Davidson's arguments reinforce Lee's evidence on the marginalisation of non-orthodox economists. In an interview, Lee claims, 'all kinds of "applied" economists would have been P[ost]K[eynesian]/heterodox if they had gone to the right schools, been taught by the right people, and gotten positions in the right departments.'

In addition to this, however, Lee (interview) makes the claim that many who would be described as ecological economists would at one point have been potential Post-Keynesians had they been in particular departments and been supervised by specific people. A corollary of this claim is to refer back to the discussion above about the interests of earlier generations of Post-Keynesians. Clearly, if the first generation of Post-Keynesians were focused on capital, accumulation, growth, distribution, etc., they would most likely have attracted students interested in those topics. This is, of course, not a deterministic progression; for example, the University of Leeds produced many students in the 1990s who are currently writing about Post-Keynesian/heterodox methodology even though they were not supervised by economists with a specific interest in that subject,[8] because of the contemporary milieu, particularly under the external influence of Sheila Dow and Tony Lawson. Also, contemporary social, political, and economic events can affect the research interests of students. However, clearly there is path dependence in research interests, as demonstrated clearly at Cambridge.[9] Thus, the foci of earlier cohorts of Post-Keynesians would have constrained the research of later generations. One respondent accused Post-Keynesianism of 'lacking leadership at the top because of a concern that the environment will conflict with jobs growth'. However, Davidson's (2002) call for more environmental work shows this not necessarily to be correct, or make Davidson an exception to that trend.

Above, it was noted that 'Post-Keynesians' do often publish in *Ecological Economics* and elsewhere. This might reflect an increasing specialisation – or perhaps ghettoisation – of environmental investigations into specialist journals in the same way in which one of the functions of the *Journal of Post-Keynesian Economics* (*JPKE*) is to counteract the ghettoisation of Post-Keynesian economics. *Ecological Economics* and the like have become the leading journals in the environmental field and are in many ways more attractive homes for economists who are inclined towards ecological issues. However, one would reasonably expect the same phenomenon to have occurred in the mainstream, as authors are attracted to, for example, the *Journal of Environmental Economics and Management*. Thus, a useful piece of evidence would be the rate at which environmental articles appear in leading orthodox journals. As an example, an audit of the *American Economic Review* (*AER*) over the same sample period was conducted (see Table 3.1). It found that 3 per cent of the articles published in the *AER* between 1999 and 2007 had a significant environmental content. Moreover, a majority of those articles were strongly focused towards the environment, and they covered a variety of topics, including the conservation of elephants. As Table 3.1 shows, on a quantitative and qualitative assessment, the *AER* scores much higher than the *JPKE* or other heterodox-friendly journals such as the *Review of Social Economy* and the *Review of Radical Political Economics*. Moreover, the other measure of incidence – i.e., the proportion of recent issues of the *AER* which contained at least one article on the environment – was 42.9 per cent. This figure is higher than any other journal audited except the *Journal of Economic Issues*. This finding suggests that there is a consistent desire to publish articles on the environment, subject to their meeting other technical requirements of the journal. Furthermore, it shows that, if Post-Keynesians are ghettoised into environmental journals, they are to an even greater extent even than orthodox economists.[10]

King's (2002: 222) explanation for the underdevelopment of a Post-Keynesian approach to the environment is that they have had weaker social contact with green economists than they have had with Institutionalists, Marxists, and feminists.[11] It seems, by simple observation, that it is true that Post-Keynesians have well-established links with Institutionalists and with Marxists. Indeed, there are many economists who appear to straddle two camps (some examples of Post-Keynesian-Institutionalists are Robert Heilbroner (1970), Frederic Lee, Mathew Forstater, and L. Randall Wray). What is clear is that, in terms of the environment, these links do not seem to have had much effect despite the apparently greater concern of both Institutionalists and Marxists with the environment. It is much easier to find Institutionalist work on green issues; for example, the main Institutionalist journal, the *Journal of Economic Issues*, has a relatively high publication rate of environmental articles (61.8 per cent of recent articles were 'environmental'). It is possible that economists sympathetic to either Post-Keynesian or Institutionalist ideas, but also focusing on the environment, have reached a decision node, at which they have chosen Institutionalism for its apparent greater concern about and openness to environmental concerns. This is a need for further research. Similarly, it would be useful to examine the career choices (and life histories) of ecological economists to ascertain if they have ever been influenced by Post-Keynesianism or considered becoming Post-Keynesian. Herman Daly, a leading ecological economist claims (private e-mail) not to have been influenced by Post-Keynesianism, except cursorily by Robinson in the sense that Post-Keynesians are an example of dissent from the orthodoxy. However, Daly thinks that the two groups do share some concerns, for example, about the need to consider distribution, which is considered prior to questions of markets and the achievement of an efficient allocation.

One objection to the above account is that many of the factors cited above apply equally to, say, Institutionalism, which has a much higher content of environmental analysis. For example, Institutionalist economists also presently face constraints imposed by the neoclassical mainstream. What features of Institutionalism make it different from Post-Keynesianism in this context? First, it has a longer heritage dating back at least to Veblen. Moreover, for long periods, it did not face institutional pressures as it currently does. In the 1930s, for example, it was included in a much broader mainstream. This allowed it to spread and to be established in various centres, which allowed a tradition to develop with its attendant institutional framework. Moreover, many of those centres were located in rural or agricultural areas, such as Texas, Colorado, and Wisconsin, in which the connection with ecological matters and issues, such as water use, was much greater than in large, urban centres. Of course, Cambridge is similarly located, but its members' focus and origins were more metropolitan. However, it is clear that personal circumstances affect one's research interests. Paul Davidson's work on oil immediately followed a period of work in the oil industry. Some respondents noted that they had been affected by various political movements, mainly in the United States, such as the conservation movement associated with President Theodore Roosevelt; and with much later 1960s movements. One respondent even cited the anthropomorphism of Disney films as a source of concern for the environment.

Furthermore, it could be argued that the Institutionalist approach differs from Post-Keynesianism in crucial ways, which lend themselves to environmental analysis. For example, Veblen's approach was characterised by systems thinking (Mearman, 2002) and an evolutionary methodology, both of which enable the type of thinking necessary for environmental analysis. Karl Polanyi could be considered similarly. He was especially proficient at seeing connections, particularly between what are traditionally referred to as economic and non-economic. As noted above, recent developments in Post-Keynesian methodology might help to incorporate more systems theories into Post-Keynesian theory and thence encourage more environmental analysis.

In sum, several factors can explain why Post-Keynesians have said relatively little on the environment. Most of these are rooted in the intellectual history of Post-Keynesianism, which has been struggling on few resources to establish itself as an alternative to the mainstream. There has been, moreover, a path dependency of research interests, so that the original interests of Post-Keynesianism remain dominant. However, a renewed interest in methodology might change this pattern. Also, broader political movements concerned with the environment might influence Post-Keynesians in ways that previously did not occur, particularly given that the original Post-Keynesians were largely disconnected from ecological concerns in ways in which American Institutionalists were not. Post-Keynesians have also been trapped in neoclassical straitjackets, such as an acceptance of the ecology–growth trade-off and marginalist tools, which may have to be shaken off for progress to be made. Thus, a combination of these factors explains Post-Keynesianism's approach to the environment. In addition to all of these factors, there are several others, which have been less significant – or perhaps not significant at all – in explaining the low volume of Post-Keynesian environmental economics.

Insignificant factors

The questionnaire results also identified factors not considered significant by respondents in explaining the relative dearth of Post-Keynesian work on the environment. Mearman (2005b) provides a fuller discussion of these factors. There was little agreement that Post-Keynesians lacked concern about the environment; indeed, there was concern that Post-Keynesians had not written more on the topic. Davidson (2002) expresses that concern explicitly and encourages them to do more (for example, by submitting to the *JPKE*). Respondents also disagreed that the age of leading Post-Keynesians was relevant to explaining the relative lack of environmental literature. Of all the questions put, Question 4g received the lowest mean score, 1.75. Its mode(s) and median were also low. Indeed, several respondents claim that older Post-Keynesians have shown much more concern with the environment than have younger Post-Keynesians. Relatedly, there seemed to be little agreement that the reason Post-Keynesianism had contributed little environmental literature was because of the newness of the subject (Question 4b). Some respondents rejected the premise that environmental economics is new. Courvisanos noted that there is a long mainstream tradition on the environment which, added to the work of, for example, Georgescu-Roegen (1971), represents at least 30 years' work. As King notes, that is 'a long time in economics!' Finally, Setterfield claims that, even if environmental economics were a new subject, 'Post-Keynesians are adept at responding to other new ideas', and thus could have engaged in environmental work had they chosen to.

Similarly, respondents did not agree that Post-Keynesians had left environmental work to other heterodox schools, even though the contribution of institutionalist economists was acknowledged. As Table 3.1 shows, the publications rate of environmental articles in recent issues of the *Journal of Economic Issues* is considerably higher than the rate for the *JPKE* (1.5 per cent). However, Marxist contributions, as measured by publications in *Capital and Class* and the *Review of Radical Political Economics* (*RRPE*), show a mixed picture. For the former, the rate of publication of articles with significant environmental content was 5.7 per cent[12] and, for the latter, the publication rate was 1.4 per cent (compared to the *JPKE*'s 1.5 per cent). Indeed, for the *RRPE*, its rate of publications by issue is much lower than the *JPKE*'s. In that light, Post-Keynesians are only a little less prolific than Marxists, who, particularly in the case of the *RRPE*, have their own themes, which dominate their journals. Over the subject period, the *RRPE* was dominated by articles on value theory.

Question 4e asked if Post-Keynesians have relatively neglected the environment because they do not believe in providing valuation of the environment. The question implies that Post-Keynesians have associated environmental economics with valuation of the environment and are sceptical of these approaches. Question 4e was informed by both neoclassical and ecological economic perspectives, which emphasise the valuation of the environment, albeit done in significantly different ways. The average score for Question 4e was 3.25, suggesting neutrality; but the mode and median were both 4, suggesting agreement. Many responses noted that Davidson, for example, had engaged in valuation of natural resources. Davidson's work on recreational demand (Davidson *et al.*, 1966, 1968), scenic enhancement (Davidson, 1967; Davidson *et al.*, 1969a) and public goods in general (Davidson, 1972) explicitly attempts to place values on non-market entities such as leisure facilities. However, some dissatisfaction was expressed at the mainstream bent of that work (see Mearman, 2005b).

Question 4e was also inspired by the interview response of Frederic Lee:

> As for pricing environmental entities, unless you are a neoclassical econo-
> mist who believes everything has a price equal to opportunity costs, then I am
> not sure what pricing environmental entities means. I can certainly provide
> evidence on how the price of iron ore or the prices of various gases are de-
> termined – but that is not what you mean I guess. Pricing something like a
> species – well if you are a neoclassical economist perhaps you can do it. I for
> one do not think that there is a price for a species.

Lee's quotation suggests a distinction between 'value' and 'price'. This distinction led to Question 4f on whether Post-Keynesians had done little environmental
work because they lack a theory of value. Alternative methods of valuation do
require some basis for attaching values to entities. Many economists would infer
from that claim that a theory of value is necessary. Of course, it has been claimed
that Post-Keynesianism lacks a theory of value and that therefore it cannot engage
in valuation even if it wanted to. This, then, would be another explanation why
Post-Keynesians have not in general engaged in environmental valuation and,
given the prominence of valuation in the environmental literature, why Post-Keynesians have said little on the environment.

Unsurprisingly, perhaps, this question provoked the strongest reactions. After
all, if, as some claim (Lichtenstein, 1983: xiv), a theory of value is the *sine qua
non* of a coherent paradigm, to claim that Post-Keynesianism lacks a value theory
is a serious charge indeed. Indeed, in an interview, Peter Howells acknowledged
that the lack of a value theory constituted a large gap in Post-Keynesianism. Many
respondents agreed that Post-Keynesians do not have a theory of value. However,
others offered work by, for example, Sraffians, as Post-Keynesian value theory.
Other respondents questioned whether a value theory is necessary for valuation of
the environment, or for environmental economics more generally. One respondent
stated that s/he does not have a theory of value, yet s/he has an 'appreciation of
value'. This suggests that there may be a need for value or ethical theory in Post-
Keynesianism. However, generally, respondents did not feel that a lack of value
theory had contributed to the low output of environmental economics in Post-
Keynesianism. A number of respondents, including King, held that other schools,
such as the Marxists (and, for some respondents, the 'other' Sraffians), have a
value theory but have said little more than Post-Keynesians on the environment.

Conclusions

Post-Keynesians have had relatively little to say about the environment. Post-
Keynesianism has, from its inception, been struggling for space and for
sympathetic economists. This trend is continuing. Post-Keynesians have had two
main goals: attacking the orthodoxy on key issues and advocating an alternative
programme. These goals have taken up nearly all their time and energy and prevented Post-Keynesians from effectively developing a distinctive approach on

the environment. However, similar things could be said about, say, Institutionalists – although they were already developed by the time the *General Theory* was published – and yet they have been much more prolific on the environment.

That would suggest that other factors have affected Post-Keynesianism. One seems to be that there is a perception that growth and the environment are in conflict – an essentially orthodox concept – and that, because Post-Keynesians are highly concerned about growth and employment, this precludes a concern with ecology. Additionally, it has been argued that Post-Keynesians have been trapped in static theorising on the environment, which is ultimately unlikely to be fruitful, and that this might have stunted the development of Post-Keynesian work. The intellectual and social history of Post-Keynesianism is also clearly a factor in explaining the relative underdevelopment of an environmental literature. Given that early Post-Keynesians were concerned with particular topics, such as growth, distribution, and money, their students followed them and remained focused on those issues. Moreover, it seems that Post-Keynesians' links with green politics and thought might have been less developed than it was with other schools, and less so than the links other schools had developed.

Of course, it could be argued that it does not matter that Post-Keynesians do not have a developed approach to the environment. If we view economics as a social science focusing on the economic aspects of society, there is no requirement for it to examine every aspect of society. There is a specialisation and division of labour; this comes from necessity, a lack of time for anyone studying society. Economists cannot and need not know sociology, political science, etc., comprehensively. Similarly, Post-Keynesian economists might be viewed as economists working on growth, distribution, money, and pricing (for example), areas in which they have already developed a considerable literature. As long as they integrate the ideas of other economists in other areas, there is no need for them to do work in the same areas.

However, given the pressing importance of environmental concerns, Post-Keynesians need to embrace the environment, for several reasons. Above all, the environment is important; also, one of Post-Keynesianism's 'selling points' is its relevance. If it has nothing to say about one of the world's most pressing issues, what is the point of it? Further, recent work on ontology in Post-Keynesianism suggests that the economic is emergent from the ecological (see Mearman, forthcoming), so some understanding of the ecological is necessary for successful economics. Christensen's (2005) argument makes this case well. However, to incorporate such insights, Post-Keynesians need to adopt methods and tools that are likely to be successful in tackling environmental questions. One of Post-Keynesianism's features, and perhaps strengths, is its pluralism. In addition the use of comparative statics, generalising methodology, and neoclassical tools (in order to attack the orthodoxy) remains a vibrant part of Post-Keynesian methodology. However, other tools, reflecting those used in Institutionalist or ecological economics approaches, might be instructive for Post-Keynesians. The recent surge in interest in open systems might provide such an opportunity, as would the development of complexity theory in Post-Keynesianism. Some of the movement in this progressive direction could come from within. Post-Keynesian work on ontology, uncertainty, and pluralism could help here; but, equally, Post-Keynesians need to engage other approaches in order to develop.

Notes

1 I should like to acknowledge all those Post-Keynesian economists who responded, many at great length, to the questionnaire, and to the two, Frederic Lee and Peter Howells, who agreed to be interviewed. I am also grateful that so many gave their permission for their responses to be quoted by name. I thank Herman Daly, Paul Davidson, Mathew Forstater, Cristina Marcuzzo, and James Swaney for useful correspondence. I should also like to acknowledge King's College, Cambridge, on whose archives I have drawn. I acknowledge the comments received at or subsequent to the Post Keynesian International Workshop, Kansas City, June 2004 and the Association for Heterodox Economics conference, Leeds, July 2004. I have received helpful comments on this paper from John King and Frederic Lee. The paper draws on material previously published in Mearman (2005a, 2005b, 2007).

2 Specifically, the editions of the *Journal of Post-Keynesian Economics* surveyed were 21(3) to 29(4) inclusive. For the other journals surveyed the editions covered were as follows: *Capital and Class*, issues 67–92; *Review of Radical Political Economics*, issues 31(1) to 39(2); *Cambridge Journal of Economics*, issues 23(1) to 31(4); *Journal of Economic Issues*, issues 33(1) to 41(2); *Review of Social Economy*, issues 57(1) to 65(2); and the *American Economic Review*, issues 89(1) to 97(3).

3 By significant content, it is meant that either the article was on an environmental (including natural resource) topic, or it contained more than a passing reference to the environment. Thus, Davidson (2002) and Forstater (2000) make reference to the environment. Davidson is counted as having significant environmental content because it makes a specific point to emphasise environmental issues; however, Forstater (2000) is not, because its discussion of social costs including environmental degradation and clean-up is merely a passing reference. This measure of environmental content has an explicitly qualitative dimension. The same measure is applied to the other journals surveyed below.

4 Winnett argues that Post-Keynesians can contribute in various ways: (a) make clear the redundancy of concepts such as externalities and market failure; (b) not treat price as a reflection of scarcity; (c) not claim that environmental entities can be valued at prices treated as allocatively efficient; (d) be sceptical about concepts of aggregate natural capital; and (e) consider environmental issues according to uncertainty.

5 To see a full version of the questionnaire, see Appendix A3.2.

6 Some concern should be noted about calculating correlations from ordinal data.

7 Thus, Post-Keynesians do not suffer from 'growthmania'. Rather, growth and employment creation might be seen as a technical problem, to which a solution can be reached which recognises environmental concerns. However, even within that schema, the environment could be relatively neglected.

8 There are several examples, such as Andrew Brown, Gary Slater, and David Spencer (see Brown *et al.*, 2002); Paul Downward (for example, 1999, 2003); Karl Petrick (2003); Stephen Dunn (see Dunn, 2001); and I. All of these students were taught and/or supervised by Malcolm Sawyer, who is not a self-identified methodologist.

9 The 'family trees' of Institutionalism are much more clearly traced out in the literature than they are in Post-Keynesianism. For example, it is possible to trace schools of Institutionalism descending from particular economists at particular universities at particular times. King's (2002) history of Post-Keynesianism plus Lee's social histories of radical economics of all strands can be considered attempts to construct such family trees for Post-Keynesianism. Yet there is little evidence of later generations of

Post-Keynesians supervising research students in environmental topics. Davidson *et al.* (1969b) is an exception.

10 Journal ranking is extremely important for UK Post-Keynesians more than for others because, under the aegis of the Research Assessment Exercise, research funding and departmental ranking are linked strongly to 'research quality', defined as publications in 'top journals'. This process does not apply in many other countries; nevertheless, universities in many countries do link salary and promotion to 'research quality', which again makes journal ranking important. Thus, journal ranking might partly explain the incidence of environmental articles in various publications. According to Kalaitzidakis, Mamuneas, and Stengos (2001), the *Journal of Environmental Economics and Management* ranks much higher than *Ecological Economics*. However, of course, the *AER* ranks higher than the *JEEM*. Thus, orthodox economists wishing to publish on the environment would aim for the *AER*. Still, the fact that such articles are accepted by the *AER* shows that it is open to environmental studies. On the other hand, journals such as *Land Economics*, which seem more open to non-mainstream work, such as Gowdy's, are ranked considerably higher than the *JPKE* according to Kalaitzidakis *et al.*'s list. *Ecological Economics* is ranked higher than the *JPKE*, but lower than the *CJE*. Also, *Energy Economics* is ranked lower than the *JPKE*. So, the picture on journal ranking is unclear: there is no clear pattern that environmentally-minded Post-Keynesians have chosen to eschew more general heterodox journals in favour of higher-ranked specialist journals.

11 This is changing, through the work of, for instance, members of the Green Economics Institute, and the instantiation of the International Journal of Green Economics. Mearman (2007) is an example of communication between greens and Post-Keynesians.

12 Much of this figure can be explained by the composition of *Capital and Class* issue 72, which was a special edition on the environment and contributed eight of the total of 12 articles with significant environmental content in the study period. The incidence of environmental articles per edition of *Capital and Class* was 18.5 per cent.

Appendix 3.1: Correlations between responses

Table A3.1   Correlation coefficients between questionnaire responses

	PK little	Growth	New	Less imp	Fight	Valuation	Value	Age	Others
PK little	–								
Growth	0.48	–							
New	0.16	0.25	–						
Less imp	0.27	0.10	0.65	–					
Fight	0.70	0.30	–0.03	0.19	–				
Valuation	0.43	0.52	0.31	0.37	0.62	–			
Value	0.00	–0.09	0.20	0.50	0.13	0.12	–		
Age	0.31	0.05	0.39	0.86	0.14	0.31	0.32	–	
Others	–0.06	0.26	0.32	0.62	0.08	0.50	0.51	0.52	–

Appendix 3.2: Questionnaire

Questionnaire on Post-Keynesian Economics and the environment

Aim: The aim of the questionnaire is to assist my research into the past, current and future contributions of Post-Keynesianism to the study of economics as related to the environment. I have selected you as a person highly able to comment on this topic – i.e., as someone with influence on Post-Keynesian Economics, either in general or on the specific topic of the environment.

Methodology:

1   I hope to exploit the advantages of both open and closed questions as they are explained in the research methods literature. Therefore, some of the questions are closed, requiring fixed answers, others are open and offer no pre-determined responses; some are closed but they allow you to comment or clarify your answer if you so wish. Please make your answers as brief or as extensive as you wish.

    a)   In the case of the closed questions, if you are replying electronically, please embolden your chosen response; if you are replying by post, please circle your response.

    b)   In the case of the open questions (including the comments or clarifications of answers to closed question), please use the space provided.

2   I should like the option to quote respondents in my final paper.
-   Do you grant me permission to quote you by name?   Yes/No
-   Do you grant me permission to quote you anonymously?   Yes/No

3   One of the advantages of open questions is that they allow the respondent to clarify their thought on a topic. Moreover, they also throw up anomalies and particular terminology, the meanings of which it might be necessary for me to clarify. I might find it useful to follow up on some of your responses by contacting you by e-mail. If you would rather I did not do this, please indicate here.

4   Please return via this e-mail to Andrew.Mearman@uwe.ac.uk; or if you prefer, by post, to:

Andrew Mearman
School of Economics
University of the West of England
Frenchay Campus
Coldharbour Lane
BRISTOL
BS16 1QY

I should be very grateful if you could complete the questionnaire. Its format should allow you to complete it very quickly if you so wish. Thank you very much in advance.

QUESTION 1: To what extent would you agree that Post-Keynesian Economics has said relatively little (in terms of the wider literature, or in terms of the amount of Post-Keynesian work being done) in the sphere of Economics and its relation to the environment (henceforth 'Environmental Economics')? (please embolden or circle your answer)

Strongly disagree ☐   Disagree ☐   Neutral ☐   Agree ☐   Strongly agree ☐

Comment (optional):

QUESTION 2: Which or whose contribution(s) to the Post-Keynesian treatment of Environmental Economics would you regard as most significant?

The next series of questions relate to the reasons why Post-Keynesian Economics has or has not had relatively little impact on Environmental Economics. Most of the questions are based on the assumption that the impact has been relatively small. Please answer question 3 before looking at question 4 because the latter gives possible answers to question 3.

QUESTION 3: What, in your view, are the main reasons that the Post-Keynesian contribution to Environmental Economics has been relatively small, or at least less than it might have been?

QUESTION 4: This question is broken down into sub-questions. All of them deal with possible reasons why the Post-Keynesian contribution to Environmental Economics has been relatively small. Please embolden or circle your answer in each case. As before, there is the opportunity to elaborate on your choice.

Question 4: Post-Keynesian Economics' (PKE) contribution to Environmental Economics has been relatively small because . . .

QUESTION 4A . . . PKE HAS TRADITIONALLY FOCUSED ON GROWTH.

Strongly disagree ☐   Disagree ☐   Neutral ☐   Agree ☐   Strongly agree ☐

Comment (optional):

QUESTION 4B . . . ENVIRONMENTAL ECONOMICS IS A RELATIVELY NEW SUBJECT.

Strongly disagree ☐ Disagree ☐ Neutral ☐ Agree ☐ Strongly agree ☐

Comment (optional):

QUESTION 4C . . . ENVIRONMENTAL ECONOMICS HAS UNTIL RECENTLY BEEN LESS IMPORTANT.

Strongly disagree ☐ Disagree ☐ Neutral ☐ Agree ☐ Strongly agree ☐

Comment (optional):

QUESTION 4D . . . POST-KEYNESIANS DEVOTED THEIR RESOURCES TO FIGHTING NEO-CLASSICAL ECONOMICS ON OTHER ISSUES.

Strongly disagree ☐ Disagree ☐ Neutral ☐ Agree ☐ Strongly agree ☐

Comment (optional):

QUESTION 4E . . . POST-KEYNESIANS DO NOT ENGAGE IN ECONOMIC VALUATION OF NATURAL RESOURCES.

Strongly disagree ☐ Disagree ☐ Neutral ☐ Agree ☐ Strongly agree ☐

Comment (optional):

QUESTION 4F . . . POST-KEYNESIANS DO NOT HAVE A THEORY OF VALUE.

Strongly disagree ☐ Disagree ☐ Neutral ☐ Agree ☐ Strongly agree ☐

Comment (optional):

QUESTION 4G . . . LEADING POST-KEYNESIANS ARE MAINLY RELATIVELY OLDER AND HAVE LESS CONCERN FOR ENVIRONMENTAL ISSUES.

Strongly disagree ☐ Disagree ☐ Neutral ☐ Agree ☐ Strongly agree ☐

Comment (optional):

QUESTION 4H . . . OTHER HETERODOX SCHOOLS HAVE DEALT WITH THE ISSUE SUF-FICIENTLY.

Strongly disagree ☐ Disagree ☐ Neutral ☐ Agree ☐ Strongly agree ☐

Comment (optional):

References

Brown, A., Slater, G., and Spencer, D. (2002), 'Driven to abstraction? Critical realism and the search for the "inner connection" of social phenomena', *Cambridge Journal of Economics*, 26 (6), 773–788.

Carabelli, A. (1988), *On Keynes's Method*, London: Macmillan.

Chick, V. (1983), *Macroeconomics after Keynes*, Oxford: Philip Allan.

Chick, V (2003), 'On open system theorising in economics', paper presented to the conference of the International Network on Economic Methodology, Leeds, September.

Christensen, P. (2005), 'Recovering and extending classical and Marshallian foundations for Post-Keynesian environmental economics', *International Journal of Environment, Workplace and Employment*, 1 (2), 155–173.

Coolican, H. (1999), *Research Methods and Statistics in Psychology*, London: Hodder and Stoughton.

Courvisanos, J. (2005), 'A Post-Keynesian innovation policy for sustainable development', *International Journal of Environment, Workplace and Employment*, 1 (2), 187–202.

Davidson, P. (1967), 'An exploratory study to identify and measure the benefits derived from the scenic enhancement of federal-aid highways', *Highway Research Record*, 182, 18–21.

Davidson, P. (1972), 'The valuation of public goods', in M. G. Garnsey and J. Hibbs (eds), *Social Sciences and the Environment* (University of Colorado Press, 1968), reprinted in R. Dorfman and N. S. Dorfman (eds), *Economics of the Environment*, New York: Norton.

Davidson, P. (2002), 'Restating the purpose of *JPKE* after 25 years', *Journal of Post-Keynesian Economics*, 25 (1), 3–7.

Davidson, P., Adams, F., and Seneca, J. (1966), 'The social value of water recreational facilities resulting from an improvement in water quality in an estuary: the Delaware – a case study', in A. V. Kneese and S. C. Smith (eds), *Water Research: Economic Analysis, Water Management, Evaluation Problems, Water Reallocation, Political and Administrative Problems, Hydrology and Engineering, Research Program and Needs*, Baltimore, MD: Johns Hopkins University Press.

Davidson, P., Adams, F., and Seneca, J. (1968), 'An analysis of recreation use of TVA lakes', *Land Economics*, 44 (4), November, 529–534.

Davidson, P., Cicchetti, C., and Seneca, J. (1969a), 'The demand and supply of outdoor recreation', Bureau of Economics Research – Rutgers University, reprinted by Bureau of Outdoor Recreation, U.S. Department of Interior.

Davidson, P., Tomer, J., and Waldman, A. (1969b), 'The economic benefits accruing from the scenic enhancement of highways', *Highway Research Record*, 285, 117–131.

Davis, J. (1989), 'Keynes on atomism and organicism', *Economic Journal*, 99, 1159–1172.

Dow, S. (1985), *Macroeconomic Thought: A Methodological Approach*, Oxford: Blackwell.

Dow, S. (1996), *The Methodology of Macroeconomic Thought: A Conceptual Analysis of Schools of Thought in Economics*, Cheltenham, UK: Edward Elgar.

Downward, P. (1999), *Pricing Theory in Post-Keynesian Economics: A Realist Approach*, Cheltenham, UK: Edward Elgar.

Downward, P. (ed.) (2003), *Applied Economics and the Critical Realist Critique*, London: Routledge.

Dunn, S. (2001), 'Whither Post-Keynesianism?', *Journal of Post-Keynesian Economics*, 22 (3), 343–364.

Eberle, D. and Hayden, G. (1991), 'Critique of contingent valuation and travel cost methods for valuing natural resources and ecosystems', *Journal of Economic Issues*, 25 (3), 649–688.

Forstater, M. (2000), 'Savings-recycling public employment: an assets-based approach to full employment and price stability', *Journal of Post-Keynesian Economics*, 22 (3), 437–451.

Forstater, M. (2004), 'Green jobs: examining the critical issues surrounding the environment, workplace and employment', *International Journal of Environment, Workplace and Employment*, 1 (1), 53–61.

Forstater, M. (2006), 'Green jobs: public sector employment and environmental sustainability', *Challenge*, 49 (4), 58–72.

Galbraith, J. K. (1958), *The Affluent Society*, London: Hamish Hamilton.

Georgescu-Roegen, N. (1971), *The Entropy Law and the Economic Process*, Cambridge, MA: Harvard University Press.

Gowdy, J. and Mayumi, K. (2001), 'Reformulating the foundations of consumer choice theory and environmental valuation', *Ecological Economics*, 39, 223–237.

Heilbroner, R. (1970), 'Ecological Armageddon', in R. Heilbroner (ed.), *Between Capitalism and Socialism: Essays in Political Economics*, New York: Random House.

Holt, R. (2005), 'Post-Keynesian economics and sustainable development', *International Journal of Environment, Workplace and Employment*, 1 (2), 174–186.

Holt, R., Pressman, S., and Spash, C. (eds) (forthcoming), *Environmental Post-Keynesian Economics: Looking at a Sustainable World*, Cheltenham, UK: Edward Elgar.

Huws, U. (1999), 'Material world: the myth of the "weightless economy"', *Socialist Register*, 29–55.

Jespersen, J. (2004), 'Macroeconomic stability: sustainable development and full employment', in L. Reisch and I. Røpke (eds), *Ecological Economics of Consumption*, Cheltenham, UK: Edward Elgar.

Kahn, R. (1935), 'Some notes on ideal output', *Economic Journal*, 45 (177), 1–35.

Kalaitzidakis, P., Mamuneas, T., and Stengos, T. (2001), 'Ranking of journals and institutions in economics', University of Leicester Working Paper Series.

Kennet, M. and Heinemann, V. (2006), 'Green economics: setting the scene', *International Journal of Green Economics*, 1 (1/2), 68–102.

Keynes, J. M. (1936), *The General Theory of Employment, Interest and Money*, London: Macmillan.

Keynes, J. M. (1937), 'The general theory of employment', *Quarterly Journal of Economics*, 51, 209–223.

King, J. (2002), *A History of Post-Keynesian Economics since 1936*, Cheltenham, UK: Edward Elgar.

Lawson, T. (1985), 'Keynes, prediction and econometrics', in T. Lawson and M. Pesaran (eds), *Keynes' Economics: Methodological Issues*, London: Croom Helm.

Lawson, T. and Pesaran, H. (eds) (1985), *Keynes' Economics: Methodological Issues*, London: Croom Helm.

Lee, F. (1998), *Post-Keynesian Price Theory*, Cambridge: Cambridge University Press.

Lee, F. (2000), 'The organisational history of Post-Keynesian economics in America, 1971–1995', *Journal of Post-Keynesian Economics*, 23 (1), 141–162.

Lee, F. (2002), 'Theory creation and the methodological foundation of Post-Keynesian economics', *Cambridge Journal of Economics*, 26, 789–804.

Lichtenstein P. M. (1983), *An Introduction to Post-Keynesian and Marxian Theories of Value and Price*, London: Macmillan.

Marangos, J. and Williams, C. (2005), 'The effect of drought on uncertainty and agricultural investment in Australia', *Journal of Post-Keynesian Economics*, 27 (4), 575–594.

Meadows, D., Meadows, D., Randers, J., and Behrens, W. (1972) *The Limits to Growth: A Report for the Club of Rome's Project on the Predicament of Mankind*, London: Earth Island.

Meadows, D., Meadows, D., and Randers, J. (1992) *Beyond the Limits: Global Collapse or Sustainable Future*, London: Earthscan.

Mearman, A. (2002), 'To what extent was Veblen an open-systems theorist?', *Journal of Economic Issues*, 36 (2), 573–581.

Mearman, A. (2004a), 'Why have Post-Keynesians had (relatively) little to say on the economics of the environment?', paper presented to the Post-Keynesian International Workshop, Kansas City, June.

Mearman, A. (2004b), 'Open systems and economic methodology', Economics Working Paper, University of the West of England, Bristol.

Mearman, A. (2005a), 'Post-Keynesian economics and the environment: introduction to the mini-symposium', *International Journal of Environment, Workplace and Employment*, 1 (2), 121–130.

Mearman, A. (2005b), 'Why have Post-Keynesians had (relatively) little to say on the economics of the environment?', *International Journal of Environment, Workplace and Employment*, 1 (2), 131–154.

Mearman, A. (2007), 'Post-Keynesian economics and the environment: waking up and smelling the coffee burning?', *International Journal of Green Economics*, 1 (3/4), 374–380.

Mearman, A. (forthcoming), 'Recent developments in Post-Keynesian methodology and their implications for Post-Keynesian environmental economics', in R. Holt, S. Pressman, and C. Spash (eds), *Environmental Post-Keynesian Economics: Looking at a Sustainable World*, Cheltenham, UK: Edward Elgar.

O'Donnell, R. (1989), *Keynes: Philosophy, Economics and Politics*, London: Macmillan.

Oppenheim, A. (1966), *Questionnaire Design and Attitude Measurement*, London: Heinemann.

Petrick, K. (2003), 'Transition in Eastern Europe: critical realism and qualitative insights', in P. Downward (ed.), *Applied Economics and the Critical Realist Critique*, London: Routledge.

Pigou, A. (1932), *The Economics of Welfare*, London: Macmillan.

Quah, D. (1997), 'Increasingly weightless economies', *Bank of England Quarterly Bulletin*, 37 (1), February, 49–56.

Robinson, J. (1972), 'The second crisis of economic theory', *American Economic Review*, 62 (2), 1–11.

Rosser, J. (1999), 'On the complexities of complex economic dynamics', *Journal of Economic Perspectives*, 13 (4), 169–192.

Spash, C. (2000), 'Ecosystems, contingent valuation and ethics: the case of wetland recreation', *Ecological Economics*, 34 (2), 195–215.

Tiryakian, E. A. (1977), 'The significance of schools in the development of sociology', in W. E. Snizek, E. R. Fuhrman, and M. K. Miller (eds), *Contemporary Issues in Theory and Research: A Metasociological Perspective*, Westport, CT: Greenwood Press.

Tymoigne, E. and Lee, F. (2003), 'Post-Keynesian economics since 1936: a history of a promise that bounced?', *Journal of Post-Keynesian Economics*, 26 (2), 273–288.

Vercelli, A. (1998), 'Sustainability, rationality and time', in S. Facheaux, D. Pearce, and J. Proops (eds), *Models of Sustainable Development*, Aldershot: Edward Elgar.

Wilson, N. and McClean, S. (1994), *Questionnaire Design: A Practical Introduction*, New-tonabbey: University of Ulster.

Winnett, A. (2003), 'Environmental economics', in J. King (ed.), *The Elgar Companion to Post-Keynesian Economics*, Cheltenham, UK: Edward Elgar.

Ziliak, S. and McCloskey, D. (2004), 'Size matters: the standard error of regressions in the *American Economic Review*', *Review of Social Economy*, forthcoming.

4 Recovering and extending classical and Marshallian foundations for a Post-Keynesian environmental economics

Paul Christensen

Introduction

It comes as little surprise that Post-Keynesian theories have paid insufficient attention to environmental economics. The primary focus of Post-Keynesian economics has been on demand-side problems of underemployment and theories of production and growth that assume the availability of resources through time. Post-Keynesians, Lavoie (2004) notes, reject supply-side arguments and insist that 'effective demand rules', even in the long run. We can safely assume that most Post-Keynesians agree that environmental sustainability is a central issue for humans and the planet. Why then have Post-Keynesians been slow to develop an environmental economics extending their understanding of the interconnections of society and economy to the issue of connections between the economy and nature? I suggest that this neglect is due in part to the neglect of 'supply-side' issues that must necessarily include a rigorous physical specification of the natural resource flows linking economy and nature. Post-Keynesian production theories have adopted a too-easy presumption of resource availability through time in their treatment of production and growth in opposition to neoclassical theories of resource scarcity.

There is no dispute that the scarcity, substitution, and equilibrium framework of neoclassical theory must be rejected. But we must be careful not to throw out the baby with the bath water. Scarcity issues remain central to understanding environmental problems and limits in the context of the rapidly increasing physical fecundity and cultural reach of modern production systems. There is an increasing contradiction between accelerating technological innovation, scientific advance, and global organisation of production fed by 'abundant' material and energy resources and the more fixed constraints of nature's robust but increasingly fragile ecosystems. Resource and production issues (the so-called supply side) have an intimate relation to environmental problems and must be taken up together in contrast to their unfortunate separation in neoclassical theory.

A central theoretical issue which continues to be ignored is that the neoclassical theory of a general or universal resource scarcity is based on an unconstrained and scientifically untenable theory of resource substitution. Unfortunately for the theory, the notion of marginal productivity adopted by the early neoclassicals violates the fundamental scientific principles governing material and energy transformations (Ayres, 1978).[1]

Neoclassical economists mistakenly assert that marginal products are positive, albeit diminishing, that anything can effectively substitute for any other input, and that human-produced capital can replace nature's 'capital'.[2] Each of these propositions as a statement about physical processes violates fundamental physical principles, including the laws of thermodynamics, which apply to material and energy transformations. The founding proposition of neoclassical economics, the principle of marginal productivity, is inconsistent with a scientific understanding of physical processes. And, as Schumpeter, Hicks, and others have noted, without marginal productivity, there is no neoclassical theory.

The general absence of any substantive treatment of natural resources in modern economic theories was noted by Georgescu-Roegen (1971), who, unfortunately, lumped Ricardo, Marx, and Keynes with the neoclassicals in his indictment. This insightful theorist failed to understand that classical and neoclassical theories of production make very different assumptions about the role of natural resources in production. Post-Keynesian theories, based on Marx and Keynes (and a mistaken reading of Ricardo), have not yet addressed fundamental issues concerning the material and energy foundations of human production systems and the links that must be established between an economy's production system and nature's production systems. These theories of production must be extended to include the metabolic flows and other services provided by the resource systems of the earth and the biosphere. A theory of economic production obeys the same physical principles governing the transformation and conversion of material and energy resources as do physical and biological systems. All production systems require negentropic material and energetic resources and obey a range of physical principles. It follows that production theory and the fields of resource and environmental economics are inseparably joined as fields of inquiry and that a basic compatibility must exist in the theories developed in each field.

The fact that Post-Keynesian economics remains incomplete on this score is not fatal. Better to have an incomplete than a wrong theory. The first question is whether Post-Keynesian theories are or can be made consistent with the construction and specification of linkages between economy and nature. A second is how to make those linkages explicit. The answer to the first question is obviously affirmative in stark contrast to the situation faced by neoclassical theories. The open nature of Post-Keynesian theory in regard to the specification of behavioural, organisational, and institutional relationships in contrast to the closed and categorical structures of neoclassical theory is well known (Dow, 1988; Lavoie, 1992). This openness obviously owes something to the historical roots of Post-Keynesian theories in a careful selection from Classical, Marxian, Institutional and Marshallian ideas and to the general production orientation of Post-Keynesianism. But what exactly is missing and how should the connections be established?

I have argued for some time that the physical connections between nature and economy that are absent in modern economic theories of production were a central feature in the development of preclassical and classical economic theories owing to the extensive influence that early modern scientific understandings of nature's productive processes and powers exerted on the formation of economic theories of production and circulation. The deep connections between science and economics have been difficult to recognise for scholars who are unfamiliar with early scientific ideas and who pass over language in economic texts that lacks resonance with modern theory with its dominating concern with market relations. These links have also been invisible because they were often camouflaged, coded, or hidden to avoid censorship or condemnation on religious grounds. They were also obscured because of the failure and even refusal of the most well-known theorists, notably Adam Smith, John Stuart Mill, and Alfred Marshall, to rigorously develop a physical foundation for production.

The recovery of the physical underpinnings of early production theory has been slow and difficult but always rewarding. It provides key concepts and connections between economy, society, and nature which have been missing from theoretical discourse yet should aid the reconstruction of more complete and powerful theories, including the construction of a robust resource and environmental foundation for Post-Keynesian production theory. It also has important implications supporting Post-Keynesian work on structural asymmetries and dynamics across industries and in macrodynamics.

The second section of the paper sketches the central role played by physical, chemical, and physiological ideas in the evolution of production ideas over three 'stages' of classical economics:

1   the physiologically-based economics that began with Thomas Hobbes and William Petty and ended with the grand detour of the Physiocratic system;
2   the hesitant steps of classical economics towards a 'more general' model of labour and industrial productivity whose most advanced formulation was given by Say (1803); and
3   the important if incomplete contributions of late classical production theory towards a physical foundation for industrial economics pioneered by Charles Babbage and the French engineers.

This era was effectively brought to a close by John Stuart Mill's shift from an effort to build a production economics based on physical foundations to the economising approach that would characterise subsequent theorising. The third section offers a sorting out of Marshall's important but also compromised effort to build on the 'classical' treatment of production returns. Although Marshall provided an important analysis of the physical and chemical requirements of agricultural production and formulation of diminishing returns, which has been virtually overlooked, he also utterly failed to provide any physical and technological foundation for the industrial sectors he treated under the headings of capital and organisation.

Obviously, we still have a great deal to learn from Marshall. A central task for Post-Keynesian theory is to rebuild a more complete physical, technological, and organisational framework for production theory along classical and Marshallian lines (Arena and Quère, 2003). Recovering and extending the physical 'foundations' of a classical-Marshallian framework provides an important pathway for building a new theoretical framework for understanding resource and environmental issues. Recent work on Marshall by Post-Keynesian writers emphasises his pioneering contributions to an emerging organisational and evolutionary economics with rich connections to Post-Keynesian ideas of firm dynamics and cost-based industrial pricing. Establishing the larger physical, biological, and ecological framework for production theory provides a new opportunity for synthesising the physical, organisational, and institutional strands that must be brought together to challenge the hegemony of neoclassical theory.

The concluding section suggests some of the lines of connection and support that Post-Keynesians and the new discipline of ecological economics offer each other. Ecological economics suffers from a too-close and uncritical association with neoclassical environmental economics and lacks an economic framework consistent with its vision of the physical and institutional interdependence of economic life. A relation between Post-Keynesians and ecological economics has a great deal to offer.

The recovery and reconstruction of the material, energy, and ecological underpinnings of economics will, it is to be hoped, aid the emergence and development of a new theoretical framework that is at once physical, ecological, psychological, social, institutional, and evolutionary in its approach. It should be clear that economics must be an interdisciplinary science that draws on the rich contributions of its border disciplines. Many economic writers such as Sismondi, Marshall, and Pareto, and institutional and evolutionary economists (old and new) have insisted that economics must include the other *social sciences* in its domain of concern. But there has been very little recognition apart from ecological economists that economics must develop a better understanding of its physical and technological connection to the natural world. Indeed, one hopes that it will be seen that the connection to nature is the key or 'missing link' that is needed to build a non-reductionist theoretical framework in economics. This is because a real-world treatment of material, energy, and informational processes involves time, entropic dissipation, historical learning, path dependency, and non-reductive relationships between sister disciplines.

Biophysical foundations of early production theory

Early physiological economics

In contrast to the highly abstract, purely quantitative, and reductionist vision of scarcity and resource substitutability developed by neoclassical theory, which based itself on nineteenth-century analytical mechanics and field theory, preclassical and classical theories of production and prices drew inspiration from the material, energetic, and organisational ideas of early scientific theories of matter, chemistry, physiology, and natural history. The 'physiological' approach that characterised the preclassical period (1650–1755), which the Physiocrats brought to a close, was initiated by Hobbes. He was, however, widely misunderstood as advocating the theory of 'possessive individualism' adopted by economics and as having made no contribution to economic theory. Both views are quite wrong. It was Hobbes's signal contribution, possibly aided by the young William Petty, that restored and extended the material-provisioning approach to production that Aristotle had initiated in his *Politics* but had failed to develop. Historians of economics have looked in vain for the 'scientific' roots of early economics in Cartesian and Newtonian mechanics and metaphysics. Although Galilean and Newtonian mechanics played important roles shaping economic methodology and ideas of equilibrium, the classical tradition had deep roots in the materialist and energetic ideas of the radical 'free Democratean philosophy' of the Italian Renaissance, the more moderate Stoic and Epicurean system of physics and psychology, Hippocratic physiology, and the political constitutionalism that Pierre Gassendi synthesised to replace Aristotelian philosophy.[3] It also had roots in the subsequent synthesis of the new Harveyan circulation physiology and the new combustion chemistry fashioned by Harvey's English and French disciples. This rich mix of clandestine physical, chemical, psychological, and political ideas was the crucible out of which early production theory emerged.

Although Hobbes is widely known as a mechanistic disciple of Galileo, his ideas about psychology, economic production, and social organisation also drew on Aristotelian ideas of generation, organic sensibility, and circulation which informed the new circulation physiology initiated by Harvey's discovery of the circulation of the blood. Hobbes used an energetic theory of subtle matter to explain the structure and activity of matter and the chemical ideas of Harvey's English disciples which connect the nutrition, respiration, and sensitive activity of living organisms. These material and physiological analogies inform the extension of the Aristotelian provisioning approach to economics that Hobbes set out in chapter 24 of *Leviathan* (Hobbes, [1651] 1968). An economy employs labour and the products of industry to obtain the materials and 'nutriment' of a commodious existence from the land and sea, 'the two breasts of our common mother.' These materials and energetic substances are carried through various stages of preparation by 'concoction' (heating) and fabrication and are circulated throughout the commonwealth by exchange for specie, which like the blood nourishes all the parts of the body (Christensen, 1989).

Hobbes' brief sketch was brilliantly extended by his former amanuensis, William Petty, whose *Treatise on Taxes* (1662; in Hull, 1889) elaborated the idea of a surplus that the ancient atomists had made the basis of social and economic evolution.[4] This 'surplus' of food and materials produced in agriculture, above the portion that must be reserved to replace the food, fodder, seed, and equipment used up, provides a fund of energy and materials that can be shifted from unproductive spending of landlords and used to develop the industrial and commercial sectors. Petty also spelt out the implications of the surplus for a theory of competitive profits across sectors (misleadingly termed 'neat rents'). Higher returns in one sector spark a flow of labour and capital goods to that sector, promoting the equalisation of rates between sectors. In addition to this equalised return, Petty advanced a concept of differential rent on favourably located lands which has gone unrecognised by historians of theory. Since the area served by transport expands geometrically with distance, whereas shipment costs increase arithmetically, this is a version of diminishing returns which lays less heavily on economic growth than the Malthus–Ricardo version.

Energy ideas inform the production approach to prices that Petty developed in his *Political Arithmetic* (1690; in Hull, 1889) and elaborated in unpublished papers (see Hull, 1899). These 'intrinsic' prices are based on the costs of food, materials, and tools employed plus profit, and then reduced to labour, land, and food, since humans and beasts 'must eat, so as to live, labour and generate.' Thus, the ultimate determinant of prices is the direct and indirect 'energy' required to bring together and produce the diverse components of a production system. Petty distinguished 'intrinsic' or production prices from the short-run prices that reflect the play of market forces. This distinction would become a basic feature in classical economics via Cantillon and Smith. Unfortunately, Petty's impressive contributions to early theory are scattered over a number of pamphlets and were never drawn together in a systematic treatise.

Petty's ideas were known to economic reformers in France, including Pierre Boisguilbert (*c.* 1700). Scientists at the Royal Academy of Science had extended Harvey's model of circulation to plants which fixed the energetic fire matter of the sun to construct a proto-ecological model of the circulation of the chemical materials of life between all the parts of nature. Recognising that human economies likewise depend on the first or primary productions of nature, Boisguilbert set out a Kaldor-like two-sector model of agricultural production and artisan manufacture. Employing the same language of a circulation that must be continuously maintained, he gave particular emphasis to the delicate balance that must be maintained between two sectors that are asymmetric in structure and behaviour and yet 'can only subsist by a common maintenance'. Prices of grain that feed the nation must be neither too high nor too low in order to sustain investments in agricultural fertility without setting off long-run oscillations in prices and investment. Since industrial goods embody the materials and nutrients of the earth in their production, there is a proportionality between the prices of each sector that must also be maintained. High and low prices in agriculture set off asymmetric and destabilising movements in manufacturing and the behaviour of workers.[5] A strong belief in the intrinsic harmony of nature led Boisguilbert to believe that nature will not only maintain the balance but punish those who interfere with it.[6] Thus, 'laisser-faire la nature.'

The most important economic writer to maintain the continuity of economic ideas that establish the classical lineage leading through François Quesnay to Adam Smith was Richard Cantillon, a banker in Paris whose Irish parents and grandparents had been dispossessed by Cromwell's invasion, which had brought Petty his land and wealth. Cantillon builds on Petty and on Boisguilbert's ideas of circulation to set out the most systematic work of economic theory before Ricardo.[7] Historians of theory have neglected his clear treatment of 'intrinsic' (production) prices, which he reduces first to land and labour before attributing regional differences in wages, etc. to institutional differences in subsistence requirements (he overlooks important productivity differences between the north and south). Cantillon's important work, written around 1730, was not published until 1755 by Mirabeau (a close associate of Quesnay).

Quesnay, who was trained as a surgeon and physician, and is part of the circle around Buffon, advanced an energetic and technological explanation of agricultural productivity. The first was laid out in earlier physiological essays which develop chemical explanations of plant and animal nutrition. Plants which fix the energetic matter of sunlight in the leaves produce the delicate organic compounds that maintain themselves and the rest of nature (see Christensen, 1994).[8] Quesnay attributed differences in agricultural productivity to differences in technology (and energy mobilised) between large animal and small animal or labour-based farming. The difference between the productivity of agriculture and the sterility of industry and transport is rooted in his energetic conception of production. The human economy, by implicit assumption, is limited to the energy produced by plants – i.e., the only source of energy in the economy comes from plants. Thus, manufacturing activity can only consume materials and food, it cannot regenerate them. Only agriculture can do that. We will see that Smith's assumption of the energy available to the economy is virtually identical to that of Quesnay.

Smithian classicism: suppressing the radical roots

It is clear from Smith's early papers on astronomy and ancient physics, his intimate knowledge of Continental science, his lecture notes on jurisprudence, and his sentiment-based psychology (he grounds *The Theory of Moral Sentiments* on an innate moral sentiment and *The Wealth of Nations* on self-interest) that Smith was well acquainted with the materialist and evolutionary ideas of ancient physics and psychology and the important role these ancient ideas played in seventeenth- and eighteenth-century Enlightenment thought.[9] Although historians have repeatedly tried to assimilate Smith to Newtonian theism, Smith's deistic ideas of nature's design and principles of operation are inconsistent with the theistic and antimaterialist cast of Newtonian 'orthodoxy'. It is the Stoic and Epicurean vision of Gassendi's system of energetic powers and self-regulating operations that he appears to be closest to. He was part of a circle of scientific friends, including the geologist James Hutton, who held very similar views. The physicist John Playfair, a member of the circle, credited him with the vision of an eternal and self-regulating universe which operates by natural laws and whose principles extend from the planetary system to organisms, society, and the economy (Wise and Smith, 1989).

Smith's early papers indicate his approval of the chemical ideas used to explain the operations of the furnace and the energetic and sensitive powers of living organisms. These ideas also provided the foundation of the sentiment psychology developed by David Hume, Smith, and his physician friends. We have seen how Quesnay used this 'organic' chemistry to explain production in nature and to deny productive status to industry. Scottish chemists likewise taught a version of the phlogiston or combustion chemistry that held that plants were the sole producers of the energy consumed by living organisms (fixing the energetic substance of sunlight in organic molecules). Although Smith began the shift to a broader theory of natural powers, we will see that he did not challenge Quesnay's physiologically based view that agricultural land is the sole source of energetic matter employed in the human economy.

A new understanding of work and natural powers, which goes back to Galileo, was being slowly advanced by late seventeenth- and early eighteenth-century physicists and engineers. It had been, at first, rather imperfectly applied to the analysis of machines employing water and wind power and early steam engines. The decisive contributions were made by the British engineer William Smeaton in the late 1750s, and a succession of French writers. This stream of theoretical insights eventually culminated in the formulation of the laws of thermodynamics by the middle decades of the nineteenth century. As Vatin (1993) observes, Smith made use of these ideas in his analysis of labour productivity, which marked an important advance over Quesnay. Adopting the new terminology of labour and work, he put the concept of labour at the heart of his theory and made human effort the source and invariable measure of value. By making the division of labour the primary source of productivity growth, he dispelled the physiocratic idea that only nature is productive.[10] Unfortunately, Smith's application of the new ideas of work is fundamentally incomplete and he does not challenge Quesnay's proposition that agricultural land is the sole source of the economy's energy. Smith initiated the application of the new ideas of work and powers, but he did not apply them to the industrial economy.[11] He can hardly be considered the prophet of the industrial revolution.

The obvious source for Smith's ideas of work is William Smeaton's pathbreaking study of the efficiency of different kinds of water wheels. Smeaton's great achievement was to construct a mechanical device which enabled him to separate the effects of work done by a machine using a given source of natural power from the work required to move the parts of machine itself. He subsequently extended his measurements of the capacity to do work to labour, animals, and steam engines. He defined work as the measure of the mechanical power 'produced' by these engines from a given natural power. This conception of work provided a universal measure of mechanical effect and value in all times and places. He also declared work as equivalent to effort or pain exerted over a defined period. Smith employed these ideas about labour and work in almost every paragraph of Book I of *The Wealth of Nations*.

Smeaton's formulation of the emerging links between energy, power, and work is pregnant with possibilities for providing an expanded foundation for production theory, but Smith made no mention whatsoever of the work done by machines harnessing nature's powers. He confined natural powers to land and the work of human labour and working animals. There is no discussion of the work done by the natural powers of wind, falling water, or the immense sources of heat from coal that were increasingly replacing wood in the industrial processes powering Britain's industrial economy and its growth (innovations that had been put in place over more than two centuries). Smith explained the invention of machines as a third consequence of the division of labour but he did not connect machines to the sources of power they require. He also failed to see technical progress in industry and transportation as a driving force extending and shaping the division of labour and thus a primary cause of increasing productivity. A possible reason for this neglect is that these transformations were incompatible with his vision of an individualistic and self-regulating system. The French economist J.-B. Say (1803) would make a pointed critique of Smith's unbalanced emphasis on labour and neglect of machinery and the forces of nature. Smith, he remarked, did not understand the true (engineering) theory of how machines contribute to producing wealth. The lack of recognition of a deep connection between nature and economy in subsequent theory obviously owes a good deal to Smith.

Smith did make a salutary contribution to the treatment of capital (in spite of the lack of clarity in his terminology) which is important to the connection between nature and economy. He divided capital into two classes:

1   the 'fixed' capital embodied in improvements to land, plant and equipment, warehouses, and skills of labour; and
2   the 'circulating' capital constituted by money (working capital) and materials, the latter covering agricultural provisions, rude produce, minerals, nearly finished, and finished goods.

He also properly insisted on the inherent physical complementarity between the two classes of capital. This has two dimensions:

•   every fixed capital is made from and thus embodies materials;
•   fixed capital and circulating capital must always be employed together.

This analysis provides an important and unnoticed application of the conservation of matter (it would also have provided a hint of the emerging idea of the conservation of energy if food and fodder had been separated from materials). Labour and machines cannot produce surplus output without a source of power and appropriate materials to process. Unfortunately, Ricardo, Mill, and Marshall each argued that there is no fundamental distinction between circulating and fixed capital – the second being merely a longer-lived version of the first. This neglects the fact that the components of capital have very different functions in production.[12]

The first general application of the new ideas of work in an economic theory of production was made by Jean-Baptiste Say (1803). He clearly saw that human production was exploiting new sources of power by inventing new machines and that production theory must include the fundamental contributions of materials and forces of nature to human production. His ideas were shaped by Lavoisier's emphasis on the importance of the conservation of matter in chemical analysis and the energetic ideas employed by French engineers and scientists, including Lazare Carnot's theory of machines; Charles Coulomb's comparisons of the work of machines, animals and labour; and Lavoisier's analysis of the energy conversions made by animals and machines.

Say defined the work of men and the work of nature as 'the continuous action which is exerted for executing an operation of industry.' He argued that all material production, whether in the field or in the factory, requires the same basic categories of elements: materials, forces of nature, and actions of labour and machines. He compared land to a machine but recognised that labour and machines are powerless to produce on their own without materials and a source of power. He understood the importance of production in economics and insisted that economic theory must begin with production before taking up the topics of value, distribution, and consumption.

Say provided the first general physical theory of production based on the new theory of work and mechanical energy. Unfortunately, his achievement was obscured by a diffuse presentation (especially in the first edition of the *Treatise*) and a failure to develop the implications of his new approach for a production-based theory of prices. Say's adoption of the older French scarcity and utility tradition of value theory ignored the interdependence between production and value of the British tradition.

The ideas of Malthus about the central role of nature in economic activity are confined to agricultural production and do not need comment here.[13] Although Ricardo would comment favourably on Say's insistence that production was the first topic to be considered in political economy, and he certainly understood the thrust of Say's physical theory of production, he did not follow Say's lead and develop an explicit physical theory of production. Ricardo had an acute understanding of the scientific ideas of Joseph Priestley and James Hutton's geology and powerful dynamical and energy-based arguments. These energy ideas clearly informed his early theories of profits and rent and the production underpinning of his theory of value and long-run dynamics of the economy. We can assume that he grasped the basic connection between material and energetic processes in plants and agricultural production as developed in the chemical thinking of his time. He certainly understood the central importance of materials and energetic resources provided by production on the land for the rest of the economy. We catch a glimpse of the importance Ricardo gave these factors in industrial production when he refuted Smith's silly declaration that nature does nothing in manufactures:

Are the powers of wind and water which move machinery, and assist navigation, nothing? The pressure of the atmosphere and elasticity of steam which move the most stupendous engines – are they not the gifts of nature? to say nothing of the effects of the matter of heat in softening and melting metals, of the decomposition of the atmosphere in the process of dyeing and fermentation. There is not a manufacture . . . in which nature does not give her assistance to man, and give it too, generously and gratuitously.

(Ricardo, 1817, ch. 2, n. 10)

Clearly, the central physical role that nature plays in Ricardo's understanding of production must be explicitly part of any 'neo-Ricardian' and Post-Keynesian approach.

Late classical theory

According to Wise, until the early 1830s economics and physical sciences had shared a common assumption that all natural processes are part of an inherently self-regulating eternal order that was explainable in terms of a balance of forces. Dynamics was subsumed under statics. By the mid-1830s, a fundamental change in scientific consciousness was under way. The nebular hypothesis, with its evidence of the resistance of light and fluids, together with the non-reversibility and decay that is connected to the second law of thermodynamics, introduced both temporality and dissipation into physics and economics. The growing importance of coal, machinery, and steam power in the British economy was an important impetus to this shift in scientific viewpoint. There was a corresponding shift in economic theory from the organic energy ideas and artisanal forms of production discussed by early classical economists to a recognition of the importance of industrial machinery and new sources of industrial power – particularly coal – in the operation and success of Britain's economy. Babbage's (1835) pioneering study of the new industrial *Economy of Machinery and Manufactures* and Ure's (1835) popular treatise on the factory system brought the importance of coal and steam engines in industrial production and transportation to widespread attention.[14]

Babbage's great study of principles of a machine economy distinguished two types of machines: those which produced power, and those designed to transmit force and execute work. The first class included water and wind mills. But it was the adoption of and ongoing innovation in steam engines employing coal that captured Babbage's imagination. Since his focus was on manufactures, he unfortunately gave very little attention to heat-based industries. The steam engine economy was characterised by increasing economies of scale and lower-cost production as larger engines and technological and operational improvements were achieved. Economics of scale in steam brought economies of scale in a host of related industries, especially in ship and rail transport. High fixed costs pushed mill owners to continuous operation and opened opportunities for new industries, such as gas lighting, and new specialisations in administration, such as accounting. New power sources and technologies created new products, new materials, and new uses for materials that formerly had little value. Production processes powered by steam were driving an expanding system of organisation and development. The principles of the machine (and coal and iron) economy extended from the factory to the larger political economy. Political economy, however, was not yet ready to come to grips with Babbage's insights.

The only British economist who attempted to apply the new theory of machines to a theory of production inputs and returns was Nassau Senior (1836). Babbage's suggestion that 'practical knowledge' would continue to grow without limit appeared in the third of Senior's 'elementary propositions of economic science', which stated that 'the powers of labor and the other instruments that produce wealth can be increased indefinitely.'[15] Senior's fourth proposition stated a classical version of production returns: first, the existence of diminishing returns to additional labour employed on the land; second, the existence of increasing returns in manufacturing. Senior clearly understood the conservation of matter in manufacturing industry when he stated that 'no additional labour or machinery can work up a pound of raw cotton into more than a pound of manufactured cotton.' But his argument that diminishing returns in agricultural production results from the employment of additional labour on the same material failed to recognise that generating additional agricultural output also requires additional materials from the soil and atmosphere plus additional solar energy. As Pietro Verri and Say insisted, the conservation laws apply to all forms of production.

Senior also used Babbage to advance Adam Smith's conception of fixed and circulating capital in terms of a distinction between structures and agents, on one hand, and material flows, on the other. Senior distinguished tools and instruments from the materials embodied in products and he subdivided machines into those that produce and those that transfer power. This led him to separate natural *powers* from ordinary *materials* on the grounds that the former are not physically embodied in output (in terms of an addition of mass). The difficulty is that he could not determine where to put food, coal, and other natural powers in his classification. Instead of establishing a subcategory of natural powers (or energetic flows) along side materials in circulating capital, Senior lumped food and coal with 'fixed capital'. Clearly, more insight about the nature of powers was needed. His efforts to grapple with a physical classification of production inputs and their implications for production returns were laudable, but were not taken up by subsequent economic writers. Indeed, Mill would later attempt to undermine Senior's classification effort.

Despite his close friendship with Babbage and his adoption of Say's injunction that production is the first topic to be considered in developing economic theory (Mill devotes Book I of his *Principles* to production), the socially progressive Mill made no attempt to apply physical or engineering insights to production theory. He followed Say and Senior in classifying production inputs under the headings of labour, natural agents, and capital, but his main concern was to emphasise *economic* and *social* aspects of production. He showed little interest in the physical foundations of economic theory. Book I of Mill's *Principles* (1848) devotes three chapters to capital and at least two to labour but none to the characteristics of land or natural agents. Mill isolated 'labour and natural objects' as the two 'requisites of production'. But in contrast to an elaborate classification of indirect labour, he treats 'natural objects' as a hodge-podge of items.

Ignoring Babbage, Senior, and William Whewell, Mill argued that 'political economists generally include all things used as *immediate* means of production either in the class of implements or [in the class] of materials to avoid a multiplication of classes . . . [and] distinctions of no scientific importance.' Mill made this assignment on the basis that an 'instrument of production can only be used once.'

Thus, he declared that a 'fleece is destroyed as a fleece' in making a garment just as a fuel is consumed to make heat. This indicates that Mill did not understand the distinction between energy and materials or the second law of thermodynamics despite his knowledge of early mechanics. In a review of the first edition of Mill's *Principles*, Senior (1848) objected to his inclusion of coals for engines and food for workers under the class of materials. Mill responded to his 'able reviewer' by admitting that although his terminology was not strictly in accord with the physical or scientific meaning of material, the distinction between materials and fuels is one that is 'almost irrelevant to political economy.'

Mill correctly recognised that tools and machinery lack productive powers of their own. But after declaring that the only productive powers are labour and natural agents, he denied this status to 'food and other materials' (and thus to fuels). The fact that steam engines burning fuels are productive and a worker lacking food is not productive exposes the hollowness of his position. Mill's defence of his untenable position had the consequence of breaking the continuity that Babbage and Senior had re-established with Smith's misunderstood classification of capital and the contribution they were making to an understanding of physical structures that process and store materials and flows from the materials and energetic powers themselves. What was now needed was an application of mid-nineteenth-century thermodynamic principles to a distinction between materials and fuels. Mill's failure to engage this distinction brought the development of engineering ideas about the machines and powers in economic production theory to a halt.

Mill recognised the existence of increasing returns in manufacturing and argued that the causes increasing 'the productiveness of [manufacturing] industry preponderate greatly over the one cause [the increasing expense of materials] which tends to diminish that productivity.' Yet he treated increasing returns as a subsidiary proposition to 'the general law of agricultural industry' – i.e., diminishing returns – which he insisted is 'the most important proposition in political economy.' Increasing returns is not given an independent development. Nor does his statement of increasing returns or diminishing returns include a consideration of the essential inputs which tie output to material and energy input and are required to increase physical output according to the conservation laws. Mill is aware of the complementarity among capital, natural powers, materials, and output, but his lack of concern with accurate scientific terminology or any systematic consideration of the physical principles of production fails to preserve or advance the physical production framework advanced by Say, Ricardo, and Senior, let alone the contributions of Babbage, William Whewell, or the French engineers who build on the work of Say, Lazare Carnot, and others. Given that Mill's work was a common point of departure for neoclassical theorists, this failure was a critical factor in the neoclassical failure to seriously grapple with energy and a physical approach to production theory.

Marshall's neglect of classical foundations

Marshall came to economics trained in mathematics and analytical mechanics. He made a close study of Mill, casting what he took to be the essential points into mathematics. Eventually, he insisted on working out the argument verbally and putting the mathematics in footnotes. But the structure of his ideas, despite his very broad perspective, remains heavily infected with individualistic and reductionist assumptions of the analytical and quantitative approach. Although he recognised the application of the conservation of matter to production when he said that 'man cannot create material things' (Marshall, 1920: 63), he neglected to articulate the scientific framework in which this has meaning.

Marshall noted Adam Smith's definition of capital but only in terms of whether 'goods change masters' and he accepted Mill's distinction between circulating capital as fulfilling 'the whole of its office . . . by a single use' from fixed capital which persists 'in a durable shape' over a number of periods. However, he declared that Ricardo 'truly remarks that the division (between circulating and fixed capital) is not essential' (Marshall, 1920: 75). Marshall's neglect of the thermodynamic principles which apply to distinctions between materials, energy, machines, and organisms is more egregious than Mill's given the state of physical knowledge in his time.

Marshall on land

Marshall's treatment of land as an agent of production showed more promise. He defined land as 'the material and the forces which Nature gives freely for man's aid, in land and water, in air and light and heat' (which develops a line of ideas that Say, Ricardo, and Mill have in common). Labour is defined as 'the economic work of man, whether with the hand or the head' (which we assume would not forget the materials and energetic matter the 'organic machine' needs to function). But the initial promise disappeared when he defined capital as simply 'the stored-up provision for the production of material goods'. Whereas his extension of the concept of capital to knowledge and organisation is salutary (Marshall, 1920: 138), the absence of any systematic treatment of the physical embodiment and essential connectedness of capital goods to nature's production is glaring, deliberate or not.

Marshall's treatment of agricultural production (under the heading of land as a factor of production) and the physical conditions which give rise to diminishing returns stands apart. He was obviously using the work of von Liebig and von Thünen as his guide. Unfortunately, he made the distinction of land from labour and capital on the basis of its limited supply (an economic rather than a physical distinction). Labour and capital can be increased essentially without limit given available materials and space. This led Marshall to insist that 'the fundamental attribute of land is its extension [i.e., its] command over a certain space . . . Man has no control over the area of the earth' (Marshall, 1920: 144).

Thus, Marshall makes extension or space 'the basis of the fundamental principle of diminishing returns' and not shortages in the specific materials or energy on which plants and animals (and other organisms) depend. Marshall certainly knew that the ability to grow agricultural products is linked to the presence or absence of basic nutrients in the soil. He would soon state a version of Liebig's law of the minimum – the principle that the growth of a biological organism will cease if any of the essential nutrients it requires are unavailable. 'Fertility', Marshall wrote, 'is limited by that element in which it is most deficient' (Marshall, 1920: 160). But he did not develop the obvious connection here of the presence or absence of essential elements in the soil (and atmosphere) to the ability to increase agricultural output. Instead, he shifted the underlying causes of diminishing returns from proximate and contingent conditions of essential nutrients to future limits of available space. This he mistakenly claims is the 'ultimate cause of the distinction . . . between land and other things' (Marshall, 1920: 145). He explained how human effort and discovery can overcome the 'short-run' limits of nutrients but, instead of basing a theory of diminishing returns on the existence of such shortages as they are experienced by farmers, he shifted the explanation to the physical 'area' or spatial extension that he defines as the fundamental feature of land. The 'limiting factor' leading to diminishing returns is the two-dimensional surface through which nature channels 'an annual income of heat and light, of air and moisture to the soil.' He understood the many physical factors that could cause diminishing returns but he focused his analysis on a feature (a future space constraint) that obscures the ongoing physical requirements that must be in place to produce in agriculture, manufacturing, and the other sectors.

Marshall on capital

One of Marshall's central contributions to economics was his important attempt to forge an organisational and evolutionary conception of economics dynamics based on a conception of production and market structures that attempted to maintain continuity with the classical framework. But entirely absent from his discussion of capital was any treatment of the physical properties of various kinds of capital goods. Marshall was presumably taking up the treatment of capital and industrial production but he never engaged the physical side of his subject. As a result, the continuity with the classical tradition was incomplete and remained to be re-established.

Organisational and evolutionary approaches to economics are, however, proliferating. Important Post-Keynesian work on markets and value theory has re-engaged the Marshallian tradition (Arena and Charbit, 1998; Arena and Quére, 2003). But the provision of a physical and ecological framework for capital parallel to his important, if misdirected, treatment of land has yet to be addressed. The capital theory controversies which were an important impetus for Post-Keynesian work have not been extended to the physical dimensions of economic activity nor to the implications of physical principles for economics. The latter is particularly important for developing a Post-Keynesian treatment of the connections between resources, production, and environment.

Our immediate concern here is the physical side of Marshall's treatment of capital and increasing returns. The chapters on capital and organisation are distressingly absent of any mention of the basic physical components of production. Although Marshall often remarks on materials or fuels it is almost always for the purpose of illustrating an economising decision or a substitution. There are very interesting discussions (Marshall and Marshall, 1879; Marshall, 1920: 386) of the influence of water power and coal on the location of industry in successive phases of Britain's economic development. Furthermore, in a lecture on competition, Marshall pointed out how increasing returns had enabled Britain to gain world dominance in trade and how industrialising countries had subsequently used protection and mercantilist policies to develop industrial capabilities (cited in Groenewegen, 2003: 125). But Marshall did not take up these issues in the *Principles*, which is built on mechanistic foundations.

Groenewegen (2003) sees Marshall 'in the classical manner, carefully analyz[ing] the contribution to output of individual factors such as land, labour and capital' and 'whose final chapters . . . introduced the importance to production of industrial organisation.' But this is mistaken. The classicals did not see output as a contribution of individual factors. The classicals understood the physical complementarity between materials, energy, and technologies of material transformations which is absent in Marshall.

As Groenewegen (2003) notes, Marshall was concerned with increasing returns from the beginning. Early on, he noted the economies to be gained 'from production on a large scale making use of extra machinery and a more elaborate scheme of the division of labour' (cited in Whitaker, 1975, I: 140–142). In 1879, Marshall linked increasing returns to the increase of capital and labour being applied to the manufacturing process. But only in a late edition of the *Principles* did he recognise that this would require 'changes in the methods of production, latest machinery, and skilled and unskilled labor of new kinds.' Although he would eventually recognise that technical change is something different than the neoclassical idea of getting more a given bundle of factors, a fact that is entirely overlooked by the neoclassical writers who pushed the Marshallian analysis back into the strait-jacket of analytical mechanics, he continued to neglect the underlying foundation of production in a material and energy analysis.

As Groenewegen notes, Mill was the main influence here. Marshall cites Babbage but only on a very limited point and did not develop Babbage's engineering-based understanding of the connections between power machinery and increases in the scale of the mechanisation of production. New designs, new skills, and increases in the speed and volume of flows of materials, energy, and new products must await the historical work of Alfred Chandler (1977). A few economic historians – namely, Brinley Thomas and E. A. Wriggley – recognise the critical importance of abundant materials and energy sources to the evolution of technology in Britain's industrial revolution but most economic historians have missed the connection.

Conclusion

Economics, as Post-Keynesians surely would agree, must be concerned with the critical role that social and institutional structures and relations play in economic life. Thanks to Keynes, they are also acutely aware of the powerful psychological dimensions of economic life and are in a position to critically evaluate and absorb the important contributions that neuroscience and new understandings of the brain are making to psychology and an understanding of the critical importance of instinct and culture in human behaviour. The plea here is that considerably more attention needs to be directed to the physical and ecological as well as technological dimensions of economic activity. Post-Keynesians have not given sufficient attention to pushing beyond the first-round assumption of the plasticity of physical production processes. If such assumptions were appropriate for conditions of underemployment facing technologically ascendant economies, they are less appropriate today given that powerful organisational and technological capacities of economic activity, which have become central to economic performance, have raised the most serious questions about the health and sustainability of ecosystem functions which are critical to life on the planet.

The past Post-Keynesian neglect of the task of developing an environmental economics is connected to a similar lack of attention to the need to establish an explicit resource foundation in production theory, along with developing the implications for production theory of the deep physical connectivity of natural systems. The methodological issues which must be engaged in building a physical, ecological, and social organisational understanding of economic activity, and its multiple interconnections, are an important arena of Post-Keynesian expertise. But an extension of this expertise to include evolutionary and ecological thinking is required.

The starkly different vision between modern economic and ecological thinking is cogently summarised by the historian of science Robert Nadeau (2003), who observes that the 'fundamental assumptions about the character of economic reality implicit in the mathematical formalism' of neoclassical and neo-Walrasian theories can provide 'no basis for positing viable economic solutions to environmental problems . . . The primary reason this is the case', he argues, is that

> [t]he conception of the relationship between parts (economic actors and firms) and wholes (market systems) in neoclassical economics is completely different from and wholly incompatible with the actual dynamics of the relationship between parts and wholes [elements, cells, organisms, populations, ecosystems, and the biosphere] in the global environment.
>
> (Nadeau, 2003: x)

Neoclassical theory, in its various incarnations, has always been predicated on reductionist assumptions about part–whole relationships that vitiate its ability to explain how actual economic systems and markets function, including the relationship between economy and environment.

The classical tradition from Hobbes to Marshall, rescued from neoclassical methodology, provides the beginning elements of a physical and ecological foundation on which a truly multi-disciplinary social, organisational, technological, and environmentally friendly economics can be established. Post-Keynesians who embrace diversity, methodological pluralism, a production orientation as opposed to an exchange orientation, and a theory of the multiple interconnections of economic relations are in a good position to consolidate the links between an 'ecological' vision of the interdependence of society and economy and the resource and environmental systems of the natural world. Concretely, this should involve an exploration of the links between Post-Keynesian theorists and the new discipline of ecological economics – the latter being a new field of study which has not managed to escape the siren call of neoclassical methods and market-based propositions.

Notes

1 I first realised the need to apply the principles of the conservation of matter and energy to production and the entropy law in the April of 1976 when I was completing my dissertation and realised that Sraffa's production system lacked any physical specification of the material and energy flows required to produce commodities. A closed production system cannot reproduce itself.

2 Coase's (1937) extension of 'Marshall's principle of substitution' to markets and firms also cannot stand as a general principle.

3 Democritus' ideas about the early evolution of the cosmos, life, and human society were known throughout antiquity by means of a group of 'histories' written by classical authors which the classical scholar Thomas Cole (1967) argues trace to a common source. Thanks to Cole's careful scholarship, we have the basic components of Democrates' philosophy of nature, his ideas of a psychology in which moral feeling and sociability were innate (which made society and social norms possible), and his schema of the basic stages of the evolution of technology and social organisation in prehistory. Salem (1996) confirms and extends Cole's important and neglected work.

4 Petty was trained in navigation and related sciences at the Jesuit college in Caen, France. He studied medicine at Leyden in Holland and Oxford. The best treatment of his economics is in Aspromourgos (1986).

5 For the physical background of Boisguilbert's ideas see Christensen (2003).

6 Boisguilbert was aware of the Stoic ideas of harmony and certainly the works of François Bernier, who presented a highly readable digest in seven volumes of Gassendi's great work of 1658. He also knew his cousin Bernard Fontenelle's ideas of nature's harmony, which were similarly based on Gassendi.

7 Because of the theoretical cast of his ideas, Cantillon has been mistakenly linked to Descartes. He was close to Montesquieu, who was a Gassendian and part of the Epicurean circle around Fontenelle and the Abbey Saint Pierre. Cantillon was part of the circle of French Newtonians and physicians around Lord Bolingbroke. The influence of Montesquieu's historical sociology, Locke's empiricism, and the inductive methodology of Newton's *Opticks* are evident.

8 Quesnay was a key figure in the revival of Gassendi's physics and psychology in the eighteenth century. As Rey (1997) observes, Gassendi's influence came in two waves: the first in the second half of the seventeenth century; and the second during the Enlightenment.

9 Smith, like Quesnay, was familiar with Gassendi's and Bernier's philosophy. He later

distanced himself from these early influences to protect his reputation and the acceptance of his ideas.

10 Vatin, who is steeped in the French engineering literature, does not identify the source of Smith's ideas of work.

11 This can be seen in his otherwise puzzling declaration in Book II of *The Wealth of Nations* that agriculture is more productive than manufacturing because it employs two powers (land and labour) whereas (artisan) manufacturing employs only one power (labour). Thus, for Smith, the energy produced by plants from the sun's energy is the sole source of energy available to human and animal labour and labour is the sole source of work in the industrial economy. Thus, the energy supplied by plants constitutes a fundamental limit on the economy's growth and increases in the size of the market driving increases in the division of labour and labour productivity, which he emphasises, are only an efficiency improvement and not a source for continuously expanding growth.

12 Ricardo's neglect of basic physical distinctions between circulating capital (materials and energy) and the fixed capital embodied in machinery, skills, etc. is most likely due to the energetic ideas of James Hutton that underlie his emphasis on dynamical processes leading to equilibrium and a corresponding neglect of intermediate states.

13 Malthus's methodological contributions are considerably richer.

14 In reviews of Babbage and Ure, the economist John McCulloch (one of the leading defenders of the classical equilibrium framework) noted the link between Britain's industrial prosperity and the exploitation of coal technologies. He sees that the increase in the quantity of iron made with coal lowers the costs of machinery (and steam engines) leading to more output and more demand for coal, iron, and machines. He does not appear to have recognised the need to incorporate these ideas into a theory of production.

15 The first two propositions addressed undiminished utility from goods and Malthusian limits on population.

References

Arena, R. and Charbit, C. (1998), 'Marshall, Andrews, and Richardson on markets: an interpretation', in N. Foss and B. Loasby (eds), *Economic Organization, Capabilities, and Coordination: Essays in Honour of G. B. Richardson*, London: Routledge, pp. 83–103.

Arena, R. and Quéré, M. (eds) (2003), *The Economics of Alfred Marshall: Revisiting Marshall's Legacy*, Basingstoke: Palgrave Macmillan.

Aspromourgos, T. (1986), 'Political economy and the social division of labour: the economics of Sir William Petty', *Scottish Journal of Political Economy*, 33 (February), 28–45.

Ayres, R. (1978), *Resources, Environment, and Economics: Applications of the Materials/ Energy Balance Principle*, New York: Wiley.

Babbage, C. (1835, repr. 1971), *On the Economy of Machinery and Manufactures*, 4th edn, New York: A. M. Kelley.

Chandler, A., Jr (1977), *The Visible Hand*, Cambridge, MA.: Harvard University Press

Christensen, P. (1989), 'Hobbes and the physiological origins of economic science', *History of Political Economy*, 21, 689–709.

Christensen, P. (1994), 'Fire, motion, and productivity: the proto-energetics of nature and economy in François Quesnay', in P. Mirowski (ed.), *Natural Images in Economic Thought, 'Markets Read in Tooth and Claw'*, Cambridge: Cambridge University Press, pp. 249–288.

Christensen, P. (2003), 'Epicurean and stoic sources for Boisguilbert's physiological and Hippocratic vision of nature and economics', in M. Schabas and N. De Marchi (eds), *Oeconomies in the Age of Newton*, Durham, NC: Duke University Press, pp. 102–129.

Coase, R. (1937), 'The nature of the firm', *Econometrica*, 4, 386–405.

Cole, T. S. (1967), *Democritus and the Sources of Greek Anthropology*, Cleveland, OH: Western Reserve University.

Dow, S. (1988), 'Post-Keynesian economics: conceptual underpinnings', *British Review of Economic Issues*, 10 (23), 1–18.

Georgescu-Roegen, N. (1971), *The Entropy Law and the Economic Process*, Cambridge, MA: Harvard University Press.

Groenewegen, P. (2003), 'Competition and evolution: Marshall's conciliation enterprise', in R. Arena and M. Quére (eds), *The Economics of Alfred Marshall: Revisiting Marshall's Legacy*, Basingstoke: Palgrave Macmillan, pp. 113–133.

Hull, C. (ed.) (1899), *The Economic Writings of Sir William Petty*, Cambridge: Cambridge University Press.

Kaldor, N. (1976), 'Inflation and recession in the World Economy', *Economic Journal*, 86 (344), 703–714.

Lavoie, M. (1992), 'Towards a new research programme for Post-Keynesianism and Neo-Ricardianism', *Review of Political Economy*, 4 (1), 37–78.

Lavoie, M. (2004), 'Post-Keynesian consumer choice theory for the economics of sustainable forest management', in S. Kant and R. A. Berry (eds), *Economics, Sustainability, and Natural Resources: Economics of Sustainable Forest Management*, New York: Springer, pp. 67–90.

Marshall, A. (1920), *Principles of Economics*, 8th edn, London: Macmillan.

Marshall, A. and Marshall, M. (1879), *The Economics of Industry*, London: Macmillan.

Mill, J. S. (1848, 7th edn 1871), *Principles of Political Economy*, London: Longmans, Green & Co.

Nadeau, R. (2003), *The Wealth of Nature: How Mainstream Economics Has Failed the Environment*, New York: Columbia University Press.

Rey, R. (1997), 'Gassendi et les sciences de la vie au XVIIIe siècle', in Sylvie Murr (ed.), *Gassendi et sa postéritié en France et en Europe 1592–1792*, Paris: J. Vrin.

Ricardo, D. (1817, repr. 1969), *The Principle of Political Economy and Taxation*, London: Dent.

Salem, J. (1996), *Démocrite: Grains de possière dans un rayon de soleil*, Paris: Vrin.

Say, J.-B. (1803), *Traité d'économique politique*, Paris.

Senior, N. (1836, repr. 1965), *An Outline of the Science of Political Economy*, New York, Augustus M. Kelley.

Senior, N. (1848), 'J. S. Mill on political economy', *Edinburgh Review*, 88, 297–325.

Ure, A. (1835), *Philosophy of Manufactures*, London: Charles Knight.

Vatin, F. (1993), *Le Travail: Economie et Physique: 1780–1830*, Paris: Presses Universitaires de France.

Whitaker, J. (ed.) (1975), *The Early Economic Writings of Alfred Marshall: 1867–1890*, 2 vols, London: Macmillan.

Wise, N. and Smith, A. C. (1989), 'Work and waste: political economy and natural philosophy in nineteenth century Britain', *History of Science*, 27, 263–301, 391–449.

5   The relevance of Post-Keynesian economics to sustainable development

Richard P. F. Holt

Introduction

Some economists have attempted to broaden the concepts of economic growth and development by considering the natural environment, the economy, and society as inextricably interrelated (Daly 1977, 1993; Norgaard 1988, 1989, 1994). Each has its own capital stock, which must be sustained. Capital stocks include not just traditional manufactured capital (private and public), but the stock of natural resources (natural capital), accumulated human skills and knowledge (human capital), and social capital. Sustainable development has been associated with the maintenance of these different types of stocks for present and future use.

The work of Jonathan Harris of the Global Development and Environment Institute at Tufts University is a good example of an environmental economist using these concepts and relating them to the principle of sustainability by separating sustainability into its economic, environmental, and social components:

> An economically sustainable system must be able to produce goods and services on a continuing basis, to maintain manageable levels of government and external debt, and to avoid extreme sectoral imbalances which damage agricultural or industrial production.

> An environmentally sustainable system must maintain a stable resource base, avoiding over-exploitation of renewable resource systems or environmental sink functions, and depleting non-renewable resources only to the extent that investment is made in adequate substitutes. This includes maintenance of biodiversity, atmospheric stability, and other ecosystem functions not ordinarily classed as economic resources.

> A socially sustainable system must achieve distributional equity, adequate provision of social services including health and education, gender equity, and political accountability and participation.

> (Harris, 2000: 5–6)

These definitions are important in understanding a Post-Keynesian approach to sustainable development, which recognises the complex relationship between the economy, environment, and society. Post-Keynesians have primarily been known for their concern about the susceptibility of economic and financial institutions to crises and collapse in a market economy, and carrying out policies that would stabilise economic growth and maintain full employment now and in the future. Given its concern about stability now and into the future, we can see the compatibility between Post-Keynesian economics and a general working definition of sustainable development given by the United Nations' Bruntland Commission (WCED, 1987: 43):

> Sustainable development is development which meets the needs of the present without compromising the ability of future generations to meet their own needs.

This definition fits nicely with Post-Keynesian analysis, but a Post-Keynesian definition of sustainable development would also include the eradicating of unemployment and poverty while securing economic and natural resources and a stable environment for future generations. To pursue and understand how Post-Keynesians would approach sustainable development, we first need to look at the neoclassical position and then compare it with the Post-Keynesian view.

The sustainability debate

Many neoclassical economists can accept the idea that we need to act appropriately to control the cost of pollutants and that our natural resources need to be prudently managed. Many would also argue that we owe future generations a living and an environmental standard at least at the same level we have today, if not higher. This means producing and consuming in a way that does not result in the net depletion of the capital needed for producing a comparable standard of living in the future. Neoclassical economists such as Solow (1992, 1994) address this issue by arguing that any depletion of natural resources must be matched by increases in manufactured capital. This potential capacity of human-made capital to substitute for declining natural capital has led to a discussion between neoclassical economists and ecological economists about what sustainable development means. The debate has led to two definitions of sustainable development. The first has been claimed as a 'weak' definition in which losses of a non-renewable or renewable resource (natural capital) can be substituted by human-made capital of equal value. The second is a 'strong' definition which demands that natural capital be kept intact given the lack of substitution possibilities arising from natural capital's unique and complementary quality (Holt, 2005: 176). This has led to a serious debate about how we should define sustainable development and what its impact is in terms of economic growth and development.

Sustainability in the neoclassical model

An example of an application of the 'weak' definition of sustainable development can be found with the work of Hartwick (1977, 1989) and Solow (1974, 1986). Both have examined the conditions under which a permanent consumption stream can be sustained from the extraction of a non-renewable resource over an infinite time horizon. Whether a permanent consumption stream is feasible depends upon the substitution possibilities that exist. If substitutes for the declining non-renewable resource are available, then the optimum extraction and substitution rate can be calculated to sustain a non-declining rate of consumption over time. Clearly, at the heart of the neoclassical model response to sustainable development is the existence of adequate substitutes or the potential to develop substitutes when required. According to neoclassical economists, although there are a few exceptions to the 'Hartwick–Solow' rule, in most cases there are sufficient substitutes to justify a weak sustainability approach to sustainable development.

A second example of the weak view of sustainability relates to environmental externalities (i.e., spillover costs involving the impact of economic activity on the environment that are not fully reflected in market prices). If, for example, there are social costs associated with pollution, advocates of the weak sustainability position argue that taxes or appropriate property rights can be used to reflect the true costs of renewable and non-renewable resources in the private sector.[1] This, in turn, will lead to the establishment of substitute forms of capital and/or the development of resource-saving technologies.

The problem, however, with the neoclassical model is that, although taxes or Coasian solutions can provide the market incentives to facilitate a more efficient use of certain resources, or reduce certain kinds of pollutants, such measures are not well suited to deal with large-scale problems in which different parties – often many in number – have difficulty negotiating an efficient arrangement (Stiglitz, 2000). Also, as ecological and institutionalist economists have pointed out (Greenwood and Holt, 2008), the neoclassical approach does not ask whether efficiency should be the only goal of resource management or the social welfare theory being invoked needs to be put in a broader context to encompass economic, environmental, and social goals. In other words, efficiency should be looked at as a means to an end rather than an end in itself. Efficiency has meaning only when one has established the goals of society, which might include sustainable development and full employment. This has been a concern for both Post-Keynesians and ecological economists.

Another important consideration – namely, power and the distribution of income and wealth – is also overlooked by the neoclassical model. Once power is brought into the picture, it is possible for one group to control the use of resources to the exclusion (or damage) of another group or groups, which cannot be dealt with unless the group at risk also has sufficient political or economic power. DeGregori (1974) writes that our mythology of free choice in free markets creates a situation in which we accept activities that take place within the 'market' that would be condemned if carried out elsewhere. He quotes Ayres's tongue and cheek comment that 'poisoning one's wife is a mortal sin, whereas poisoning thousands of people by selling adulterated food or drugs is a mere business misadventure' (DeGregori, 1974: 55–56). This can readily be extended to the long-term sustainability problems we face today, in which the people being 'poisoned' are those who will emerge in future generations yet have no power to influence current decisions (Greenwood and Holt, 2008).

The Post-Keynesian position is able to deal with these issues better than the neoclassical model given its pluralistic approach, which has long incorporated notions of power, institutions, and the unequal distribution of income and wealth. Given the concern about long-term economic and social stability, Post-Keynesians would also embrace a 'strong' definition of sustainability (which recognises lack of substitutability for some resources) and quality of life issues in ways that the neoclassical model cannot. Let's now examine how the Post-Keynesian public policy approach would be different.

Main features of Post-Keynesian economics related to public policy[2]

This section covers the main features of the Post-Keynesian approach and explains how it differs from the neoclassical position. These characteristics of Post-Keynesian thought are important in understanding the Post-Keynesian position on sustainable development. Three facets of Post-Keynesian economics related to sustainable development are:

1   the future is uncertain rather than being known or known with some probability distribution;
2   individual decision-making is dependent on social factors, such as human relations, conventions, habits and emulation rather than individual rational choice;
3   economic analysis involves an examination of economies moving and evolving through historical time rather than economies effortlessly and mechanically adjusting from one equilibrium point to another.

Uncertainty versus risk

One important characteristic of the Post-Keynesian approach is its focus on uncertainty rather than risk in the real world. In the early 1920s, both Keynes (1921) and Knight (1921) grappled with the questions of risk and uncertainty. Knight argued that risk involves measurable probabilities whereas uncertainty involves immeasurable and unknowable probabilities. He suggested that the key difference is that we can insure against risk but not against uncertainty, and that this has important real world implications. Writing at the same time as Knight, Keynes accepted this distinction and stressed the importance of uncertainty in many economic decisions. Later, in Chapter 12 of *The General Theory*, Keynes (1936) argued that uncertainty has implications for investment given that investment decisions cannot be confidently based on some objective assessment of probable outcomes and the likely profitability of each possible outcome. Consequently, investors must to some degree rely on 'animal spirits' or the average state of confidence when deciding whether to invest and in what. In a world where ignorance is a fact of life, individuals follow norms, rules, conventions and habits which are rational responses to an uncertain and complex environment. Given this, people tend to act in a manner based on the behaviour of others (i.e., they observe and imitate other people). Because one can never be certain about the expectations and the behaviour of others, many Post-Keynesians (Carabelli, 1988; Arestis, 1996) believe this merely accentuates the level of uncertainty.

We can therefore regard sustainable development as an example in which the future consequences of environmental damage cannot be known because, until we do something repeatedly to the environment, we cannot assess the probability of environmental damage from these actions. In other words, we cannot perform controlled experiments with the Earth and a parallel Earth to see how pollution affects one but not the other, keeping everything else constant. Nor can we undertake the second best action and use a large sample of past experience to make probability judgments. We are currently experiencing the worldwide consequences of certain forms and quantities of pollution for the first time in history. Thus the results are to some extent uncertain; yet we must make some decisions regarding pollution and resource depletion in the face of this uncertainty. This is a role that government policy can play and not the market.

Social rationality versus individual rationality

Neoclassical analysis makes a number of assumptions regarding how individuals think and behave. They see people as knowing the choices and options available to them and the probabilistic outcomes of making each choice. People then act rationally and make decisions to maximise their utility. In contrast, Post-Keynesians see individuals confronting uncertainty when they have to make decisions. People do not know their options, the consequences of their actions, or the utility that will accrue to them from different choices. When people are not sure of what they want and not sure of what to do, the seemingly rational response is to look to others when making decisions and to follow their lead, despite the fact that they too are equally ignorant.

Post-Keynesians do not see people as isolated individuals. Rather, Post-Keynesians see people as social beings and recognise the interdependence of human well-being as a general rule. Human relations are important in making decisions. The difference between social rationality and individual rationality is clearest in the so-called prisoner's dilemma, which shows how two isolated (non-communicating) individuals pursuing their own best interest end up in a less than optimal situation. In the typical prisoner's dilemma, two men guilty of a serious crime that would normally attract a 10-year prison sentence are captured and ushered into separate rooms. If neither confesses, they are convicted of a lesser crime and given three-year prison terms. If both confess, they each receive a five-year sentence – a reward for confessing for the more serious crime they have committed. However, if one confesses and testifies against the other, who continues to plead his innocence, the confessor receives a one-year sentence while the non-confessor incurs a 10-year prison term. In this situation, we would expect both men to do what is necessary to avoid a 10-year sentence. Hence we would expect them to confess to the serious crime and receive the five-year prison term. However, if the two men were able to communicate beforehand, they could both agree not to confess and each would receive a three-year term. The inability to communicate (i.e., being forced to act independently) leads to a sub-optimal outcome.

Prisoner's dilemma situations are common in everyday life and are particularly evident with environmental problems related to sustainable development. They are the heart of the free-rider problem.[3] Like the prisoner who confesses, the free rider does not pay to support community services that everyone regards as desirable, such as clean air, on the basis that everyone else will contribute and one less contribution to the common good will have little if any impact on air quality. Of course, if everyone adopts this form of logic and free-rides, the aggregate outcomes involving open-access resources are serious environmental problems that can affect existing and future generations.

The overall result of the prisoner's dilemma is that, when individuals rationally maximise their own self interest, they can make choices which, in the aggregate, are sub-optimal. To achieve an outcome much nearer to the optimum, stakeholders need to be able to cooperate and enforce cooperation. This opens the door to government policy – for example, taxes to discourage carbon emissions and to protect and rehabilitate environmental goods that society believes are critical to achieving sustainability. In addition to the prisoner's dilemma, there are clearly dictator and ultimatum games which markets, themselves, cannot resolve.

Following Galbraith (1969, 1974, 1996), Post-Keynesians recognise that needs and choices are influenced by publicity, by fashion, by culture, and by friends and family. This can lead to behaviour and consumption habits that are unsustainable and environmentally harmful. Following the work of the psychologist Abraham Maslow (1954) and the economist Nicholas Georgescu-Roegen (1971), Post-Keynesians see needs as not all being equal (see Lavoie, 1992, 2006). Peter Earl (1983) has been most responsible for bringing these ideas into a Post-Keynesian theory of individual choice. According to this view, some needs are more important than others; and we form a hierarchy of needs. At the bottom of the hierarchy is the need for survival: the need for food, shelter, and clothing. Next comes the need for comfort and social interaction. Finally, there are the needs of self-actualization and improvement. As Lavoie (2006) points out, it is one's income which determines where one is and how rapidly one can move from one level of need to another. When we are poor, the only things that matter are the goods necessary for survival. As our income increases, and our survival is no longer in jeopardy, we concern ourselves with other, higher needs, such as comforts and friends. This view about a hierarchy of needs is important for both Post-Keynesians and ecological economists in terms of understanding the development of consumption and production behaviour that can be manipulated by market forces yet can adversely affect the environment.

Historical time versus equilibrium

Post-Keynesians focus on history rather than equilibrium. Joan Robinson (1974) emphasised that neoclassical economics has an obsessive preoccupation with equilibrium analysis or logical time. This analysis ignores the fact that the equilibrium reached may depend on how the economy reaches that equilibrium. It also ignores the fact that the transition path itself may affect parts of the economy (and the environment) and, thus, the equilibrium position that the economy reaches. In physics, this phenomenon is referred to as 'hysteresis' – it recognises that there may be several possible outcomes to a system, and that the actual outcome depends upon the historical path taken (Holt and Setterfield, 1999).

Robinson criticised the equilibrium approach and suggested that economists should focus more on how economies evolve over time than on how they move to some timeless equilibrium point. Kahn (1972), Robinson (1976) and Kaldor (1985) all believed that economies could not be described in terms of some equilibrium at which the economy stabilises once it is reached. Historical time means that economic systems do not have an equilibrium or point of rest (Kaldor 1985); rather, disequilibrium and instability are the normal state of affairs for industrial economies. Economies move through time; where we are now depends on our past, and where we are going depends on both the past and the present. Economists need to analyse this process rather than deducing properties of some equilibrium position.

In this sense, what neoclassical analysis fails to address is the issue of what happens during the transition from one equilibrium position to the next, and whether anything that transpires during the transition process will affect either the preferences of individuals or the ability to produce goods. Overlooking historical time means that neoclassical economics ignores the reality of the real world since it is erroneous to assume that economies in transition have no impact on consumers' and firms' behaviour, the natural environment, governments, etc. Furthermore, neoclassical economics ignores the path dependency of economic systems. Consider, for example, unemployment. If we have an unemployment problem, it may take a considerably long time before full employment is restored. Abstracting from this, and focusing on just the current situation and the eventual equilibrium, neoclassical theory ignores the fact that worker skills may deteriorate during the time they are unemployed. The same thing can be said about the use of environmental goods: markets readjust during the time it takes to find substitutes to replace exhausted non-renewable resources.

Thus, economies do not gravitate to a new equilibrium position containing the original level of worker skills. Nor are we endowed with the same stock of non-renewable resources that society needs. There are, as a consequence, social implications arising from the evolution of economies. Because unemployed workers lose skills, contacts, etc., their health can deteriorate. If we move from one equilibrium stressing growth as a primary objective, and we later become concerned about environmental degradation, we continue to be impacted upon by the degradational consequences of our earlier behaviour. Moving to a new equilibrium position does not erase the manifestations of past indiscretions.

The Post-Keynesian approach to policy

For Post-Keynesians, the state must provide what the private sector cannot and will not provide (Pressman, 2006). At the aggregate or macroeconomic level, the state needs to assure full employment and stable prices. From a sustainable development perspective, policies are required to guarantee that we do not deplete the natural resource base or the ecosystem services needed to generate the economic opportunities for future generations.

Given the Post-Keynesian perspective on risk and uncertainty, one important function of the government is to reduce uncertainty and, whenever possible, to help convert uncertainty into risk. There are many ways that governments can do this, and many ways they actually do. For example, deposit insurance safeguards individual depositors and eliminates the uncertainty of losing bank deposits during a financial crisis. Federal disaster relief helps victims of natural catastrophes. There are also consumer product safety laws, banking standards, and workplace safety regulations that reduce or shift risk. Governments can do likewise when dealing with economic and social issues associated with sustainable development by protecting the stock of natural capital and developing policies to limit greenhouse gas emissions.

Through government policies and institutional structures, we are able to decrease the level of uncertainty for individuals as they make choices and decisions about the future. Consider, for example, regulations imposed by the government to promote safe water and air quality standards. Government regulations on environmental quality mean that people do not have to worry about the safety of their water and air most of the time. They do not have to test the water before they drink it. We need to recognise that, on the whole, markets have failed to appropriately manage environmental problems because of uncertainty and because of individual inabilities to process information correctly. In these cases, government support is necessary and highlights the clear disparity between Post-Keynesian public policies and traditional public policy recommendations, of which the latter rely on the neoclassical view that wrongly equates risk with uncertainty.

In a world of uncertainty and irrational human tastes and behaviour, it is also important for governments not only to reduce uncertainty, but also to prevent irrational behaviour at both the individual level and the aggregate level. In essence, governments must prevent prisoner's dilemma situations that emerge in areas such as healthcare and the environment. And, in the absence of future generations being able to register their preferences in markets today, the government must also make sure that development is sustainable in the long run. It is the institution that is able to account for the likely preferences of future generations who do not get to vote today – either with their money or in the ballot box.

Another key area where neoclassical and Post-Keynesian approaches to public policy differ is in relation to *merit* goods. The notion of merit goods was introduced by Musgrave (1957, 1959). Musgrave defined merit goods as commodities that a society in general believes all people should consume, regardless of an individual's preferences, because of the ascribed value attached to them. To ensure merit goods are provided in sufficient quantities to all people, government intervention in the economy is invariably required at the microeconomic level.

More recently, Amartya Sen (1985) has taken the notion of merit goods and developed it into the idea of 'capabilities'. According to this approach, well-being depends on the things people can do and the things they can do well. Sen has argued that the purpose of life and of an economic system is to develop a certain set of potentials or abilities in all human beings. All people warrant being able to read and receive a decent education. In addition, all people are deserving of numerous political and human freedoms. Such things that fall under this rubric include education and, of course, a clean and sustainable environment. The demand for these goods may not be adequately expressed for a variety of reasons – invariably because of individual preferences and, in some instances, a lack of affordability. Thus, the main way to assure merit goods are produced and equitably provided is to have governments produce them and make sure they are available to everyone. This dovetails with Sen's (1984) arguments that, rather than enhancing utility, we need to focus on developing capabilities.

The neoclassical response to the issue of merit goods has been to improve market performance by having the state supply the necessary information to individuals so they can make informed choices (McLure, 1968). They assume that this will be less costly and lead to a more optimal result than having the government provide so-called merit goods directly. The Post-Keynesian response has been to have the government provide merit goods or, in the case of the natural environment, do what is necessary to ensure it remains in a state that enables people to thrive both now and into the future. The essence of the Post-Keynesian approach is to maintain a portfolio of public investments to provide merit goods and to also deal with economic, social, and environmental problems. Public investment, in the Post-Keynesian sense, should therefore be undertaken not simply to maintain government spending, but to increase spending in areas where the private sector is failing. At the end of *The General Theory*, Keynes (1936) discussed the role of government by talking about the public provision of education, healthcare, etc. To this we can add spending to improve the environment and to promote sustainable development. These investments have a number of different positive effects. They help stabilise the macroeconomy, they reduce the impact of economic activity on the natural environment, they improve microeconomic performance, and they assist greatly in increasing the general welfare of a nation's citizens. These policies, by reducing uncertainty, also minimise fluctuations in the business cycle and its negative side-effects (e.g., the loss of worker skills) and thus promote more sustainable forms of development.

Given these general and broad categorisations of how Post-Keynesian policy would be different from the neoclassical approach, let's look specifically how it relates to sustainable development.

Sustainable development and Post-Keynesian economics[4]

Can the views of Post-Keynesians be reconciled with sustainable development? I believe they can. Of course, Keynes did not talk about sustainable development, but I think it would be something he would understand and appreciate. In fact, Keynes does touch on it, though not directly, in his essay 'The Future':

> [Of] the absolute needs – a point may soon be reached, much sooner perhaps than all of us aware of, when these (economic) needs are satisfied in the sense that we prefer to devote our further energies to non-economic purposes. . .I draw the conclusion that, assuming no important wars and no important increase in population, the economic problem may be solved. . .[This] means that the economic problem is not – when we look into the future – the permanent problem of the human race. . .The pace at which we can reach our destination of economic bliss will be governed by four things – our power to control population, our determination to avoid wars and civil dissensions, our willingness to entrust to science the direction of those matters which are properly the concern of science, and the rate of accumulation as fixed by the margin between our production and our consumption; of which the last will easily look after itself, given the first three.
>
> (Keynes, 1963: 363–364, parentheses added)

What Keynes is saying here can, without controversy, be related to sustainable development. That is, he was deeply concerned with controlling population growth, avoiding world-wide conflicts, trusting in science (where applicable), and, finally, humankind's ability to understand the relationship between production and consumption and its impact on sustaining capital for economic and social prosperity. Also evident in Keynes's essay is the extension of his concern for normative issues which can be related to sustainable development – for example, the quality of human life and ability to sustain development for the benefit of present and future generations.

From Keynes, as reviewed earlier in this chapter, we can now see how many elements of Post-Keynesian economics can inform our understanding of sustainable development and what is required to achieve it. In the first instance, there is the Post-Keynesian methodology, which is based on realism in contrast to the neoclassical view of constrained maximization and instrumentalism. Post-Keynesians hold onto a form of organicism or holism that recognises the interdependency and connection between the environment, society, and the economy as compared with the mechanical and methodological individualism of neoclassical economics (Norgaard, 1988).

Second, because of historical time, Post-Keynesians do not obligatorily resort to neoclassical marginal analysis since, as we have seen, they rely heavily on notions of path dependency and irreversibility – a key concern in understanding the evolution of economic systems and the behaviour of people living within them from a sustainable development perspective. In historical time, then, the impact of past events on the present cannot be completely undone. As Georgescu-Roegen (1971) pointed out, unlike logical time, historical time is irrevocable; we move strictly from the present to the future, which plays an important part in the dynamics of sustainable development.

Another area in which Post-Keynesian economics can provide useful insights in relation to sustainable development is the idea of uncertainty. The work done by Post-Keynesians on institutions, knowledge, bounded rationality, and uncertainty (Rosser, 2004) – all of which look at complex dynamics and the lack of predictability about the future – compels all policy-makers to concern themselves with non-market factors and to adopt a more cautionary approach when assessing the legitimacy of current economic activity.

Finally, there is the recent work of Marc Lavoie (2009). Lavoie has looked closely at consumer theory within Post-Keynesian economics by employing a framework that embodies the following aspects of reality:

- Procedural rationality: bounded knowledge and uncertainty undermine optimizing behaviour even at the individual level.
- Satiable wants: some needs are more basic than others (the principle of a needs hierarchy). A distinction between wants and needs is therefore necessary, particularly in regards to whether and how much the 'wants' of presently existing people should take precedence over the 'needs' of future generations.
- Separability of needs: needs are separable from each other, implying there is a restriction to the degree to which the substitution of one good for another can satisfy a particular need.
- Needs hierarchy: needs are subordinate and hierarchical.
- Growth of needs: absolute income is more important than the substitution of one good for another in terms of one's ability to progress to higher forms of need (e.g., self-actualisation).
- Non-independence: preferences are not made independently of social norms, customs, and objective values.

All of these conditions are compatible with the work that is being done by ecological economists and the methodological approach they are using to promote ways to achieve sustainable development. Where there seems to be tension between Post-Keynesians and many sustainable development practitioners is with the role that effective aggregate demand plays in maintaining full employment in a modern, money-using, entrepreneurial economy. Post-Keynesians view the demand side of the economy rather than the supply side as the main determinant of the growth in Gross Domestic Product (GDP). Since government expenditure constitutes a large proportion of all demand-side spending within the economy, Post-Keynesians believe that government spending needs to be sufficient to guarantee the full employment level of GDP. Furthermore, just as GDP growth at the macroeconomic level requires greater government expenditure in general, progress at the microeconomic level in solving key economic problems also demands specific and well-targeted forms of government spending. Post-Keynesians might therefore regard these considerations as paramount in trying to reconcile the goals of GDP growth, full employment, and sustainable development. But, in dealing with such critical real world problems, Post-Keynesians unquestionably place the greatest emphasis on the macroeconomic aspects of policy issues.

An example of the attention that Post-Keynesians give to macroeconomics is the recent work that a number of Post-Keynesians have undertaken on an 'employer of last resort' (ELR) policy. Under this policy, the government provides employment at a liveable wage to anyone who is conventionally unemployed yet willing and able to work. The number of people employed under the ELR policy expands/contracts around a steady state of full employment as the economy contracts/expands (i.e., more people are employed by the ELR policy as conventional unemployment rises following economic contraction). Post-Keynesians believe that the concept of using buffers or guaranteeing levels of full employment can also be applied to guarantee a steady state of natural capital over time. To ensure we do not run down our existing stock of natural capital, we might use the following principle advocated by Herman Daly (1977, 1993):

> Never reduce the stock of natural capital below a level that generates a sustained yield unless good substitutes are currently available for the services generated.

Given the history of Post-Keynesian economics as it relates to employment issues, this is an idea that Post-Keynesians readily relate to.

Another area where Post-Keynesian policies can be developed is with regard to recent Post-Keynesian work with complexity theory (Rosser, 2004). By developing policies that deal with non-linear complexities in a global ecologic–economic system, this work considers how critical boundaries and threshold levels can be established by taking into consideration a series of principles called the Lisbon Principles (Constanza *et al.*, 1999). They include:

- the responsibility principle;
- the scale-matching principle;
- the precautionary principle;
- the adaptive management principle;
- the cost allocation principle;
- the full participation principle.

These principles are similar to the above 'Daly Rule' in that they establish social guidelines and institutions to deal with uncertainties that could lead to catastrophic outcomes. Finally, the work of Barkley Rosser, Jr. (2004) with fisheries and forest systems juxtaposes complex non-linear dynamics with traditional policy-making approaches. All these efforts are contingent on the emergence of appropriate institutions and arrangements for dealing with policy issues, something that Post-Keynesian economists have been practicing for some time and to which they have much to contribute.

Conclusion

This chapter has looked at some of the fundamental principles of Post-Keynesian and neoclassical economics and how they both relate to sustainable development. Given the current methodological approach of neoclassical economics, it is ill-equipped to deal with the many economic and social complexities associated with achieving sustainable development goals. Although there are limitations with Post-Keynesian economics in terms of understanding and dealing with sustainable development, it provides a theoretical framework considerably more amenable to the assimilation of the sustainability concept into its models than its neoclassical counterpart. For this reason alone, Post-Keynesian economics has much to offer, particularly in relation to the environment–employment dilemma, and should not be overlooked in any attempt to simultaneously achieve the goals of ecological sustainability and full employment.

Notes

1 Property rights solutions are based on the work of Ronald Coase (1960).
2 This section borrows from a new book I am writing with Steven Pressman on Post-Keynesian economics and public policy (forthcoming).
3 The free-rider problem emerges because of the *public goods* nature of most environmental issues.
4 This section is based on Holt (2005).

References

Arestis, P. (1996), 'Post-Keynesian economics: towards coherence', *Cambridge Journal of Economics*, 20, 111–135.

Carabelli, A. (1988), *On Keynes's Method*, London: Palgrave/Macmillan.

Coase, R. (1960), 'The problem of social cost', *Journal of Law and Economics*, 3, October, 1–44.

Costanza, R., Andrade, F., Antunes, P., van den Belt, M., Boesch, D., Boersma, D., Catarino, F., Hanna, S., Limburg, K., Low, B., Molitor, M., Pereira, J. G., Rayner, S., Santos, R., Wilson, J., and Young, M. (1999), 'Ecological economics and sustainable governance of the oceans', *Ecological Economics*, 31, 171–187.

Daly, H. (1977), *Steady State Economics*, San Francisco: W. H. Freeman & Co.

Daly, H. (1993), 'Sustainable growth: an impossibility theorem', in H. Daly and Kenneth Townsend (eds), *Valuing the Earth: Economics, Ecology, and Ethics*, Cambridge, MA: MIT Press.

DeGregori, T. R. (1974), 'Power and illusion in the marketplace: institutions and technology', *Journal of Economic Issues*, 8 (4), 759–770.

Earl, P. (1983), *The Economic Imagination: Towards a Behavioural Analysis of Choice*, Brighton: Wheatsheaf Books.

Galbraith, J. K. (1969), *The Affluent Society*, 2nd edn, Boston: Houghton Mifflin.

Galbraith, J. K. (1974), *Economics and the Public Purpose*, Boston: Houghton Mifflin.

Galbraith, J. K. (1996), *The Good Society: The Humane Agenda*, Boston, MA: Houghton Mifflin.

Georgescu-Roegen, N. (1971), *The Entropy Law and the Economic Process*, Cambridge, MA: Harvard University Press.

Greenwood, D. T. and Holt, R. P. F. (2008), 'Institutional and ecological economics: the role of technology and institutions in economic development', *Journal of Economic Issues*, 42 (2), 445–452.

Harris, J. M. (2000), 'Basic principles of sustainable development', Global Development and Environment Institute, Tufts University, Working Paper 00-04, June.

Hartwick, J. M. (1977), 'Intergenerational equity and the investing of rents from exhaustible resources', *American Economic Review*, 66, 972–974.

Hartwick, J. M. (1989), *Non-Renewable Resources Extraction Programs and Markets*, Chur: Harwood.

Holt, R. P. F. (2005), 'Post-Keynesian economics and sustainable development', *International Journal of Environment, Workplace, and Employment*, 1 (2), 174–186.

Holt, R. P. F. and Setterfield, M. (1999), 'Time', in P. A. O'Hara (ed.), *Encyclopedia of Political Economy*, London: Routledge.

Kahn, R. (1972), *Selected Essays on Employment and Growth*, Cambridge: Cambridge University Press.

Kaldor, N. (1985), *Economics without Equilibrium*, Armonk, NY: M. E. Sharpe.

Keynes, J. M. (1921, repr. 1973), *Treatise in Probability*, London: Macmillan.

Keynes, J. M. (1936), *The General Theory of Employment, Interest and Money*, New York: Harcourt Brace & World.

Keynes, J. M. (1963), 'The future', *Essays in Persuasion*, New York: Norton Press.

Knight, F. (1921), *Risk, Uncertainty, and Profit*, Chicago: University of Chicago Press.

Lavoie, M. (1992), *Foundations of Post-Keynesian Economic Analysis*, Aldershot, UK: Edward Elgar.

Lavoie, M. (2006), *Introduction to Post-Keynesian Economics*, London: Palgrave/Macmillan.

Lavoie, M. (2009), 'Post-Keynesian consumer choice theory and Ecological Economics', in R. P. F. Holt, S. Pressman and C. Spash (eds), *Post Keynesian and Ecological Economics: Confronting Environmental Issues*, Aldershot, UK: Edward Elgar.

McLure, C. E. (1968), 'Merit wants: a normatively empty box', *Finanzarchiv*, 27, 474–483.

Maslow, A. (1954), 'Normality, health and values', *Main Currents*, 10, 75–81.

Musgrave, R. (1957), 'A multiple theory of budget determination', *Finanzarchiv*, 17, 333–43.

Musgrave, R. (1959), *The Theory of Public Finance*, New York: McGraw-Hill.

Norgaard, R. (1988), 'Sustainable development: a co-evolutionary view', *Futures*, December, 606–620.

Norgaard, R. (1989), 'The case for methodological pluralism', *Ecological Economics*, 1, 37–57.

Norgaard, R. (1994), *Development Betrayed: The End of Progress and a Coevolutionary Revisioning of the Future*, New York: Routledge.

Pressman, S. (2006), 'A Post Keynesian theory of the state', in S. Pressman (ed.), *Alternative Theories of the State*, London: Palgrave/Macmillan.

Robinson, J. (1974, repr. 1980), 'History versus equilibrium', in J. Robinson, *Collected Economic Papers*, volume 5, Cambridge, MA: MIT Press.

Robinson, J. (1976), 'The age of growth', in *Collected Economic Papers of Joan Robinson*, volume 4, Oxford: Basil Blackwell.

Rosser, Barkley, Jr. (2004), 'Forestry complex dynamics and policy problems', *Studies in Regional Science*, 34 (2), 3–18.

Sen, A. (1984), *Resources, Values and Development*, Oxford: Basil Blackwell.

Sen, A. (1985), *Commodities and Capabilities*, Amsterdam: North Holland.

Solow, R. (1974), 'Intergenerational equity and exhaustible resources', *American Economic Review*, 64, 1–14.

Solow, R. (1986), 'On the intergenerational allocation of natural resources', *Scandinavian Journal of Economics*, 88, 141–149.

Solow, R. (1992), 'An almost practical step toward sustainability', Resources for the Future Working Paper, Washington, DC.

Solow, R. (1994), 'Perspectives on growth theory', *Journal of Economic Perspectives*, 8 (1), 45–54.

Stiglitz, J. (2000), *Economics of the Public Sector*, 3rd edn, New York: W. W. Norton & Co.

World Commission on Environment and Development (WCED) (1987), *Our Common Future*, Oxford: Oxford University Press.

Part III
Guaranteed employment versus guaranteed income

6 The Basic Income Guarantee and the goals of equality, efficiency, and environmentalism

Karl Widerquist

Michael A. Lewis

Introduction

The most important issue in equality – if not in all economic policy – is the persistence of poverty. This chapter argues that anti-poverty policy needs to move away from the categorical approach towards universalism, specifically in the form of a Basic Income Guarantee. This chapter argues that the Basic Income Guarantee, in any of its various versions (for example, a negative income tax, a universal Basic Income, or the social dividend) is the most efficient and comprehensive method to attack poverty. It can also be used as part of a strategy for environmental protection.

The following section, entitled 'The definition of poverty and the goal of poverty policy', defines poverty and our goal for poverty policy. The section entitled 'Views on the causes of poverty' critically examines five theories of the causes of poverty: the physical inability to work; single parenthood; inadequate demand for labour; inadequate human capital; and a poor work ethic. The section entitled 'Social policies to address poverty' assesses the current system of poverty alleviation in the United States and two proposed reforms: publicly guaranteed employment, and the Basic Income Guarantee. The section entitled 'The Basic Income Guarantee and environmental protection' considers whether the Basic Income Guarantee can be made part of an overall strategy for environmental protection. The final section concludes and summarizes the arguments in the chapter.

The definition of poverty and the goal of poverty policy

This chapter focuses on an absolute definition of poverty, according to which 'the poverty line' is the amount of income needed for a person or family to purchase their minimum needs of food, shelter, and clothing.[1] A family with less income than the poverty line is considered to be living in poverty. We focus on this rather than relative poverty because we believe society's first priority should be to meet everyone's basic needs before addressing the question of whether there is enough equality in the consumption of luxuries.

The question of where the poverty line ought to be has been extensively debated (Schiller, 1989; Schwarz and Volgy, 1992; Mishel and Bernstein, 1994), but this is not a debate we intend to join here. For present purposes, we accept the US government's standard of the poverty line. There are good reasons to believe it is inadequate, but arguments that the Basic Income Guarantee is the best policy to reach that line would not differ significantly if the line were drawn higher.

We believe that there is a broad consensus among all but the most radical property rights advocates that the ultimate goal of policy should be to reduce poverty as much as possible and eliminate it, if possible. People who argue for less generous forms of redistribution most often couch their arguments in terms of such programmes being counter-productive or ineffective. The goal of this chapter is to question not the sincerity of that argument, but its validity. The wide differences of opinion about poverty policy largely reflect differences about how best to achieve the goal of poverty reduction, which in turn depends on people's beliefs about the causes of poverty.

Views on the causes of poverty

There are many differing views on the cause or causes of poverty, including the physical inability to work, inadequate demand for labour, inadequate human capital, lack of work ethic, and single parenthood. There is no clear consensus about the relative importance of each of these possible causes. We discuss each of them and then discuss our own view.

Physical inability to work

Some people are physically incapable of holding a job and, hence, providing for their own subsistence because of old age or disability. The House Committee on Ways and Means (1992) defines the disabled as 'those unable to engage in any substantial gainful activity by reason of medically determined physical or mental impairment expected to result in death or that has lasted or can be expected to last for a continuous period of at least 12 months'. Although this is, in some ways, the most straightforward and widely accepted cause of poverty, there is a considerable grey area about how disabled one must be to be incapable of working (Dolgoff *et al.*, 1993).

Single-parenthood

One cause of poverty could be that single parents cannot afford the time away from their children to work (Ellwood, 1988).[2] Pearce (1978) found that female-headed families have become a disproportionate share of the impoverished population. Kelso (1994) found that, between 1960 and 1991, the percentage of poor families headed by single women increased from 18.3 per cent to 38.7 per cent. There is disagreement on whether this should be viewed as a root cause of poverty or not (Garfinkel and McLanahan, 1986; Mishel and Bernstein, 1994; Mayer, 1997). Some authors (Murray, 1984; Magnet, 1993; Tanner, 1996) argue that welfare causes single parenthood by encouraging women who would not otherwise become single parents to do so. Even if this cause and effect is plausible, we are not sympathetic to the belief that single mothers should be kept in poverty to discourage others from becoming single mothers. According to Kim (1997), whereas most single parents with children under the age of six years did not work, 46 per cent of those who did work had incomes below the poverty line, which suggests that the reason that so many single parents do not work is because, if they do, they may have a high probability of remaining below the poverty line.

Inadequate demand for labour

According to one view, the demand for labour is presently not high enough to employ, at above poverty wages, all those who are willing and able to supply their labour. Two consequences can follow from this: high unemployment and/or low-wage employment. Keep in mind that, according to this view, low-wage employment is caused not by a lack of human capital but by inadequate demand. Just as is the case in any other market, when demand is less than supply, there is downward pressure on price, which in this case is the wage (Harvey, 1989; Harrison and Bluestone, 1990; Rose, 1994; Wilson, 1996). Some neoclassical economists reject the idea that unemployment, as usually defined by economists, can exist for very long. According to this view, what appears to be unemployment is really a result of people choosing not to offer their labour at the going wage, perhaps because they are searching for a better-paid job. In this sense, their unemployment is 'frictional' rather than 'structural'. In other words, when the demand for labour is low, wages simply fall until an equilibrium level is reached at which all workers who are willing to work at the much lower wage can find a job (Munday, 1996). There is, according to neoclassical economists, no unemployment except for the fact that some would-be workers have opted to exit the labour market. As such, the ensuing unemployment is entirely 'voluntary'.

The problem with the neoclassical position is that, even if a full-employment equilibrium can be shown to exist, there is no reason to believe that the equilibrium wage will constitute a living wage. There is no economic theory assuring that everyone who wants to work can find a job that pays above poverty wages. It has been pointed out, at least as long ago as Smith (1976, originally published in 1776), but also by many others, that workers have a disadvantageous position in the labour market. That is, workers need a job to survive but the owners of natural resources do not need employees to survive. This could explain the tendency for wages to be low in some sectors of the economy. This 'lack of market power' in the hands of workers often leads to poverty, but tends to be overlooked. We therefore recommend that any poverty policy should be evaluated in terms of its effect on the market power of labourers. The lack-of-market-power argument can be expressed in an imperfect model of the labour market or by use of the perfect-competition model. In the latter case, the need to work causes a large amount of competition for a limited number of employment opportunities which, in turn, leads to the bidding down of wages.

Low level of human capital

Human capital refers to the skills, knowledge, and abilities that make people more productive in their work. If the labour market is competitive, economic theory predicts that the people with more human capital (i.e., those that are more productive) will find more work and better-paying jobs. This theory is the basis of one influential view of the cause of poverty: people with poor human capital skills end up either unemployed or employed in low-wage jobs (Atkinson, 1983; Becker, 1993; Ehrenberg and Smith, 1994).

Lack of work ethic

Some people may choose to behave in ways that cause their own poverty. For example, Mead (1986) contends that an insufficient work ethic causes poverty. Able-bodied persons might choose not to work because they become disenchanted, they find the work on offer demeaning, they consider the wage an insufficient form of compensation, or they find it difficult to hold down a job. Individuals who choose not to work are considered 'out of the labour force', because they voluntarily choose not to participate at the going wage.

Our view of the causes of poverty

Considering all of the possible causes mentioned above, we adopt a largely agnostic approach in this chapter. Some of the possible causes of poverty are clearly more important than others but, because the problem has many possible causes, we would be ill-advised to ignore any of them. We believe that the widespread characterisation of the poor as 'bad' people with no work ethic is clearly false, but we believe it would be a mistake to go so far as to assume that no-one has an insufficient desire to work or that certain kinds of policies do not discourage this desire.

We believe that a significant problem of formulating effective public policy is caused by the fact that many people on all sides of the political spectrum find it appealing to focus on only one or a few causes. The left side of the political spectrum tends to focus on unemployment, whereas the right side tends to believe that people do not value work sufficiently. What tends to be left out of the discussion is that the extent to which people value work often depends upon wages and working conditions. People may not value work, not because they lack the work ethic, not because the alternatives to work are more appealing, but because the jobs available are not adequately rewarding. Policies designed to foster a work ethic sufficient to make workers accept a lifetime of working for poverty wages cannot end poverty, but they can do much to boost the profits of those who pay poverty wages to their employees.

The causes of poverty are many and complex, but the problem of poverty is a simple one to comprehend: people are poor if they do not have enough money to buy the basic necessities of life. Policies should be evaluated on the basis of their effects on the living standards of the working poor, the living standards of those who do not or cannot work, and the number of affected people. In 2002, there were 7.4 million people in the United States below the poverty line who had been in the labour force for at least 27 weeks. This amounted to 5.3 per cent of the US labour force (US Department of Labor/Bureau of Statistics, 2004). The problem we address in the next section is to design a policy that takes all of the causes of poverty into account.

Social policies to address poverty

The current social support system in the United States, as in many other industrialised nations, involves a categorical approach to poverty alleviation in which different policies are tailored to deal with the different causes of poverty. The overall system is very complex and usually involves a great deal of overhead cost. The US version of the categorical approach heavily involves separating the 'deserving' and the 'undeserving' poor. We discuss the merits of this strategy and two proposals to broaden and simplify anti-poverty policy, guaranteed public employment, and the Basic Income Guarantee. We argue that the Basic Income Guarantee is the most comprehensive and efficient policy to address poverty.

Separating the 'deserving' and 'undeserving' poor

Many policy-makers believe that those who cannot work (either because of disability or unemployment) are the 'deserving' poor, whereas those who simply do not work, are the 'undeserving' poor (Zastro, 1986). The strategy then becomes one of categorising the poor in terms of the cause of their poverty, creating a different solution for each deserving category, and encouraging the undeserving poor to get a job; this, to a large extent, requires good jobs to be available through policies such as the minimum wage, labour market regulation, and the promotion of full employment. If the strategy works perfectly, those who cannot work will be supported, and all those who can work will have their work disincentives eliminated. As we discuss below, this definition leaves out the person who does not work because of unacceptable working conditions.

The United States has an enormous yet incomplete system of overlapping poverty-alleviation programmes, as summarised in Table 6.1. Despite the large number of programmes, they are currently unable to eliminate all poverty or even draw all workers out of poverty. To recall, 5.3 per cent of the labour force in 2002 had incomes below the poverty line (US Department of Labor/Bureau of Statistics, 2004). Each programme has its own eligibility requirements, making it difficult for people in need to know what form of assistance they might qualify for. Simply having low or no income does not qualify someone for these programmes; thus, many poor people may fail to qualify for any assistance at all.

The categorical approach has been the basis for the US social welfare system since the Great Depression. Although it has had many successes, and has helped to reduce poverty, especially among the elderly, we believe that this approach

Table 6.1   Poverty-alleviation programmes in the United States

Category (cause)	Programme
Physically unable to work	Social Security, SSI, Medicare, Worker's Compensation, Medicaid
Single parenthood	TANF, public housing, Medicaid, Food Stamps
Unemployment	Unemployment Insurance, food stamps, public housing, Medicaid
Low wages	Minimum wage, food stamps, public housing, Medicaid, earned income tax credit
Inadequate human capital	Public education, some counselling as a part of TANF and other programmes
Lack of work ethic	Employment Counselling, denial of benefits

has proven to be extremely expensive and not completely effective (i.e., very inefficient). The rest of this section discusses four reasons why the categorical approach is not efficient or effective:

- the problem with defining the 'deserving' poor;
- the cost of categorising each person;
- the harsh penalty for the so-called 'undeserving' poor;
- and the effect the strategy has had on the market or bargaining power of workers.

First, how can one accurately define 'deserving'? Even if we accept the distinction between those who cannot and those who will not work, how can we agree on who is able to work? Most would agree that a person with a severe developmental disability or someone with a profound case of schizophrenia is unable to work, but it is harder to agree about milder disabilities. A blind psychiatrist can still work but not a blind factory worker. Does being blind make a person deserving? What if the blindness was caused by complications due to diabetes that resulted from eating too many sweets? The arbitrariness of this categorisation is exemplified by the fact that single mothers were once considered 'deserving' but now they are not.

Second, once a definition of need is determined, it is costly to separate people into categories of need. The effort involved in categorisation is expensive and there are significant costs associated with correcting mistakes. The US social welfare system has numerous overlapping programmes all with the same ultimate goal. Each programme has its own eligibility requirements making it expensive for the government to determine who is qualified for which programme. It is also difficult for needy persons to determine which programmes they may be eligible for. Programmes vary greatly in the portion of total spending taken up by administrative costs. Some are extremely high; others quite low. The administrative cost of unemployment insurance, for example, is more than 85 per cent of the total programme budget whereas the administrative cost of social security is less than 1 per cent of the total budget (House Committee on Ways and Means, 1992).

Third, the impact on individuals of making and correcting misjudgments is critically important. People who are deserving, as currently defined, are often wrongly classified as non-deserving (Type 2 error); others who are non-deserving are sometimes classified as deserving (Type 1 error). A Type 2 error is someone 'falling through the cracks', such as a homeless person with an undiagnosed mental disorder. Type 1 errors include giving benefits to someone who has a high income, such as sending a social security cheque to a retired billionaire. Type 1 errors also include giving benefits to someone who has a low income but would otherwise be earning a higher private income if in work, such as people who wait until their unemployment payment runs out before looking for a new job.

Separating the deserving from the undeserving involves a very high penalty for laziness. Even if a person is 'truly undeserving', should they face imminent starvation? This makes the penalty for laziness more severe than the penalty for most crimes, except murder. It seems also to retreat from the goal of eliminating poverty. Saving (1997) characterises this as 'tough love', saying that less redistribution will get more of the poor into the labour force, reducing the number of the poor at the cost of increasing the severity of poverty. Even if this were an acceptable trade-off, we doubt that it would work once we seriously consider its effects on the labour market.

This brings us to the fourth problem with the categorical strategy. It hurts the market position of all labourers. Requiring everyone to work increases the supply of labour. This not only places downward pressure on wages, it also reduces the market power of labour, often causing workers to seek a job quickly rather than seek a job commensurate with their human capital. Policy-makers have inadequately attempted to solve these problems by other government actions, such as the minimum wage and labour regulations, but none solve the underlying problem that, whereas workers are forced to desperately compete for jobs, employers do not have to desperately compete for workers. The distinction between deserving and undeserving does not allow a person the freedom to refuse a job because the pay is too low or the working conditions are unacceptable. The strategy of imposing 'tough love' undermines our belief that people who work hard should be rewarded for it. The condition that those who work are 'deserving' implies that no-one who works full-time should live in poverty, yet, as we have highlighted, many workers in the United States do – not because they are lazy, but because of their weak bargaining position.

This problem can lead to a paradox of hard work. As workers work harder, more labour is supplied to the market, and the downward pressure on wages increases. This, in turn, forces workers to work even harder, thereby fuelling the cycle. The current system over-emphasises 'bad values' as the cause of poverty. Workers may have good values but few opportunities, and 'bad values' may be the result, not the cause, of poverty. People at the low end of the job market know that the jobs available to them pay very little and offer little hope of advancement. A minimum-wage job requires a single parent with two children to work two jobs just to make ends meet. To simply reach the poverty line, many single parents on low hourly wages are required to work 70 to 80 hours per week. Even then, their capacity to work this number of hours is dependent upon their access to a large amount of free childcare. Certainly, a person in this situation would be unable to save the money needed to start a small business or the time needed outside of work to learn skills to improve his or her situation. If it is at all possible, it can take years to advance out of this situation. It is not surprising that people faced with these options do not develop a strong work ethic. If we want people to value work, we must make work valuable to them in the short run, not as a distant promise of reward after years of poverty wages.

We believe that one should not be called 'undeserving' for choosing not to work if the only jobs open to them would leave their families in poverty. We, therefore, search for a solution that will give workers greater market power. The guaranteed income would increase the market power of workers and thus help the unemployed and working poor alike.

Guaranteed public employment

Because inadequate demand for labour is a significant cause of poverty and unemployment, government-provided jobs have been proposed as a solution. A comprehensive version could replace all transfer payments to those able to work (including Temporary Assistance for Needy Families (TANF), unemployment insurance, the minimum wage, food stamps, and public housing) with a government guarantee to hire anyone willing and able to work. This idea is known as the public jobs approach, the guaranteed job, or the government acting as an Employer of Last Resort (ELR). Minsky (1986) proposed a version in 1986; another version, the Works Progress Administration, operated in the United States during the Great Depression.

Several Post-Keynesian economists have recently put forward ELR proposals as a systematic method to balance the demand and supply of labour without creating inflationary pressure, including Wray (1998) in *Understanding Modern Money*. The comments here are directed at that proposal. An evaluation of ELR as an economic stabilisation tool is beyond the scope of this chapter. We will be evaluating it as a tool to reduce poverty. To the extent that ELR can stabilise the economy in ways that other policies do not, this could at least partially mitigate the inefficiency effects that we point out below.

There are two important differences between ELR and workfare. First, ELR is comprehensive: the government promises to hire anyone who is willing and able to work at a pre-determined wage. They do not need to demonstrate that they are poor or single parents, as workfare requires. Second, ELR pays higher wages. Wray argues that the ELR should involve a living wage and include fringe benefits such as healthcare, childcare, and retirement. He uses $6.25 per hour for illustration and asks the reader to 'assume' that that is a living wage while admitting that that assumption is unlikely to be true unless wages are supplemented with other sources of income, possibly including a second job (Wray, 1998).

Obviously public employment is not aimed at those unable to work; it would have to be combined with programmes for the elderly and disabled as part of a more comprehensive strategy to eliminate poverty. As a poverty-alleviating policy, it must, therefore, be seen as part of a larger targeted system of benefits whereby the associated costs of determining who is eligible for a public job and who is eligible for other kinds of aid would count as the inevitable inefficiency of a poverty-alleviating strategy incorporating an ELR. Although the ELR would seem to eliminate the problem of separating the unemployed from those unwilling to work, it would not do that perfectly. Since the ELR offers a uniform wage, some people might be genuinely unemployed from higher-skilled occupations and thus be unwilling to accept the underemployment associated with an ELR job.

The ELR could help single parents in poverty, but not without serious side-effects. For example, the jobs could: (a) pay enough to enable workers to obtain private daycare; (b) include daycare as a fringe benefit; or (c) involve flexible hours and work-sharing arrangements so that groups of workers could take turns caring for each other's children. However, all of these possibilities create the problem of separating parents from children for a significant amount of time, which might not be the best thing for those families. The alternative would be to classify single parents as those 'unable to work' because of child-rearing commitments and responsibilities. But, because single parents and their children make up the majority of the poor, doing so would mean that a Job Guarantee would not help most people who live in poverty.

It has been suggested that the ELR could eliminate the problems of low wages and unemployment caused by a low demand for labour. It would directly eliminate unemployment, and, if it pays higher than poverty wages, it would nearly eliminate low wages as a source of poverty. An ELR with health benefits, daycare, and a living wage would greatly reduce poverty, but a low wage would not reduce the number of people living in poverty and would verge on being exploitative.

Although, at one point, Wray (1998) argues that the ELR should pay a living wage, he is not very optimistic that an ELR could or should attempt to increase the going wage in the labour market. He takes the position that the purchasing power of the going wage in the low-wage sector is beyond the control of policy. With a very small discussion of how and why the purchasing power of wages is determined, and whether it can be influenced by other policies, Wray states that increasing the ELR wage is equivalent to devaluing the currency and that other wages and prices will adjust upward to reflect the devaluation (Wray, 1998: 135–136). This implies that, if the going wage in the labour market is a poverty wage, the ELR alone is powerless to give low-wage workers a higher standard of living. Furthermore, if ELR jobs at the going wage are poverty-wage jobs, why is it so important to make sure that conventionally unemployed labourers have such an occupation rather than making sure that they, along with everyone else, have the power to refuse such a job? We are not suggesting that proponents of guaranteed public employment are of the view that stabilising the price level has the necessary benefit of leaving the working class with no other option but to work for poverty wages; however, they need to spell out how their strategy would get the poor back to work as well as haul them out of the poverty they are already having to endure. That said, we shall assume that, for the rest of this section, the

ELR system can be designed to pay the wages sufficient to bring workers out of poverty.

Proponents of the low level of human capital view might give qualified approval of the public jobs approach if the ELR could be shown to have the power to set higher wages. The policy could directly eliminate the symptom (low wages), but would less directly address its cause. ELR employees might or might not gain valuable work experience and the skills necessary to increase earnings if and when they return to the private sector. An extreme proponent of the low human capital view might fear that ELR jobs would become 'make work', and would not eventually lead to better private sector jobs. However, if such a problem arises, the system could be adjusted to include a job-training programme.

People who think that the poor lack sufficient values might also voice qualified approval of this approach. They would see its major weakness as being the difficulty to both guarantee a job and give people an incentive to work hard on that job. Could workers be fired for poor performance? If not, it wouldn't be much of a job. But if so, the job would not be a truly guaranteed job, and what would happen to the people who were fired? If a worker does not perform his or her job adequately, the problem resurfaces of separating those who cannot perform on account of mental disability from those who simply do not perform. An employer of last resort may be reluctant to fire employees, but workers who least value hard work would have incentives to try to work as little as possible. One solution would be to take a judgmental position and treat such workers as 'undeserving', 'bad' people, who ought to be poor or homeless. Another solution would be to heavily supervise employees, but this could increase cost, reduce productivity, and develop an antagonism between employees and management. A third solution would be to combine the ELR with a smaller, universal system, such as the Basic Income Guarantee, so that people who did not accept the jobs as they are, or did not perform well enough to keep them, would not be paid as much as ELR workers, but would not remain completely destitute.

Like workfare, public employment could socialise the poor into recognising the value of work. However, it would do this more effectively than workfare if it positively rewarded work with the payment of a higher-than-poverty income. Thus, participants would directly and immediately see a positive reward for their labour.

Our view is that public employment would be a vast improvement over the current state of affairs. Like the guaranteed income, it would act as an automatic stabiliser on the economy and would eliminate many of the sources of poverty. However, there are four reasons why public employment is not as appealing as the guaranteed income. First, it relies on an extreme version of the work ethic, similar to workfare. We say this because, like workfare, unless it is accompanied by some universal support system, an ELR would require able-bodied persons to work in return for assistance. We hasten to add, however, that public employment with a living wage would apply the extreme version of the work ethic more fairly than the current system. This is because it would create a reciprocal moral obligation rather than a one-sided moral obligation. It would require people to work for assistance but would assure that the level of assistance was high enough to allow them to escape poverty. Yet it would put workers in the position in which they have to accept the employer's decision about what is a fair wage. Public employment in the context of a society in which poor individuals have no access to the means of survival unless they work for people who control property leaves the workers with no options but to accept whatever the employers decide is fair. We would like to hope that the market wage is always fair, or that public employers will always decide to pay good wages, but we have no reason to believe this would eventuate. Isn't it rather one-sided to believe that the class of people who control access to jobs and government assistance can judge the poor as 'deserving' or 'undeserving', while the class of people who work are not given the power to judge employers as being 'deserving' of having employees?

Second, a major disadvantage of public employment is that this would be significantly more expensive than the guaranteed income. In addition to the wage costs and the costs of separating those who can work from those who should be eligible for other programmes, plus the administrative costs of other programmes, the ELR would have enormous overhead costs of its own. These would include the cost of administration, supervision, materials, transportation, and planning. Every town and neighbourhood would require facilities and managers to manage peak levels of demand for ELR jobs during periods of high unemployment. These facilities would sit idle during periods of relatively low unemployment. If the ELR was replaced by a Basic Income Guarantee, all of these costs could be turned into higher payments to the poor or greater government services without putting any additional pressure on prices from the demand side of the economy.

Guaranteed public employment also has external costs that, despite being difficult to measure in pecuniary terms, are costs just the same. A public-employment-induced net increase in the supply of labour would also mean an increase in traffic congestion, crowded subways/buses, a rise in the negative health effects of commuting (e.g., stress and the respiratory problems associated with inhaling automobile fumes), and an increase in the environmental depletion of any scarce resource assets used in production. Traffic congestion and some types of work also tend to create noise pollution, which, if not a threat to health (see Godish, 2000), is certainly a cost.

Considering all of these costs, a public jobs programme could ultimately cost many times more than its wage cost. Thus, it is likely to be the most expensive of all programmes that we will be discussing in this chapter. The guaranteed income, because of its simplicity, would have low administrative costs comparable with social security, as discussed above.

One could counter that the cost of public employment would be compensated for by the fact that participants would be producing worthwhile goods and services that would justify the higher costs. However, participants would also be giving up the time that they could spend in job training, starting a business, volunteering, getting an education, raising children, or doing whatever it is they find valuable. There is no objective way to judge whether participants would make more valuable use of their time with a guaranteed job or a guaranteed income and thus no a priori way to say that the increased production of the ELR approach would be worth its cost.

The third less appealing aspect of public employment is that, although it and the guaranteed income would create an effective bed for private sector wages, the guaranteed income could have a greater impact on private sector wages for a given level of benefits. For instance, to establish $300 a week as the effective minimum wage, public wages would have to be $300 to make workers indifferent between private and public sector jobs. However, if people preferred leisure to labour, the guaranteed income could be less than $300 to make workers indifferent between private sector jobs and living off the guaranteed income.

Fourth, public employment would be a logistical nightmare. Imagine all the resources the government would have to expend deciding what public employees would do and all of the political fights over what district would get which jobs and the benefit of the subsequent output. Unemployment is erratic and, presumably, so would be the number of applicants for public jobs. How would public employment ensure enough work for all applicants, in all locations, at all times, without resorting to making work for work's sake?

The Basic Income Guarantee

In this section, we argue that the Basic Income Guarantee is the most efficient and comprehensive poverty-alleviation policy because it can eliminate poverty no matter what the cause. There are different versions of the Basic Income Guarantee, including the citizen's income, the Basic Income, the negative income tax, the social dividend, and others (see Lapman, 1965; Lord, 2003; Van Parijs, 2004). For our purposes, we need not go into detail about the technical differences between them. All of them are essentially a form of income insurance, thus providing a guarantee that no-one's income falls below the poverty line, for any reason. More than that, a Basic Income Guarantee would ensure that, the more one works outside of the home, the better off one is.

There are two important numbers in a Basic Income Guarantee scheme: the grant level and the marginal tax rate. The grant (or the minimum income or the maximum supplement) is the amount of money received by a person earning no income through their own private means. The marginal tax rate is the rate at which the grant is reduced (in the case of a negative income tax) or private income is taxed (in the case of a Basic Income) as private income rises. The Basic Income Guarantee would replace most of the current tax and benefit system operating in most countries with a simple equation – that is, after-tax income equals the untaxed proportion of one's private income plus the government grant:

$$D = Y(1 - t) + G \tag{6.1}$$

where:

- D = after-tax income;
- Y = private income;

- t = the marginal tax rate;
- G = the government grant.

If the grant is greater than a person's or a family's income tax liabilities, net taxes (T) are negative (i.e., the person or family is a net recipient of transfers). Hence:

$$T = Yt - G \tag{6.2}$$

For example (see Table 6.2), suppose we constructed a system with a $10,000 grant for a family of three and a 50 per cent marginal tax rate – meaning that for every dollar a family earns they would lose $0.50 of their supplement or they would pay $0.50 tax on their private income. A family with no private income would receive the $10,000 transfer. If the family began earning $5,000 privately, its benefits would be reduced by $2,500 (50 per cent of $5,000), amounting to an after-tax income of $12,500 ($10,000 – $2,500 + $5,000 = $12,500). If this family increased its private earnings to $10,000, its after-tax income would be $15,000. If this family increased its earnings to $20,000 (the break-even point), it would receive no net subsidy, giving it an after-tax income of $20,000. Notice that this family is always financially better off increasing its private earnings rather than relying solely on the Basic Income Guarantee.

These numbers are purely for illustration. The minimum income level and the marginal tax rate would have to be chosen based on the poverty line and the government revenue available. Notice that, although the marginal tax rate is fairly high at 50 per cent, the average tax rate is much lower for most families. Notice also that, although the marginal tax rate is the same for all families, the overall effect of the tax benefit system is quite progressive. The marginal tax rate could, if necessary, be reduced by collecting revenue from other sources, such as property, sales, or wealth taxes, thereby reducing the need to raise revenue from the income tax.

Those who believe poverty stems from disability or single-parent status might find the Basic Income Guarantee appealing. A Basic Income Guarantee would assure that everyone unable to work, for any reason, would not become impoverished. Retirees could live off of the minimum income, but would be assured that,

Table 6.2 Hypothetical tax and income schedule

Private income ($)	Net tax ($)	After-tax income ($)	Average tax rate
0	−10,000	10,000	–
5,000	−7,500	12,500	−150%
10,000	−5,000	15,000	−50%
20,000	0	20,000	0
30,000	5,000	25,000	17%
50,000	15,000	35,000	30%
100,000	40,000	60,000	40%

the more private savings they have accumulated, the better off they would be. Some, however, advocate combining the Basic Income Guarantee with a retirement programme or providing a higher maximum supplement to retirees. The Basic Income Guarantee would eliminate the possibility of Type 2 categorisation errors. Someone truly unable to work, but who does not qualify for a particular programme under the current system, would be guaranteed assistance under the system we propose.

The guaranteed income would work very well to prevent poverty if inadequate demand for labour led to low wages or high unemployment and this was the primary cause of poverty. The unemployed would be able to live off of the minimum income until they found another job, while low-wage workers would receive an income supplement to bring their total income above the poverty line, thereby making them better off at all times than those who are not working.

The guaranteed income would also eliminate many of the negative side-effects arising from current policies employed to overcome the inadequate demand for labour. Unlike the minimum wage, a guaranteed income would not adversely effect labour demand. And unlike unemployment insurance, a guaranteed income would not encourage workers to remain unemployed until their benefits expire, nor leave them desperate to find any job once their benefits have expired. Workers on unemployment benefits must give up their entire supplement to take a job, and risk not being able to receive the benefits again if they choose to quit their job. For example, suppose that someone received $200 per week in unemployment insurance. If the recipient were offered a $250 per week job, s/he would lose all unemployment benefits and start paying income taxes. This would leave him/her little better off and possibly worse off than staying on unemployment benefits. A person in the same situation, but receiving a Basic Income Guarantee, could take the job and enjoy a rise in after-tax income from $200 to $325 per week without risking the loss of benefits if s/he feels the need to quit the job. Thus, the Basic Income Guarantee ensures that, the more one works, the more income one receives, while never having to fear complete destitution.

People who believe inadequate human capital causes poverty might voice qualified approval of the Basic Income Guarantee. A Basic Income does not treat the cause of poverty, but it effectively treats the symptom. It does little to directly enhance human capital, since it merely provides people with enough money to meet their subsistence needs. However, the Basic Income's potential appeal is that it would free up people's time to enhance their levels of human capital. If people were assured that their subsistence needs would be met, whether they worked or not, they would be in a position to devote more of their time to training and other activities which would increase their levels of human capital. Such a person would have more opportunity to increase his/her human capital than a minimum-wage worker today, who would potentially have to work two jobs to keep a family of three above the poverty line. This would leave very little time available to increase their skills. Also, the Basic Income Guarantee could be combined with increased job training, placement, and educational funding. This combination would be superior to workfare because it would offer both a long-term and a short-term solution to poverty caused by inadequate human capital.

The strongest opposition to the guaranteed income is likely to come from the perspective that a lack of work ethic causes poverty. Some might make this argument directly, others indirectly. People who directly contend that the lack of a work ethic causes poverty argue that a policy providing enough money for people's basic needs would result in a severe work disincentive. As a consequence, society would not be able to get enough people to work to create the things needed for society to be sustained. This is an important objection. However, there are three problems with it. First, it relies on a very strong and unrealistic assumption about people's aversion to work. People do not simply work to earn money. Second, it relies on an extreme and one-sided version of the work ethic. Third, it ignores the incentive effects on businesses. These arguments are supported in the following discussion.

Unlike the present system, the guaranteed income would always provide an incentive for people to work if they could because, no matter what a person earned, one would always be financially better off earning more. The guaranteed income is a lump sum transfer (the poor receive it as a grant, others receive it as a tax deduction) and hence it does not result in an inefficiency; inefficiency could be caused only by collecting taxes to support it. It has a work disincentive only in the sense that one is not completely destitute if one does not work, but it counters that with a significant reward if someone does work. As mentioned above, the incentive to work for a person receiving a guaranteed income removes some work disincentives that many current anti-poverty programmes have. TANF, food stamps, unemployment insurance, and even public housing are all very difficult to qualify for. If something is difficult to obtain, it is risky to give it up. In a guaranteed income system, a worker takes no risk when accepting a job. This would greatly reduce the 'cycle of dependency' problem. A supporter of the 'bad values' view of poverty might respond by using the extreme version of the work ethic – that is, able-bodied persons are obligated to work for their subsistence. Those who hold this view tend to be ambivalent about or oppose poverty-alleviation policies that provide able-bodied poor people with assistance without requiring them to work for it (Mead, 1986).

We are neither ambivalent about nor opposed to such policies. As we have said, it is one-sided to hold individuals who do not own property to a moral obligation to work without holding society to a reciprocal moral obligation. There are two ways to solve this inconsistency – either increase the moral obligation of employers (as the minimum wage and the ELR attempt to do) or decrease the moral obligation on the part of workers. We believe the second is more effective because the belief that large numbers of people will not work, even if offered a good wage, relies on an unrealistic assumption about human behaviour – it is based on a belief that 'every man does not have his price'. On the whole, people will work if given an incentive to do so, and people are happier and better performed workers if they *choose* to work rather than if they are *forced* to work. Remember, as cited above, that 5.3 per cent of the labour force in 2002 lived in poverty. Since some of those who made up this 5.3 per cent were actually working, instead of simply looking for work, this implies that some Americans had such a strong work ethic that they were willing to work even though they had little pecuniary incentive to do so. Even before TANF, when the Aid to Families with Dependent Children (AFDC) had no time limits, most recipients were no longer on public assistance within three years. The 'cycle of dependency' tends to be most severe where there are few work opportunities in the private sector (Handler and Hasenfeld, 1997).

Recall that neither Keynesian nor neoclassical economic theory implies that the labour market will provide above-poverty wages for everyone who wants to work. In the absence of redistribution, workers are desperate to work but employers are not as desperate to find workers, which leads to low wages in the least skilled labour markets. As a consequence, this thrusts upon workers an obligation to work. Although the Basic Income Guarantee provides a supplement for non-workers and workers alike, it gives low-wage workers the market power to command higher wages. If, as people so often fear, a large number of low-wage workers attempted to quit their jobs to live off the minimum income alone, the market would respond with higher wages to induce them back to work. Even if wages did not rise sufficiently for everyone to re-enter work, wages would rise enough for the hard-working to be significantly better off than they are under the current system. Furthermore, they would certainly be better off than those who just lived off the minimum income.

Many people make the values argument against the Basic Income indirectly, saying that, because the work ethic is so strong in our society, we should advocate poverty-alleviation policies that are consistent with it. A guaranteed income is not consistent with the work ethic because it provides people with 'something for nothing'. To avoid eroding the work ethic, a guaranteed income, if enacted, would have to be set at a very low level. This would prevent the guaranteed income from meeting subsistence needs and thus defeat the main purpose of it. In all, if politicians and the public wish to avoid putting the work ethic at risk, they are unlikely to be willing to provide generous levels of governmental assistance to non-working people.

An ELR system would not, however, run into this problem. Poor persons who took the ELR jobs would be working for their subsistence, and politicians and the public would be willing to reward them with higher income than would be the case under a Basic Income Guarantee. The implication is that, thanks to our societal adherence to the work ethic, public assistance beneficiaries would end up better off under a public employment scheme than with a guaranteed income plan.

We agree that politicians and the public might be willing to give more money under a public employment approach than under a Basic Income Guarantee. This does not necessarily mean, however, that recipients would receive more money or would be better off. As we argued above, the public employment approach is very expensive. Taxpayers must be willing to forgo enough to cover the added expense of supervisors, materials, and all the other overhead costs associated with the public employment programme. In addition, there are the externalities discussed earlier that must also be taken into account. Because public jobs are likely to be so much more expensive and involve so many more costs, it is doubtful whether the public at large would be willing to bear the burden of making sure recipients receive a higher income than under the guaranteed income. Even if they did, the recipients might not be better off because of the high cost of engaging in work. Work often comes with travel costs, childcare costs, and other costs. The money used to cover these expenses cannot be used to purchase food, shelter, clothing, and other goods and services. If these private costs were taken into account by the designers of a public employment programme, the ELR wages would have to be *significantly* higher to ensure recipients were better off with a guaranteed job than a Basic Income Guarantee.

The Basic Income Guarantee and environmental protection

The Basic Income Guarantee has been endorsed by Green parties around the world, largely because of its potential environmental benefits. However, it is not directly an environmental policy. It can be used as part of an environmental strategy, but presenting it as an environmental panacea is a gross mischaracterisation. It is instead something which can help reduce the human costs of environmental policies.

Some proponents of the Basic Income Guarantee promote it as an environmental policy because it can free people from the necessity of engaging in environmentally harmful production activities to meet their basic needs (e.g., Offe, 1992). This argument is plausible, but one must not forget that the other side is also true – namely, the Basic Income Guarantee makes it possible for people to consume products that might be environmentally unfriendly without having to conduct work that would otherwise be environmentally beneficial. An issue that is not often addressed in discussions about production and the environment is the environmental cost of transportation to work. Many people commute to and from work by car, which is one of the most environmentally damaging of all activities. This is true even in an era when emissions from cars are heavily regulated. Emissions such as hydrocarbons, sulphur dioxide, nitrogen oxides, carbon monoxide, and carbon dioxide cause major damage to the environment and to public health. If a Basic Income Guarantee resulted in a net reduction in labour supply, this might lead to a net reduction in the distances travelled in cars. On the other side of the coin, the Basic Income Guarantee provides people with more disposable income with which they can purchase more environmentally damaging forms of transportation.

Overall, whereas some people might use their Basic Income to live Thoreau's simple life, others might choose to live the most environmentally costly lifestyle that a Basic Income can afford them. Since the Basic Income Guarantee does not regulate what people can spend their income on, the aggregate effect of a Basic Income Guarantee is not unambiguously towards a lower environmental impact. One cannot, as a consequence, conclude that a Basic Income Guarantee is an environmental policy in itself. It is therefore better thought of as a tool to aid environmental policies.

As Chapters 1 and 2 have revealed, one of the great debates about environmental policies concerns the allegation that they will 'cost jobs.' In our opinion, this allegation is not necessarily true. Better environmental policies may simply involve only a shift of employment into more environmentally friendly occupations, although the allegation of jobs losses is plausible at least in the short run. Nevertheless, jobs are not the measure of the health of a society. The most important function of an economic system is to make sure everyone has enough food to eat, adequate shelter, clothing, a meaningful life, and a sustainable future. A job does not ensure that a person has any of these things, nor is it essential to having all of these things. The Basic Income Guarantee can ensure that everyone has access to basic necessities such as food, shelter, and clothing, and it also provides access to resources with which to pursue a meaningful life. It does so whether or not environmental policies cause disruptions in the labour market.

Ecological tax reform – to be discussed in Part IV of the book – can be used to discourage pollution and the depletion of natural resources without forcing the poor to suffer the greatest costs of such a policy. Ecological tax reform can be combined with a Basic Income Guarantee both to lessen the impact of the cost of the taxes on the poor and to reflect the collective claim that society has on the scarcity rents which ordinarily accrue to the owners of resources. If, for example, firms pay a heavy tax for pollution, they have an incentive to avoid polluting in the first place. If firms pay a heavy tax for the ore they mine or the forests they deplete, they have an incentive to use less of these resources and to recycle what is already in use. If landowners pay a heavy tax on the value of land, they have an incentive to build more compact and manageable cities. However, these taxes also create an incentive for firms to pass on the added cost to consumers. If all else is equal, the relative cost of such taxes is greater for those with the lower incomes. However, if the revenue from these taxes is distributed equally to all citizens in the form of a Basic Income Guarantee, they provide a net gain to anyone who has less than average impact on the environment and a net cost for anyone who has a greater than average impact on the environment.

Estimates of how much revenue can be raised from such taxes vary between 2 per cent and 30 per cent of GDP. Whereas the lower end of the scale is far less than would be needed to support a Basic Income Guarantee, the upper end is more than enough. Encouraging evidence does exist in relation to the Alaska Permanent Fund. The state of Alaska has a small Basic Income Guarantee supported by a fund created out of the state's oil revenues. Each Alaskan resident usually receives between $1,000 and $2,000 a year from this fund. This is not enough to live on, but $8,000 a year makes a big difference to a family of four living on the margin. Alaska has enormous oil wealth but this fund was created from just one-eighth of the state's oil taxes, which are low by international standards. If a fund were created out of all oil taxes plus similar taxes on other mining, pollution, land values, the use of the broadcast spectrum, and other activities, a great deal more revenue could be raised, quite possibly enough to support a substantial Basic Income Guarantee.

However, there are political risks associated with this kind of policy. People might become more willing to permit greater depletion of natural resources, particularly if they are being paid from the proceeds it generates. The taxes would have to be seen as something to help preserve resources for future generations, not simply to raise revenue for the current generation. Another potential problem is the contradiction that lies in financing a policy that society desires by means of taxing activities it would rather discourage. If taxes effectively discourage polluting activities, they would reduce the revenue for the Basic Income Guarantee. If the goal of such a policy is to reduce environmental degradation, with minimal cost to the poor, such a situation would mean that the goal was successfully achieved. But the goal is also to provide a guaranteed income support for the poor. Hence, the better the policy achieves one goal, the less successful it is at achieving the other.

Conclusion

Programmes which require the poor to prove their worth by demonstrating a willingness to accept employment require the government to spend large amounts of money on things other than direct payments to the poor. This is an inefficiency in itself that is also compounded by a second inefficiency which can emerge if selection errors result in people falling through the cracks of the welfare system. The Basic Income Guarantee has no cracks to fall through. It involves a simple, effective payment system which assists the needy without wasting funds on support structures. Therefore, in our view, if we want poverty reduction to be the central goal of poverty-alleviation policies, the Basic Income Guarantee is the most efficient means of achieving it.

We also believe that the biggest barrier to a more effective poverty-alleviation policy is the predilection that modern society has for judging the poor, which invariably penalises a great number of honest yet needy people. Currently, US law requires those on welfare to work in return for the benefits they receive although it limits the time recipients are eligible to receive such benefits to five years over one's lifetime. We are doubtful whether this approach will do much to curtail poverty. In fact, we believe it might actually exacerbate it. As more people are pushed off the welfare rolls, they face increased pressure to compete in the labour market, putting downward pressure on wages. Thus, at best, the welfare reform laws might simply swell the ranks of the working poor who have already endured 30 years of stagnating material standards of living at a time when significant GDP growth has substantially increased the material standards of living of the wealthier classes.

Anyone who believes that, above all else, work can provide workers with a better life should be distressed by this evidence. It is not necessary for poverty to exist to the extent that it does in a country as wealthy as the United States. If the goal is to eliminate poverty, the Basic Income Guarantee is the most comprehensive means to achieving it. In the end, the issue is a normative one. Should society be so committed to the work ethic that it forces the poor to work at poverty wages? If the answer is yes, is society not putting enforcement of a very strong version of the work ethic ahead of a shared desire to possess an economy that provides a decent life for everyone? We should instead adopt the position that eliminating poverty is important enough for everyone to deserve the resources required to meet their basic needs. With a Basic Income Guarantee in place, there is still plenty of scope to provide adequate work incentives by ensuring there is a sufficient supply of good quality jobs. There is no need to force people into poverty-maintaining forms of work by using destitution as the penalty for not working. Society should certainly reward the work ethic, but it should never enforce the work ethic.

Notes

1 Medical care, though important to one's standard of living, we treat as a separate issue.
2 Neoclassical economists regard *work* as time spent doing something in return for a money wage. Non-market labour, such taking care of children, is not considered work from this point of view. But even though something is not considered work or labour, as most economists define it, it would be a mistake to assume, therefore, that it is not socially valuable.

References

Atkinson, A. B. (1983), *The Economics of Inequality*, New York: Oxford University Press.

Becker, G. (1993), *Human Capital*, Chicago: The University of Chicago Press.

Dolgoff, R., Feldstein, D., and Skolnik, L. (1993), *Understanding Social Welfare*, New York: Longman.

Ehrenberg, R. and Smith, R. (1994), *Modern Labor Economics: Theory and Public Policy*, New York: HarperCollins College Publishers.

Ellwood, D. T. (1988) *Poor Support*, New York: Basic Books.

Garfinkel, I. and McLanahan, S. (1986) *Single Mothers and their Children: A New American Dilemma*, Washington, DC: Urban Institute Press.

Godish, T. (2000), *Air Quality,* New York: Lewis Publishers.

Handler, J. and Hasenfeld, Y. (1997), *We the Poor: Work, Poverty and Welfare*, New Haven, CT: Yale University Press.

Harrison, B. and Bluestone, B. (1990), *The Great U-Turn*, New York: Basic Books.

Harvey, P. (1989), *Securing the Right to Full Employment: Social Welfare Policy and the Unemployed in the United States*, Princeton, NJ: Princeton University Press.

House Committee on Ways and Means (1992), *Overview of Entitlement Programs: Green Book*, Washington, DC: US Government Printing Office.

Kelso, W. (1994), *Poverty and the Underclass: Changing Perceptions of the Poor in America*, New York: New York University Press.

Kim, M. (1997), 'The working poor: lousy jobs or lazy workers?', Jerome Levy Economics Institute of Bard College Working Paper No. 194.

Lapman, R. (1965), 'Approaches to the reduction of poverty', *American Economic Review*, 55, 521–529.

Lord, C. (2003), *A Citizens Income: A Foundation for a Sustainable World*, Oxfordshire: John Carpenter Publishing.

Magnet, M. (1993), *The Dream and the Nightmare: The Sixties' Legacy to the Underclass*, New York: William Morrow and Company Inc.

Mayer, S. (1997), *What Money Can't Buy*, Cambridge, MA: Harvard University Press.

Mead, L. (1986), *Beyond Entitlement: The Limits of Benevolence*, New York: Free Press.

Minsky, H. (1986), *Stabilizing an Unstable Economy*, New Haven, CT: Yale University Press.

Mishel, L. and Bernstein, J. (1994) *The State of Working America: 1994–1995*, New York: M. E. Sharpe.

Munday, S. (1996), *Current Developments in Economics*, New York: St. Martin's Press.

Murray, C. (1984), *Losing Ground: American Social Policy 1950–1980*, New York: Basic Books.

Offe, C. (1992), 'A non-productivist design for social policies', in P. Van Parijs (ed.), *Arguing for Basic Income*, London: Verso, pp. 61–78.

Pearce, D. (1978), 'The feminization of poverty: women, work, and welfare', *Urban Sociological Change*, 2, 128–136.

Rose, N. (1994), *Put to Work: Relief Programs in the Great Depression*, New York: Monthly Review Press.

Saving, J. (1997), 'Tough love: implications for redistributive policy', *Economic Review*, The Federal Reserve Board of Dallas, Third Quarter, 2 October.

Schiller, B. (1989), *The Economics of Poverty and Discrimination*, Upper Saddle River, NJ: Prentice Hall.

Schwarz, J. and Volgy, T. (1992), *The Forgotten Americans*, New York: W. W. Norton and Company, Inc.

Smith, A. (1976), *An Inquiry into the Nature and Causes of the Wealth of Nations*, Oxford: Oxford University Press.

Tanner, M. (1996), *The End of Welfare: Fighting Poverty in the Civil Society*, Washington, DC: Cato Institute.

US Department of Labor/Bureau of Statistics (2004), *A Profile of the Working Poor, 2002, Report 976*, www.bls.gov.cps/cpswp2002.pdf.

Van Parijs, P. (2004), 'Basic income: a simple and powerful idea for the twenty-first century,' *Politics and Society*, 3, 1, 7–39.

Wilson, W. (1996), *When Work Disappears: The World of the New Urban Poor*, New York: Vintage Books.

Wray, R. (1998), *Understanding Modern Money*, Northampton, MA: Edward Elgar.

Zastro, C. (1986), *Introduction to Social Welfare*, Homewood, IL: Dorsey Press.

7 Evaluating the economic and environmental viability of Basic Income and Job Guarantees

Pavlina R. Tcherneva

Introduction

Basic Income and Job Guarantees are two proposals in the public interest, which rest on the conviction that universal and unconditional policies are more effective and fair than targeted and means-tested programmes. Supporters of these proposals consider modern welfare and labour market policies to be inequitable and inefficient, and therefore advocate an open-ended commitment to guarantee the right to livelihood for all individuals. Both policies aim to enhance individual freedom, economic opportunities, democratic citizenship, and promote social inclusion via poverty eradication, human capital investment, community revitalisation, and environmental renewal. How to reach these goals, however, is vigorously contested.

Briefly, Basic Income supporters see modern economies as moving towards increasingly precarious labour markets and argue that jobs cannot be the answer to a better life (Aronowitz and DiFazio, 1994). In addition, whereas some individuals are exempt from having to work (thanks to inheritance, for example), others are compelled to work, often in 'bad' jobs, for their livelihood. Therefore, it is argued that any social policy which enhances *real freedom* must give individuals equal access to nature's endowments via a guaranteed income but without the coercion to work for it (Van Parijs, 1995). Such a policy would further emancipate them from obligatory employment by empowering them to say 'no' to demeaning or compulsory labour (Widerquist, 2004). In this sense, capitalism is viewed as inherently unjust, in large part because of the dependency on work for income. Thus, the core objective of the Basic Income policy is to sever the link between the two.

By contrast, Job Guarantee supporters argue that Basic Income advocates have misconstrued the problem of income insecurity (Harvey, 2003; Mitchell and Watts, 2004). A well-structured guaranteed employment that offers opportunities for meaningful work at a living wage counters the precariousness of the labour market by eliminating unemployment, drastically reducing poverty, and enhancing the individual freedom to say 'no' to bad jobs. In other words, in a monetary market economy, many of the observed labour market problems stem from an insufficient quantity and quality of jobs. Only after the right to work has been secured for all can we adequately evaluate the failures of the market and welfare policies (Harvey, 2003). Securing the right to work is the over-riding objective for Job Guarantee advocates.

Some important criticisms have been levelled at the economic viability of Basic Income proposals. The main charge is that they are inherently inflationary with potentially disastrous consequences for a nation's currency. Additionally, the strong destabilising effect of Basic Incomes on labour markets and wages makes the policy potentially stagflationary and hyperinflationary (Mitchell and Watts, 2004; Tcherneva 2006a).

The goal of this chapter is therefore threefold. First, it explores the macroeconomic viability of each programme in the context of modern, monetary, production economies. Second, it elaborates on their environmental merits. Finally, in the hope of consensus building, it advances a joint policy proposal that is economically viable, environmentally friendly, and socially just.

Can we pay for Basic Income or Job Guarantees?

Throughout this chapter, two specific policy proposals will be discussed. The first is the Basic Income Guarantee (BIG) and involves a universal payment to each citizen irrespective of race, gender, marital status, or labour market participation, which is set at a level sufficient to afford everyone the basic material standard of living.[1] The second is the Job Guarantee proposal, which offers a federally funded job to anyone ready, willing, and able to work but who has not found desired private sector employment. It provides a living wage and decent working conditions. The programme is modelled after the following proposals: the public service employment (PSE) scheme; the government acting as an employer of last resort (ELR); and the buffer stock employment (BSE) model.[2]

False notions of public finance are perhaps the single most important obstacle to implementing important government policies. Much has been written on how governments can finance Basic Income and Job Guarantees.[3] Such discussion is technically relevant only for countries which have given up sovereign control over their currencies (e.g., where the currency is under the control of a currency board or some other fixed exchange rate regime). Sovereign currency nations, which the majority of the countries in the world are, do not face operational financing constraints. To be sure, they face political constraints, which could be shaken off with full appreciation of the workings of sovereign currencies. Although the ideology of the 'tax-payer's money' is entrenched in all contemporary discourse, it is crucial to dispel its false premises and to understand adequately the nature of the universal guarantees. This is the purpose of this section.

There is a large body of literature that has examined the principles of sovereign finance.[4] Three specific tenets need to be emphasised here. First, taxation and spending are always two independent operations but, under flexible exchange rate regimes, the former does not and cannot finance the latter. A sovereign currency nation can always pay for its public programmes of choice, be they Basic Income or Job Guarantees, or any other programme, irrespective of tax collections. This does not mean, however, that tax collections are unimportant.

The second point to emphasise is that, although money emission does not depend on taxes, tax collections are crucially important for maintaining the viability of the currency. In fact, in monetary production economies, the value of the currency is linked to what one must do to obtain it (for repayment of taxes or other obligations), and the public sector can directly set its terms of exchange and, in doing so, affect its value. Third, in a modern market economy, unemployment is always and everywhere a monetary phenomenon that can be effectively addressed with a proper application of sovereign finance.

Sovereign currency control

A common mistake made by many observers is to conflate government with non-government finance. Whereas the private sector is indeed restricted by revenue or by borrowing for its spending, this is not the case for the public sector since it 'finances' its expenditures in its own money. This simply reflects the single-supplier (or currency monopoly) status of a central government. As the tax-driven approach to money has made clear, the purpose of taxation is not to 'finance' state spending, but rather to create a demand for the currency of the sovereign. In modern economies, such as in the United States, the United Kingdom, and Japan, the currency (the dollar, the pound, and the yen, respectively) is not a 'limited' resource of the government (Mosler, 1997–1998: 169). The consolidated government (with the treasury and the central bank as its agents) conducts its spending by crediting private bank accounts. It taxes the private sector by debiting them. Thus, taxation functions not to finance government spending but to create demand for otherwise unbacked state currencies. This way, the money-issuing authority can purchase requisite goods and services from the private sector. Taxation is, in a sense, a vehicle for moving resources from the private to the public domain.

If the purpose of taxation is to create demand for state money then, logically and operationally, tax collections cannot occur until the government has provided that which it demands for payment of taxes. In other words, not only are spending and taxation two entirely independent operations, but the former must necessarily precede the latter. Another way of seeing this causality is to say that government spending 'finances' private sector 'tax payments' and not vice versa.[5]

In sum, sovereign governments have a public monopoly over the domestic currency. Government spending precedes taxation whereas spending always creates new high-powered money (HPM). Taxation, on the other hand, always destroys HPM. Therefore taxes are never stockpiled and cannot be re-spent to 'finance' future expenditures. This also means that a government's budget status is an *ex post* accounting result. A 'budget-neutral' policy aims to gauge some subsequent accounting result but provides no a priori knowledge of the economic consequences of that policy.

Although governments may not be operationally constrained in their spending, it is crucially important what programmes they choose to finance. As sole suppliers of a fiat currency, they also have the responsibility for maintaining its value, and certain policies are better suited to doing this than others.

The value of the currency

Taxes not only create private sector demand for government money, but also impart value to it. Innes (1913: 165) stresses that: 'A dollar of money is a dollar, not because of the material of which it is made, but because of the dollar of tax which is imposed to redeem it.' He also argues that 'the more government money there is in circulation, the poorer we are' (161). In other words, if government money in circulation far exceeds the total tax liability, the value of the currency will fall (i.e., inflation will take place). Thus, it is not only the requirement to pay taxes, but also the difficulty of obtaining that which settles the tax obligation, that gives money its value.

This important relationship between leakages and injections of HPM is difficult to gauge. Since the currency is the product of a public monopoly, the government has a direct method at its disposal for determining a currency's value. For Knapp, payments with state fiat measure a certain number of units of value (Knapp, [1924] 1973: 7–8). For example, if the state required that, to obtain one unit of HPM, a person must supply one hour of labour, then money will be worth exactly that – one hour of labour (Wray 2003: 104). Thus, as a monopoly issuer of the currency, the state can determine the value of the latter by setting 'unilaterally the terms of exchange that it will offer to those seeking its currency' (Forstater and Mosler, 1999: 174).[6]

What this means is that the state has the power to exogenously set the price at which it will provide HPM – i.e., the price at which it buys assets and goods and services from the private sector. Although it is hardly desirable for the state to set the prices of all goods and services it purchases, it nonetheless has this prerogative. As will be discussed later, through the Job Guarantee, the money monopolist need only set *one* price to anchor the value of its currency. By contrast, the Basic Income Guarantee does not set any terms of exchange for the sovereign currency; instead, it provides it unconditionally.

Unemployment is a monetary phenomenon

The last point to make in this section is that unemployment is a monetary phenomenon. This has been well demonstrated by Keynes in the *General Theory*, but the tax-driven approach to money sheds new light on what Keynes meant by 'money is a bottomless sink of purchasing power . . . [and] there is no value for it at which demand [for it] is diverted . . . into a demand for other things' (Keynes, 1936: 231).

Government deficit spending necessarily results in increased private sector holdings of net financial assets. If the non-government sector chronically desires to save more than it invests (i.e., run a budget surplus), the result will be a widening demand gap (Wray, 1998: 83). This demand gap cannot be filled by other private sector agents because, in order for some people to increase their holdings of net savings, others must decrease theirs. In the aggregate, an increase in the desire to net save can be accommodated only by an increase in government deficit spending. Mosler explains:

> Unemployment occurs when, in aggregate, the private sector wants to work and earn the monetary unit of account, but does not want to spend all it would earn (if fully employed) on the current products of industry . . . Involuntary unemployment is evidence that the desired holding of net financial assets of the private sector exceeds the actual [net savings] allowed by government fiscal policy.
>
> (Mosler, 1997–98: 176–177)

Similarly, Wray concludes that

> unemployment is *de facto* evidence that the government's deficit is too low to provide the level of net saving desired. In a sense, unemployment keeps the value of the currency, because it is a reflection of a position where the government has kept the supply of fiat money too scarce.
>
> (Wray, 1998: 84)

Although mainstream economists argue that governments must force slack on the economy in order to maintain the purchasing power of the currency, as this chapter will explain, well-designed full employment policies can do the job.

To sum up, a sovereign government is not operationally constrained in terms of funding public programmes. But the money monopolist also has the responsibility of maintaining the value of the currency. Because, at present, it does not set the terms of exchange for its currency, it uses unemployment to maintain its purchasing power. Unemployment is a monetary phenomenon and a reflection of keeping the currency too scarce. With this in mind, we can evaluate the economic impacts of implementing Basic Income and Job Guarantees.

Macroeconomic consequences of the Basic Income Guarantee

A focal point of the Basic Income proposal is its budget-neutral stance (Atkinson, 1995; Van Parijs, 2004). Such an analysis presumably stems from efforts to quash neoliberal objections to government deficit spending (Mitchell and Watts, 2004: 8). This section argues that a preoccupation with budget neutrality is wrong-headed for two reasons. First, it obfuscates the inflationary nature of a BIG by relying on conventional notions of public finance. Second, because taxes are largely endogenous, attempts to 'raise' sufficient tax revenue to counterbalance the increased spending on a BIG are likely to be self-defeating with perverse macroeconomic effects.

Inflation: an inherent feature of the BIG

As the tax-driven approach to money makes clear, taxes impart value to the currency by creating demand for it. Additionally, a currency's value is determined by what is required to obtain it. In the case of a BIG, there is no such requirement, since income payments are disbursed universally and unconditionally. If a programme is instituted whereby the population can obtain freely the unit which fulfils the tax obligation, the value of the currency will deteriorate sharply. Although this may not happen immediately, over time the value of an unconditionally provided currency will ultimately tend to zero. It must be stressed that the Basic Income is inflationary not because it is financed by 'fiat' money but because the currency is essentially 'free' (Tcherneva and Wray, 2005a) and is supplied on demand to all. Therefore, it effectively invalidates the purpose of taxation – to create demand for the government's currency. We can then easily envision a scenario in which the currency loses its value and private sector agents re-price their transactions in terms of some other (stronger) currency. History is replete with such examples: the inability to collect income and corporate taxes in Russia in the late 1990s; the provision of 'free' currency through uncollateralised lending in Eastern Europe during the transition period; and the accelerating interest rate payments on public debt in Turkey in the 1990s. In each case, the policy instituted resulted in a collapsing domestic currency and the 'flight' to stronger foreign currencies (for details, see Mitchell, 2002; Hudson, 2003; Tcherneva, 2006a).

It is not only the fact that the currency is free that produces a destabilising effect. A Basic Income Guarantee that buys the minimum standard of living (suppose that amount is equal to $20,000 in the United States) will cause an exodus of those workers in the labour force who previously 'earned' their minimum standard of living by working. In other words, workers in most $20,000-paying jobs will opt out of the labour force, especially if they are 'bad' jobs. Given this, the next issue to investigate is the impact of Basic Income Guarantees on labour force participation and economic activity.

The impact of the BIG on government budgets, wages, prices, and the labour force

Since tax collections are largely endogenous, the preoccupation with the budget neutrality of BIG policies can produce tax schedules that may have perverse market effects. In fact, it may prove impossible for the BIG proposal to remain budget neutral.

Some have proposed, for example, that the Basic Income Guarantee be 'financed' by a flat tax (Atkinson, 1995; Clark, 2004). It is reasonable to expect that a guaranteed Basic Income of $20,000 will induce some people in 'bad' $20,000-paying jobs to exit the market – a desirable effect, according to BIG advocates. The resulting impact on employment, income, and tax collections will be negative. As tax revenues fall, a budget deficit results and, although the deficit does not pose a problem in itself, the compulsion will be to raise tax rates to achieve the originally intended budget neutrality. This tax increase will induce a new cohort of workers previously earning an after-tax income of $20,000, but now earning less than $20,000 because of the tax increase, to leave the labour market to live off the BIG benefit. All additional tax increases that are imposed to recoup the cost of rising BIG payments will further erode employment and output (again, with a logical limit of zero).

If taxes are progressive, as advocated by Aronowitz and Cutler (1998) and Aronowitz and DiFazio (1994), this substitution effect may take somewhat longer to materialise. However, if they are regressive, as proposed by Van Parijs (1995) and Meade (1989), the labour force drop-out rate will be considerably higher, since regressive taxes carry larger disincentives to work in low-wage jobs. In any event, the BIG will be unlikely to achieve budget neutrality because tax collections are endogenous and forever unable to catch up with the rising BIG benefit payments.

The impact on the labour force and output is also negative. This seemingly 'voluntary' exit from the labour force is the BIG's solution to unemployment. This is a contrived result, however, as full employment is achieved by conceiving an artificial reduction in the labour supply (Mitchell and Watts, 2004: 13). In effect, full employment takes the form of 'forced inactivity'. In order to coax BIG recipients back into the labour market, some employers will need to offer higher wages. At first approximation, this appears to be a desirable effect. However, soon thereafter, the same employers will also raise prices to cover their increasing wage costs. As a consequence, rising prices will erode the purchasing power of the BIG payment and undermine the economic conditions of its recipients. To maintain the objective of the universal guarantee and to provide a minimum necessary standard of living, there will be pressure to revise the BIG benefit upward. Such a move will induce an additional exit of workers from the labour market, lower output levels, and lead to another compensatory rise in wages and prices. The latter, of course, will further reduce the BIG's purchasing power. This vicious cycle renders the income guarantee self-defeating. Note that, if the benefit is continually increased, the income guarantee becomes not just inflationary, but hyperinflationary.

Consider the impact if the government continues to increase taxes to achieve budget neutrality. Workers remaining on the margins of the labour market will exit the labour force. This will further reduce the labour force participation rate and leads to increasingly lower output, lower employment, and much higher prices than before the BIG was implemented. Should policy-makers continually increase the BIG to compensate recipients for the loss of purchasing power and simultaneously increase taxes to 'fund' the ensuing rise in expenditures, the likely result is stagflation – the dreaded combination of low employment and high prices.[7]

Since the BIG never quite manages to give people the purchasing power necessary to meet their basic material requirements, some individuals will be forced back into the labour market, quite possibly into 'bad' jobs. Hence the implementation of BIG is likely to produce an environment characterised by involuntary unemployment and higher prices.

In sum, we have to be mindful of how the government supplies the currency to the population. Misconceptions about public finance produce unwarranted attempts to achieve a budget-neutral BIG, which serves only to gauge some *ex post* accounting identity but says nothing about the impact of the BIG on economic performance.[8]

Macroeconomic effects of the employer of last resort

Keynes argued that 'unemployment develops . . . because people want the moon; men cannot be employed when the object of desire (i.e., money) is something which cannot be produced and the demand for which cannot be readily choked off' (Keynes, 1936: 235). As the tax-driven approach to money further makes clear, unemployment results from the chronic desire of some private sector agents to hoard net financial assets – a desire which can only be accommodated by the public sector. Minsky (1986) recognised that unemployment was a monetary phenomenon and indicated how desired financial resources can be supplied by simultaneously implementing a successful full employment strategy. For Minsky, it is the role of government to divorce the determination of full employment from the profitability of hiring. This can be accomplished only when the government creates an infinitely elastic demand for labour (Minsky 1986: 308).

Lerner (1943: 9) also argued that it was the government's job to keep spending 'neither greater nor less than that rate which at the current prices would buy all the goods that it is possible to produce.' Spending below this level results in unemployment, whereas spending above it causes inflation. The goal is to always keep government spending at the 'right' level to ensure full employment and price stability.

Two policies, virtually identical in design, which embrace Minsky's full employment strategy and Lerner's functional finance approach are the employer of last resort (ELR) proposal (Mosler, 1997–98; Wray, 1998) and the buffer stock employment model (Mitchell, 1998).[9] These policy prescriptions aim to eliminate unemployment and simultaneously stabilise the value of the currency. The proposals are motivated by the recognition that sovereign states have no operational financial constraints, can discretionarily set one important price in the economy, and can provide an infinitely elastic demand for labour.

Through the ELR, the government sets only the price of public sector labour, allowing all other prices to be determined in the market (Mosler, 1997–1998: 175). The fixed public sector wage provides a sufficiently stable benchmark for the value of the currency (Wray 1998: 131). Since governments are not fiscally constrained, the programme is implemented on a fixed-price/floating-quantity rule – namely, the hiring of labour in the ELR is not limited by budget caps, and spending on the ELR fluctuates counter-cyclically. Therefore, the key macroeconomic merits of the ELR, which are missing from BIG proposals, are its ability to stabilise the business cycle as well as the value of the currency and the overall price level. We shall now consider these macroeconomic benefits of the ELR in more detail.

The ELR stabilises the business cycle

With the Job Guarantee, government spending on public employment fluctuates counter-cyclically. During downturns in the business cycle, when private business establishments shed workers, the unemployed labour is able to find employment in the public sector. Government spending automatically increases, thereby providing the necessary economic stimulus to ensure full employment is maintained. Conversely, as the economy improves, and private sector employment expands, workers are lured away from the ELR pool, thus reducing government deficit spending. This counter-cyclical spending behaviour serves as a powerful automatic stabiliser that ensures government spending is always at the 'right' level to maintain full employment. By contrast, the Basic Income Guarantee has a destabilising effect on the business cycle due to its inflationary bias and the negative impact on labour force participation rates and aggregate output.

The ELR fixes the value of currency

Since the value of the currency is determined by what must be done to obtain it, with an ELR in place, it is linked to the public sector wage. Suppose the government pays an ELR employee $20,000 per year (for approximately 2,000 hours of work). The value of the currency will be anchored by the effort expended to earn this income. That is, the benchmark value of the currency will be $10 per hour of work. Now, suppose the government decides to pay $40,000 to ELR workers. The hourly wage jumps from $10 to $20 per hour. It now takes workers half the time to earn what they previously earned before the increase in the ELR wage. All else being equal, the purchasing power of the currency falls by half (i.e., $10 now purchases half an hour of work). By contrast, if the government cuts the yearly salary to $10,000, workers will need to work twice as much to obtain the same amount in dollars, which raises the value of the currency.

Purchasing power is measured in terms of the labour units the currency can buy. As with the BIG, the implementation of an ELR will cause a one-time jump in prices. However, since the purchasing power of the currency is tied to the labour hours it can buy, and thus its value does not deteriorate progressively as it does with BIG, there is no imperative to continually redefine the wage upward. The public sector wage provides an internally stable benchmark for prices.

The ELR enhances price stability

Policies of 'priming the pump', such as military Keynesianism, are inflationary, since they primarily hire 'off the top' of the labour pool by competing with the private sector for the most desirable workers (Wray 1998: 179). The ELR, by contrast, hires 'from the bottom' of the labour pool and thus prevents inflationary pressures from building. In fact, the ELR enhances price stability for two main reasons. First, the ELR is a buffer stock programme, which operates on a fixed-price/floating-quantity rule. Second, deficit spending on public service employment is always set at the right level (i.e., never more than the level necessary to ensure full employment is maintained).

The ELR is a buffer stock programme operating on a fixed-price/floating-quantity rule

Economists usually fear that high levels of employment can introduce uncontrollable wage-price spirals. It is therefore necessary to show how the ELR contributes to wage stability, which, in turn, promotes price stability. As Mitchell (1998) and Wray (1998) have stressed, the key is that the ELR is designed as a buffer stock programme and that it operates on a fixed price/floating quantity rule. The idea of the rule is to utilise labour as a buffer stock so that, like any buffer stock commodity, the programme will stabilise the commodity's price.

In a nutshell, during recessions, jobless workers find employment in the public sector at the fixed ELR wage. Total government spending rises to relieve deflationary pressures. Alternatively, when the economy recovers and non-government demand for labour increases, ELR workers are drawn back into private sector jobs at a premium over the ELR wage. Government spending automatically contracts, thereby relieving any inflationary pressures that might ensue. In other words, when there is an upward pressure on the buffer stock's price, the commodity is sold (i.e., ELR workers return to the private sector), and when there are deflationary forces at work it is bought (i.e., unemployed labour is hired under the ELR scheme). Public sector employment thus acts as a buffer stock that shrinks and expands counter-cyclically.

The ELR programme operates on a fixed-price/floating-quantity rule because the price of the buffer stock (the ELR wage) is fixed and the quantity of the commodity (public sector employment) is allowed to float. The exogenous public sector wage is internally stable and, since labour is a basic commodity (employed directly and indirectly in the production of every commodity type), it serves as a perfect benchmark for all other commodity prices.[10] It is in this sense that the public sector wage provides a stable anchor for prices in the economy. This important inbuilt feature of the ELR programme has no comparable counterpart in income guarantee proposals.

Deficit spending on the ELR is always at the right level

The buffer stock feature of the ELR ensures that government spending is, as Lerner had originally instructed, always at the 'right' level. The tax-driven approach to money explains why there is nothing inherently wrong with government budget deficits.[11] For ELR advocates, the 'right' level of deficit spending is that which ensures full employment, and no more. Furthermore, because of its counter-cyclical nature, the Job Guarantee programme also ensures that deficit spending will counteract inflationary or deflationary pressures, not create them.

Inflation and deflation occur when aggregate demand is either too large or too small relative to aggregate production and the productive capacity of the economy. The key to offsetting these pressures is to boost income and spending to the level sufficient to purchase the entire full employment level of output – no more and no less. By design, the ELR programme guarantees that any resulting budget deficit is never too big or too small. Government spending will increase until unemployment is eliminated, at which point deficits cease growing, thereby ensuring that aggregate demand does not exceed the full employment level of aggregate supply. Conversely, if private sector unemployment grows once more, so does the deficit spending required to bring aggregate demand and the full employment level of output back into equilibrium. In other words, the automatic counter-cyclical and stabilising feature of the ELR programme guarantees that spending will grow only up to the full employment level of output.[12] By contrast, Basic Income programmes cannot claim any such countervailing force to demand-side inflationary pressure.

Employer of last resort projects also support a non-inflationary environment by enhancing human capital and private sector efficiency. Unlike the BIG, the ELR can directly provide for the maintenance and appreciation of human capital by ensuring that training and education are explicit features of any ELR programme. Furthermore, by addressing the problem of unemployment head-on, ELR also reduces the social and economic costs associated with it. Finally, private sector productivity is enhanced by directing ELR projects towards the development of public infrastructure and costly environmental rehabilitation, and by reducing production rigidities linked to high levels of capacity utilisation.

It has been increasingly recognised that public policies must enhance not only macroeconomic stabilisation but also environmental sustainability. The next section specifically focuses on the environmental merits of the BIG and ELR programmes.

Environmental aspects of the Basic Income and Job Guarantees

There is significant common ground that informs the environmental concerns of BIG and ELR advocates. Much of it rests on a rejection of contemporary growth-at-all-costs macroeconomic policies which lead to an unequal distribution of income, wasteful over-consumption in higher income cohorts, and poverty and destitution in lower cohorts.

Growth, income distribution, and the environment

Advocates of the ELR view policies which aggressively and indiscriminately aim to stimulate private investment as destabilising, inflationary, and environmentally damaging. Hence, the private sector is unable to guarantee the attainment and preservation of either full employment or environmental sustainability. For this reason, the public sector has an important role to play in addressing both objectives. The specific proposal advanced by most ELR supporters is that of 'green' public sector jobs (Forstater, 2004). For Basic Income supporters, on the other hand, eco-friendly outcomes spring naturally from: (a) the expected redistribution toward more equal incomes; (b) subsequent reductions in GDP growth rates;[13] and (c) the financing of the BIG through pollution and/or resource taxes. I will discuss growth and income distribution first and will return to eco-friendly taxes later.

Continuous growth rests on sustained and rising rates of economic expansion, increasing resource extraction, and their maximum utilisation. The underlying competitive forces of cost minimisation often imply large-scale industrial pollution (as environmental cleanup is expensive and unprofitable), and the uneven income distribution that accompanies modern pro-growth policies induces environmentally damaging activities among the poor (e.g., Haitian and Amazon deforestation). These forces are at odds with environmental sustainability since they ultimately lead to the 'tragedy of the commons' (Lord, 2003).

The BIG is expected to produce environmentally desirable outcomes by equalising the income distribution at the bottom of the income scale. It is therefore argued that the BIG would, for example, eliminate the need for indigenous people in Brazil to log the Amazon rainforests for subsistence. However, it is likely that the wasteful consumption at the top of the income scale would continue unimpeded unless there were both a considerable redistribution of income away from the rich and a decline in overall growth rates.

Advocates of the BIG also believe that growth in GDP would be checked by the fact that the BIG provides an opportunity for workers to withdraw from the labour market and engage instead in non-market activities – an outcome which some believe should be celebrated (e.g., Murray, 1997). If this is a likely scenario, all the negative consequences from a reduction in the labour force discussed above will apply with full force, making the BIG economically infeasible.

An important question to consider is whether the BIG would trigger eco-conscientiousness. For example, will the logging of the Amazon rainforests cease if a BIG is introduced in Brazil or will the BIG be treated as a source of extra income that could be used to boost consumption above and beyond what is afforded by the minimum guaranteed income? Will a BIG induce American consumers to buy more organic food and fewer sport-utility vehicles, or will the BIG simply enable the poor to join the queues for the next (now affordable) gas-guzzler? And in what way will the BIG encourage companies to opt for environmentally clean technology, especially in the face of rising labour costs caused by a mass exodus of workers from the labour force? None of the supposed environmental benefits envisaged by BIG proponents are guaranteed by the provision of a Basic Income. To be fair, BIG supporters have argued that the programme should be supplemented by other socially desirable policies (e.g., environmental regulations) but, in this case, any environmental benefits will stem from the regulations and not from the provision of the Basic Income. To this end, it is hard to believe that, in modern capitalist economies, the sole provision of income will set in motion an extraordinary chain of events that will entice individuals to voluntarily opt for 'simpler and more environmentally-friendly lifestyles', as it is argued, for example, in Van Parijs *et al.* (2001). The stark reality is that those with the simpler lifestyles are generally those who have no income. Access to a guaranteed income will allow these people to partake more actively in mainstream society and culture, which is likely to lead to more complex consumption patterns. In such circumstances, the environmental outcomes arising from the introduction of a BIG are ambiguous.

ELR proponents agree that creating jobs at any price – particularly, at the expense of the environment – is not a viable policy option. Minsky (1986) has long argued that getting to full employment by stimulating aggregate demand could lead to inequitable and destabilising outcomes, especially given that indiscriminate pump priming tends to be environmentally unsustainable, inflationary, and an overall unreliable means of achieving and maintaining full employment.

It seems that BIG advocates reject Job Guarantees largely because they falsely equate them with contemporary pro-growth, pro-investment, pro-profit practices. It is perhaps not well understood that ELR programmes are designed to decouple the determination of full employment from any specific level of GDP. At the margin, full employment is secured by the public sector directly hiring all who wish to work, and does not necessarily depend on GDP growth, aggregate demand, investment subsidies, or tax incentives. Growth in GDP is a consequence of, and not a precondition for, full employment. Furthermore, when ELR jobs are designed with the environment in mind, one is effectively redefining growth to include environmentally friendly output and employment.

Note that BIG proposals are still dependent on growth for the source of their financing (e.g., income taxes). Thus, the desire of BIG proponents to check growth is fundamentally at odds with the BIG's dependence on rising GDP to ensure it is adequately financed. Such a conundrum cannot be satisfactorily resolved. As argued above, nations with sovereign and freely floating currencies do not face operational financing constraints, and thus the financing of the BIG need not depend on a particular level of growth. But this is cold comfort for BIG supporters because the same tenets of modern finance immediately render their policy inflationary.

Furthermore, if the BIG indeed proves to be inflationary (or hyperinflationary), it will produce a more unequal income distribution as the poor opt out of 'bad' jobs to live on the Basic Income that, as a consequence of the rising price level, would gradually be eroded. In this case, it is likely that the poor will be anything but emancipated from compulsory work. Indeed, they are likely to be forced back into the labour market. In addition, even if the poor so desire, they may be unable to engage in more environmentally sensitive activities, such as buying locally grown food or ecologically friendly appliances, since most of them will be prohibitively expensive. If so, any environmentally friendly consequences that the access to a Basic Income might generate will evaporate along with the deflated real value of that income.

By contrast, the ELR does not depend on specific levels of GDP growth for its implementation, but stabilises the business cycle, enhances human capital, and improves the investment environment. In addition, its commitment to eco-friendly public service jobs contributes to environmental improvements. What an eco-friendly ELR programme looks like is explored in the next section.

Public service employment and the environment

Advocates of ELR are interested not only in offering unconditional employment, but also in structuring the programme in a way to addresses very specific economic concerns – namely, environmental degradation, urban blight, gender inequality, deficient elderly and childcare services, and inadequate training and education. The strong environmental concerns stem specifically from the acknowledgement that there is an immediate need to rehabilitate the environment and restore its health which, owing to its open access status, the private sector has no incentive to perform at the requisite level. ELR jobs should be part of a comprehensive programme to assist in achieving environmental sustainability and can be the first and immediate step toward environmental rehabilitation and conservation. Many of these tasks can be undertaken by relatively unskilled labour. Forstater (2004) has called for a 'Green Jobs Corps' as an important model for ELR work, whereby an environmental tax is incorporated explicitly in the proposal and a detailed application of eco-friendly tasks is advanced. Some of the ELR jobs would include reforestation, water, soil, and air restoration, aggressive recycling efforts at the local and national level, insulation and weatherproofing for residential and some commercial buildings, and the conversion to alternative energy of all public industries and institutions.

Separately, evidence is now emerging which shows that cities, municipalities, and nations alike are beginning and will continue to face increasing costs to their economies as they deal with the pressing issue of climate change (Stern, 2006). It has been predicted that moderate sea level increases caused by rising temperatures will inundate coastal regions, thus causing flooding, infrastructure damage, and the possible forced migration of hundreds of millions of people worldwide (Goodstein and Doppelt, 2006). Such large-scale problems will require a timely and comprehensive response. The recent experience in the United States with Hurricane Katrina has demonstrated that it is the public sector which must be best prepared to ameliorate these problems. An organised and ready public Jobs Corps could respond before, during, and after a crisis to minimise its impact. In the case of Hurricane Katrina, ELR workers, had they been available, could have fortified levies and evacuated residents in advance of the storm. Following the disaster, they could have reconstructed ports, piers, and other much needed infrastructure in both the devastated and healthy communities overwhelmed by migrating population. At the time, Vanden Heuvel (2005) called for a new 'New Deal' to rebuild New Orleans. Much of the work that would have been required could have been performed by ELR workers.

Infrastructure in many developed nations is crumbling. For example, in 2007, one-eighth of all highway bridges in the United States were structurally deficient and close to one-seventh were functionally obsolete (Department of Transportation, 2007). In much of the underdeveloped world, non-existent infrastructure is a major obstacle to economic development. An ELR programme can undertake repair and construction of infrastructure at the needed level. In sum, a well-structured ELR can ensure full employment which does not necessarily conflict with environmental goals. In fact, it can enhance the chances of achieving them.

Environmental aspects of the BIG

The environmentally friendly outcomes of a BIG policy are likely to emerge not from the provision of a guaranteed minimum income, but from the resource use and pollution taxes that the BIG's proponents advance as a means to financing it. There are already numerous policies which promote equitable land use and egalitarian resource allocation, including the Sky Trust, the Alaska Permanent Fund, and the Earth Dividend, just to name a few. Each of these represents either equal access by all citizens to Earth's resources (Earth Dividend) or equal access to the profits generated from exploiting these resources (Sky Trust and Alaska Permanent Fund). These programmes, however, are not the same as the BIG discussed in this chapter. Some scholars have proposed that the BIG should be financed through pollution or other ecological taxes (e.g., Van Parijs, 1995).

I would argue that the agenda for tax reform which BIG supporters advocate can be an essential feature of any policy for social reform. What BIG supporters must deal with is the fact that resource or pollution taxes do not suffice as financing instruments for the BIG. If the BIG supporters insist that pollution or any other resource or environmental taxes are required to 'pay' for the BIG programme, the policy will be self-defeating since resource-based taxes cannot be relied upon to provide an income that will afford the minimum necessary standard of living for all citizens.

To demonstrate this, consider the following. A resource-based tax aims to discourage the use of a particular resource. With regard to taxes on pollution or resource use, the most effective tax policy is one which manages to generate the least amount of revenue. That is, it is one which, as intended, deters pollution or depletion of the targeted resource. To therefore link the BIG to such a tax would mean either that: (a) when the tax is successful in protecting the environment, sufficient revenue is not generated to cover all recipients; or (b) the tax is ineffective, and more pollution and environmental abuse is taking place in order to generate sufficient revenue for the BIG coverage. In the latter case, especially if the BIG is very popular, there may even be a perverse incentive to encourage, for example, oil production so that its increased output can later be taxed to keep the BIG fund 'solvent'.

In sum, an environmental tax policy is an important policy objective, but it would be a mistake to structure either the BIG or the ELR so that it is dependent on ecological taxes for its financing. Of course, if a 'bad' resource is taxed (e.g., oil) and the funds are invested in a 'good' resource (e.g., solar or wind energy), then, over the long run, there will be a greater incentive to move from dirty to clean energy. But this is a case of good environmental policy, not an example of how to best secure the minimum required standard of living for all citizens, as has already been demonstrated by the Alaska Permanent Fund, for example, from which individual payments have never exceeded $2,000 per person annually. Such a 'fund' has proven to be an effective environmental policy, but not an effective Basic Income policy.[14] Again the proposition of this chapter is that, if the Basic Income cannot buy the minimum standard of living for all, the policy is neither effective nor just.

To summarise, as far as BIG supporters are concerned, the universal provision of a Basic Income is the over-riding objective and its 'green' consequences can be expected to ensue naturally. However, it seems more plausible that the environmental benefits of the BIG stem from the tax mechanisms proposed to finance it and not from the provision of income to all. By contrast, for ELR advocates, guaranteeing full employment is essential through targeted job creation into areas that repair, support, and enhance the environment. Eco-friendly activities are explicitly incorporated in the institutional setup of the ELR job programme. Since there are no operational constraints to the funding of either policy, tax reform for environmental purposes is an entirely different matter – a worthy goal in its own right.

The road to participation and the promise for a joint proposal

Since the objective is to provide for all members of society, and not just for the economically active population, a joint proposal is necessary. To be economically viable and environmentally friendly, however, the proposal needs to embody several key ingredients. First, it must tie the provision of income to public service work, in the form of fixed hourly wage. Second, it needs to provide unconditional income support for the young, the elderly, and the disabled. Third, it must be carefully structured to accommodate the biophysical conditions of the environment and to support environmental preservation, rehabilitation, and renewal.[15]

Such a proposal is desirable because individual human inactivity, especially due to involuntary unemployment, has far-reaching consequences beyond the single dimension of a loss of income (Sen, 1999: 94). Therefore, the BIG's focus on the provision of income alone will not provide the necessary remedy. By contrast, the ELR's concern with currency stability should not take precedence over the objective of creating 'good' jobs. Given the many common goals that income and Job Guarantees share, a joint proposal that is environmentally sustainable is a promising alternative for providing the requisite material standard of living to all.

There are many sources we can consult when designing such a proposal. For example, Atkinson's 'participation income' (1995) and White's 'civic minimum' (2003) offer some possibilities for marrying the ELR with the BIG.[16] These proposals emphasise the need to define work very broadly, foster social inclusion, enhance human capital, and improve the overall socio-economic situation (Clark, 2003; Fitzpatrick, 2003). Minsky's discussion of the 'the road to participation' also provides some of the ingredients for such a joint policy. For Minsky, the road to participation means creating permanent programmes whose main purpose is to provide 'public services, environmental improvements . . . as well as the creation and improvement of human resources' (Minsky, 1986: 312).

This chapter has explained the economic imperatives that make it necessary to tie the hourly income benefit to an hour of public work. Nonetheless, this coercive feature will still trouble BIG advocates. The challenge therefore remains to design a proposal which enhances individual freedom by allowing people to determine their own pursuits. One way to do this is to allow the individuals to choose, and even define, the kind of activities they wish to perform. Thus, although involvement in the community is compulsory, the kind of work performed is not.

To see how this can be accomplished, we can turn to the Job Guarantee programme that was recently implemented in Argentina.[17] Although this programme was available only to unemployed heads of households, it offers insights for designing a joint policy. The Argentinean programme (usually referred to as *Jefes*) was intended to deal with the massive poverty, unemployment, and social dislocation that resulted from the 2001–2002 economic crisis.

After the decision was made to fund the Job Guarantee, the Argentinean federal government provided the general guidelines for administering the programme. It devolved the actual management and administration of the programme to the local government level. The municipalities evaluated the general needs of their communities and their available resources. Subsequently, they made requests for proposals for specific projects that would provide the goods and services that were most needed in their communities.

The *Jefes* plan was, nevertheless, started as a form of Basic Income. After all the unemployed heads of households registered for the programme, they immediately started receiving income. In the early transition period, many recipients did not work since it took some time to design, approve, and implement the proposed projects. However, the programme was up and running in four months, and soon thereafter beneficiaries started taking up the newly created public sector jobs.

In fact, most of the actual activities were designed and proposed by NGOs, local government organisations, labour movements, and the unemployed themselves. Importantly, they were provided with the forum and institutional support to allow them to engage in activities of their own choice. Because nutrition was a top priority in the poorest communities, many such projects included community kitchens, bakeries, or pastry shops. Other projects involved conversion of previously barren plots into arable land, where the beneficiaries set up their own agro-cooperatives. Where pollution was a major concern, activities centred solely on landfill cleanup and recycling. Indeed, in some of the poorest areas, residents organised *en masse* to recycle cardboard and plastic from Buenos Aires's large garbage dumps. Some projects used recycled plastic to make toys and Christmas tree ornaments; others collected and repaired old and ragged books and clothes from wealthier neighbourhoods, which were then distributed to newly built community centres in the city's poorest neighbourhoods.

Official surveys of programme participants indicate that receipt of an income is not among the main reasons for satisfaction with the *Jefes* plan. Beneficiaries enjoy being in the programme because they have the opportunity 'do something', to work in a 'good environment', to 'help the community', and to 'learn' (Figure 7.1).

In other words, it is possible to design a programme that will guarantee an income to all, but will require able-bodied persons to participate in community work. Such a programme can be structured to give people considerable freedom (subject to some general guidelines) to determine the kind of community work they would like to perform. Such activities can include not only helping in the community, but also engaging in individual artistic pursuits. Programmes of this nature can also be motivated by concerns for the environment.

By marrying the participation income with the Job Guarantee, it is possible to design a policy which offers the institutional vehicle for achieving a wide range of desirable social goals. ELR jobs can be oriented to assist in achieving the objectives of environmental rehabilitation, reforestation, and recycling, to provide assistance to young parents with family planning, and to address issues of domestic violence, high school drop-out rates, and spousal and child abuse. In fact, Argentina already provides many examples of public sector projects that deal with all of the above. Once the institutional framework for community work is established, it can be directed to address other social problems as well.

Finally, a joint policy will enjoy prolonged success if motivated by an awareness that valuable work is not only that which is profitable, but also that which is socially useful and environmentally sustainable. In other words, the activities in this programme should be targeted toward adequate social provisioning and not toward profit-making. The 'production for use' in the public sector ought not to compete with the 'production for profit' of the private market. Government jobs should provide services that are presently outside the purview of profit-making enterprises (e.g., environmental rehabilitation, childcare, elderly care, homeless shelters, community kitchens, to name a few).

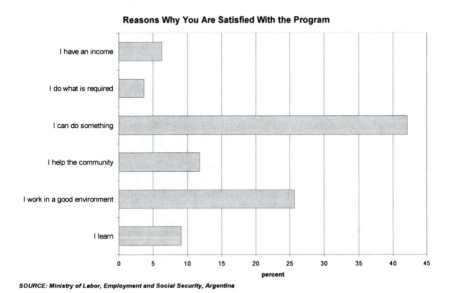

SOURCE: Ministry of Labor, Employment and Social Security, Argentina

Figure 7.1 Survey of participants of the Argentinean Jefes plan

Conclusion

The dichotomy between policies that target 'only income' or 'only employment' is no longer constructive. An effective safety net must provide both a guaranteed source of income and a guaranteed source of work opportunities in meaningful, life-enhancing activities. In a monetary production economy, however, it is important to tie the provision of income to participation in the community of everyone who is willing and able to contribute. But it should be confined to people who are able to contribute. This way, the socio-economic situation can be improved by creating an economically viable policy which stabilises the price level and the business cycle, while also enhancing the meaning of work and individual freedom.

Whether universal guarantees stand a chance depends largely on the political will and dominant ideology; however, the first step is to gain a full appreciation of their macroeconomic consequences and institutional aspects. Only then can we constructively move forward to design economically viable and environmentally friendly universal assurances in the public interest.

Notes

1 There are many incarnations of the Basic Income Guarantee. Partial Basic Income and the negative income tax (NIT), for example, will not be discussed here because they are, respectively, either deficient to buy the minimum standard of living or contingent on labour market participation. A full Basic Income, by contrast, is that which is set at the subsistence level (Van Parijs, 1992: 237 n27) or at the official poverty line (Clark, 2004), although, for Van Parijs, maximisation of individual opportunities and freedom requires that it be set at the *highest sustainable* level (Van Parijs, 1992, 1995, 2004).

2 There is broad general consensus over the purpose and design of these programmes (see, for example, Harvey, 1989; Wray, 1998; Mitchell, 1998). Although history is replete with direct job creation programmes, they tend to be of limited duration and subject to punitive means tests – two features which Job Guarantee supporters strongly oppose.

3 See, for example, debates between Clark (2003) and Harvey (2003).

4 This work is largely part of the modern money approach, also known as chartalism, neochartalism, tax-driven money, or money as a creature of the state. The approach is most closely associated with the writings of George F. Knapp ([1924] 1973) and Abba P. Lerner (1947), but finds support in much of the economic literature ranging from Adam Smith to Keynes. For a detailed survey of chartalism, see Tcherneva (2006b).

5 It has also been demonstrated that bonds also do not 'finance' government spending. Bond sales maintain the target interest rate by draining excess reserves of high-powered money (HPM), which have been created through government spending (Mosler, 1997–1998; Wray, 1998; Bell, 2000).

6 Wray (2003: 104) notes: 'If the state simply handed out HPM on request, its value would be close to zero as anyone could meet her tax liability simply by requesting HPM.'

7 Mitchell and Watts (2004: 13) also argue that stagflation is a likely result because of the expected income redistribution and deteriorating inducement to invest caused by the BIG policy.

8 See also Abba Lerner (1947), whose proposal for 'functional finance' upheld that policy should be guided not by antiquated notions of 'sound finance', but by the effect of finance on economic activity.

9   Employer of last resort (ELR) is Minsky's terminology, which is used throughout this paper as a generic term for direct Job Guarantees.

10 This is a key point. If a government attempted to use the price of something not always used in the production and delivery of goods and services to anchor the currency (e.g., silver), it would fail miserably.

11 In fact, if the non-government sector runs a surplus (i.e., hoards net financial assets), the government sector, by accounting logic, must run a deficit.

12 There has been some confusion about the operation of the ELR (see Sawyer, 2003). It is important to note that ELR eliminates unemployment by offering a job to everyone willing and able to work, not by increasing aggregate demand. Although a rise in aggregate demand may result as a consequence of the program, this does not have to be the case. The government can eliminate unemployment via the ELR while simultaneously reducing its spending on other programmes and raising taxes. This is hardly a desirable recommendation, but it illustrates that ELR can eliminate unemployment in the face of falling aggregate demand. It does so by offering a job, not by 'pump priming' (for details, see Mitchell and Wray, 2005).

13 There is no consensus around this outcome.

14 Even this outcome is debatable. The Alaska Permanent Fund invests its oil earnings into a portfolio of assets, many of which are in industries that are not eco-friendly. The dividend payment to Alaskans is therefore linked to how profitable these industries are.

15 For explanation of these biophysical conditions, see Forstater (2004).

16 Fitzpatrick (2003), Galston (2001), and Anderson (2001), among others, support some conditionality purporting that there must be a reciprocal obligation on the part of the Basic Income recipient.

17 The institutional details and macroeconomic effects of this program have been discussed in detail in Tcherneva and Wray (2005b).

References

Anderson, E. (2001), 'Optional freedoms', in P. Van Parijs, J. Cohen, and J. Rogers (eds), *What's Wrong with a Free Lunch?*, Boston, MA: Beacon Press, pp. 70–74.

Aronowitz, S. and Cutler, J. (1998), *Post-Work*, London: Routledge.

Aronowitz, S. and DiFazio, W. (1994), *The Jobless Future*, Minneapolis, MN: University of Minnesota Press.

Atkinson, A. B. (1995), *Public Economics in Action: The Basic Income/Flat Tax Proposal*, Oxford: Oxford University Press.

Bell, S. (2000), 'Do taxes and bonds finance government spending?', *Journal of Economic Issues*, 34 (3), September, 603–620.

Clark, C. M. A. (2003), 'Promoting economic equity: the Basic Income approach,' in M. R. Tool and P. D. Bush (eds), *Institutional Analysis and Economic Policy*, Boston, MA: Kluwer Academic Publishers, pp. 133–156.

Clark, C. M. A. (2004), *Ending Poverty in America: The First Step*, USBIG Discussion Paper No. 80.

Department of Transportation (2007), 'Conditions of US Highway Bridges: 1990–2007,' August 14, http://www.bts.gov/current_topics/2007_08_02_bridge_data/html/bridges_us.html.

Fitzpatrick, T. (2003), *After the New Social Democracy*, Manchester: Manchester University Press.

Forstater, M. (2004), 'Green jobs: addressing the critical issues surrounding the environment, workplace and employment', *International Journal of Environment, Workplace and Employment*, 1 (1), 53–61.

Forstater, M. and Mosler, W. (1999), 'General framework for the analysis of currencies and commodities,' in P. Davidson and J. Kregel (eds), *Full Employment and Price Stability in a Global Economy*, Cheltenham: Edward Elgar, pp. 166–177.

Galston, W. (2001), 'What about reciprocity?' in P. Van Parijs, J. Cohen, and J. Rogers (eds), *What's Wrong with a Free Lunch?*, Boston, MA: Beacon Press, pp. 29–33.

Goodstein, E. and Doppelt, B. (2006), 'Abrupt climate change and the economy: a survey with application to Oregon,' in University of Oregon, *Report on Climate Change by the Climate Leadership Initiative*, http://www.lclark.edu/~eban/CEPSpr06.pdf.

Harvey, P. (1989), *Securing the Right to Employment: Social Welfare Policy and the Unemployed in the United States*, Princeton, NJ: Princeton University Press.

Harvey, P. (2003), *The Right to Work and Basic Income Guarantees: A Comparative Assessment*, USBIG Discussion Paper No. 57.

Hudson, M. (2003), 'The creditary/monetary debate in historical perspective,' in S. Bell and E. Nell (eds), *The State, the Market and the Euro*, Cheltenham: Edward Elgar, pp. 39–76.

Innes, A. M. (1913), 'What is money?' *Banking Law Journal*, May, 377–408.

Keynes, J. M. (1936), *The General Theory of Employment, Interest and Money*, New York: Harcourt-Brace & World, Inc.

Knapp, G. F. ([1924] 1973), *The State Theory of Money*, Clifton, NY: Augustus M. Kelley.

Lerner, A. P. (1943), 'Functional finance and the federal debt,' *Social Research*, 10, February, 38–57.

Lerner, A. P. (1947), 'Money as a creature of the state', *American Economic Review*, 37, May, 312–317.

Lord, C. (2003), *A Citizens' Income: A Foundation for a Sustainable World*, Oxfordshire: Jon Carpenter Publishing.

Meade, J. E. (1989), *Agathotopia: The Economics of Partnership*, Aberdeen: Aberdeen University Press.

Minsky, H. (1986), *Stabilizing an Unstable Economy*, New Haven, CT: Yale University Press.

Mitchell, S. (2002), 'Turkey: another disaster in the making', *Jubilee Research Analysis*, 3 October.

Mitchell, W. F. (1998), 'The buffer stock employment model,' *Journal of Economic Issues*, 32 (2), June, 547–555.

Mitchell, W. F. and Watts, M. J. (2004), 'A comparison of the macroeconomic consequences of Basic Income and Job Guarantee schemes,' *Rutgers Journal of Law and Urban Policy*, 2 (1), 1–24.

Mitchell, W. F. and Wray, L. R. (2005), 'In defense of Employer of Last Resort: a response to Malcolm Sawyer,' *Journal of Economic Issues*, 39 (1), 235–245.

Mosler, W. B. (1997–98), 'Full employment and price stability,' *Journal of Post Keynesian Economics*, 20 (2), Winter, 167–182.

Murray, M. (1997), *. . . And Economic Justice for All: Welfare Reform for the 21st Century*, Armonk, NY: M. E. Sharpe.

Sawyer, M. (2003), 'Employer of last resort: could it deliver full employment and price stability?', *Journal of Economic Issues*, 37 (4), 881–908.

Sen, A. (1999), *Development as Freedom*, New York: Alfred A. Knopf.

Stern, N. (2006), *The Economics of Climate Change: The Stern Review*, Cambridge: Cambridge University Press.

Tcherneva, P. R. (2006a), 'Universal assurances in the public interest: evaluating the economic viability of Basic Income and Job Guarantees,' *International Journal of Environment, Workplace and Employment*, 2 (1), 69–88.

Tcherneva, P. R. (2006b), 'Chartalism and the tax-driven approach to money,' in P. Arestis and M. Sawyer (eds), *Handbook of Alternative Monetary Economics*, Cheltenham: Edward Elgar, pp. 69–86.

Tcherneva, P. R. and Wray, L. R. (2005a), 'Common goals – different solutions: can Basic Income and Job Guarantees deliver their own promises,' *Rutgers Journal of Law and Urban Policy*, 2 (1), 125–163.

Tcherneva, P. R. and Wray, L. R. (2005b), *Employer of Last Resort: A Case Study of Argentina's Jefes Program*, C-FEPS Working Paper No. 41, Kansas City, MO: Center for Full Employment and Price Stability.

Van Parijs, P. (ed.) (1992), *Arguing for Basic Income*, New York: Verso.

Van Parijs, P. (1995), *Real Freedom for All*, Oxford: Oxford University Press.

Van Parijs, P. (2004), 'Basic income: a simple and powerful idea for the twenty-first century,' *Politics and Society*, 32 (1), 7–39.

Van Parijs, P., Cohen, J. and Rogers, J. (eds) (2001), *What's Wrong with a Free Lunch?*, Boston, MA: Beacon Press.

Vanden Heuvel, K. (2005), 'It's time for a new "New Deal"', *The Nation*, 9 August, *http://www.thenation.com/blogs/edcut?bid=7&pid=20690*.

White, S. (2003), *The Civic Minimum*, Oxford: Oxford University Press.

Widerquist, K. (2004), *Freedom as the Power to Say No*, USBIG Discussion Paper No. 88.

Wray, L. R. (1998), *Understanding Modern Money: The Key to Full Employment and Price Stability*, Cheltenham: Edward Elgar.

Wray, L. R. (2003), 'Functional finance and US government budget surpluses,' in E. Nell and M. Forstater (eds), *Reinventing Functional Finance*, Cheltenham: Edward Elgar, pp. 141–159.

8 A comparison of the macroeconomic consequences of Basic Income and Job Guarantee schemes

William Mitchell

Martin Watts

Introduction

This chapter contrasts two policy responses to rising income insecurity: the introduction of a universal Basic Income Guarantee (BIG) and the implementation of a Job Guarantee (JG).[1] Both initiatives challenge the prescriptions of the dominant neoliberal policy agenda.[2]

In his 1987 Ely Lecture to the American Economics Association, the Princeton economist Alan Blinder described the failure to provide productive employment for all those willing and able to work as one of the 'major weaknesses of market capitalism.' He argued that the failure had been 'shamefully debilitating' since the mid-1970s, and that the associated costs make 'reducing high unemployment a political, economic and moral challenge of the highest order' (Blinder, 1989: 139).

In the last three decades, most governments have abandoned the goal of full employment and are content to pursue the diminished goal of full employability. Policy-makers have followed the dominant economic orthodoxy and consistently constrained their economies under the pretext that the economy should operate at the so-called natural rate of unemployment. These policies have prevented economies from generating enough jobs (and hours of work) to match the preferences of the labour force. The result has been persistently high unemployment and rising levels of underemployment (Mitchell and Muysken, 2008). Ironically, highly desirable, labour-intensive projects have not been undertaken, to the detriment of all of society (see Mitchell, 1998; Wray, 1998). The cumulative costs of the forgone output and unemployment are huge and dwarf the costs of alleged microeconomic inefficiency (Watts and Mitchell, 2000). A key outcome of these disturbing labour market trends has been rising income insecurity for individuals and families. It is in this context that we consider the BIG and the JG.

The provision of an unconditional BIG, set at a 'liveable' level and payable to all citizens, is advocated by a number of public policy theorists as a means of addressing income security (see Van Parijs, 1997; Widerquist and Lewis, 1997; Clark and Kavanagh, 1996; Lerner, 2000; Tomlinson, 2000). Most BIG proponents are motivated by a belief that full employment is now unattainable (e.g., Nogeura, 2004). We argue that this solution is a palliative one at best. It is based on a failure both to construct the problem of income insecurity appropriately and to understand the options that a government, which issues its own currency, has available to maintain full employment.

We argue that there are no economic constraints to achieving full employment. Only ideological and political constraints exist. In fact, each policy response requires that the same ideological and political barriers relating to philosophical notions of citizenship and individual rights be confronted and overcome. But when compared to a full-scale public sector employment programme, the BIG is a second-rate option and is inherently inflationary.

We prefer to solve income insecurity by focusing on the root causes of unemployment. The solution lies in restoring the role of the state as an 'employer of last resort' and thereby introducing a JG (Mitchell, 1998).

The second major section of this chapter outlines the BIG and JG models and the different ways they construct the income security problem. The third section explores the operation of the labour market under these two models, and the associated rights and obligations of citizenship. The fourth section considers the nature of coercion under the BIG and JG and the possibility for dynamic transitions to a broader and more inclusive notion of work. The following section briefly considers whether chronic income insecurity in developing economies requires a different policy response. Conclusions are presented in the final section.

Constructing the problem[3]

How we construct a problem conditions the way we attempt to solve it. It is easy to pose a false problem and then outline a false solution. Both advocates of income guarantees and advocates of employment guarantees seek to address the problem of income insecurity. What exactly is the nature of this problem?

The problem of income insecurity

Advocates of a BIG concentrate on income insecurity whereas JG proponents argue that income insecurity is just one aspect of the broader problem of unemployment in a mixed capitalist economy that is constrained by inflationary biases. The BIG construction is consistent with the neoliberal economics of individualism and competitive markets constrained by market imperfections. We argue that it is based on a false premise and a curious inconsistency. The false premise is that fiat currency-issuing governments are financially constrained. The inconsistency is that the political conditions that would have to be present for the BIG to be a reality require the state to recognise the philosophical values of citizenship and individual rights. But these are also the constraints preventing a return to full employment. However, BIG advocates claim that full employment is no longer achievable 'by reasonable means, and necessitates lower wages, less social protection, more stress, social illness and inequality' (Standing, 2002: 272, quoted in Harvey, 2003: 16).

In exposing this false premise and logical inconsistency, we argue that the BIG can never be a superior option to a JG in a monetary economy in which the fiat currency-issuer is a monopoly and private markets are constrained by inflationary biases.

The Basic Income approach to income insecurity

Our attention in this chapter is on what Clark and Kavanagh (1996: 400) describe as a 'full Basic Income' in which the BIG is set above the poverty line, replaces all other forms of public assistance, and is financed through an increase in tax rates or a widening of the tax base. In crafting a case for an unconditional Basic Income, the BIG literature gives little attention to the causes of income insecurity, although they are associated with the rise of mass unemployment identified earlier. Van Parijs, for example, approaches the problem by drawing on a liberal egalitarian conception of justice. He argues that individuals must be afforded 'real freedom; a state marked by both the absence of constraints on action and the means to realise one's projects' (cited in Gintis, 1997: 181). This requires that scarce social resources, including access to paid employment, should be so distributed as to maximise the value of opportunities available to the least well-off. Van Parijs (1997: 5) concludes that capitalism can be justified by redistributing wealth in the form of a BIG payable to all individuals irrespective of their household situation and whether or not they engage in paid work.

Although macroeconomic analysis within the BIG literature is limited to the 'financing' of the scheme, its advocates, nonetheless, argue that the BIG will provide poverty relief and full employment (see Clark and Kavanagh, 1996; Van Parijs, 2000; Basic Income European Network, 2004). How then will a BIG, and the decoupling of income from work, lead to full employment?

The existence and persistence of unemployment in BIG models is generally accepted, but rarely explained. However, Van Parijs (1991) presents both an explanation of unemployment and a model of BIG financing. Drawing from orthodox neoclassical theory, Van Parijs considers that unemployment arises because wage rigidities impede atomistic competition and prevent the labour market from clearing (see also Seekings, 2006). Various explanations for the wage rigidities include trade union power, minimum wage legislation, and bargaining processes, which generate efficiency wages (insider–outsider arrangements). Thus, according to Van Parijs, unemployment is caused by the departure from competitive equilibrium rather than any macroeconomic failure.

Van Parijs then proposes a rather bizarre and very neoclassical solution in terms of a redistribution of the 'property right' represented by the alleged existence of 'employment rents' that are associated with scarce jobs.[4] Van Parijs (1991: 124) says 'let us give each member of the society concerned a tradable entitlement to an equal share of those jobs.'

Accordingly, BIG payments can be 'financed' by taxing workers who enjoy employment rents. Van Parijs (1991: 124) claims that these rents are given by the difference between the income (and other advantages) the employed derive from their jobs, and the (lower) income they would need to get if the market were to clear. In a situation of persistent massive unemployment, there is no doubt that the sum total of these rents would greatly swell the amount available for financing the grant.

In this way, a BIG enables workers to live a decent, if modest, life without paid employment. Van Parijs concludes that the claim that Malibu surfers are living off others is a serious misrepresentation because they live off

> their share, or less than their share, of rents which would otherwise be monopolized by those who hold a rich society's productive jobs.
>
> (Van Parijs, 1991: 130–131)

But the implicit full employment concept is unacceptable, because it is engineered through an artificial withdrawal of labour supply, so that some of the unemployed are reclassified as not in the labour force. There are insurmountable problems with this representation of income insecurity and the BIG financing model. They are:

1   Within the BIG logic, efficiency wage bargains reflect freedom of association and maximising decisions for both parties to the contract. Productivity falls if firms offer only the competitive wage. Recruitment becomes more difficult and turnover rises. The wage outcomes are not dysfunctional and are not imperfections that can be eliminated to restore an otherwise (perfectly) competitive labour market.
2   If workers are willing to work at the efficiency wage, and there are queues for jobs, there must be insufficient demand for the output they produce. Unemployment is demand-deficient in this case and firms are unwilling to hire more workers at lower wages.
3   Justice, as Van Parijs (1991) sees it, occurs when there are no employment rents, which means wages equal their (textbook) competitive levels. If we assume that the imperfections (which create the rents) could be eliminated, then, within the logic of the competitive neoclassical model, there would be equal endowments, market-clearing real wages, and zero involuntary unemployment. There would also be zero employment rents and zero employment envy, but also no tradable commodities to support the Basic Income. In other words, this form of BIG financing would depend on the existence of market imperfections.
4   The BIG literature presumes that the good life enjoyed by the employed worker is at the expense of the unemployed and that scarcity is the problem. But, although jobs might be scarce at present, are there no useful activities in which the unemployed could be engaged?

The final point is at the heart of the difference between the BIG and JG approaches to income insecurity. The solution to income insecurity has to go beyond palliative care. Unemployment is the most significant source of income insecurity (Sen, 1997). A more efficacious, and less apologetic, response to unemployment requires an understanding of why some people do not have access to paid employment and to thus alter the conduct of macroeconomic policy so that it achieves sustainable full employment at reasonable wages. This requires, in part, the implementation of a JG.

The Job Guarantee approach to income insecurity

In contradistinction to BIG explanations, the JG model explains unemployment persistence in terms of systemic failure – the result of erroneous macroeconomic policies which have failed to generate enough jobs (hours of work) to match the preferences of the labour force (Mitchell, 1998; Wray, 1998; Mitchell and Muysken, 2008). The level of unemployment at any point in time is a choice made by the national government through its budgetary stance. Persistent unemployment is the product of inadequate budget spending. *Ipso facto*, JG advocates argue that the state must use its power as the issuer of currency to ensure there are enough jobs available at all times. We note that countries that avoided the plunge into high unemployment in the 1970s maintained a 'sector of the economy which effectively functions as an employer of last resort, which absorbs the shocks which occur from time to time, and more generally makes employment available to the less skilled, the less qualified' (Ormerod, 1994: 203).

The JG model, which is underpinned by the buffer stock principle, and outlined in Mitchell (1998), can be summarised as follows:

1   *Full employment*: The public sector operates a buffer stock of jobs to absorb workers who are unable to find employment in the private sector. The pool expands (declines) when private sector activity declines (expands). There is thus an open-ended offer by government to purchase labour.

2   *JG wage*: The JG wage rate is set at the minimum wage level to avoid disturbing the private wage structure. Thus, the government 'hires off the bottom' and does not compete for purchases at market prices.

3   *Social wage*: The state supplements the JG earnings with a wide range of social wage expenditures, including adequate levels of public education, health, childcare, and access to legal aid. Further, the JG policy does not replace the conventional use of fiscal policy to achieve social and economic objectives.

4   *Family income supplements*: The JG is not based on family units. Anyone above the legal working age is entitled to receive the benefits of the scheme. We would supplement the JG wage with benefits reflecting family structure. In contrast to workfare, there would not be pressure applied to single parents to seek employment.

5   *Inflation control*: When the level of private sector activity is such that wage-price pressures form as the precursor to an inflationary episode, the government manipulates fiscal and monetary policy settings to reduce the level

of private sector demand. The ratio of JG employment to total employment (the buffer employment ratio (BER)) that is consistent with stable inflation is the outcome of this redistribution of workers from the inflating private sector to the fixed-price JG sector. It is called the non-accelerating-inflation-buffer employment ratio (NAIBER). Its microeconomic foundations are different to those underpinning the neoclassical NAIRU.[5]

6 *Workfare*: The JG is not workfare. Workfare does not provide secure employment with conditions (non-wage benefits and the like) consistent with community norms. Workfare is a programme whereby the state extracts a contribution from the unemployed for their welfare payments. The state, however, takes no responsibility for the failure of the economy to generate enough jobs. Under the JG, the state assumes this responsibility.

7 *Unemployment benefits*: These could be phased out, remain optional, or be immediately abandoned. The JG per se can operate with any option. However, we would abandon unemployment support after a short period because the JG offers paid work instead.

8 *Administration*: The JG would be financed by the national government, which has a monopoly on currency issuance, but would be organised and implemented locally (see CofFEE, 2006).

9 *Type of jobs*: JG workers would work in many socially useful activities including urban renewal projects and other environmental and construction schemes (e.g., reforestation, sand dune stabilisation, and river valley erosion control), personal assistance to pensioners, and other community schemes (see Cowling *et al.*, 2003; CofFEE, 2006).

In contrast to the BIG model, the JG approach provides a secure liveable income via a guarantee of a job for every person who is able to work. Those unable to work are provided with a living income. Full employment is attained by maintaining an open-ended job offer to ensure that the economy provides sufficient work opportunities rather than by engineering labour supply adjustments, which define the problem away. The JG also differs from a standard Keynesian approach because it does not rely on generalised demand expansion per se (spending at market prices and multipliers) to achieve full employment (Mitchell and Wray, 2005). Mitchell and Muysken (2008) provide a critique of the generalised Keynesian expansion in terms of its lack of an inflation-proofing mechanism.

The BIG approaches the question of income security from the pessimistic view that unemployment is inevitable and a result of market imperfections rather than macroeconomic failure. By failing to address the macroeconomic issues, BIG advocates have been, and continue to be, reluctant to engage in a meaningful debate on the merits of restoring full employment.

False premises lead to false conclusions[6]

In addition to constructing the problem of income insecurity incorrectly, the mainstream BIG literature advocates the introduction of a BIG within a 'budget neutral' environment. This is presumably to allay the criticism of the neoliberals who eschew government deficits. When we use the term *government*, we are referring to the level of government that has a monopoly over the issue of fiat currency. One of the sensitive issues for BIG proponents is thus its perceived 'cost'. In this section, we show that much of this debate is conducted on the false premise that the government is financially constrained.

The realities of modern money

A modern monetary system is characterised by a floating exchange rate (so monetary policy is freed from the need to defend foreign exchange reserves) and the monopoly provision of fiat currency. The monopolist is the national government. The following macroeconomic principles explain the fundamental flaws in the arguments used to justify the abandonment of full employment, as a policy objective.

First, under a fiat currency system, the monetary unit defined by the government has no intrinsic worth. It cannot be legally converted by the government, for example, into gold as it was under the gold standard. The viability of the fiat currency is ensured because it is the only unit which is acceptable for payment of taxes and other financial demands of the government.

Second, as a matter of national accounting, the federal government deficit (surplus) equals the non-government surplus (deficit). The failure to recognise this relationship is a major oversight of neoliberal analysis. In aggregate, there can be no net savings of financial assets of the non-government sector without cumulative government deficit spending. All transactions between private entities, such as commercial banks, net to zero because, for every asset created, a matching liability is created. Thus the federal government, via net spending (deficits), is the only entity that can provide the non-government sector with net financial assets (net savings) and thereby simultaneously accommodate any net desire to save and eliminate unemployment. Also, and contrary to neoliberal rhetoric, the systematic pursuit of government budget surpluses is necessarily manifested as systematic declines in private sector savings.

Third, the decreasing levels of net private savings which finance the government surplus increasingly leverage the private sector. The deteriorating debt-to-income ratios which ensue eventually result in the system succumbing to ongoing demand-draining fiscal drag through a slow-down in real activity.

Fourth, the analogy neoliberals draw between private household budgets and the government budget is false. Households must finance their spending of the currency *ex ante*. However, the government, as the issuer of the currency, must spend first (credit private bank accounts) before it can subsequently tax (debit private accounts). Government spending is the source of the funds the private sector requires to pay its taxes and to net save. Government is not revenue constrained through a 'government budget constraint' (GBC) (Mitchell, 1998; Wray, 1998; Mitchell and Mosler, 2002).

Fifth, unemployment occurs when net government spending is too low. As a matter of accounting, for aggregate output to be entirely sold, total spending must equal total income. Involuntary unemployment is idle labour unable to find a buyer at the current money wage. In the absence of net government spending, unemployment arises when the private sector, in aggregate, desires to spend less of the monetary unit of account than it earns. Nominal (or real) wage cuts *per se* do not clear the labour market, unless they somehow eliminate the private sector's desire to net save and the latter subsequently increases its spending. Thus, unemployment occurs when net government spending is too low to accommodate the need of the non-government sector to pay taxes and its desire to net save.

Sixth, although the federal government is not financially constrained, it still issues debt to control its liquidity impact on the private sector. Government spending and purchases of government bonds by the central bank add liquidity, whereas taxation and sales of government securities drain private liquidity. These transactions influence the system's daily cash position. A system surplus (deficit) occurs when the outflow of funds from the official sector is above (below) the funds inflow to the official sector. Budget deficits result in system-wide surpluses (excess bank reserves). The system cash position has crucial implications for the central bank, which targets the level of short-term interest rates as its monetary policy position. Competition between the commercial banks to create better earning opportunities on the surplus reserves puts downward pressure on the cash rate. If the central bank desires to maintain the current cash rate, it must drain this surplus liquidity by selling government debt. In other words, government debt functions as interest rate support via the maintenance of the desired level of reserves in the commercial banking system and not as a source of funds to finance government spending. The private sector purchases the debt to earn a market yield on their reserve holdings. Thus, far from pushing interest rates up, debt issue maintains existing rates, which would otherwise fall.

In summary, the government, as the issuer of money, cannot be financially constrained and has an obligation to ensure that its net spending is sufficient to maintain full employment. Thus any 'policy package' underpinned by a government financial constraint is based on erroneous foundations.[7]

The implications of modern money for the Basic Income approach

Once it is recognised that there is no financial constraint on government spending, many of the problems created by BIG theorists can be avoided. First, if the budget impact is kept to a minimum, there would only be a small increase in aggregate demand resulting from a modest BIG scheme, which would be unlikely to provide sufficient hours of work to meet labour force preferences. Second, it is highly unlikely that labour participation rates would fall with the introduction of the BIG, given the rising participation by women in part-time work (desiring higher family incomes) and the strong commitment to work among the unemployed (Widerquist and Lewis, 1997). But there could be an increase in the supply of part-time labour as full-timers reduce work hours and combine the BIG with earned income. Third, employers in the secondary labour market will probably utilise this increase in part-time labour supply to exploit the large implicit BIG subsidy by reducing wages and conditions (Van der Veen, 1998). Fourth, some full-time jobs may be replaced with low-wage, low-productivity, part-time jobs leading to falling investment, skill accumulation, and ultimately falling average living standards. Finally, to 'finance' a more generous BIG, higher taxes would be necessary, which could impact on labour supply if substitution effects dominate.[8]

Under budget neutrality, the maximum sustainable BIG would be modest. Aggregate demand and employment impacts are likely to be small and, even with some redistribution of working hours, high levels of labour underutilisation are likely to persist. Overall, this strategy does not enhance the rights of the most disadvantaged, nor does it provide work for those who desire it (see Cowling *et al.*, 2003; Little, 1998).

However, more profound problems emerge if a BIG is introduced into a functional finance paradigm (Wray, 1998). The value of the currency is determined by 'what is required to obtain it for payment of the given tax liability' (Tcherneva, 2003). Persistent unemployment can be avoided by the introduction of the BIG through a net government stimulus (deficit). But the value of the currency will fall given that nothing is provided in return for the government spending. The resulting inflationary bias, in the current context of inflation-first central bank policy, would invoke interest rate adjustments that would constrain the economy from achieving sufficient output levels to offer real employment options to all aspiring workers.

Demand for labour would clearly increase more through a net government deficit than under a budget-neutral regime. However, it is the impact on labour supply that is of critical importance. If the level of BIG is increased, total labour supply is likely to decrease, whereas the impact of lower tax rates on the labour supply of incumbent workers would depend on the relative magnitudes of their income and substitution effects. Given the net stimulus to employment and output, there is the logical possibility of an excess demand for labour occurring at full employment[9] as a consequence of the artificial reduction of the full employment level of output. This would serve to compound the inflationary pressure.

In the absence of an inbuilt counter-inflation mechanism, rising wages would make the BIG relatively less attractive. This may lead to some 'life-stylers' choosing to return to the labour market. Meanwhile, the government may respond by raising taxes and/or reducing government expenditure, which would tend to raise unemployment. In both cases, demand pressure would decline. However, to the extent that the inflationary process has assumed a cost-push form, wage and price inflation may decline only slowly.

It is thus possible that an unsustainable dynamic could be generated in which there are periodic phases of demand-pull inflation and induced cost-push inflation at low rates of unemployment, followed by contractionary policy and high rates of unemployment. These economic outcomes are consistent with the indiscriminate Keynesian policy of the past. The dynamic efficiency of such a pattern is highly questionable given that the hysteretic consequences of unemployment keep being manifested. Even if this Keynesian expansion could achieve full employment, considerable economic inflexibility is created. The ebb and flow of the private sector cannot be readily accommodated, and the likelihood of inflation is thus increased (Forstater, 2000). In addition, the inflationary process at full employment could threaten to change the distribution of real income, weakening the inducement to invest, and making the achievement of sustained full employment even more difficult (Rowthorn, 1980). Over time, there would be political pressure to raise the BIG in line with changing community expectations that reflect higher wage levels. Policy-makers would need to correctly anticipate the impact on labour supply.

Thus, the introduction of a BIG policy designed to achieve full employment is likely to be highly problematic with respect its capacity to deliver both sustained full employment and price stability.[10]

The JG is the only way to generate and sustain full employment with price stability. The JG is, in effect, a buffer stock that operates under a fixed-price/floating-quantity rule (Mitchell, 1998; Wray, 1998). Given that the JG hires at a fixed price in exchange for hours of work and does not compete with private sector wages, employment redistributions between the private sector and the buffer stock can always be achieved to stabilise any wage inflation in the non-JG sector.[11] The JG pool thus adjusts according to private sector demand levels.

Finally, we need to consider the effect of a BIG on social attitudes to work and non-work. Although BIG advocates argue that the universality of the payment will make it more acceptable to the community, this claim ignores the distinction between BIG recipients who choose to work and those that choose more leisure and no paid work. Beder (2000: 2) observes that work is still at

> the heart of capitalist culture . . . [and] . . . to make sure there is no identity outside of employment, the unemployed are stigmatised. They tend to be portrayed in the media as either frauds, hopeless cases, or layabouts who are living it up at taxpayers' expense. Work is seen as an essential characteristic of being human. No matter how tedious it is, any work is generally considered to be better than no work.

In summary, the BIG fails to satisfy the essential criteria for an effective and sustainable full employment policy. The imposition of a liveable BIG violates attitudes to work and non-work. A BIG policy that achieves full employment, in part by engineering an artificial reduction in labour supply, is likely to be unsustainable because of frequent episodes of stagflation, which could impact on the real distribution of income. Thus a BIG is unable to solve the central problem of income insecurity.

The labour market and the welfare system: rights and obligations

Noguera (2004) notes that the welfare states of post-war Europe recognised a form of social and economic citizenship firmly anchored in formal employment. The Keynesian full employment commitment was buttressed by the development of the welfare state, which defined the state's obligation to provide security to all citizens and replaced the deserving–undeserving poor dichotomy (Timmins, 1995). Transfer payments were provided to disadvantaged individuals and groups and a professional public sector provided standardised services to all citizens.

Accompanying the neoliberal attacks on macroeconomic policy have been the concerted attacks on supplementary institutions, such as the industrial relations system and the apparatus of the welfare state, because the move to persistently high labour underutilisation has placed pressure on the capacity of the welfare state to support itself. This, in turn, has led to a move towards user-pays approaches to income support.

To force individuals to become accountable for their own outcomes, welfare policy changes have introduced recipient responsibilities to counter-balance existing rights while promoting the movement from passive to active welfare. Individuals now face broader obligations and their rights as citizens have been replaced by compulsory contractual relationships with behavioural criteria imposed as a condition of benefit receipt.

Unemployment has been reconceptualised as an individual problem of welfare dependence rather than a consequence of a deficiency of jobs, reflecting systemic policy failure. Increasingly, governments are imposing tighter controls on the 'victims' of unemployment in exchange for ongoing receipt of income support. The preoccupation with instituting behavioural requirements and enforcing sanctions for welfare recipients implies that dependence is an individual preference. Unfortunately, there is no reciprocal obligation on government to ensure there are enough jobs.

The BIG school considers that the solution to this systemic policy failure is not the re-introduction of a full employment policy, but rather the recognition by the state of the philosophical values of citizenship by the introduction of an unconditional income. If governments introduce a BIG, but maintain their obsession with the maintenance of budget surpluses, then this form of income support is likely to be subject to the same type of pressure that has reduced the coverage, duration, and level of public benefits over the last decade in many Western economies.

BIG advocates also make claims about the impact of a BIG on the functioning of the macroeconomic labour market, which warrant serious examination.

Noguera (2004) asserts that the introduction of a BIG brings about a more rational distribution of jobs and working time according to citizens' preferences. These improved labour market outcomes are alleged to result from individuals being liberated from the need to work and the ability to veto bad jobs, thereby forcing a restructuring of jobs and improved matching so that quality jobs are available to more workers. Noting the presence in many written constitutions of the freedom to choose one's profession and/or job, Noguera (2004: 20–21) concludes that such freedom is better guaranteed by a BIG than any 'workfarist, welfare to work or activation policy'.

Noguera seems to be confusing the alleged freedom to refuse a job under a liveable BIG, a concept which is in itself highly problematic,[12] with the presence of sufficient jobs and hence the ability to exercise real choice over which job to undertake. Meaningful job choice necessarily implies the presence of full employment and a pool of jobs that are accessible to the most disadvantaged workers in the labour market. In this context, the provision of a JG with stable pay and conditions is an essential component.

In addition to this, there must be sufficient paid work undertaken in aggregate to produce goods and services in the domestic economy in response to aggregate demand arising from consumption and the other forms of expenditure. Why should an employed worker, who is not responsible for the plight of the unemployed, be prepared to sacrifice income to pay for the non-work of another, irrespective of whether unemployment is voluntary or involuntary? One person's freedom from the work imperative under capitalism is another worker's alienation. With their individualistic perspective, BIG advocates never address this macroeconomic constraint on *real freedom*. In this context, the later analysis of the claim that a JG is coercive is important.

This failure to explore the macroeconomics of the BIG is shown in even sharper relief when the ecologists' arguments for BIG are analysed. Fitzpatrick (2002: 144) is quite clear:

> For ecologists, people should be opting out of the labour market: the fewer people that are actually contributing to GDP growth then the more the brakes will be applied to such growth. In fact, we should aim at a full BIG as soon as possible in order to provide people with the incentive to abandon wage-earning.

This quotation fails to understand that the implementation of a BIG is not supposed to be a deflationary policy that curtails consumption and other components of aggregate expenditure. Even under budget neutrality, there is likely to be a modest increase in consumption arising from the shift in the distribution of income to low-income groups, who typically have a higher propensity to consume than high-income earners. The individual freedom to reduce hours of work is presumed to aggregate to a collective reduction in hours worked and output. This represents another example of the fallacy of composition which bedevils orthodox macroeconomics. Significantly, there is no discussion of the long-term trends in labour market participation and the presence/absence of anti-consumerist sentiment amongst populations in developed Western economies.

Humphrey (2002) sees the implementation of a BIG as a means of achieving ecologically appropriate behaviour through the removal of material insecurity. Certainly, the imperative to maintain environmentally destructive forms of employment, such as logging in rural areas, is removed by the implementation of a BIG. However, its introduction within a stimulatory or budget neutral policy does nothing to curtail desired levels of consumption and, hence, the collective imperative to work, as noted above.

There is a presumption in the BIG literature that the good (employed) life that the worker has is at the expense of the unemployed and that the scarcity of jobs is the problem. We cannot say that the provision of an income without work is equivalent to the provision of an income with a job when there is evidence of significant social needs in local communities (Allen *et al.*, 2007) which remain unmet because levels of spending are inadequate to fund the jobs. Scarcity of jobs is the chosen policy position of government, rather than being a natural occurrence.

Payment of a BIG to all citizens would signify a further withdrawal by the state from its responsibility to manage economic affairs and care for its citizens. Young people must be encouraged to develop skills and engage in paid work, rather than be the passive recipients of a social security benefit. The failure to engage in paid work cannot be narrowly construed as an inability to generate disposable income which can be addressed through a benefit, but entails a much broader form of exclusion from economic, social, and cultural life, which has highly detrimental consequences (see, for example, Kieselbach, 2003). Harvey (2003) has also reported the benefits of stable work with decent wages, health, and retirement benefits.

Advocates of the BIG fail to explain how its availability will promote meaningful engagement on the part of the disadvantaged, who have limited income-earning opportunities. The universal availability of the BIG does not overcome the stigma associated with voluntary unemployment of the able-bodied who do not have caring or other responsibilities. The achievement of full employment would rule out the need for a BI if those citizens who are unable to work on account of illness, disability, or caring responsibilities were eligible for social security benefits. This is precisely the JG solution.

Coercion and the future of work

Although the JG satisfies the essential conditions for a successful full employment policy within a monetary capitalist system, two important issues remain to be discussed: (a) is a compulsory JG overly coercive?; and (b) does the JG or BIG model introduce dynamics that can take us beyond the oppressive reliance on work for income security?

Coercion

The JG is a source of freedom (capitalist property relations notwithstanding) if workers prefer to work, because the JG overcomes the shortage of jobs. But it is possible that some people – the 'sea-changers' – do not value work in any intrinsic sense and, if confronted with the choice between the JG and a BIG, would always take the latter option. A blanket JG is evidently coercive in its impact on this particular group.

We note that the underlying unit of analysis in the BIG literature is an individual who appears to resemble McGregor's (1960) theory X person. Theory X people, according to neoclassical textbooks, are self-centred, rational maximisers. Reinforcing this conception of human behaviour is a libertarian concept of freedom. Proponents of a BIG see a decoupling of income from work as an essential step towards increasing choice and freedom. From a Marxist perspective, a BIG offers the hope of taking subsistence away from any necessity to produce surplus value, at least for an individual who chooses the BIG. The JG thus represents the antithesis of individual freedom. Even if the vast majority of individuals desire to be employed, a flexible system would also permit those who did not want to work to enjoy the income guarantee.

However, if the orthodox, government budget constraint version of the BIG is taken at face value, BIG proponents are confronted with a major dilemma. To finance the scheme, some people have to work. It is difficult to believe that all those who are working are choosing to work in preference to not working. However, under capitalist property relations, workers in general have to work to survive. Van Parijs (1993: 179) asks:

> what is 'unfair' about living off the labour of others when everyone is given the same possibility? Facing this possibility, some will choose to do no or little paid work. Others will want to work a lot, whether for the additional money or for the satisfaction of working. They finance the universal grant. If the latter envy the former's idleness, why don't they follow suit?

There are a number of problems with this conception of a free and fair system. First, our lives will not all begin at the time of the inception of the BIG. Individuals who, under different circumstances, might have taken the no-work option have entered into commitments, such as undertaking further education and having children. In that sense, prior constraints prevent them from enjoying real freedom. Second, the financing logic fails on account of the inherent fallacy of composition. The BIG system would be undermined if everyone chose to take the non-work option. So we are left with the uncomfortable conclusion that, under the BIG, the coercion of work is neatly transferred to those who continue to undertake paid work, whereas under the JG the coercion of work is shared by all. No form of wage labour is non-coercive under capitalism.

Transition to the future of work

Following this logic, the correct question is what forms of coercion are most likely to lead to changes in the mode of production over time. The importance of the work ethic in reinforcing capitalist social relations cannot be underestimated. Proponents of a BIG argue that the introduction of a universal income guarantee contains a dynamic that can steer society away from capitalism towards a communist state (*ceteris paribus*) 'as defined by distribution according to needs' (Van Parijs, 1993: 162). Marxist supporters of the BIG see this as a major advantage, a palliative under capitalism, but also containing the seed for its own destruction. Is this claim valid?

The future of paid work and the traditional moral views about the virtues of work – which are exploited by the capitalist class – need to be recast given the failure of most economies to provide enough work. It is likely that a non-capitalist system of work and income generation would be needed before the yoke of the work ethic and the stigmatisation of non-workers is fully expunged.

The question is how to make this transition in light of the constraints that capital places on the working class and the state. Advocates of the BIG believe that their approach provides this dynamic. Clearly, there is a need to embrace a broader concept of work in the first phase of decoupling work and income. However, to impose this new culture of non-work onto society, given its current attitudes about paid work, is unlikely to be a constructive approach. The patent hostility towards the unemployed will be transferred to the Malibu surfers.

Social attitudes take time to evolve and are best reinforced by changes in the educational system. The change in mode of production through evolutionary means will not happen overnight, and concepts of community wealth and civic responsibility that have been eroded over time by the divide-and-conquer individualism of the neoliberal era have to be restored.

The JG provides a stronger evolutionary dynamic in terms of establishing broader historical transitions away from the unemployment and income insecurity that are intrinsic to the capitalist mode of production. In this context, we see the JG as a short-run palliative but a longer-term force for historical change – as part of a dynamic agenda to take us beyond capitalism.

Employment guarantees and income guarantees in developing countries

Does our logic apply to developing countries? Seekings (2006) claims that in high-unemployment countries, such as South Africa, where there is already a high-wage sector defended by vested interests, the introduction of an employment guarantee based on public works projects would be unsustainable. This is a common argument made by development economists against employment guarantees as a solution to poverty arising from mass unemployment. However, these criticisms are typically based on notions of financial unsustainability underpinned by a government budget constraint. We consider there to be nothing intrinsically different in a developing economy that maintains sovereignty of its own currency that would prevent the introduction of a JG, particularly when such economies lack adequate social and economic infrastructure. There are political and ideological issues that need to be confronted, but these are common to both policy suggestions.

Conclusion

Work remains central to identity and independence, and persistent unemployment remains the central cause of income insecurity. Although the introduction of an unconditional BIG has superficial appeal – by allowing individuals to subsist without work – the model fails to come to grips with the failure of macroeconomic policy to provide paid employment opportunities and secure incomes for all.

In this chapter, we have set out the conditions that must be met if a full employment strategy is to be both effective and sustainable. Unlike the BIG model, the JG model meets these conditions within the constraints of a monetary capitalist system. It is a far better vehicle to rebuild a sense of community and the purposeful nature of work, which can extend beyond the creation of surplus value for the capitalist employer. It also provides the framework whereby the concept of work itself can be broadened to include activities that many would currently dismiss as being leisure, which is consistent with the aspirations of some BIG advocates.

Notes

1 The JG is much the same as the employer of last resort (ELR) referred to by Tcherneva in the previous chapter.
2 We use the terms neoclassical, orthodox, and neoliberal interchangeably here.
3 Several sections of this chapter are based on previous work that the authors have done in partnership with Sally Cowling. We acknowledge her input on this topic.
4 An employment rent is the difference between the actual wage a worker receives and the lowest wage an employer would need to pay to entice the worker to supply his or her labour.
5 The NAIRU refers to the non-accelerating-inflation rate of unemployment and is the unemployment rate at which, under particular circumstances, the inflation rate is stable.
6 This section draws heavily on Mitchell and Mosler (2002) and Mitchell and Muysken (2008).
7 In this respect, Harvey's argument (2003: 11) that job creation to achieve full employment is the preferred option, because its fiscal cost is less than Clark's BIG programme, signifies a misunderstanding of fiscal policy. The two programmes should be based on their respective consequences for resource allocation, income distribution, employment and inflation, rather than their consequences for fiscal outlays.
8 Whereas some BIG advocates, such as Widerquist and Lewis (1997: 35–36), argue that there will be little impact on the participation rate of the recipients of BIG who are on low pay or are unemployed, Lerner (2000) points to the liberating impact on individuals who can make real choices about whether or not to participate in paid work.
9 The alternative is that the excess demand for goods would be increasingly met through imports with consequential effects for the exchange rate and the domestic price level, which would accentuate the inflationary pressure.
10 Some BIG supporters recommend financing the BIG through other forms of taxes to avoid alienating workers, but there appears to be no consensus. If taxes were shifted from labour to capital – bringing about a nominal redistribution of income – this may induce price increases to restore the real distribution of income, or could weaken the inducement to invest. Reliance on environmental taxes, such as those based on resource use, is problematic, since the revenue stream is likely to be inadequate given the incentive for resource conservation (Tcherneva, Chapter 7 in this book).
11 The payment of market wages to JG workers undermines this counter-inflation mechanism (cf. Harvey, 2003: 8), so that the full employment policy is reduced to an indiscriminate Keynesian expansion.
12 By assumption, there is a critical liveable level of the BIG at which the balance of power in the labour market fundamentally changes, but there are differences in reservation incomes of individuals according to their respective potentials to earn wage income. Thus, setting a BIG at a liveable level for the majority of workers would cause a massive distortion in the functioning of the labour market and would be unsustainable.

References

Allen, E., Cook, B., Mitchell, W. F., and Watts, M. (2007), *The Failed Full Employability Paradigm*, Working Paper No. 07-04, Centre of Full Employment and Equity, University of Newcastle.

Basic Income European Network (2004), 'What is Basic Income?', http://www.etes.ucl.ac.be/bien/BI/Definition.htm.

Beder, S. (2000), *Selling the Work Ethic: From Puritan Pulpit to Corporate PR*, Carlton North, Vic.: Scribe Publications.

Blinder, A. S. (1989), *Macroeconomics under Debate*, London: Harvester Wheatsheaf.

Clark, C. M. A. and Kavanagh, C. (1996), 'Basic income, inequality, and unemployment: rethinking the linkage between work and welfare', *Journal of Economic Literature*, 30 (2), June, 399–407.

CofFEE (2006), *The Job Guarantee in Practice*, Working Paper 06-15, Centre of Full Employment and Equity, University of Newcastle.

Cowling, S., Mitchell, W. F., and Watts, M. J. (2003), *The Right to Income versus the Right to Work*, Working Paper 03-08, Centre of Full Employment and Equity, University of Newcastle.

Fitzpatrick, T. (2002), 'With no strings attached? Basic income and the greening of security', in T. Fitzpatrick and M. Cahill (eds), *Environment and Welfare: Towards a Green Social Policy*, Basingstoke: Palgrave Macmillan, pp. 138–154.

Forstater, M. (2000), 'Full employment and economic flexibility', in W. F. Mitchell and E. Carlson (eds), *The Path to Full Employment*, Sydney: University of NSW Press, pp. 49–88.

Gintis, H. (1997), 'Review of *Real Freedom for All* by Philippe Van Parijs', *Journal of Economic Literature*, 35, 181–182.

Harvey, P. (2003), *The Right to Work and Basic Income Guarantees: A Comparative Assessment*, USBIG Discussion Paper No. 57, February.

Humphrey, M. (2002), 'The ideologies of green welfare', in T. Fitzpatrick and M. Cahill (eds), *Environment and Welfare: Towards a Green Social Policy*, Basingstoke: Palgrave Macmillan, pp. 61–80.

Kieselbach, T. (2003), 'Long-term unemployment among young people: the risk of social exclusion', *American Journal of Community Psychology*, 32 (1–2), 69–76.

Lerner, S. (2000), 'The positives of flexibility', paper presented at the Eighth International Congress of the Basic Income European Network, Berlin, October.

Little, A. (1998), *Post-Industrial Socialism: Towards a New Politics of Welfare*, London: Routledge.

McGregor, D. M. (1960), *The Human Side of Management*, New York: McGraw-Hill.

Mitchell, W. F. (1998), 'The buffer stock employment model – full employment without a NAIRU', *Journal of Economic Issues*, 32 (2), 547–55.

Mitchell, W. F. and Mosler, W. (2002), 'The imperative of fiscal policy for full employment', *Australian Journal of Labour Economics*, 5 (2), 243–259.

Mitchell, W. F. and Muysken, J. (2008), *Full Employment Abandoned: Shifting Sands and Policy Failures*, Aldershot: Edward Elgar.

Mitchell, W. F. and Wray, L. R. (2005), 'In defence of the employer of last resort', *Journal of Economic Issues*, 39 (1), March, 235–245.

Noguera, J. (2004), 'Citizens or workers? Basic income vs. welfare to work policies', paper presented at Life beyond Work Workshop, International Institute for the Sociology of Law (IISL), Onati, April.

Ormerod, P. (1994), *The Death of Economics*, London: Faber and Faber.

Rowthorn, R. (1980), *Capitalism, Conflict and Inflation: Essays in Political Economy*, London: Lawrence and Wishart.

Seekings, J. (2006), 'Employment guarantee or minimum income? Workfare and welfare in developing countries', paper presented at the Fifth Congress of the US Basic Income Guarantee Network: Resources and Rights, Philadelphia, 24–26 February.

Sen, A. (1997), 'Inequality, unemployment and contemporary Europe', *International Labour Review*, 136 (2), 161–172.

Standing, G. (2002), *Beyond the New Paternalism: Basic Security as Equality*, London: Verso.

Tcherneva, P. (2003), *Job or Income Guarantee*, CFEPS Working Paper 29, August, http://www.cfeps.org/pubs/wp/wp29/wp29.html.

Timmins, N. (1995), *The Five Giants: A Biography of the Welfare State*, London: Harper-Collins.

Tomlinson, J. (2000), 'The basic solution to unemployment', paper presented to the Seventh National Unemployment Conference, University of Western Sydney, December.

Van der Veen, R. (1998), 'Real freedom versus reciprocity: competing views on the justice of unconditional Basic Income', *Political Studies*, 46 (1), 140–163.

Van Parijs, P. (1991), 'Why surfers should be fed: the liberal case for an unconditional Basic Income', *Philosophy and Public Affairs*, 20, 101–131.

Van Parijs, P. (1993), *Marxism Recycled*, Cambridge: Cambridge University Press.

Van Parijs, P. (1997), 'Reciprocity and the justification of an unconditional Basic Income: reply to Stuart White', *Political Studies*, 45 (2), June, 372–330.

Van Parijs, P. (2000), 'A Basic Income for all', *Boston Review*, October–November, 4–8.

Watts, M. J. and Mitchell, W. F. (2000), 'The costs of unemployment', *Economic and Labour Relations Review*, 11 (2), December, 180–197.

Widerquist, K. and Lewis, M. (1997), *An Efficiency Argument for the Guaranteed Income*, Working Paper No. 212, Jerome Levy Economics Institute.

Wray, L. R. (1998), *Understanding Modern Money*, Northampton: Edward Elgar.

Part IV

Ecological tax reform and the double dividend

9 An applied general equilibrium analysis of a double dividend policy for the Spanish economy

Antonio Manresa

Ferran Sancho

Introduction[1]

There is growing empirical evidence and increasing scientific consensus that CO_2 emissions play a significant role in the escalation of the greenhouse effect. Authorities have tried to respond to this concern by proposing different control mechanisms and policies, with the Kyoto Protocol high on the international political agenda. In the European Union (EU), as a whole, the stated target is an 8 per cent reduction in CO_2 emissions from their 1990 levels by 2012. The preferred policy tool in the EU for achieving this target has been the creation of a market for emission permits whereby the permits can be traded among polluting firms. Another tool under consideration is the enactment of 'green' tax reforms by way of levying an eco-tax on CO_2-polluting goods. There is, however, a considerable tax load already in existence in the EU. To prevent the overall tax load from rising, it is widely felt that any new tax category should satisfy some neutrality requirement regarding total government tax income. In addition, any new tax intended to reduce emissions is likely to increase production costs and possibly lower production levels. All things considered, a new eco-tax should, if enacted, be finely tuned to accommodate other tax instruments and overall tax and spending policies.

The reduction of CO_2 emissions via a new neutral tax instrument raises the question of whether or not there would be an efficiency gain if an existing tax were replaced by an eco-tax. This is the central concern of most of the tax reform literature, which aims at identifying what changes in the tax rates of an existing tax system would promote partial efficiency improvements (e.g., Feldstein, 1976; Atkinson and Stiglitz, 1980; Ahmad and Stern, 1984).

Consider, for instance, the likely consequences of enacting an eco-tax (a tax on CO_2 emissions) and a corresponding reduction in the tax on labour use by firms. There will be, on the one hand, an increase in the production costs due to the new indirect tax and upward pressure on prices. On the other hand, the reduction in the labour tax will lower the contribution of the wage bill to total production costs, thus generating downward pressure on prices. The final effect on prices is not at all clear and will depend on the extent of the cost changes and the behavioural responses of the economic agents involved. Collateral to how prices adjust, there will also be quantity adjustments in both final output and input factor markets. As a possibility, if the demand for labour were to fall relative to labour supply, and the labour market were subject to frictions or rigidities, unemployment might increase. A careful general equilibrium accounting of cost increases and cost reductions is obviously needed to determine the probable final effects. Since the net effects are unclear, the realisation of a double dividend – namely, the reduction in CO_2 emissions and the boost in employment levels – turns out to be an empirical question.

In this chapter, we consider the double dividend question within the context of the Spanish economy using an applied general equilibrium framework. We have built a computable model which allows us to evaluate how resource allocation, prices, and quantities might respond to ecological tax reform policies. The model is calibrated to two different databases: for 1990 and 1995. This double calibration has the advantage of giving us a measure of the overall robustness of the simulation results to the numerical specification. The model simulates alternative fiscal scenarios and sums up the results in terms of CO_2 emissions, employment levels, and a money metric measure of private welfare. Although we shall present the results in greater detail soon, it would appear that a double dividend policy outcome is feasible, but not under all scenarios. A second relevant result links the presence of a double dividend to the degree of flexibility in the economy. By flexibility, we mean technological adaptability in terms of higher substitution possibilities as well as some adaptability in the labour market in terms of unemployment responsiveness to the real wage rate. Summing up, more flexibility increases the likelihood of observing a double dividend result. The type of applied general equilibrium model we use in this study is well known in the literature and has become a widespread tool for policy analysis. The popularity of this family of models can be traced to the seminal contributions of Scarf (1973) and Shoven and Whalley (1984).

The chapter is organised as follows. In the second section, we describe, very briefly, the state of the double dividend literature. In the third section, we outline the structure of the simulation model. The fourth section presents the main empirical results and the final section concludes the chapter.

The double dividend

The public economics literature regards environmental quality as a public good and pollution as a negative externality.[2] In terms of optimal taxation, the imposition of a Pigouvian tax[3] on a polluting agent equal to the marginal environmental damage (MED) is generally recommended to internalise the associated externality. In theory, the Pigouvian tax allows the competitive equilibrium to again correspond to a Pareto-efficient outcome. In reality, however, taxes distort economic decisions, and some markets do not behave according to the competitive norm. A line of research has therefore explored how best to design an optimal environmental tax under competitive conditions in the presence of existing market-distorting taxes. This procedure is referred to as a 'second best' approach in the sense that the aim of the environmental tax is to ensure the existing welfare level is not reduced (Sandmo, 1975; Bovenberg and Van der Ploeg, 1994; Parry, 1995; Bovenberg and Goulder, 1996).

The theoretical answer states that the optimal tax (t), in the second best sense, should satisfy the equation of $t = MED/MCPF$, where $MCPF$ denotes the marginal cost of public funds. From a theoretical perspective, it is shown that a new tax interacts with the existing taxes, creating additional distortions, which ultimately affect private welfare. The key question is therefore this: do these ensuing interactions increase or decrease welfare? The double dividend hypothesis states that the neutral substitution of an existing tax by a new environmental tax may indeed give rise to a double dividend – namely, a reduction in CO_2 emissions and an improvement in efficiency and employment levels. Yet, in many ways, this hypothesis is nothing but a restatement of the standard tax reform position concerning partial welfare improvements plus the obvious effect of reducing CO_2 emissions if the new tax is directed towards emission-producing goods. In other words, we will be considering what we call a 'third best' scenario, whereby a (non-optimal) tax substitution within an existing tax system may prove welfare-promoting if conveniently and accurately calculated. The double dividend issue is therefore one that needs to be studied and perhaps settled empirically.

There are several versions of the double dividend hypothesis ranging from 'weak' to 'strong' possibilities regarding efficiency gains following the enactment of an environmental tax (Goulder, 1995). The 'weak' double dividend hypothesis states that an improvement in efficiency may be possible if there is a lump-sum devolution of the collections of the environmental tax. The 'strong' double dividend hypothesis states that an efficiency gain may occur as a consequence of tax recycling (i.e., where revenue raised from the imposition of a new tax can be used to reduce an existing tax) (Pearce, 1991; Bovenberg and de Mooij, 1994). Finally the 'strongest' or 'employment' double dividend assumption takes the view that tax recycling between a new environmental tax and an existing tax on labour use may boost employment levels (Drèze and Malinvaud, 1993). Recent surveys and reviews of the different versions of the double dividend hypothesis can be found in Bovenberg (1999), Bosello *et al.* (2001), and Schöb (2005).

There is contradicting empirical evidence of the possibility of implementing a double dividend outcome, although most contributions conclude that, when previously attempted, no double dividend can be observed. Goulder (1992, 1995), Parry (1995), Bovenberg and Goulder (1996), and Parry *et al.* (1998) are good examples of negative empirical evidence. On the other hand, Jorgenson and Wilcoxen (1993) and Denis and Koopman (1995) provide positive evidence in favour of a double dividend under certain assumptions and conditions. Most of the models used to explore the double dividend hypothesis assume perfect competition with frictionless market adjustments. The frictionless assumption is particularly difficult to justify for the labour market in view of the considerable unemployment levels in most European economies. Models designed to address the employment (or unemployment) question have tended to favour the presence of a double dividend. The critical issue seems to be whether any new environmental tax can be shifted to agents that do not receive labour income (Bovenberg and de Mooij, 1994; Bovenberg and van der Ploeg, 1994, 1998). When the tax can be shifted forward to other agents, the tax load over labour is reduced and an employment double dividend is more likely to arise. It is not surprising, then, that partial and general equilibrium models featuring one type of good and one type of agent are not especially conducive to observing a double dividend. This is because, implicit in these models, the room that the policy-maker has for shifting forward any tax is limited or simply non-existent.

Fully fledged general equilibrium models, on the other hand, can provide enough flexibility for interactions to take place and adjustments to be realised, particularly labour market adjustments. A characteristic of labour markets in Europe is the presence of involuntary unemployment. Workers may be inelasticly offering their labour endowment at a given wage rate but, if labour demand is not enough to absorb the supply of labour, involuntary unemployment will unavoidably arise. Of course, it may be argued that the wage rate should be lowered to clear labour markets and reduce unemployment. However, the going wage may have been negotiated by unions and, to ensure workers can live a decent existence, may be well above the full employment (market-clearing) wage. Unions, however, may react to the unemployment rate with some adjustment flexibility in wages. This labour market friction introduces a feedback relationship between the real wage and the unemployment rate that renders both the wage rate and the unemployment levels endogenous variables. Thus, a specific unemployment equilibrium structure can be incorporated into an otherwise standard general equilibrium model to allow the model to identify frictions and extend the notion of equilibrium to encompass the unique features of the labour market in question.

The modelling facility

We have built a disaggregated general equilibrium model of the Spanish economy and have implemented it by using two different social accounting matrices: one for 1990; the other for 1995. By employing two independently constructed databases, we can compare and validate the robustness of the simulation results. In our analysis, we have simulated: (a) the introduction of a new environmental tax (eco-tax) modelled as an *ad valorem* tax[4] on energy-related goods; and (b) the reduction of labour taxes across all production sectors under a constant tax collections assumption. Owing to data restrictions, the model contemplates a single representative consumer; this, admittedly, precludes us from considering any distributional effects of the enacted policies. Our analysis therefore focuses exclusively on efficiency issues.

All our tax simulations depict two main scenarios for two periods (1990 and 1995). The first scenario takes into account a so-called 'rigid' version of the economy in which there is no technological adjustment to changing prices, and unemployment is kept fixed at the baseline level. The second scenario depicts a 'flexible' version of the economy in which we allow for choice of technique in primary input factors and for labour market adjustments in response to changing prices and market conditions. The comparison of the results in both limiting scenarios allows us to infer the extent to which technological and behavioural flexibilities matter in terms of attaining a double dividend.

The model we use follows the tradition of applied general equilibrium modelling as developed by Shoven and Whalley (1984) and Ballard *et al.* (1985). Both these instances emphasise, unlike the World Bank trade-oriented models, the role of the government as a spending and tax-collecting agent. These models offer a comprehensive representation of the circular flow of income with agents such as producers, consumers, the government, and the foreign sectors explicitly following a set of behavioural rules for the attainment of their specific goals. The level of disaggregation in the model is consistent with the detail in the Social Accounting Matrices (SAM) database for Spain on a number of production sectors, consumer types, etc.

The production side of the economy includes 35 constant returns-to-scale sectors with a subset of six of them being energy-supplier sectors. The total output supply of a sector is an aggregation of domestic and imported goods. Domestic output is the result of combining an aggregate primary factor (value added) with intermediate goods; value-added is the aggregation of labour and capital. It is assumed that the productive technology adopts the nested structure familiar in computable general equilibrium models. Profit maximisation and a competitive market environment guide the behaviour of producers.

On the demand side, the single representative consumer maximises utility over present and future consumption (savings) under a budget constraint. Gross income is the result of selling the endowments of labour and capital owned by the consumer in the factor markets plus transfers that the consumer receives from the government and the foreign sectors. Disposable income is gross income less the income tax which has been deducted (i.e., after-tax income).

The government plays a singular role in the model and a more detailed description of its activities follows. On the income side, we distinguish five different tax categories. They are:

- an income tax with collections denoted by *INC*;
- an indirect production tax (*IND*);
- a value-added tax (*VAT*);
- a payroll tax (*PRT*); and
- tariffs on imports (*TAR*).

In addition, we aim to include a hypothetical eco-tax (*ECO*) in the counterfactual scenarios (note: *ECO* = 0 in the baseline). We add up tax income from all sources and denote it by *TI*. Besides total tax income (*TI*), the government also obtains capital income (*KG*) from its properties and assets. The government uses its income for expenditure on public consumption (*GPC*) and public investment (*GPI*), and provides social transfers (*GST*). The difference between income and expenditures is the government deficit (or surplus) (*GDF*). That is:

$$GDF = (TI + KG) - (GPC + GPI + GST) \tag{9.1}$$

We can rearrange this expression to obtain:

$$GPC + GPI + GST = TI + KG - GDF \tag{9.2}$$

Under this budget constraint representation, a government deficit can be financed by the sale of government securities (bonds) to the private sector. The sale of bonds permits the government to execute an expenditure level higher than its total income. Notice that, under this representation, the level of the government discretionary spending (public consumption and public investment) can be made exogenous or endogenous. In the first case, the spending level is fixed and the deficit is endogenously determined at equilibrium. In the second case, the government modifies its expenditure levels in accordance to its income to maintain a target deficit/surplus.

The labour market also has a special role in the model. Since we want to model unemployment, we do so by assuming involuntary unemployment in a simple way. That is, we assume that the representative consumer is endowed with labour that is elastically offered at the current real wage rate up to the point of full labour utilisation. At this point, the labour supply is depleted and becomes fully inelastic. Demand for labour is the result of profit maximisation by firms. Under competitive conditions and constant returns to scale, firms formulate their conditional demand for labour. If aggregate conditional demand for labour intersects the labour supply function in the elastic zone, unemployment arises since not all of the labour endowment is employed. In addition, we include a feedback reaction between the real wage and the unemployment rate (u) that aims at picking up wage flexibility in the labour market. The feedback reaction is denoted by:

$$\frac{w}{cpi} = \left(\frac{1-u}{1-\bar{u}}\right)^{1/\beta} \tag{9.3}$$

where w is the nominal wage rate; cpi is a consumer price index; $\bar{u}$ is the baseline unemployment rate; and β is an elasticity parameter that measures the sensitivity of the real wage rate (w/cpi) to the unemployment rate (u). For instance, when $\beta = \infty$, the real wage is fully rigid and unemployment is fully flexible; when $\beta = 0$, unemployment is fully rigid (fixed) and the real wage is fully flexible. In between these polar cases (i.e., $0 < \beta < \infty$), a rise in β increases represents a decline in the sensitivity of the real wage to unemployment.

As is standard in general equilibrium analysis, the description of an equilibrium state includes a vector of prices and an allocation of resources such that all markets for goods, services, and input factors clear. With the possible exception of the labour market, all private agents maximise their objective functions under the restrictions they face, the government fulfils its expenditure plan under its income constraint, and all macro-accounting identities are satisfied (in particular, the 'savings = investment' identity).

Once the price and allocation equilibrium values are known, all national income and product account variables can, if necessary, be calculated (e.g., GDP, tax revenues, etc.). In addition, from the equilibrium values, it is possible to estimate the level of CO_2 emissions using emission coefficients adapted from EuroStat statistics (www.ec.europa.eu/eurostat). We distinguish between emissions that originate from production activities and those from final demand. Emissions levels depend upon the respective emissions 'technology' and the levels of output and final demand. Since output and demands are equilibrium magnitudes within the model, and the observed equilibrium is dependent on the tax rate structure, we are able to ascertain the link between the tax instruments and the level of CO_2 emissions. As the government explores new tax policies (even if only counterfactually), each possible new equilibrium is associated with a particular level of (counterfactual) emissions. Each new possible equilibrium outcome can also be assessed in terms of the welfare effects on consumers and the unemployment rate. We base private welfare on money metric utility using an equivalent variation index. Thus, for each equilibrium, we are able to generate two measures that relate to the double dividend issue we are exploring – one measuring environmental quality in terms of CO_2 emissions; the other measuring possible efficiency gains in terms of welfare or employment levels.[5]

Policies and simulation results

As previously mentioned, the model is calibrated to two SAM databases of the Spanish economy (1990 and 1995). Calibration entails the specification of all technological, behavioural, and tax parameters so that the empirical data reported in both SAMs corresponds with all the equilibrium conditions of the model. We refer to this equilibrium as the baseline or benchmark equilibrium, and we use it as a yardstick to appraise the effects of any change in the tax instruments – particularly, in our case, the introduction of the eco-tax. The model has an exogenous elasticity with a reference value of $\beta = 1.25$ that is drawn from the empirical econometrics literature (Andrés *et al.*, 1990).

All tax rates used in the model are effective, *ad valorem* tax rates. When these rates are applied to the database tax base, all observed tax collections are recuperated. In the simulated equilibrium, the tax bases are endogenous and price- and quantity-dependent. This affects the income side of the government budget constraint. Expenditures on public consumption and investment are also price-dependent and therefore endogenous. Social transfers from the government are also price-dependent since, in actual practice, transfers are adjusted in accordance with changes in the consumer price index in order to maintain their purchasing power.

We consider two versions of the model that represent two polar cases. The first version is, as mentioned earlier in the chapter, the 'rigid' model in which there is no technological substitution and no change in the level of unemployment. In the second 'flexible' version of the model, firms can adjust their demands for primary factors over a smooth isoquant. Hence there is the possibility of adjustments in the labour market that can lead to endogenously determined employment levels or, alternatively, an endogenously determined unemployment rate.

234 Manresa and Sancho

Within each of the two model versions, we contemplate the outcomes of two main tax policy scenarios. The first one consists of the introduction of a new set of eco-taxes on top of the existing tax system. The second scenario is the same as the first except the increased tax pressure/liability is offset by a reduction in the labour tax to maintain total tax collections constant in real terms. The reduction in the labour tax amounts to a homogenous lowering of the social security contributions paid by employers across all productive sectors. We choose this tax as the compensating tax because of its likely positive effect on the labour market.

The tax policy scenarios that we examine include the adoption of a new 10 per cent eco-tax on the use of energy products as well as a 15 per cent increase in the effective tax rate on petroleum products. We consider these policies, by themselves, and then jointly. A summary of the simulation results appear in Tables 9.1 to 9.5.

A first impression suggests that the numerical results for 1990 and 1995 follow very similar patterns – an indication that, despite using two different and independently built databases, there is enough built-in robustness in the results to transcend them. We will use the 1995 numerical results (i.e., the results in parentheses) for clarity of exposition and to lead the discussion.

Table 9.1 displays the simulated effects of the new energy tax policies under the rigid version of the model with no compensating labour tax reduction to offset the increased tax revenues. It is estimated that total CO_2 emissions would fall by about 4 per cent from the baseline figure. Of this decline, 21 per cent can be attributed to the change in final demand and less than 2 per cent to adjustments in production. Total utility and money metric utility – as measured by the equivalent variation index – both fall. Since the levels of employment and capital are kept at the initial levels, the observed change can be explained by a small contraction in

Table 9.1 Estimated eco-tax effects on the Spanish economy (rigid model; no labour tax compensation)

Indicators	Base situation	10% eco-tax (a)	15% petrol tax (b)	(a) + (b)
Unemployment rate (%)	16.3 (22.9)	16.3 (22.9)	16.3 (22.9)	16.3 (22.9)
% Δ in utility	–	–0.013 (–0.015)	–0.002 (–0.003)	–0.016 (–0.018)
Equivalent variation (billions of Euro)	–	–3.385 (–5.775)	–0.607 (–1.099)	–4.047 (–7.009)
% Δ in production-related CO_2 emissions	–	–1.028 (–1.408)	–0.055 (–0.160)	–1.083 (–1.562)
% Δ in demand-related CO_2 emissions	–	–15.195 (–15.518)	–4.329 (–6.506)	–18.921 (–21.148)
% Δ in total CO_2 emissions	–	–3.382 (–3.251)	–0.765 (–0.989)	–4.046 (–4.121)

Δ = change.
Figures not in parentheses are 1990 values; values in parentheses are 1995 values.

aggregate activity levels but with a considerable allocation shift conducive to a substantial reduction in CO_2 emissions. Because consumers cannot shift forward the new taxes, their real income declines, thus explaining the fall in demand and utility. The reduction in CO_2 emissions is not accompanied by an efficiency gain and no double dividend is observed.

Table 9.2 is based on the same eco-taxes as Table 9.1 except it is assumed that a revenue-neutral reduction in the labour tax has been enacted. Total emissions again fall but slightly more than in the previous case. However, in this situation, emissions linked to production fall a little more while emissions linked to final demand fall slightly less. Price adjustments are spread over all sectors and the fall in real income is substantially lower. Indeed, the equivalent variation loss is about one-quarter of the previous example.

The results of the simulations in this second scenario give us a hint to the efficiency cost of the eco-tax policies. Strictly speaking, emissions can be reduced and the efficiency cost in terms of equivalent variation can be interpreted as a shadow cost of the respective policies. When a tax compensation scheme is contemplated, the efficiency cost accompanying the associated emission reductions is much smaller. Because of the assumed rigidity of the model, Table 9.2 does not reveal the existence of a double dividend.

Moving on to Tables 9.3 and 9.4, we analyse the same simulations as in Tables 9.1 and 9.2, but under the flexible version of the model. Here, unemployment is endogenous and the choice of technique takes place over smooth Cobb–Douglas isoquants defined on labour and capital. Table 9.3 examines the same unrestricted tax policies of Table 9.1, whereas in Table 9.4 we add the compensated reduction

Table 9.2   Estimated eco-tax effects on the Spanish economy (rigid model; with labour tax compensation)

Indicators	Base situation	10% eco-tax (a)	15% petrol tax (b)	(a) + (b)
% Δ in labour tax	–	−11.416 (−12.280)	−1.728 (−2.258)	−13.044 (−16.641)
Unemployment rate (%)	16.3 (22.9)	16.3 (22.9)	16.3 (22.9)	16.3 (22.9)
% Δ in utility	–	−0.003 (−0.003)	−0.001 (−0.001)	−0.004 (−0.005)
Equivalent variation (billions of Euro)	–	−0.673 (−1.244)	−0.222 (−0.389)	−0.943 (−1.726)
% Δ in production-related CO_2 emissions	–	−1.091 (−1.601)	−0.064 (−0.191)	−1.155 (−1.788)
% Δ in demand-related CO_2 emissions	–	−13.878 (−14.715)	−4.125 (−6.373)	−17.469 (−20.273)
% Δ in total CO_2 emissions	–	−3.214 (−3.315)	−0.739 (−0.999)	−3.865 (−4.203)

Δ = change.
Figures not in parentheses are 1990 values; values in parentheses are 1995 values.

Table 9.3   Estimated eco-tax effects on the Spanish economy (flexible model ($\beta = 1.25$); no labour tax compensation)

Indicators	Base situation	10% eco-tax (a)	15% petrol tax (b)	(a) + (b)
Unemployment rate (%)	16.3	17.1	16.4	17.3
	(22.9)	(23.8)	(23.1)	(24.0)
% Δ in utility	–	–0.162	–0.298	–1.954
		(–1.897)	(–0.374)	(–2.326)
Equivalent variation	–	–4.076	–0.749	–4.911
(billions of Euro)		(–7.348)	(–1.446)	(–9.005)
% Δ in production-related	–	–1.573	–0.158	–1.749
CO_2 emissions		(–2.176)	(–0.337)	(–2.538)
% Δ in demand-related	–	–15.064	–4.337	–18.806
CO_2 emissions		(–16.164)	(–6.430)	(–21.886)
% Δ in total CO_2 emissions	–	–3.810	–0.852	–4.582
		(–4.004)	(–1.161)	(–5.066)

Δ = change.
Figures not in parentheses are 1990 values; values in parentheses are 1995 values.

in the labour tax. In Table 9.3, CO_2 emissions fall slightly more than in the rigid model (5 per cent), with the main reduction taking place in emissions related to production activities. This is an indication that the eco-tax policy has induced a substitution towards labour–capital combinations (particularly capital) with a lesser indirect energy content. The welfare indicators fall, and do so to a larger extent than in the rigid model. A possible explanation is the fall in labour use now that unemployment is endogenous. Just over a 1 per cent increase in the unemployment rate is observed. This reduces labour income and private consumption and thus has a negative effect on welfare.

In sharp contrast to this uncompensated tax scenario, we find, in Table 9.4, that unemployment decreases under all tax policies and that welfare improves under the 10 per cent eco-tax policy. The total level of CO_2 emissions is smaller than the equivalent policy scenario in the rigid model (Table 9.2). There is, therefore, a clear double dividend in terms of a welfare gain, a reduction in the unemployment rate, and diminished CO_2 emissions. In fact, there is an employment double dividend under all three tax policies and a strong double dividend under the selective 10 per cent eco-tax policy.

The revenue-neutral tax policies of Table 9.4 do indeed provide a positive drive in terms of efficiency gains. The reduction in the labour tax across all productive sectors proves to be stimulative enough to bring about a substitution of labour for capital, as well as a lesser indirect energy content of production, which can potentially alleviate any high unemployment levels that may exist. Moreover, since the results carry over to both empirical databases for 1990 and 1995, this serves as good empirical evidence in support of the overall effectiveness of the studied tax policies. The policy conclusion is that there is probably enough room to redesign

Table 9.4 Estimated eco-tax effects on the Spanish economy (flexible model ($\beta = 1.25$); with labour tax compensation)

Indicators	Base situation	10% eco-tax (a)	15% petrol tax (b)	(a) + (b)
% Δ in labour tax	–	−11.420 (−15.028)	−1.730 (−2.095)	−13.040 (−17.174)
Unemployment rate (%)	16.3 (22.9)	15.6 (22.1)	16.2 (22.9)	15.6 (22.2)
% Δ in utility	–	0.050 (0.031)	−0.047 (−0.110)	−0.043 (−0.128)
Equivalent variation (billions of Euro)	–	−0.126 (0.122)	−0.119 (−0.427)	−0.110 (−0.498)
% Δ in production-related CO_2 emissions	–	−0.688 (−1.017)	−0.023 (−0.181)	−0.737 (−1.224)
% Δ in demand-related CO_2 emissions	–	−13.520 (−14.497)	−4.081 (−6.395)	−17.110 (−20.107)
% Δ in total CO_2 emissions	–	−2.820 (−2.778)	−0.697 (−0.993)	−3.457 (−3.691)

Δ = change.
Figures not in parentheses are 1990 values; values in parentheses are 1995 values.

the actual tax system to achieve efficiency gains at no cost in terms of the tax collections to the government. With the revenue-neutral assumption driving the redesigned tax policy, all government expenditure policies (public consumption, public investment, and social transfers) can continue unabated. The economy, however, would reach a different equilibrium with a double dividend in terms of environmental quality and efficiency improvements. Flexibility, therefore, seems to be the leading factor behind the achievement of a double dividend.

In Table 9.5, we check this flexibility assertion by way of measuring the economic and environmental impact under different labour market scenarios (i.e., $\beta = 5$ and $\beta = \infty$). We have simplified matters by confining the results to the most recent database (1995) and by assuming a 10 per cent eco-tax across the board.

Although increasing labour market flexibility gives rise to better efficiency indicators, in terms of both less unemployment and more real income, it comes at a cost in terms of decreasing emissions. Examining the effects of a value of $\beta = \infty$ in relation to the reference elasticity of $\beta = 1.5$, we can see that there is a gain of nearly 2 per cent in the level of employed labour. However, total emissions of CO_2 decrease by around half the total level for the reference elasticity (i.e., from a 2.78 per cent fall at $\beta = 1.5$ to a 1.49 per cent fall at $\beta = \infty$). Interestingly, the composition of CO_2 emissions shows that production-related emissions rise rather than decline (a 1.01 per cent fall at $\beta = 1.5$; a 0.34 per cent increase at $\beta = \infty$). What this suggests is that the eco-tax would initially induce a substitution effect which would reduce CO_2 emissions. Eventually, the labour market flexibility would bring about a volume or output effect that would offset the substitution

Table 9.5   Estimated eco-tax effects on the Spanish economy (10% energy tax; flexible model ($\beta = 1.25, 5, \infty$); with labour tax compensation)

Indicators	Base situation	($\beta = 1.25$) (i)	($\beta = 1.25$) (ii)	($\beta = \infty$) (iii)
Unemployment rate (%)	22.9	22.1	21.3	20.3
% Δ in utility	–	0.031	0.534	1.083
Equivalent variation (billions of Euro)	–	0.122	2.068	4.194
% Δ in production-related CO_2 emissions	–	–1.017	–0.369	0.338
% Δ in demand-related CO_2 emissions	–	–14.497	–14.087	–13.660
% Δ in total CO_2 emissions	–	–2.778	–2.162	–1.490

Δ = change.
All figures in 1995 values.

effect. Thus, more labour market flexibility may not generate dominant double dividend outcomes. The parametric trade-off between real income and emissions can thus be traced to a higher degree of labour market flexibility.

Concluding remarks

We have used a computable general equilibrium model of the Spanish economy to examine the likelihood of achieving the double dividend following the enactment of ecological tax reform measures. This methodology is well known for its modelling versatility and its ability to capture the detail of decision-making at the level of basic agents – namely, producers, consumers, and the government. The inclusion of labour market dynamics was especially important given our desire to capture some empirical characteristics of the Spanish labour market. Two other key features built into the model were: (a) the possibility of involuntary unemployment; and (b) the linking of the real wage rate to the unemployment rate using a labour market elasticity parameter to represent the prevailing degree of labour market rigidity in the Spanish economy.

Taking into account two kinds of eco-taxes and a compensating labour tax reduction, two main conclusions can be deduced from this study. The first conclusion is that an employment double dividend – i.e., lower CO_2 emissions and a lower unemployment rate – is an empirical possibility under a standard set of model characteristics and policy options. The second conclusion is that, up to a point, a flexible labour market will respond well to tax policies directed at containing CO_2 emissions and improving labour utilisation (lowering unemployment). Beyond such a point, increased labour market flexibility may work against the lowering of CO_2 emissions. Overall, however, revenue neutral tax policies are necessary, but not always sufficient, to achieve the double dividend.

It should be said that simulation results showing a double dividend outcome illustrate what is empirically and theoretically possible, but do not necessarily indicate what will actually happen. Results depend always on the structure of the model, the behavioural rules of private agents, the different expenditure policies of the government that often accompany new tax policies, and many other implicit and explicit assumptions that are needed to make a model operational. For instance, we assumed no substitution among intermediate energy inputs in both the rigid and flexible versions of the model. Our justification for this assumption was that we wanted to observe the equilibrium outcome in the short run. Of course, this restrictive modelling assumption is a least favourable scenario if one of the policy goals is to lower CO_2 emissions. However, even under this restriction, a double dividend could in principle be observed in our model. Thus, what appears to be a restrictive assumption turns out to support the argument that governments, in their efforts to reconcile the environment–employment dilemma, should seriously consider introducing ecological tax reform to achieve the double dividend.

Notes

1 Institutional support from research grants SEJ2006-07884 and SGR2005-00984 (Manresa) and SEC200-712 and SGR2005-0712 (Sancho) is gratefully acknowledged. Stated opinions are those of the authors and therefore do not reflect the viewpoint of the supporting institutions. We thank Jordi Roca and José Maria Labeaga for comments on an earlier draft.
2 A public good has two main characteristics: (a) non-rivalry of consumption/use; and (b) non-excludability of consumption/use. Environmental quality is a public good because one's enjoyment of it does not affect another's ability to enjoy it (i.e., non-rivalry) and because it is not possible to exclude someone from enjoying the benefits of environmental quality (e.g., the breathing of clean air) should they refuse to pay for such benefits (i.e., non-excludability). A negative externality occurs when the actions of one party imposes uncompensated costs on another party. Pollution is a prime example of a negative externality.
3 A tax to internalise the cost of a negative externality was labelled a Pigouvian tax following the work of Pigou (1924).
4 An *ad valorem* tax is a tax levied as a percentage of the final price of a particular good.
5 A more detailed technical description of the model and the overall equilibrium conditions can be found in Manresa and Sancho (2005).

References

Ahmad, E. and Stern, N. (1984), 'The theory of tax reform and Indian indirect taxes', *Journal of Public Economics*, 25, 259–298.

Andrés, J., Dolado, J. J., Molinas, C., Sebastián, M., and Zabalza, A. (1990), 'The Influence of Demand and Capital Constraints on Spanish Unemployment', in J. Drèze and C. Bean (eds), *Europe's Unemployment Problem*, Cambridge, MA: MIT Press.

Atkinson, A. N. and Stiglitz, J. (1980), *Lectures in Public Economics*, New York: McGraw-Hill.

Ballard, C., Fullerton, D., Shoven, J., and Whalley, J. (1985), *A General Equilibrium Model for Tax Policy Evaluation*, Chicago: NBER and University of Chicago Press.

Bosello, F., Carraro, C., and Galeotti, G. (2001), 'The double dividend issue: modeling strategies and empirical findings', *Environmental and Development Economics*, 6, 9–45.

Bovenberg, L. (1999), 'Green tax reforms and the double dividend: an updated reader's guide', *International Tax and Public Finance*, 6, 421–443.

Bovenberg, L. and de Mooij, R. A. (1994), 'Environmental levies and distortionary taxation', *American Economic Review*, 94, 1085–1099.

Bovenberg, L. and Goulder, L. H. (1996) 'Optimal environmental taxation in the presence of other taxes: general equilibrium analyses', *American Economic Review*, 86 (4), 985–1000.

Bovenberg, L. and Van der Ploeg, F. (1994), 'Environmental policy, public finance, and the labor market in a second-best world', *Journal of Public Economics*, 55, 349–390.

Bovenberg, L. and Van der Ploeg, F. (1998), 'Tax reform, structural unemployment and the environment', *Scandinavian Journal of Economics*, 100 (3), 593–610.

Denis, C. and Koopman, J. (1995), 'Differential treatment of sectors and energy products in the design of a CO_2/energy tax: consequences for employment, economic welfare, and CO_2 emissions', Working Paper 32/95, Fondazione Enrico Mattei.

Drèze, J. H. and Malinvaud, E. (1993), 'Growth and employment: the scope of an European initiative', *European Economic Review*, 38, 489–504.

Feldstein, M. S. (1976), 'On the theory of tax reform', *Journal of Public Economics*, 6, 77–104.

Goulder, L. H. (1992), 'Do the costs of a carbon tax vanish when interactions with other taxes are accounted for?', NBER, Working Paper 4061.

Goulder, L. H. (1995), 'Environmental taxation and the "double dividend": a reader's guide', *International Tax and Public Finance*, 2, 155–182.

Jorgenson, D. W. and Wilcoxen, P. J. (1993), 'Reducing U.S. carbon emissions: an econometric general equilibrium assessment', *Resource and Energy Economics*, 15 (1), 7–25.

Manresa, A. and Sancho, F. (2005), 'Implementing a double dividend: recycling ecotaxes towards lower labour taxes', *Energy Policy*, 33, 1577–1585.

Parry, I. W. H. (1995), 'Pollution taxes and revenue recycling', *Journal of Environmental Economics and Management*, 29, 564–577.

Parry, I. W. H., Willians, R. C., III, and Goulder, L. H. (1998), *When can Carbon Abatement Policies Increase Welfare? The Fundamental Role of Distorted Factor Markets*, Resources for the Future Discussion Paper 97-18-REV

Pearce, D. W. (1991), 'The role of carbon taxes in adjusting to global warming', *Economic Journal*, 101, 938–948.

Pigou, A. C. (1924), *The Economics of Welfare*, London: Macmillan.

Sandmo, A. (1975), 'Optimal taxation in the presence of externalities', *Swedish Journal of Economics*, 77, 86–98.

Scarf, H. E. (1973), *The Computation of Economic Equilibria*, New Haven, CT: Cowles Foundation, Yale University Press.

Schöb, R. (2005), 'The double dividend hypothesis of environmental taxes: a survey', in H. Folmer and T. Tietenberg (eds), *The International Yearbook of Environmental and Resource Economics 2005/2006*, Cheltenham: Edward Elgar.

Shoven, J. and Whalley, J. (1984), 'Applied general equilibrium analysis of taxation and trade', *Journal of Economic Literature*, 22 (3), 1007–1051.

10 An empirical assessment of ecological tax reform and the double dividend

Philip Lawn

Introduction

Many ecological economists adopt a lukewarm position with respect to conventional ecological tax reform (ETR) measures. The reason for this is straightforward – although ecological economists believe that conventional ETR measures are likely to improve resource use efficiency and increase the attractiveness of employing labour, they are unable to: (a) guarantee that economic activity is ecologically sustainable; and (b) reduce unemployment sufficiently to achieve full employment. Given this, ecological economists believe that conventional ETR measures are unlikely to deliver the double dividend of ecological sustainability and low unemployment (or full employment).

The principal aim of this chapter is to offer support for the ecological economic position on ETR. To achieve this aim, empirical evidence is provided of the efficiency, employment, and CO_2 emissions performances of Sweden, Denmark, the Netherlands, and Finland. These four countries have been chosen because they, more than any other countries, have come closest to explicitly implementing a package of ETR measures (Hoerner and Bosquet, 2001). All four countries introduced CO_2 taxes in the early 1990s, which were either immediately or later accompanied by decreased tax rates on income and/or labour.

For the purposes of this chapter, the efficiency performance of the above four nations is reflected by the ratio of real GDP to CO_2 emissions. Both the total number of people employed and the unemployment rate were used to indicate the employment impact of ETR measures, while total CO_2 emissions were used as an indicator of environmental stress.

Total CO_2 emissions was the preferred environmental indicator for three reasons. Firstly, the environmental element of the ETR packages of all four counties focused primarily on subduing CO_2 emissions in order to meet Kyoto obligations. Secondly, since CO_2 emissions are highly correlated to energy consumption, and energy is necessary to fuel the economic process, total CO_2 emissions constitute a good macro indicator of a nation's environmental impact. Finally, climate change – of which CO_2 emissions are the principal cause – is regarded as one of humankind's most pressing environmental concerns.

What is the conventional approach to ETR?

In conventional terms, ETR involves the imposition of taxes on such 'bads' as resource depletion and pollution and reduced tax rates on such 'goods' as labour and income (see, for example, O'Riordan, 1997; Roodman, 1998; Hoerner and Bosquet, 2001; Schöb, 2005). In most cases, ETR is promoted as a revenue-neutral means of achieving the double dividend of ecological sustainability and low unemployment (Daly, 1996; Hoerner and Bosquet, 2001; Schöb, 2005).

How does ETR supposedly deliver the double dividend? Firstly, ETR proponents believe that taxing resource depletion and pollution creates an immediate incentive for producers to reduce resource wastage and a long-term incentive to develop and install resource-saving technologies. Thus, by reducing the rate of resource throughput per unit of economic activity, depletion and pollution taxes are able to alleviate the growing pressure that economic activity currently imposes on the natural environment.

From an employment perspective, conventional ETR proponents believe that reduced tax rates on labour and income will encourage the employment of labour and reward value-adding in production (Lawn, 2007). Indeed, by rewarding better rather than more production, ETR advocates believe that reduced tax rates on income can boost real wages and enable workers to increase their leisure time (i.e., permit workers to reduce the number of hours spent at work). In turn, this can promote job sharing and thus reduce the unemployment rate. In all, conventional ETR proponents argue that ETR can overcome the common fear that depletion and pollution taxes will result in rising unemployment (Bosquet, 2000; Forstater, 2004; Lawn, 2004a; Victor and Rosenbluth, Chapter 13 of this volume).

It is important to recognise, at this point, that conventional ETR measures rely entirely on the role that tax-adjusted market prices play in altering the incentives and disincentives of producers, consumers, and workers alike in order to achieve the desired goals of ecological sustainability and low unemployment. Clearly, an important assumption underlying the claim made by conventional ETR advocates is that ecological sustainability can be achieved by internalising the spillover costs of resource depletion and pollution. In other words, by ensuring the prices of material goods reflect the marginal social cost of production (resource inputs) and consumption (waste outputs), it is assumed that all ensuing outcomes will be ecologically sustainable. As we shall soon see, it is here where some ecological economists depart, not from the concept of ETR itself, but from the conventional ETR approach.

What do some ecological economists have to say about conventional ETR measures and why?

Conventional ETR measures and the Jevons effect

Many ecological economists are quite comfortable with the idea that conventional ETR measures can have positive employment implications. As such, they believe that tax reductions on income and labour should remain an essential feature of any ETR package. However, they are much less confident that the depletion/pollution tax element of a conventional ETR approach can achieve ecological sustainability. These misgivings stem from the ecological economic argument that sustainability is essentially a resource throughput problem yet the beneficial function of market prices, and this includes tax-adjusted resource prices, is strictly confined to improving the efficiency with which a given rate of resource throughput – whether it be ecologically sustainable or not – is allocated to alternative product uses.

There is no doubt that a more efficient allocation of natural resources is socially desirable with obvious environmental benefits *per unit of economic activity*. The problem, according to ecological economists, is that any efficiency gains secured in an economic system devoid of any explicit limitation on the rate of resource throughput are likely to be overwhelmed by the scale impact of increased economic activity – the so-called 'Jevons effect'. When this occurs, the aggregate rate of resource throughput and any subsequent environmental stress increases rather than diminishes. Because the conventional ETR approach does not involve an explicit limitation on the rate of resource throughput, ecological economists argue that conventional ETR measures cannot prevent the intensity of environmental stress from eventually exceeding the ecosphere's biophysical carrying capacity.

There are two main factors underpinning the argument put forward by ecological economists. The first factor relates to the first and second laws of thermodynamics. As explained in Chapter 2, both laws preclude 100 per cent production efficiency, which means that the matter–energy embodied in newly produced goods must be something less than the matter–energy embodied in the low-entropy resources used in their production.[1] As an added constraint, the first and second laws of thermodynamics prohibit the 100 per cent recycling of matter and forbid the recycling of energy altogether. Thus, taken together, the first and second laws of thermodynamics ensure that, as production efficiency nears its asymptotic value of 100 per cent (i.e., $E < 1$), efficiency advances are subject to diminishing returns.

The main ramification of diminishing returns is destined to apply if nations attempt to continuously increase the physical volume of economic activity. This is because a reduction in the aggregate impact on the environment is only possible if the percentage increase in resource use efficiency continues to exceed the percentage increase in the quantity of new goods produced. Since the inevitability of diminishing returns precludes this situation from occurring indefinitely, the continued growth in real GDP must eventually be unsustainable.

Of course, the problem of unsustainability need not arise if tax-adjusted resource prices can put a brake on the physical volume of economic activity to ensure it remains within biophysical limits. But, in order to achieve this, tax-adjusted resource prices must reflect the *absolute scarcity* of the total resource stock and its constituent resource types. For reasons soon to be explained, ecological economists stress that market prices reflect *relative* not absolute scarcities, and are thus incapable of ensuring ecological sustainability.

To achieve ecological sustainability, many ecological economists believe it is necessary for an ETR package to include a separate policy instrument in the form of quantitative throughput controls that are based on ecological rather than economic criteria (Daly, 1991; Lawn, 2000, 2007). Ecological economists are therefore in favour of tradeable resource use and pollution permits – essentially 'cap and trade' systems – rather than direct depletion and pollution taxes.[2]

How can permit systems successfully deal with the sustainability issue in a manner that depletion/pollution taxes cannot? Unlike conventional ETR packages, a restriction on the number of permits auctioned by a government authority automatically limits the throughput of matter–energy to a rate consistent with the regenerative and waste assimilative capacities of the natural environment.[3] This immediately resolves the sustainability goal. The revenue raised from the sale of the permits can be redistributed to the poor and those directly harmed by depletion/pollution activities. This assists in the resolution of society's equity goals. Finally, the premium paid by resource buyers for the limited number of permits – which is determined by demand and *constrained* supply forces in the various resource markets – serves as a throughput or absolute scarcity tax to facilitate the efficient allocation of the incoming resource flow.[4] Hence, permit systems achieve everything that is likely to be generated by depletion and pollution taxes except they go one step further and ensure ecological sustainability.[5]

Why can't tax-adjusted resource prices achieve ecological sustainability?

As just mentioned, whether tax-adjusted resource prices can negate the Jevons effect and bring about ecological sustainability depends essentially on whether they can adequately reflect the absolute scarcity of the total resource stock. Ecological economists believe they cannot. Their position can be summarised by the following. Firstly, relative prices are generated by interacting market demand and supply forces, which are essentially flow-based forces. By flow-based forces I mean the inflowing quantity of low entropy resources demanded at various prices by resource buyers and, on the supply side, the inflowing quantity of the various types and grades of low entropy resources supplied at various prices by resource sellers.

Secondly, although the stock of a particular resource has some bearing over the inflowing quantity being supplied, the supply of a particular incoming flow at any point in time is much less restricted than the supply of the same incoming flow over time. For example, if timber suppliers double the quantity of timber supplied to a particular timber market, they can continue to do this for some limited period even if the rate of supply exceeds the capacity of forests/timber plantations to supply the same quantity of timber over time. As for the suppliers of a non-renewable resource, any quantity supplied at a particular point in time cannot be continued indefinitely. However, until the stock of the resource is close to exhaustion, it is still possible for its short-term supply to be increased.

Thirdly, in the short term, when a larger yet unsustainable quantity of a particular resource is being supplied, it is possible, at least during the initial depletion phase of the resource, for the price-influencing effect of flow-based forces to dominate the stock effect. Should this be occurring, the relative price of a dwindling resource falls rather than rises – as one would expect of the short-run price for crude oil if, for example, OPEC countries immediately increased oil production. Would this fall in price be a reflection of its declining absolute scarcity? No. It would be a reflection of a higher inflowing quantity (declining relative scarcity) at a time when the remaining stock was shrinking (increasing absolute scarcity).

It is true that the stock effect on resource prices must eventually outweigh the flow effect since, on the supply side, resource prices are also influenced by the cost of extraction/harvesting. This cost is likely to rise sharply as it becomes increasingly difficult to sustain the same inflowing quantity from an ever-diminishing stock. Clearly, resource prices must eventually rise to reflect an increase in the absolute scarcity of low entropy matter–energy. But there are three main reasons why the conveyance of this information in markets is likely to be delayed or not be properly conveyed at all. To begin with, resources themselves are required to extract/harvest resources. If the prices of the resources used to extract/harvest new resources are understated, so is the cost of extraction. This, in turn, understates the cost of future extraction, and so on. Secondly, futures markets are imperfect at best and non-existent at worst. Thirdly, where futures markets exist, they are designed to capture the stock effect on the future supplies of particular resources. For example, if the stock of a particular resource is severely limited, so are future supplies. One would expect the price of a rapidly dwindling resource in a futures contract to be very high to reflect the shortage of future supplies. Although the price might well be higher, it is unlikely to be sufficiently high because people have the tendency to discount future values, including the cost to future generations of having smaller resource stocks. Furthermore, future generations, the very people most likely to be adversely affected by increasing resource scarcity, have no way of bidding in the present for the future availability of resources. Taken together, these factors may or may not threaten the intergenerational efficiency of resource use. However, intergenerational efficiency does not guarantee intergenerational equity (sustainability) in the same way intragenerational efficiency need not coincide with intragenerational equity (Howarth and Norgaard, 1990; Daly, 1991). In all, the price signals generated by resource markets, including futures markets, are likely to be ineffective at ensuring natural capital maintenance and a sustainable resource flow.

I might also point out that a recent simulation exercise (Lawn, 2004b) appears to theoretically support the ecological economic position on resource prices and resource scarcity. Based on a welfare-maximising natural resource model, the exercise suggests that the price of an increasingly scarce resource is likely to decline in the initial depletion phase. Only as stock-based supply-side forces eventually overwhelm flow-based supply-side forces does the price of the resource begin to rise rapidly. Importantly, this occurs only once the stock of the resource approaches total exhaustion. To make matters worse, the initial fall in the resource price and the rapid rate of depletion are accentuated by a number of factors. The first occurs whenever the resource price is in some way a function of its past price – something that is critical given that the extraction of many resource types requires the use of the resource being extracted (e.g., oil is invariably used to power the oil extraction process). The second involves the use of high discount rates, which markedly devalue the future impact of dwindling resource stocks, and the third occurs when governments, as they have a tendency to do, subsidise resource extraction industries in order to promote the growth of a nation's GDP.

Evidence of ETR performances

Previous assessments

In this sub-section, I shall briefly reveal some of the evidence already obtained regarding the success or otherwise of ETR policies. A great deal of the work conducted on ETR has focused on simulation exercises designed to predict the likely outcome of various ETR measures. Much less has involved the analysis of data to assess the efficacy of ETR measures previously implemented in various countries. Consequently, very little of the work has led to conclusive statements about the role and value of ETR.

One of the most significant recent surveys on ETR was conducted by Bosquet (2000). The survey consisted of 56 studies of *ex ante* modelling exercises (i.e., simulation studies designed to predict the likely impact of ETR measures rather than *ex post* studies examining the actual economic and environmental impacts of ETR measures already imposed). On the whole, the simulation exercises predicted that ETR measures should lower carbon emissions, reduce the rate of energy use, and relieve environmental stress. Moreover, since CO_2 emissions taxes and energy taxes have considerable revenue potential, it was expected that environmental taxes would allow governments to lighten the tax burden on personal income and on the employment of labour (Bosquet, 2000).[6] This, it seemed, provided widespread support for the ability of ETR to deliver the double dividend of ecological sustainability and low unemployment.

One of the more obvious limitations of *ex ante* analyses is that simulation models cannot fully incorporate the impact that dynamic efficiency, technological progress, and complex feedback processes can have on future outcomes. As such, their predictive power is somewhat questionable. In all, the success of any policy can be ascertained only via an *ex post* examination of relevant data. Unfortunately, *ex post* assessments of ETR are few in number. One such example is a study by Larsen and Nesbakken (1997), which claims that, from 1991 to 1993, carbon taxes assisted Norway to reduce carbon emissions from stationary sources in the manufacturing and service sectors by 3–4 per cent, with similar reductions observed in relation to household stationary and mobile sources.[7] With the benefit of time, it can be revealed that Norway's CO_2 emissions rose significantly between 1993 and 1997 and were tempered only by the introduction of a new round of carbon taxes in 1999 (Statistics Norway, various). Overall, Norway's

CO_2 emissions increased by over 10 per cent between 1990 and 2002 (Statistics Norway, various).

A study by the Swedish EPA (Swedish EPA, 1997) also claims that Swedish ETR measures have reduced CO_2 emissions. Unfortunately, the Swedish EPA provides no quantitative estimate of the reductions. As we shall see in an upcoming section of the chapter, Swedish ETR measures in the mid-1990s were successful at reducing CO_2 emissions in the short term only. Increases in real GDP after 1999 appeared to overwhelm the efficiency benefits induced by the Swedish ETR measures that, in turn, led to a rise in CO_2 emissions in each year from 2000 to 2003.

The same has also occurred where ETR has been used to target other pollutants. Ekins (1999) has shown that a Swedish nitrogen oxide (NO_x) tax announced in 1990 and imposed in 1992 led to massive reductions in NO_x emission levels between 1990 and 1995. However, by 2000, Swedish NO_x emissions had risen by 23.1 per cent on their 1995 levels (WRI, www.earthtrends.wri.org). Interestingly, most of the initial decline in NO_x emissions between 1990 and 1995 occurred in 1991, the year following the announcement of the tax. Hence, the announcement effect proved to be more powerful than the tax itself.

In what appears to be a clear example of the Jevons effect, Ekins (1999) has also provided evidence of the impact of a 5 per cent per annum increase in road fuel duties that was introduced by the UK government in 1993. In 1995, petrol and diesel demand fell by 1 per cent despite a rise in the volume of economic activity (as measured by real GDP). However, between 1995 and 1997, the rise in economic activity more than offset any efficiency gains so that the consumption of petrol and diesel increased by 5 per cent over this two-year period. This pattern has persisted in the UK, indicating that higher fuel taxes have failed to prevent a rise in petrol and diesel usage.

Analysis of the ETR performances of Sweden, Denmark, the Netherlands, and Finland

In this sub-section of the chapter, the ETR measures of Sweden, Denmark, the Netherlands, and Finland are summarised, as is the timing of their introduction. Empirical evidence is then provided in both tabulated and diagrammatical form with an assessment made of the impact of the respective ETR packages.

Sweden

Sweden first introduced ETR measures in 1991, which entailed a range of environmental taxes and levies, such as an excise tax on CO_2 emissions and a reduction in income tax rates. In 1993, following claims by energy-intensive industries that the 1991 measures were impacting on international competitiveness, the CO_2 tax rate for industry and horticulture was significantly reduced (Hoerner and Bosquet, 2001). However, by 1997, and following a small rise in the CO_2 tax rate in 1996, CO_2 taxes were increased to just short of their 1991 rates. In addition, it was decided that CO_2 tax rates should be adjusted to take account of inflation. This aside, fuels used for electricity generation remained exempt from CO_2 taxes and other energy taxes, while many other energy-intensive industries continued to enjoy a cap on CO_2 tax obligations provided that their total CO_2 tax impost exceeded 0.8 per cent of sales (Hoerner and Bosquet, 2001).

In 2001, in an attempt to quell the rise in CO_2 and other emissions, the Swedish Government decided to widen the scope of its environmental taxes. In addition, CO_2 tax rates were further increased. These tax rises were matched by income tax rate reductions and a cut to employers' social security contributions to the national pension fund.

Both the environmental and employment elements of Sweden's ETR measures and the timing of both their introduction and modifications are summarised in columns *j* and *k* of Table 10.1. The notes below the table indicate the exact nature of the tax rates. Columns *a–h* of Table 10.1 also reveal the various indicators relevant to Sweden's ETR performance over the period 1990–2004.

Figure 10.1, which is drawn from the data in Table 10.1, graphically illustrates both the CO_2 emissions of Sweden (column *b* of Table 10.1) and the ratio of Sweden's real GDP to CO_2 emissions (column *d* of Table 10.1). Interestingly, the initial introduction of a CO_2 tax did little to increase the efficiency ratio or reduce Sweden's CO_2 emissions. Only following the increases in CO_2 tax rates in the mid- and late 1990s did the efficiency performance of Sweden improve. Nevertheless, it was short-lived. For example, between 1996 and 2000, the ratio of Sweden's real GDP to CO_2 emissions rose steadily from 33,680.6 SEK per tonne to 45,292.5 SEK per tonne – a 34.5 per cent increase. This contributed to a decline in CO_2 emissions over the same four-year period from 56.9 to 48.9 million tonnes – a 14.0 per cent reduction. However, between 2000 and 2003, the ratio of Sweden's real GDP to CO_2 emissions remained almost unchanged (in fact, fell by 0.6 per cent), while CO_2 emissions rose slightly from 48.9 million tonnes in 2000 to 51.6 million tonnes in 2003 – a 5.4 per cent increase. In 2004, the final year of the study period, the efficiency ratio jumped sharply (45,028.6 SEK per tonne to 47,747.3 SEK per tonne). Correspondingly, CO_2 emissions declined.

Figure 10.2 again illustrates Sweden's CO_2 emissions and efficiency ratio except that the data in both cases have been set to an index value of 100 for the first year of the study period (columns *c* and *e* of Table 10.1). This provides a better demonstration of the trend change in both indicators as well as their comparative change in each year. It can be seen quite clearly from Figure 10.2 that both indicators moved in opposite directions in almost every year during the study period. This suggests that efficiency increases were able to reduce Sweden's environmental stress. In other words, the ETR measures implemented by the Swedish government appear to have prevented the scale impact of a growing real GDP from entirely overwhelming the efficiency improvements induced. Having said this, the relative rise in the efficiency ratio over the study period was far more pronounced (+35.1 per cent) than the overall fall in Sweden's CO_2 emissions (−2.4 per cent). Given the small margins involved, it cannot be concluded that ef-

Table 10.1 Ecological tax reform performance of Sweden, 1990–2004

Year	Real GDP (billion SEK) (2000 prices)	CO_2 emissions (000s tonnes)	CO_2 emissions (1990 = 100.0)	Real GDP/CO_2 ratio (SEK per tonne) (a/b)	Index of GDP/CO_2 (1990 = 100.0)	Employment numbers (000s)	Unemployment rate (%)	Real GDP/employment ratio (SEK per emp. person) (a/f)	ETR environmental element	ETR employment element
	a	b	c	d	e	f	g	h	j	k
1990	1,828.6	51,733.64	100.0	35,346.5	100.0	4,636.1	1.8	394,426.5		
1991	1,808.9	52,484.16	101.5	34,464.9	97.5	4,536.3	3.1	398,752.6	CO_2 tax imposed (A)	Income tax cut (B)
1992	1,787.5	52,397.47	101.3	34,113.7	96.5	4,351.9	5.1	410,734.0		
1993	1,751.8	51,850.19	100.2	33,786.0	95.6	4,087.4	9.6	428,587.4	CO_2 tax modified (C)	
1994	1,820.2	54,268.90	104.9	33,539.9	94.9	4,080.9	8.8	446,022.0		
1995	1,891.3	53,310.37	103.0	35,476.3	100.4	4,173.7	8.3	453,136.3		
1996	1,916.6	56,905.56	110.0	33,680.6	95.3	4,133.9	8.8	463,633.4	CO_2 tax increased (D)	
1997	1,961.3	52,551.64	101.6	37,322.2	105.6	4,091.5	9.1	479,370.4	CO_2 tax increased (E)	
1998	2,033.2	53,006.47	102.5	38,357.5	108.5	4,160.4	8.0	488,701.6	CO_2 tax indexed (F)	
1999	2,125.2	50,402.79	97.4	42,164.4	119.3	4,253.0	6.4	499,694.8	CO_2 tax indexed (F)	
2000	2,217.3	48,954.92	94.6	45,292.5	128.1	4,320.2	5.2	513,237.8	CO_2 tax indexed (F)	
2001	2,241.0	49,437.24	95.6	45,329.9	128.2	4,396.7	4.2	509,697.0	CO_2 tax increased (G)	Income tax cut (H)
2002	2,285.7	50,716.01	98.0	45,069.1	127.5	4,393.5	4.3	520,251.7		
2003	2,324.4	51,621.09	99.8	45,028.6	127.4	4,390.9	5.0	529,373.2		
2004	2,411.5	50,504.80	97.6	47,747.3	135.1	4,402.9	5.6	547,699.7		

Notes

A Industry & horticulture 250 SEK/tCO_2; h/holds, commercial & motor fuels 250 SEK/tCO_2.

B Reduction in income tax rates and highest marginal tax rate capped at 50%.

C Industry & horticulture 80 SEK/tCO_2; h/holds, commercial & motor fuels 320 SEK/tCO_2.

D Industry & horticulture 92.5 SEK/tCO_2; h/holds, commercial & motor fuels 370 SEK/tCO_2.

E Industry & horticulture 185 SEK/tCO_2; h/holds, commercial & motor fuels 370 SEK/tCO_2.

F New excise taxes on energy and CO_2; annual inflation indexation of all CO_2 tax rates.

G H/holds, commercial & motor fuels 530 SEK/tCO_2.

H Reduction in income tax rates and employees' social security contributions.

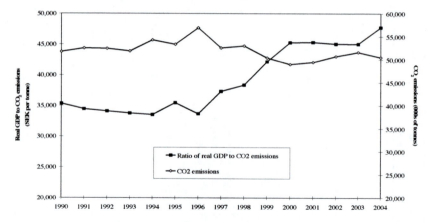

Figure 10.1 CO$_2$ emissions and CO$_2$ efficiency of Sweden, 1990–2004.

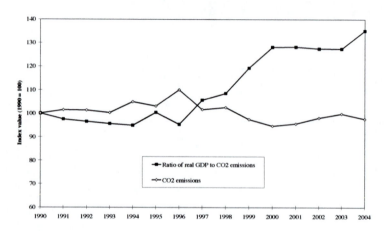

Figure 10.2 CO$_2$ emissions and CO$_2$ efficiency of Sweden, 1990–2004 (index values).

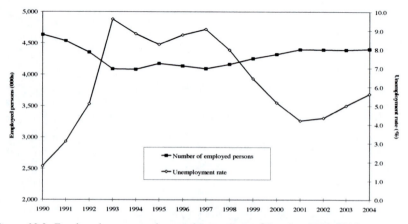

Figure 10.3 Employed persons and unemployment rate of Sweden, 1990–2004.

ficiency gains induced by ETR policy measures will prevent total CO_2 emissions from rising in the future.

As for the employment impact of Sweden's ETR measures, such an assessment is more difficult to make. Between 1990 and 1993, employment numbers declined by over half a million while, during the same time, the unemployment rate jumped dramatically from 1.8 per cent to 9.6 per cent (Figure 10.3 and columns *f* and *g* from Table 10.1). With real GDP falling in each year between 1990 and 1993 (column *a* in Table 10.1), this employment outcome can be attributed almost entirely to the early-1990s recession experienced in Sweden.

Although Sweden's real GDP rose from 1993 to 1997, the unemployment rate recovered only marginally over the same period (falling from 9.6 per cent in 1993 to 9.1 per cent in 1997). Beyond 1997 and until the new ETR measures in 2001, the unemployment rate fell rapidly to 4.2 per cent. This is despite very modest increases in real GDP. Whether the 1997 ETR measures were responsible for the apparent attractiveness of employing labour is difficult to conclude.

Unfortunately, and despite continued annual increases in real GDP to 2004, the 2001 ETR measures appear to have overturned the attractiveness of labour, with the unemployment rate at the end of the study period finishing at 5.6 per cent. With employment numbers rising between 2001 and 2004, the income tax rate cuts of 2001 may have increased the labour force participation rate to such an extent that the net increase in available jobs was unable to keep pace with the rise in the number of people seeking employment. If this is the case, future ETR policies of the Swedish Government will need to do more to: (a) encourage people to exit the labour market; and/or (b) provide public sector jobs to absorb the unemployed labour. Failure of future ETR policies in this regard may result in a growing conflict between CO_2 emissions objectives and the goal of low unemployment.

Denmark

Incentives to promote energy efficiency have long been a feature of the Danish taxation system (Hoerner and Bosquet, 2001). However, the 'Energy Package' introduced in the early 1990s not only involved a broader range of energy and emissions taxes, it included subsidies to encourage the development and uptake of resource-saving technologies and the use of environmental tax revenues to reduce social security contributions.

As part of the Energy Package, a CO_2 emissions tax was introduced in 1992, although the tax rate imposed on manufacturers was halved in the following year because of fears that the initial tax rate (100 DKK per metric tonne of CO_2 emissions) was affecting the international competitiveness of Denmark's manufacturing sector (Hoerner and Bosquet, 2001). Despite these concerns, energy tax rates were later increased and a host of new energy-based tax rates were introduced in 1996. The CO_2 emissions tax rate, in particular, was increased in every year from 1996 to 2002.

One of the main policy measures that enabled the Danish government to allay fears concerning the increase in the CO_2 emissions tax rate was the 1994 reduction of labour and income taxes. Indeed, with further modifications to income tax rates in 1997 and 1999 through to 2002 the Danish government had shifted much of the tax based from earned income onto natural resource depletion and pollution – the very theoretical basis underpinning the concept of ETR (Hoerner and Bosquet, 2001).

Columns *j* and *k* in Table 10.2 summarise the environmental and employment elements of Denmark's ETR measures as well as the timing of their introduction and subsequent modifications. As with Table 10.1 for Sweden, the notes below Table 10.2 spell out the exact nature of the tax rates in Denmark over the period 1990–2002. Columns *a–h* of Table 10.2 reveal the various indicators relevant to Denmark's ETR performance over the study period.

Denmark's CO_2 emissions (column *b* of Table 10.2) and the ratio of Denmark's real GDP to CO_2 emissions (column *d* of Table 10.2) are graphically illustrated in Figure 10.4. Prior to the introduction of a CO_2 tax in 1992, Denmark had experienced a significant rise in CO_2 emissions and a sharp decline in its efficiency ratio (1990 to 1991). Although the initial CO_2 tax imposition appears to have had a positive impact in terms of reducing emissions and increasing the efficiency ratio, the change to the CO_2 tax rate in 1993 seems to have reversed this effect. For example, CO_2 emissions increased from 60.1 million tonnes in 1993 to 74.0 million tonnes in 1996 (a 23.3 per cent rise), while the real GDP/CO_2 emissions ratio declined from 15,514.0 DKK per tonne to 13,982.4 DKK per tonne over the same period (a 9.9 per cent reduction).

Following the increases in CO_2 tax rates in 1996 and the subsequent annual increases to 2002, the ratio of Denmark's real GDP to CO_2 emissions increased by a dramatic 55.3 per cent between 1996 and 2000 (13,982.4 DKK per tonne to 21,719.2 DKK per tonne). The ratio declined slightly in 2001 but increased marginally in 2002. As one might expect, Denmark's CO_2 emissions fell sharply between 1996 and 2000 (74.0 million tonnes down to 53.1 million tonnes). Emissions increased slightly in 2001 to 54.6 million tonnes but effectively stabilised in 2002 (54.3 million tonnes).

Figure 10.5 illustrates Denmark's CO_2 emissions and efficiency ratio with both indicators set in 1990 to an index value of 100 (columns *c* and *e* of Table 10.2). The figure reveals that both indicators moved in opposite directions in every year during the study period. There is little doubt that efficiency improvements played a key role in whatever reductions in environmental stress Denmark secured during the 1990s.

There are, however, two noteworthy aspects to consider. Firstly, during the 'efficiency boom' of 1996–2000, the relative decline in CO_2 emissions between 1996 and 2002 (−26.7 per cent) was not nearly as large as the rise in the real GDP to CO_2 emissions ratio (+54.6 per cent). Secondly, and perhaps more importantly, total CO_2 emissions increased by 2.6 per cent over the entire study period despite there being an overall efficiency increase of 24.8 per cent. Although the scale effect of a rising real GDP did not exceed the 1996–2000 efficiency improvements induced by the more stringent ETR measures of the mid-1990s, it can be concluded that: (a) efficiency gains were becoming more difficult to secure towards the end of the study period (i.e., in 2001 and 2002); and (b) over the entire

Table 10.2 Ecological tax reform performance of Denmark, 1990–2002

Year	Real GDP (billion DKK) (1995 prices)	CO$_2$ emissions (000s tonnes)	CO$_2$ emissions (1990 = 100.0)	Real GDP/ CO$_2$ ratio (DKK per tonne) (a/b)	Index of GDP/CO$_2$ (1990 = 100.0)	Employment numbers (000s)	Unemployment rate (%)	Real GDP/ employment ratio (DKK per emp. person) (a/f)	ETR environmental element	ETR employment element
	a	b	c	d	e	f	g	h	j	k
1990	915.9	52,886	100.0	17,318.7	100.0	2,066.2	9.7	443,286.7		
1991	926.1	63,559	120.2	14,571.2	84.1	2,044.3	10.6	453,030.4		
1992	931.8	57,755	109.2	16,133.4	93.2	2,059.0	11.3	452,543.0	CO$_2$ tax imposed (A)	
1993	931.8	60,060	113.6	15,514.0	89.6	2,046.1	12.4	455,389.8	CO$_2$ tax modified (B)	
1994	982.7	63,663	120.4	15,436.0	89.1	2,056.9	12.3	477,759.7		Lab/income tax cut (C)
1995	1,009.8	60,609	114.6	16,660.2	96.2	2,088.2	10.4	483,553.3		
1996	1,035.2	74,035	140.0	13,982.4	80.7	2,121.6	8.9	487,928.5	CO$_2$ tax increased (D)	
1997	1,065.9	64,524	122.0	16,519.9	95.4	2,194.0	7.9	485,838.2	CO$_2$ tax increased (E)	Income tax cut (F)
1998	1,092.2	60,409	114.2	18,080.7	104.4	2,244.4	6.6	486,649.9	CO$_2$ tax increased (G)	
1999	1,121.0	57,523	108.8	19,488.2	112.5	2,238.7	5.7	500,745.5	CO$_2$ tax increased (H)	Income tax cut (I)
2000	1,152.8	53,076	100.4	21,719.2	125.4	2,251.2	5.4	512,067.8	CO$_2$ tax increased (J)	Income tax cut (I)
2001	1,167.8	54,615	103.3	21,382.7	123.5	2,261.2	5.2	516,458.1	CO$_2$ tax increased (J)	Income tax cut (I)
2002	1,173.7	54,287	102.6	21,620.0	124.8	2,231.9	5.2	525,869.0	CO$_2$ tax increased (J)	Income tax cut (I)

Notes

A Many energy taxes replaced with 100 DKK/tCO$_2$ (effective for h/holds on 15 May 1992; effective for industry and commercial sectors on 1 January 1993).
B Reduction in tax to 50 DKK/tCO$_2$ for manufacturers; other energy tax refunds for industry.
C Labour taxes reduced by 2.2% of GDP; marginal tax rates on income to fall by 10% by 1998.
D 200 DKK/tCO$_2$ with concessions for some production processes.
E 400 DKK/tCO$_2$ with reduced concessions for some production processes.
F Employee's social security contributions reduced (0.11% in 1997; 0.27% in 1998; 0.32% in 1999; 0.53% in 2000).
G 600 DKK/tCO$_2$ with reduced concessions for some production processes.
H Further reduced concessions on CO$_2$ taxes for some production processes.
I Income tax rates reduced from 1999 to 2002 (–6.2 bn DKK by 2002).
J Increases in green taxes from 2000 to 2002 (+5.6 bn DKK by 2002).

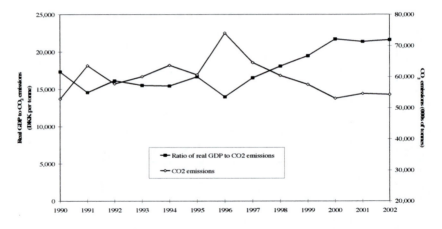

Figure 10.4 CO_2 emissions and CO_2 efficiency of Denmark, 1990–2002.

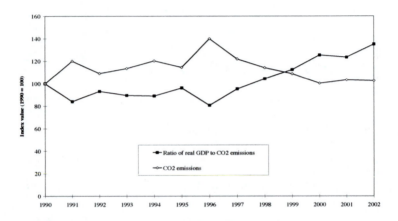

Figure 10.5 CO_2 emissions and CO_2 efficiency of Denmark, 1990–2002 (index values).

study period, the efficiency improvements were more than offset by the weight of increase in real GDP. In Denmark, at least, it would appear that the Jevons effect may have occurred as a consequence of conventional ETR measures being unable to limit the overall rate of resource throughput.

Not unlike the Swedish case, the employment impact of Denmark's ETR measures is inconclusive (see Figure 10.6). Similarly to Sweden, Denmark also suffered a recession in the early 1990s, although less severe, which led to employment numbers falling and a resultant rise in the unemployment rate. However, because the unemployment rate was already high in 1990 at 9.7 per cent, the rise to 12.4 per cent by 1993 was smaller in magnitude than the Swedish case (column *g* of Table 10.2).

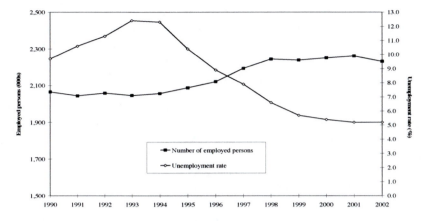

Figure 10.6 Employed persons and unemployment rate of Denmark, 1990–2002.

From 1993 to the end of the study period, Denmark's unemployment rate declined in each year. By 2002, it had fallen to 5.2 per cent. In stark contrast to Sweden, the fall in the unemployment rate, particularly following the 1997 ETR measures, was accompanied by only a very small increase in employment numbers. Indeed, the unemployment rate declined in 1999 and remained steady in 2002 despite employment numbers falling slightly. This suggests that the Danish government's ETR policies have been relatively successful in reducing the labour force participation rate and increasing the attractiveness of employing labour. The Danish approach therefore appears to have been partially successful in averting the policy conflict between unemployment and environmental goals.

The Netherlands

Although a general fuel charge was first introduced in the Netherlands in 1988, it was not until 1992 that it was transformed by the Dutch government into a general fuel tax as a means of collecting tax revenues on all fossil fuels (Hoerner and Bosquet, 2001). Notwithstanding this, fuels used as a raw material were exempted from the tax. Importantly, this meant that electricity remained tax-exempt although the energy resources used to generate electricity were not.

As of 1 January 1996, a new approach to fuel taxes was adopted by the Dutch government. Rather than having a general fuel tax, a regulatory tax was introduced. This new tax was specifically targeted to alter energy-use behaviour with the express aim of increasing the rate of energy efficiency in light of an apparent stagnation in efficiency advances in the first half of the 1990s (see real GDP/CO_2 emissions ratio from 1990 to 1996 in Table 10.3).

One of the key features of the new regulatory tax was its focus on small users of energy. The decision made by the Dutch government to minimise the burden on large energy-intensive corporations was based on the understanding that: (a) the majority of large companies were already bound by agreements to adopt energy-saving measures; (b) a unilateral CO_2 emissions tax would adversely affect export competitiveness; and (c) large energy-intensive corporations were covered by the general fuel tax. Despite the focus on small energy users, the economic activities of 95 per cent of all Dutch companies and individuals were covered by the regulatory fuel tax (Hoerner and Bosquet, 2001).

Other important features of the 1996 ETR measures adopted by the Dutch government were the reductions in the rate of employers' social security contributions, the rise in the tax credit for the self-employed, the 3 per cent cut in the corporate tax rate, and the 0.6 per cent reduction in the personal income tax rate. Designed to be revenue-neutral, these measures ensured the 1996 ETR package incorporated both labour and income tax cuts.

In order to complement the 1996 ETR measures, a 40 per cent tax credit on corporate and personal income was introduced in 1997 for companies and individuals investing in energy-saving measures. A system of voluntary agreements to encourage additional resource-saving investments was also introduced, thereby allowing firms to choose their preferred depreciation schedule for environmental investments (Hoerner and Bosquet, 2001).

Table 10.3 describes the nature and the timing of the environmental and employment elements of the Netherlands ETR policy (columns *j* and *k*), and the various indicators in columns *a–h* reveal the ETR performance of the Netherlands over the period 1990–2002. The more precise details are again found in the notes below Table 10.3.

Figure 10.7 graphically reveals both the CO_2 emissions of the Netherlands (column *b* of Table 10.3) and the ratio of its real GDP to CO_2 emissions (column *d* of Table 10.3). It can be clearly seen that, prior to the introduction of the regulatory fuel tax in 1996, the 1992 transformation of the general fuel charge to a general fuel tax did little to increase the Dutch efficiency ratio (1,735.7 euros per tonne of CO_2 emissions in 1992 and 1,750.1 euros per tonne of CO_2 emissions in 1996[8]). The adoption of the general fuel tax also failed to drastically reduce CO_2 emissions. As it turned out, emissions rose from 163.7 million tonnes in 1992 to 178.3 million tonnes in 1996 – an 8.9 per cent increase in just four years.

Initially, at least, the 1996 introduction of the regulatory fuel tax appears to have had a positive impact on both the Dutch efficiency ratio and total CO_2 emissions. Between 1996 and 1999, the efficiency ratio grew steadily from 1,750.1 to 2,072.4 euros per tonne of CO_2 emissions. At the same, total CO_2 emissions fell from 178.3 to 169.2 million tonnes.

However, the potency of the regulatory fuel tax waned considerably after 1999. Whereas the efficiency ratio rose marginally in 2000, it fell in both 2001 and 2002. Not surprisingly, Dutch CO_2 emissions increased from 1999 to 2002. Worse still, at 178.5 million tonnes in 2002, CO_2 emissions were slightly higher than the 1996 spike.

Table 10.3 Ecological tax reform performance of the Netherlands, 1990–2002

Year	Real GDP (million euros) (1995 prices)	CO_2 emissions (000s tonnes)	CO_2 emissions (1990=100.0)	Real GDP/CO_2 ratio (euros per tonne) (a/b)	Index of GDP/CO_2 (1990=100.0)	Employment numbers (000s)	Unemployment rate (%)	Real GDP/employment ratio (euros per emp. person) (a/f)	ETR environmental element	ETR employment element
	a	b	c	d	e	f	g	h	j	k
1990	272,633	157,893	100.0	1,726.7	100.0	–	6.2	–		
1991	279,442	166,542	105.5	1,677.9	97.2	–	5.6	–		
1992	284,182	163,726	103.7	1,735.7	100.5	–	5.1	–	Fuel tax imposed (A)	
1993	286,707	167,144	105.9	1,715.3	99.3	–	5.8	–		
1994	294,140	169,846	107.6	1,731.8	100.3	–	6.9	–		
1995	302,804	170,990	108.3	1,770.9	102.6	–	6.7	–		
1996	312,004	178,281	112.9	1,750.1	101.4	6,954	6.2	44,866.8	Fuel tax change (B)	Income taxes cut (C)
1997	323,981	175,812	111.3	1,842.8	106.7	7,171	5.0	45,179.3	Energy tax credit (D)	
1998	338,073	174,440	110.5	1,938.0	112.2	7,371	3.8	45,865.3		
1999	350,614	169,180	107.1	2,072.4	120.0	7,554	3.5	46,414.4		
2000	362,772	173,886	110.1	2,086.3	120.8	7,733	2.9	46,912.2		
2001	366,857	178,213	112.9	2,058.5	119.2	7,830	2.5	46,852.7		
2002	367,224	178,524	113.1	2,057.0	119.1	7,867	2.8	46,679.0		

Notes
A General fuel tax collected on all fossil fuels; fuels used as raw materials not subject to tax.
B New general fuel tax regime; tax rates on various fuels based on CO_2/energy content; Special exemptions apply.
C Employers' social security contributions reduced by 0.19%; tax credit for self-employed increased to NLG 1,300; corporate profits tax reduced; Personal tax rate reduced by 0.6%.
D 40% tax credit applied to corporate or personal tax base for investment in energy-saving measures.

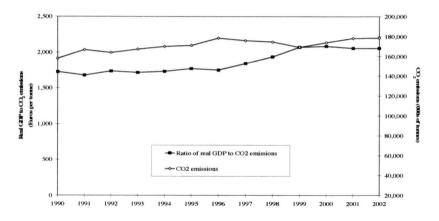

Figure 10.7 CO_2 emissions and CO_2 efficiency of the Netherlands, 1990–2002.

The trend change in the efficiency ratio and CO_2 emissions is starkly evidenced by the index values of both indicators presented in Figure 10.8 (also columns *c* and *e* of Table 10.3). Although both indicators moved in opposite directions in most years during the study period, this was not the case during the short period prior to the introduction of the regulatory fuel tax in 1996. The same occurred following the apparent impotency of the tax after 1999. As a consequence, it was only during the rapid efficiency-advancing period of 1996–1999, which initially followed the imposition of the regulatory fuel tax, that efficiency increases reduced environmental stress levels in the Netherlands.

Over the entire study period (1990–2002), the real GDP/CO_2 emissions ratio increased by 19.1 per cent while Dutch CO_2 emissions rose by 13.1 per cent. Clearly, the scale impact of a rising real GDP completely overwhelmed the efficiency improvements induced by the ETR measures implemented by the Dutch government. Almost without question, something resembling the Jevons effect took place after 1999.

It should be noted, however, that the efficiency advances achieved in the Netherlands (+19.1 per cent) were much lower than the gains experienced in both Sweden (+35.1 per cent) and Denmark (+24.8 per cent). Given this, one might reasonably question whether the ETR measures introduced in the Netherlands were as potent and/or as appropriately targeted as those imposed in both Sweden and Denmark. Furthermore, it begs the question as to whether a better designed ETR package in the Netherlands might have increased efficiency levels enough to have prevented the rise in Dutch CO_2 emissions, particularly after 1999. Thus, despite the strong evidential support for the ecological economic position on conventional ETR measures, the position is not conclusively proven in the Dutch case.

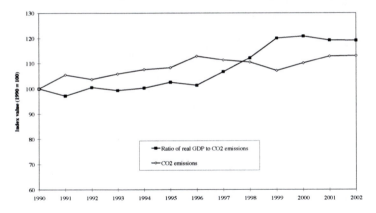

Figure 10.8 CO_2 emissions and CO_2 efficiency of the Netherlands, 1990–2002 (index values).

The employment implications of the Dutch ETR measures are difficult to assess because of the lack of employment numbers for the period 1990–1995. This aside, Figure 10.9 suggests that the Dutch unemployment rate was much less volatile than in Sweden and Denmark. In addition, the unemployment rate never reached the 1993 heights of 9.6 per cent in Sweden and 12.4 per cent in Denmark (note: the Dutch rate peaked at 6.9 per cent in 1994). The lower unemployment rate in the Netherlands can be largely attributed to institutional factors and labour market programmes explicitly undertaken by the Dutch government to keep unemployment as low as possible.

Figure 10.9 and column *g* in Table 10.3 indicate that the Dutch unemployment rate fell sharply following the income tax rate cuts and the reduction in employers' social security contributions in 1996. Indeed, without any additional rate of growth in real GDP from 1996 to 2001, the unemployment rate rapidly declined from 6.2 per cent to 2.5 per cent. It is also interesting to note that the real GDP/employment ratio of the Netherlands (column *h* in Table 10.3) did not vary much between 1996 and 2002. There were, conversely, much greater increases in the real GDP/employment ratio for both Sweden and Denmark during this period (column *h* in Tables 10.1 and 10.2). In a relative sense, this indicates that the employment elements of the Dutch ETR measures were better able to maintain if not increase the attractiveness of labour as real GDP grew and as CO_2 emissions predominantly fell in the post-1996 period. In other words, there was a greater degree of substitution between labour and energy in the Netherlands than in Sweden and Denmark.[9]

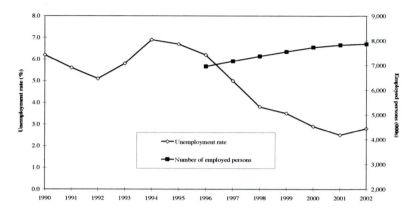

Figure 10.9 Employed persons and unemployment rate of the Netherlands, 1990–2002.

Finland

In 1990, Finland became the first country to introduce an environmentally-motivated CO_2 tax. However, the tax was, until 1994, based entirely on a fuel's carbon content. During the period 1994–1996, the Finnish government varied the environmental component of the tax to reflect a fuel's carbon and energy content (based on a 60:40 ratio). Except for electricity generation, this variation of the tax was reversed in 1997 (Hoerner and Bosquet, 2001). Nevertheless, the tax rate on the carbon content was increased significantly at the beginning of each year between 1996 and 1999 (from 14 FIM per tonne of CO_2 emissions in 1996 to 102 FIM per tonne of CO_2 emissions by 1999).

Finland's tax-shifting measures began to resemble the conventional ETR model in 1997 following cuts to personal income tax rates and employers' social security contributions. Subsequent to an agreement between private corporations and labour unions to limit wage rises in 1998 and 1999, the Finnish government cut labour taxes by a further 1.5 billion FIM in 1998 and 3.5 billion FIM in 1999 (Hoerner and Bosquet, 2001). Apart from increasing the attractiveness of employing labour, these tax cuts enabled the Finnish government to allay any public fears of an increased tax burden that might have resulted from the rise in the tax on carbon.

Columns *j* and *k* in Table 10.4 summarise the environmental and employment elements of Finland's ETR. Columns *a–h* reveal the various indicators relevant to Finland's ETR performance over the study period (1990–2002), and the precise nature of the ETR measures are explained in the notes below the table.

Finland's CO_2 emissions (column *b* of Table 10.4) and the ratio of Finland's real GDP to CO_2 emissions (column *d* of Table 10.4) are graphically presented in Figure 10.10. Figure 10.10 shows that the CO_2 tax introduced in 1990 and its modification in the mid-1990s had no positive effect on Finland's efficiency ratio.

Table 10.4 Ecological tax reform performance of Finland, 1990–2002

Year	Real GDP (billion euros) (2000 prices)	CO₂ emissions (000s tonnes)	CO₂ emissions (1990 = 100.0)	Real GDP/ CO₂ ratio (euros per tonne) (a:b)	Index of GDP:CO₂ (1990 = 100.0)	Employment numbers (000s)	Unemployment rate (%)	Real GDP/ employment ratio (euros per emp. person) (a:f)	ETR environmental element	ETR employment element
	a	b	c	d	e	f	g	h	j	k
1990	108.5	70,500	100.0	1,539.0	100.0	–	–	–	CO₂ tax introduced (A)	
1991	102.2	69,500	98.6	1,469.9	95.5	–	–	–		
1992	99.0	66,800	94.8	1,481.8	96.3	–	–	–		
1993	98.2	67,900	96.3	1,446.5	94.0	–	–	–	CO₂ tax increased (B)	
1994	101.1	74,400	105.5	1,358.4	88.3	–	–	–	CO₂ tax modified (C)	
1995	104.8	71,600	101.6	1,463.4	95.1	2,099	15.4	49,919.0		
1996	108.7	76,900	109.1	1,412.9	91.8	2,127	14.6	51,081.3	CO₂ tax increased (D)	
1997	115.3	76,000	107.8	1,516.7	98.5	2,169	12.7	53,143.4	CO₂ tax increased (E)	Income tax cut (F)
1998	121.2	72,900	103.4	1,663.2	108.1	2,222	11.4	54,566.2	CO₂ tax increased (G)	Labour tax reduced (H)
1999	126.0	72,500	102.8	1,737.4	112.9	2,296	10.2	54,860.6	CO₂ tax increased (I)	Labour tax reduced (J)
2000	132.3	70,200	99.6	1,884.2	122.4	2,335	9.8	56,647.5		
2001	135.8	75,800	107.5	1,791.0	116.4	2,367	9.1	57,354.9		
2002	138.0	77,300	109.6	1,785.1	116.0	2,372	9.1	58,174.1		

Notes

A Energy tax on various fuels based on the fuel's carbon content (6.7 FIM/tCO₂).

B Tax rates on carbon component of fuels increased to 14 FIM/tCO₂.

C Energy tax rates adapted to be based on both carbon and energy contents (60:40 ratio).

D Energy tax based solely on carbon component, except for electricity; tax rates on carbon component of fuels increased to 38 FIM/tCO₂.

E Tax rates on carbon component of fuels increased to 71 FIM/tCO₂.

F Reductions in personal income tax rates; reduced employer social security contributions.

G Tax rates on carbon component of fuels increased to 82 FIM/tCO₂.

H Labour taxes reduced by FIM 1.5 bn (0.25% of GDP).

I Tax rates on carbon component of fuels increased to 102 FIM/tCO₂.

J Labour taxes reduced by FIM 3.5 bn (0.5% of GDP).

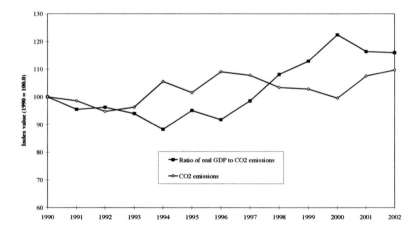

Figure 10.10 CO$_2$ emissions and CO$_2$ efficiency of Finland, 1990–2002.

Between 1990 and 1996, the real GDP/CO$_2$ emissions ratio actually declined slightly from 1,539.0 to 1,412.9 euros per tonne – an 8.2 per cent fall. At the same time, total CO$_2$ emissions rose from 70.5 million to 76.9 million tonnes – effectively, a 9.1 per cent increase.

The more significant CO$_2$ tax rate rises imposed between 1996 and 1999 triggered an immediate and dramatic reversal of the pre-1996 trend. Between 1996 and 2000, the real GDP/CO$_2$ emissions ratio shot up by 33.3 per cent from 1,412.9 to 1,884.2 euros per tonne, while total CO$_2$ emissions fell to 70.2 million tonnes – an 8.7 per cent decrease over the four years and an emissions level in 2000 lower than that generated in 1990. Strangely, despite no change to the CO$_2$ tax rate, the efficiency of resource use fell slightly in both 2001 and 2002. With real GDP still rising, CO$_2$ emissions increased beyond their 2000 levels to 77.3 million tonnes by the end of the study period.

Figure 10.11 graphically presents the index values of the efficiency ratio and CO$_2$ emissions to reveal the trend change in both indicators (also columns *c* and *e* of Table 10.4). In the very early stages (1990–1993), both indicators trend downwards – largely the consequence of a sharp recession experienced by Finland in the early 1990s. From this point until the end of the study period, both indicators moved in opposite directions. Overall, Finland's CO$_2$ emissions rose by 9.6 per cent between 1990 and 2002. What's more, Finland's real GDP/CO$_2$ emissions ratio increased by a mere 16.0 per cent, the lowest of all the four countries examined in this chapter.

Conclusions regarding the ecological economic position on conventional ETR measures are difficult to draw in the Finnish case. This is because in each of the years when Finland's efficiency ratio increased, it was accompanied by a fall in Finland's CO$_2$ emissions. However, efficiency gains were made in only six of the twelve years during the study period. Thus, although at no stage did the scale of economic activity in these six years more than offset the environmental stress-

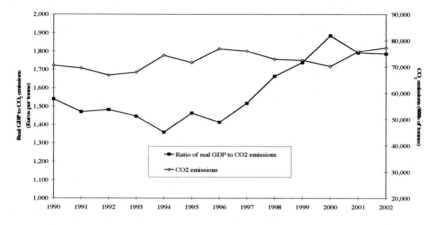

Figure 10.11 CO_2 emissions and CO_2 efficiency of Finland, 1990–2002 (index values).

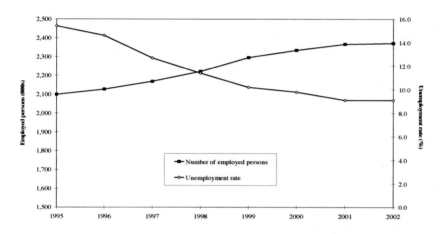

Figure 10.12   Employed persons and unemployment rate of Finland, 1995–2002.

relieving impact of increased efficiency, the efficiency performance of Finland was weak over the study period. Of greater concern is the fact that the Finnish case constitutes a clear example of total CO_2 emissions rising in the face of ETR policies designed to quell their increase. This evidence leans more strongly towards the Jevons effect having taken place in Finland than it having been averted.

Consider Figure 10.12, which shows the employment impact of the ETR measures introduced by the Finnish government from 1995 to 2002. Owing to a recession as severe as anywhere else in the industrial world, the unemployment rate in Finland reached 15.4 per cent in 1995. By 2002, the unemployment rate had declined to 9.1 per cent – still very high when compared with the other three counties examined in this chapter. The fall in the unemployment rate can be mostly attributed to the recovery of the growth rate in real GDP from 1995 to 2002. Although the reduction in labour tax rates in 1997, 1998, and 1999 may have had a positive impact on the unemployment rate and the attractiveness of labour, this certainly cannot be concluded from a casual observation of the data in Table 10.4. If anything, the employment elements of Finland's ETR measures appear to have had very little impact given that the real GDP/employment ratio increased at about the same rate before and after the policies were implemented.

Comments on the evidence

When the evidence of all four countries is considered together, a relatively clear and uniform picture emerges. It is one which reveals that conventional ETR measures – i.e., taxes on pollution rather than quantitative throughput controls – led to greater efficiency and lower CO_2 emissions, *but only in the short term*. Whether it was the consequence of diminishing efficiency advances or the scale impact of increased economic activity, conventional ETR measures failed to prevent CO_2 emissions from eventually rising. Worse still, the CO_2 emissions of Finland and the Netherlands were significantly higher at the end of the study period than they were at the beginning. Only in Sweden did CO_2 emissions fall but, as previously highlighted, the decline was a meagre 2.4 per cent. One can therefore conclude that the Jevons effect generally took place within three to four years of introducing the environmental elements of an ETR package.

The employment impact of the tax cuts to labour and income was much less conclusive. About all that can be said about the employment elements of the respective ETR packages is that: (a) the possible tension between the policy goals of ecological sustainability and low unemployment might be far less in Denmark than elsewhere; and (b) some limited degree of substitutability between labour and energy may have occurred in the Netherlands.

In summary, the evidence provided in this chapter supports the ecological economic position that conventional ETR measures cannot achieve the double dividend of ecological sustainability and low unemployment. However, a few things should be borne in mind. Firstly, the empirical analysis conducted in this chapter is based on casual observation of the data presented. The inferences made are not based on rigorous statistical tests.[10] Secondly, it has been assumed that the impact of the introduced policy measures is immediate rather than lagged. Clearly, the duration it takes for ETR policies to impact fully on the economy is a crucial consideration when judging their success or failure. Having said this, the apparent impotency of the ETR measures some three to four years following their imposition suggests that any lagged effect is more than likely negligible – reflecting, quite possibly, an initial response to the ETR measures but no continuous or progressive efficiency improvements. On the other hand, it is possible that the policy lag could be a decade or more in length, in which case the long-term implications of the ETR measures may have yet to fully materialise.

Thirdly, the potential influence of exogenous factors has been overlooked or ignored. There is little doubt that international forces, domestic institutional factors, and government decisions in other policy domains can greatly affect the environmental and employment outcomes of a particular country (Bosquet, 2000). It is conceivable that one or more of these factors, and not the lack of quantitative throughput controls recommended by many ecological economists, may have contributed to the medium-term failure of the conventional ETR measures introduced.

Finally, it is possible that the ETR measures imposed in all four countries were feeble or inappropriately targeted. If so, it still leaves open the possibility that better devised ETR policies of the conventional kind could have achieved more in terms of reducing environmental stress and lowering unemployment. But it is highly unlikely that they would have achieved both ecological sustainability and full employment.

Concluding remarks

Despite considerable benefits arising from the ETR packages implemented in Sweden, Denmark, the Netherlands, and Finland, their success in terms of reducing CO_2 emissions was short-lived. In each country, it appears that producers responded rapidly to the sporadically introduced CO_2 and energy taxes. However, the tax impositions were unable to induce a continuation of the efficiency-advancing process. As a consequence, the scale effect of the increase in economic activity quickly exceeded the efficiency improvements obtained. This invariably resulted in a return to, or a rise in, the pre-reform stress levels on the environment.

Although the ETR packages introduced in each of the studied nations may have had a positive employment effect, the ultimate success of any ETR policy is likely to depend, as many ecological economists believe, on the inclusion of cap-and-trade systems that ostensibly involve the use of tradeable resource use permits. In addition, a substantial lowering of the unemployment rate or, more particularly, the achievement of full employment, will require more than just tax cuts on labour and income. It will also necessitate some of the measures previously outlined in Part III of the book. Having said this, conventional ETR measures constitute a major advance over present policy approaches and, although inadequate to some extent, could prove to be the ideal means of preparing a nation's economy, and its citizens, for the more radical measures needed to simultaneously resolve the ecological sustainability and full employment goals.

From the point of view of CO_2 emissions and their contribution to global climate change, there would appear to be an urgent need to go beyond suggested carbon taxes and establish carbon trading systems at both the intra- and international levels. The introduction of carbon-trading initiatives in Europe and moves afoot to install similar systems in California and the Australian states of New South Wales, Victoria, and South Australia are all positive developments.

Above all, this chapter supports the view that appropriate responses to environmental and employment concerns must not be corrupted by mainstream economic arguments that allocative efficiency – facilitated by the internalisation of environmental spillover costs into market prices (i.e., conventional ETR measures) – can deliver sustainable environmental outcomes. Nor should we be fooled into believing that a natural rate of unemployment is the best possible employment outcome and that a nation's moral obligation to those deprived of paid employment amounts to nothing more than providing an often inadequate level of public welfare assistance. Once and for all, we must immediately abandon the idea that mainstream economic policies can deliver the double dividend of ecological sustainability and low unemployment.

Notes

1 See note 8 in Chapter 2.
2 A more detailed description of a system of tradeable resource use permits can be found in Lawn (2007: ch. 11).
3 This is not entirely true. Although the quantity of matter–energy passing through an economic system is crucial to achieving sustainability, so is the quality of the high-entropy waste exiting the economy. Tradeable permits do not prevent the generation of highly toxic forms of pollution that could have devastating impacts on the natural environment. It is therefore necessary to prohibit the generation of certain substances and minimise the environmental impact of the remainder, of which the latter can be achieved through the introduction of assurance bonds. For more on assurance bonds, see Costanza and Perrings (1990).
4 It is the constrained supply forces that ensures ecological limits are internalised into resource prices.
5 Of course, whether permit systems achieve ecological sustainability still depends on the rate of throughput being within the regenerative and waste assimilative capacities of the natural environment. This, moreover, depends upon the human capacity to determine such a rate and auctioning the appropriate number of permits. Should the sustainable rate of throughput be overestimated and too many permits be auctioned, ecological sustainability will not be achieved. Since the natural environment is a complex system whereby exact knowledge of the sustainable limit is infeasible, a precautionary approach should be adopted. That is, for example, the number of permits auctioned should approximate around 75 per cent of the estimated sustainable rate of throughput.
6 For those interested in a few of the more elaborate simulation exercises, see Goulder (1995), Cansier and Krumm (1997), Tindale and Holtham (1996), Baron et al. (1996), and Harrison and Kriström (1999).
7 Stationary sources in the manufacturing and services sectors along with stationary and mobile sources generated by households represent approximately 40 per cent of Norway's CO_2 emissions.
8 Euro values are based on the exchange rate of the Dutch guilder (NLG) at the time of the conversion into the euro.
9 There is, nonetheless, a severe limit on the substitutability of labour for energy. To understand why, see Lawn (2003).
10 Rigorous statistical analysis of the impact of ETR is the subject of my current research in this area. More conclusive results can be expected in the foreseeable future.

References

Baron, R., Dower, R., Morgenstern, D., Martinez-Lopez, M., Johansen, H., Johnsen, T., Alfsen, K., Ezban, R., and Gronlykke, M. (1996), *Policies and Measures for Common Action*, Paris: Annex I Experts Group on the UNFCCC, International Energy Agency.

Blanchard, O. (2002), *A Macroeconomic Survey of Europe*, place: publisher.

Bosquet, B. (2000), 'Environmental tax reform: does it work? A survey of the empirical evidence', *Ecological Economics*, 34, 19–32.

Cansier, D. and Krumm, R. (1997), 'Air pollution taxation: an empirical study', *Ecological Economics*, 23, 59–70.

Costanza, R. and Perrings, C. (1990), 'A flexible assurance bonding system for improved environmental management', *Ecological Economics*, 2, 57–76.

Daly, H. (1991), *Steady-State Economics*, 2nd edn, Washington, DC: Island Press.

Daly, H. (1996), *Beyond Growth*, Boston: Beacon Press.

Ekins, P. (1999), 'European environmental taxes and charges: recent experience, issues, and trends', *Ecological Economics*, 31, 39–62.

Forstater, M. (2004), 'Green jobs: addressing the critical issues surrounding the environment, workplace and employment', *International Journal of Environment, Workplace, and Employment*, 1 (1), 53–61.

Goulder, L. (1995), 'Effects of carbon taxes in an economy with prior tax distortions: an intertemporal general equilibrium analysis', *Journal of Environmental Economics and Management*, 29 (3), 271–297.

Harrison, G. and Kriström, B. (1999), 'General equilibrium effects of increasing carbon taxes in Sweden', in R. Brännlund and I.-M. Gren (eds), *Green Taxes*, Cheltenham, UK: Edward Elgar.

Hoerner, J. A. and Bosquet, B. (2001), *Environmental Tax Reform: The European Experience*, Washington, DC: Centre for a Sustainable Economy.

Howarth, R. and Norgaard, R. (1990), 'Intergenerational resource rights, efficiency, and social optimality', *Land Economics*, 6, 1–11.

Larsen, B. and Nesbakken, R (1997), 'Norwegian emissions of CO_2 1987–1994: a study of some effects of the CO_2 tax', *Environmental and Resource Economics*, 9 (3), 275–290.

Lawn, P. (2000), 'Ecological tax reform: many know why but few know how', *Environment, Development, and Sustainability*, 2, 143–164.

Lawn, P. (2003), 'How important is natural capital in terms of sustaining real output? Revisiting the natural capital/human-made capital substitutability debate', *International Journal of Global Environmental Issues*, 3 (4), 418–435.

Lawn, P. (2004a), 'Environment, workplace, and employment: an introduction', *International Journal of Environment, Workplace, and Employment*, 1 (1), 4–39.

Lawn, P. (2004b), 'How well are resource prices likely to serve as indicators of natural resource scarcity?', *International Journal of Sustainable Development*, 7 (4), 369–397.

Lawn, P. (2007), *Frontier Issues in Ecological Economics*, Cheltenham, UK: Edward Elgar.

O'Riordan, T. (ed.) (1997), *Ecotaxation*, London: Earthscan.

Roodman, D. (1998), *The Natural Wealth of Nations*, Washington, DC: Worldwatch Institute.

Schöb, R. (2005), 'The double dividend hypothesis of environmental taxes: a survey', in H. Folmer and T. Tietenberg (eds), *The International Yearbook of Environmental and Resource Economics 2005/2006*, Cheltenham, UK: Edward Elgar.

Statistics Norway (various), 'National accounts and the environment: Table 1 – Norway's total value added, employment, and air emissions, 1999–2002', http://www.ssb.no.

Swedish Environmental Protection Agency (EPA) (1997), *Environmental Taxes in Sweden: Economic Instruments of Environmental Policy*, Report No. 4745, Swedish EPA, Stockholm.

Tindale, S. and Holtham, G. (1996), *Green Tax Reform: Pollution Payments and Labour Tax Cuts*, London: Institute for Public Policy Research.

World Resources Institute (WRI) (n.d.), 'EarthTrends – climate and atmosphere', http://www.earthtrends.wri.org.

Part V

Jobs versus the environment

11 A city that works

Employment patterns and urban ecosystem service requirements in Greater Christchurch, New Zealand

Nigel Jollands

Nancy Golubiewski

Garry McDonald

Introduction

The early inhabitants of Christchurch, New Zealand, would hardly recognise Christchurch City today. The large forests of matai and totara trees that once grew along the coast are gone, and the partially forested Canterbury Plains are largely treeless. In the past 150 years, the Christchurch area has evolved into a bustling urban environment of some 360,000 people covering an area of 143,000 ha.

The growth of the Greater Christchurch area has brought with it some significant urban development issues that, if not addressed, are likely to undermine the current quality of life. These issues include continued population growth, disbursed patterns of residential development, increased demand for employment opportunities, growth in traffic, and increasing demands on infrastructure services (Urban Development Strategy Working Group, 2004).

The growth in the Greater Christchurch Urban area is not unique. The UN Population Division (1997) notes that urbanisation is a dominant demographic trend around the world. In 1800, fewer than 3 per cent of the global population lived in urban settlements (Newcombe *et al.*, 1978). Currently, around half the world's population is urbanised, and the proportion is projected to rise to 61 per cent in the next 30 years (Grimm *et al.*, 2000). According to Folke *et al.* (1997: 167), 'the population of the world's cities are [sic] growing by about 1 million people each week.'

As a result, many metropolitan areas have been forced to develop strategies to cope with this ongoing urban growth process. A common focus of many of these strategies is consideration of the need to create employment opportunities. For example, in New Zealand, the Auckland Regional Growth Forum's vision and desired outcome include the promotion of a 'diversity of employment and business opportunities' (Regional Growth Forum, 1999). Interestingly, one issue that was not addressed in this employment focus is the impact changing employment patterns will have on the ecosystem service demands of that city.

The imperative to understand the biophysical implications of employment patterns in urban settlement has been articulated by many academics in recent decades (e.g., Wolman 1965). For example, Newcombe *et al.* (1978: 3) stated that:

we must come to understand and appreciate the nature of the inputs of urban settlements; their transportation networks; the capacity of their natural and man-made circulatory systems; the generation, disposal and resource potential of their wastes – in short, we must become familiar with the metabolism of our cities.

This understanding is important because a city's planners need to be aware of the limits imposed on a city by impending resource constraints and the degree of dependence of their city on imported resources (Folke *et al.*, 1997).

Despite these arguments for understanding resource use, Huang and Hsu (2003) note that such information has rarely been used in urban policy-making. Furthermore, few studies have studied the impact of employment patterns on a city's resource requirements.

The purpose of this chapter is to ask: what impact does employment structure have on a city's ecosystem service requirements? To address this question, the chapter investigates the notion of ecosystem services and their link to employment. The Greater Christchurch area is used as a case study to investigate 'how the city works' or, equivalently, the link between employment structure and the city's resource use.

Ecosystem service appropriation and employment

Employment has long been a focus of research, and much has been made of the links between employment and other economic variables, such as inflation and welfare. Yet there are close ties between employment and the use of ecosystem services.

Ecosystem services represent the direct and indirect benefits that human populations derive from natural processes (de Groot, 1987; Daily, 1997). Natural processes provide many obvious services by way of goods used directly in the economy (e.g., coal, wood, and water). Ecosystem services can also be less obvious in their contribution to human populations. For example, natural processes regulate the climate, treat human waste, and provide habitat for pollinating species.

Urban systems critically depend on ecosystem services. In fact, urban systems cannot be fully understood in isolation from the ecological system in which they exist. As Huang (1998: 39) states, 'it has become evident that the urban economic system not only affects the environment but is also a heterotrophic system that has to depend on the surrounding natural environment for life-supporting services.' Urban socio-economic and ecological systems are physically connected by the throughput of energy and matter from natural ecosystems and by other ecosystem goods and services that sustain human activity. In this way, urban socio-economic systems capture (or appropriate) many essential ecosystem services, such as freshwater, energy carriers, and waste treatment services provided by the environment.

The ecosystem services captured by a city are directly related to how people are employed (i.e., employment structure) in that city. Employment in this chapter is defined as people working for hire or reward across all economic sectors. The measure of employment used in this chapter is full-time equivalent employees (FTEs).

Employment has a significant influence on a city's ecosystem service appropriation, for three reasons. First, people necessarily use goods and services derived from the environment when they are employed in economic activity. There are no exceptions. An obvious example is a person employed in a wood-product manufacturing plant. Such a person relies on a constant flow of electricity generated from either fossil fuels or renewable sources to keep the plant operating; on the timber grown in forests to provide the raw materials; and on decomposition processes to deal with the waste produced by the plant. A less obvious example is a clerk working in a bank. This person also relies on ecosystem services – energy for the computing system, cellulose-based paper, and, indirectly, waste treatment services to treat office waste and garbage. Thus, regardless of the sector, all employment relies on the capture of ecosystem services.

Second, employment affects ecosystem service use through actual decisions on the 'factory floor'. That is, employees directly make decisions about when to switch a machine on or off, when to throw material into the rubbish bin, or how much land is required to produce the required tonnage of a crop. For this reason, employees have a high degree of control over ecosystem service use.

Finally, employment is a useful proxy for economic activity. Generally, as economic activity increases or decreases the level of employment follows. Employment is often a better proxy for economic activity than value-added measures, because employment data do not suffer from exchange rates, inflation, or changing relative prices. For these reasons, employment can be used as a useful measure of economic activity.

It is important to understand the level of ecosystem goods and services appropriated by employment in the urban system. As Folke *et al.* (1997: 171) argue, 'the capacity of ecosystems to generate non-market natural resources and ecological services is increasingly becoming a limiting factor for social and economic development.' It is not wise to take the ecological resource base of any city for granted since the productive potential of this resource base is becoming increasingly limited and stressed (Folke *et al.*, 1997). In this context, estimates of appropriated ecosystem services by cities become important. Although ecosystem-service demand measures are static and do not provide an estimate of ecological carrying capacity, they do supply insight into the hidden human requirements for ecosystem services. This, in turn, sheds light on the scale of city growth – an essential aspect of the sustainability of an urban system (Folke *et al.*, 1997).

A second reason why it is important to understand ecosystem service use by cities is that this information can improve policy development in several ways (Sahely *et al.*, 2003). Such an analysis can provide important information for infrastructure planning. The more resources required by different economic sectors in a city, the larger the infrastructure systems must be to provide such resources.

An understanding of ecosystem service requirements can also assist with state-of-the-environment reporting. One of the strengths of this type of information is that it provides parameters which meet the criteria for good sustainability indicators (Jollands and Patterson, 2004). Specifically, measures of ecosystem service requirement per employee are: (a) scientifically valid (based on principles of conservation of energy and mass); (b) policy relevant (to urban planners and dwellers); and (c) available and comparable over time, understandable, and unambiguous.

Presenting ecosystem service appropriation information to planners assists them to be proactive. Sahely *et al.* (2003: 472) state that:

> material flow analysis or urban metabolism is a useful tool for early recognition, priority setting, effective policy-making, and communication. As a tool for early recognition, ecosystem service appropriation information does not rely on signals for environmental stress but rather highlights potential future problems by demonstrating changes in flows and stocks of the urban system.

Finally, information on ecosystem service demand can potentially enhance the effectiveness of policy-making by forcing decision-makers to consider the whole system: both the urban domain and the wider ecological context. This helps decision-makers establish ecosystem service implications of employment structure, such as legitimate policy issues, alongside the (often) more visible economic and social agenda.

The case of Greater Christchurch

The challenging issues facing Greater Christchurch have in the past been exacerbated by a lack of coordination among relevant planning agencies. At present, five local government agencies operate in the Greater Christchurch metropolitan area: Christchurch City Council, Selwyn District Council, Waimakariri District Council, Banks Peninsular District Council, and the Regional Council (Environment Canterbury). These councils have tended to address the range of growth-related issues independently with a diverse range of solutions, which are not necessarily compatible.

In response to the increasing pressure from urban growth in the Greater Christchurch area, the five councils joined forces to prepare a Greater Christchurch Urban Development Strategy (UDS). The purpose of the UDS is 'to ensure an excellent quality of life in the Greater Christchurch through an integrated and collaborative planning approach for future metropolitan urban development' (Urban Development Strategy Working Group, 2004: 2). In other words, the UDS specifically takes a metropolitan approach, with adjoining local authorities working to address the cross-boundary planning and urban development issues.

The Greater Christchurch area is the largest urban area in the South Island of New Zealand and is located at 43° South and 174° East. It covers all of Christchurch city and includes urban parts of the adjoining areas of Waimakariri, Selwyn, and Banks Peninsula, thus including a large area of Environment Canterbury's jurisdiction (Figure 11.1).

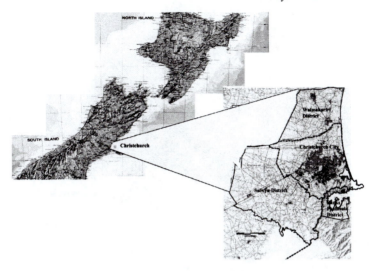

Figure 11.1 Map of UDS boundary showing its location in relation to the South Island of New Zealand.

The boundaries of the UDS area are the Ashley River to the north, the Selwyn River to the south, and the Lyttelton basin to the east. This encompasses a principal commuter, household, and job catchment area between Christchurch and surrounding areas.

In the 2001 population census, the Greater Christchurch area was home to 366,438 people (Statistics New Zealand, 2004). The gross regional product of the Greater Christchurch area in 2001 was $11.1 billion. The Greater Christchurch economy is dominated (in terms of employment) by the retail trade, business services, health and trade, and other auxiliary service sectors (Figure 11.2).

Employment features as a central issue in the UDS Issues Document (Urban Development Strategy Working Group, 2005). Specifically, the Issues Document notes that employment patterns are already moving away from manufacturing towards service sectors, such as information technology and tourism. The Issues Document also notes that an increase in population in the area is likely to influence employment and provide 'a greater variety of jobs'. The question then is: what will be the implications of this employment structure on ecosystem service requirements?

Method and data used in the analysis

This research focuses on understanding the impact of changing employment patterns on the ecosystem service requirements of Greater Christchurch. In order to conduct this analysis, our research involves three key steps:

1 identifying the ecosystem services covered in this research and quantifying their respective 'resource accounts';

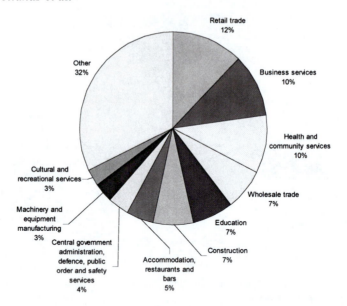

Figure 11.2   Full-time equivalent employee by sector for Greater Christchurch, 2001.

2   calculating sectoral employee numbers for the Greater Christchurch area;
3   calculating and analysing the ecosystem service requirements per employee
    (direct and indirect).

The terms 'direct' and 'indirect' require clarification. This chapter attempts to account for the full-system effect of employment on ecosystem service requirements. These full-system effects are often referred to as direct and indirect effects.

Direct effects (or requirements) can be defined as the actual inputs (employees or ecosystem services) that the production process, or sector, uses. As well as direct requirements, economic activities also indirectly use other resource inputs or employees from other sectors. This is because sectors draw on many kinds of inputs from a multitude of other sectors in order to generate their output. Indirect inputs, therefore, represent the system flows that were necessary to produce the direct inputs (Hannon, 1973). These indirect requirements arising from inter-industry dependencies must be taken into account to gain a full system-wide understanding of ecosystem service use (Di Pascoli *et al.*, 2001; Guo *et al.*, 2001).

An example given by Herendeen (1998: 147) serves to illustrate the distinction between direct and indirect inputs. Herendeen asks: how much energy is required to drive a car 1 km? The possible answers are:

•   the fuel burned;
•   plus the energy to extract, refine, and transport the fuel;
•   plus the energy to manufacture the car (pro-rata'd to 1 km use);
•   plus the energy to produce tyres, replacement parts, etc.;

- plus the energy to build and maintain roads;
- plus the energy to maintain auto repair shops, government regulation, and registration services.
- plus the energy to produce and maintain that portion of the health system used to care for the consequences of auto accidents and auto-related health problems.

The first input can be regarded as the direct input, whereas the remaining inputs are indirect requirements to drive the car. Most analyses consider only the direct requirements of a production process. However, ignoring indirect requirements is analytically myopic. Economic systems are highly interrelated, and commodity production depends on both direct and indirect inputs. Furthermore, indirect inputs can be a significant component of total inputs. For example, Patterson and McDonald (2004) have calculated the total (direct plus indirect) emissions of carbon dioxide from the New Zealand tourism sector in 1997/98. Total CO_2 emissions from the tourism sector are estimated at 6.8 million tonnes. Of this, 26 per cent of the emissions are from 'indirect' emissions.

Ecosystem services covered in this research and their respective resource accounts

Twenty-three major categories of ecosystem services have been identified by de Groot *et al.* (2002). Ideally, the appropriation of all of these services should be measured. However, given the availability of data, we have concentrated on appropriation estimates for land and energy inputs and solid waste outputs (Figure 11.3). The first two can be referred to as 'raw materials', and solid waste output can be regarded as a 'proxy' for the ecosystem service of waste treatment (Jollands, 2003).

The first step of estimating ecosystem service requirements involves estimating the physical resource accounts for the UDS area. These accounts are two-dimensional matrices of order m (physical resource) × n (economic sectors) in physical units. The information sources for generating the resource accounts are summarised in Table 11.1.

Calculating employee numbers for the Greater Christchurch area for 2001

Employee numbers by sector are usually reported according to local government units (i.e., City and District Council). To develop the sectoral employee account for the Greater Christchurch area – which brings together parts of four local authority areas – we had to use meshblock-level employee data (full-time equivalents or FTEs) from Statistics New Zealand. A meshblock is the smallest geographical area for which official statistics are publicly available. Using spatial overlay analysis, we identified which meshblocks lay within the Greater Christchurch boundary. Sectoral employment was then aggregated by ANZSIC code.

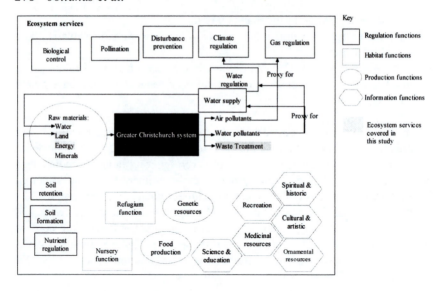

Figure 11.3 Ecosystem services covered in this area (Jollands, 2003).

Table 11.1 Data sources for resource accounts

Resource account	Information source
Land	Market Economics (derived data set from Quotable Value, Agribase, Ministry of Agriculture and Forestry's National Exotic Forest Description, and Transit New Zealand's national traffic database)
Energy	Energy Efficiency and Conservation Authority
Waste	Christchurch City Council (survey conducted by New Zealand Centre for Ecological Economics)

Calculating direct and indirect ecosystem service requirements per employee

Calculating direct resources use per employee is relatively straightforward. We begin with the following:

$$D_{kj} = \frac{q_{kj}}{D_{FTEj}} \tag{11.1}$$

where D_{kj} = direct employee to resource or pollutant (k) for sector j; q_{kj} = the quantity of resources or pollutant k in physical units in sector j; and D_{FTEj} = direct FTEs in sector j.

Calculating the indirect, or flow-on, intensities is more complicated. Once the generation of resource accounts is complete, we estimate total system ecosystem service requirements using an inverse Leontief matrix (ILM) approach (Hite and Laurent, 1971). The two essential elements of the ILM approach are: (a) the inverse Leontief matrix of the input–output matrix of the Greater Christchurch economy; and (b) the resource accounts showing the flow of environmental inputs to, and outputs from, the economy. Algebraically, the approach is outlined below. Consider the following equation:

$$e_{kj} = \frac{q_{kj}}{X_j} \tag{11.2}$$

where e_{kj} is the output (or direct) ecological multiplier of resource inputs or pollution outputs k in sector j; q_{kj} is the physical quantity of resource inputs or pollution outputs k used by sector j; and X_j is the total output of sector j in dollars.

Rearranging (11.2) yields the following:

$$q_{kj} = e_{kj} X_j \tag{11.3}$$

Consider a situation of m resource inputs to, or pollution outputs from, n economic sectors. The set of all e_{kj} arranged in a matrix of order $m \times n$ is called $\mathbf{E}$. In matrix notation:

$$\mathbf{q} = \mathbf{Ex} \tag{11.4}$$

where $\mathbf{q}$ is a vector of order $m \times 1$ resource inputs, or pollution outputs, and $\mathbf{x}$ is a vector of gross economic output of order n 1. It can be shown that (see Jollands, 2003):

$$\mathbf{x} = (\mathbf{I} - \mathbf{A})^{-1}\mathbf{y} \tag{11.5}$$

where $(\mathbf{I} - \mathbf{A})^{-1}$ is the inverse Leontief matrix of order $n \times n$; and $\mathbf{y}$ is an $n \times 1$ vector of final demand. By substituting equation (11.5) into equation (11.4), we obtain:

$$\mathbf{q} = \mathbf{E}(\mathbf{I} - \mathbf{A})^{-1}\mathbf{y} \tag{11.6}$$

Furthermore, substituting $\mathbf{F}$ for $(\mathbf{I} - \mathbf{A})^{-1}$ yields:

$$\mathbf{q} = \mathbf{Fy} \tag{11.7}$$

where $\mathbf{F}$ is a matrix of order $m \times n$ of the system-wide eco-efficiency (direct and indirect) multipliers of final demand expressed in terms of physical units per dollar. We can now calculate the indirect resource requirement per sector as follows:

$$\mathbf{F} - \mathbf{E} = \mathbf{I} \tag{11.8}$$

where **I** is a matrix of order $m \times n$ indirect resource or pollutant intensities in physical units per dollar. We are now in a position to calculate the actual physical quantity of the indirect resource requirement. This is achieved by element-wise multiplying **I** by **x**:

$$I * x = U \tag{11.9}$$

where **U** is a matrix of order $m \times n$ in physical units and $*$ denotes element-wise multiplication. The elements of **U** are u_{kj}.

It is also necessary to calculate Type 1 employment multipliers (L_j) for the n sectors. Employment multipliers were supplied by Market Economics Ltd and were calculated using standard procedures (Richardson, 1972). Thus, we now have a set of n L_j, such that:

$$L_j = \frac{\left(D_{FTEj} + I_{FTEj} \right)}{D_{FTEj}} \tag{11.10}$$

where I_{FTEj} is the indirect employment of sector j. Given that we know D_{FTEj}, then:

$$I_{FTEj} = \left(D_{FTEj} \times L_j \right) - D_{FTEj} \tag{11.11}$$

Thus, indirect employ intensity (N_{kj}) can be calculated as:

$$N_{kj} = \frac{u_{kj}}{I_{FTEj}} \tag{11.12}$$

The D_{kj} and N_{kj} are important. We use sectoral land use (i.e., where $k =$ land) as an example of how they can be interpreted. Land-use intensity implies the area of land required per employee. For each sector, we calculate two types of land-use intensities:

1   the **direct** land-use intensity (D_{kj}), which is the amount of actual land a sector uses per employee;
2   the **indirect** land-use intensity, which is the amount of land used indirectly by the sector by way of the land required to produce the inputs necessary per indirect employee.

For example, the mixed livestock sector uses land directly. But this sector also purchases items such as fence posts that require land (for growing trees). Indirect land use is sometimes referred to as 'embodied land'. Likewise, the purchases of the mixed livestock sector require employees to produce the goods. The labour contribution to these goods can be regarded as indirect employment (or is sometimes called 'embodied labour').

Assumptions, limitations, and strengths of the method

Assumptions

The method used in this chapter to calculate employment multipliers and ecosystem service requirements relies on the standard Leontief matrix and, therefore, relies on the same assumptions as standard economic input–output (IO) tables. For the accounting identities and mathematics in IO algebra to hold in static analyses, two crucial assumptions must be made.[1]

1   *Homogeneity.* For calculation purposes, it is assumed an IO sector consists of processes producing a single homogenous product with similar techniques. The main reason for the homogeneity assumption is to avoid negative entries in the $(I - A)^{-1}$ matrix (Costanza and Hannon, 1989). A negative value in the $(I - A)^{-1}$ matrix implies the column sector directly or indirectly produces (rather than requires) the row commodity. This is contrary to IO accounting conventions. Furthermore, a negative entry would imply that production of an additional unit of a commodity would result in a decrease in total (direct and indirect) input requirements rather than more. This is clearly absurd.

   The assumption of homogeneity is a gross simplification of a complex economic–environment system where multi-product plants make it difficult to group together plants with similar output and input structures. The pragmatic approach is 'to group processes and products which differ in some respects but which behave sufficiently uniformly to be used as a basis for aggregation' (Richardson, 1972: 8). The issue is even more acute when dealing with environmental outputs from the economy. The assumption of no joint products is at odds with a model where industries produce pollutants as well as commodities.

2   *Additivity.* It is assumed that the total effect of carrying out several types of production is the sum of their separate effects. The additivity assumption, therefore, rules out external economies or diseconomies associated with production (Burton, 1985).

Limitations

In addition to the simplifying assumptions, the method based on the inverse Leontief matrix could be criticised because of its heavy data requirements, restrictive boundary definition, and its assumptions about the relationship between prices and physical flows.

A common criticism of the ILM-based approach is that it is expensive to implement because it requires a significant quantity of data. However, economic IO data are available for most countries. A greater challenge involves gathering sectoral data on ecosystem services. As was demonstrated by the *Eco*Link database (McDonald and Patterson, 1999), these data are generally available in New Zealand at an acceptable cost. Consequently, the ILM-based approach provides an implementable method for calculating the ecosystem service requirements of the total system.

A further limitation relates to the boundary of the approach based on the ILM. The method traces the direct and indirect use of ecosystem services through the economic system. Further links back through the ecological system are not accounted for.

A simple example serves to illustrate this point. Consider Figure 11.4, showing a simplified process for the production of butter. Butter production requires wood indirectly because of the need for paper packaging. The ILM-based approach estimates the ecological multiplier of wood use per unit of butter by accounting for the flow of wood through the various economic processes as it is transformed into butter packaging. However, the ILM-based approach does not trace the links through the environment which produced the wood in the first place. That is, the solar energy, soil, and nutrient inputs are not accounted for in the ILM-based method of calculating eco-efficiency indicators. Figure 11.4 shows that the scope of the ILM-based approach is confined to the boxes lying within the shaded area. This restrictive boundary definition is necessary to make the ILM approach tractable. Data on the complex links in an ecosystem are not readily available.

Another limitation of the IO framework relates to the assumption about the relationship between prices and physical flows. Generally, the IO technique assumes that a producing sector charges all purchasing sectors the same for its product. This assumption allows the analyst to use monetary flows as a proxy

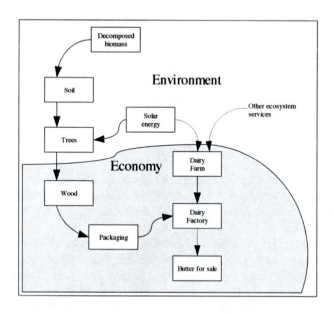

Figure 11.4   The boundaries of the inverse Leontief matrix approach to calculating direct and indirect ecosystem service requirements (butter production as an example).

for material flows (Bicknell *et al.*, 1998: 158). If sectoral prices are constant, the analyst can infer physical output between sectors by using the monetary flows in the transactions table. If, however, a producing sector is able to charge one sector more for its product than another, use of the transaction table to infer physical product flows may lead to false conclusions.

A final criticism of using an IO framework to calculate a system's total ecosystem service requirements is that the ecosystem services embodied in the capital being employed are not accounted for. Conceptually, one would like to treat the ecosystem services required to manufacture plant and equipment in the same way as one treats the ecosystem services used to make the end products themselves. However, capital formation and depreciation are not included in the inter-industry matrix (Bullard and Herendeen, 1975). Although these factors could be endogenised into the framework, this creates further problems in itself. For example, to balance the IO matrix, capital formation must equal capital depreciation, which may not actually be the case if capital accumulation is taking place. The standard approach is to exclude capital from the transaction matrix. However, it must be acknowledged that excluding resource requirements of capital from the analysis means the calculated ecological multipliers will underestimate the 'true' value of the multipliers.

Strengths

The apparent naivety of IO analysis is misleading. The simplifying assumptions are offset by many compensating advantages, the most important of which is that they allow empirical estimation of indirect flows in a complex system. Consequently, a number of authors in different fields have used the IO framework to analyse the requirements for natural resources, particularly energy, in the production of various commodities (see for example Hite and Laurent, 1971; Bullard and Herendeen, 1975; Wright, 1975; Peet, 1987).

There are several reasons why IO tables are useful for economic-environmental analysis in general. First, the assumptions are not always too far from reality. For example, Richardson (1972: 9) notes that 'it is possible for money values to be used as a measure of physical purchases in real terms, since relative price changes do not distort too much the input purchase pattern per unit of output.'

Second, IO tables can answer the call of authors, such as Billharz and Moldan (1997), and tie ecosystem services directly to the economic sectors that use them. Although IO models are based on economic transaction tables denominated in dollars, Victor (1971: 5) has demonstrated that ecological inputs and outputs, such as pollution, can be 'conveniently included in IO models, without upsetting the accounting identities.' Therefore, the links between final demand, the production of goods and services, and the use of ecosystem services can be explored using IO methods (Bicknell *et al.*, 1998). The IO framework also imposes much-needed discipline on economic-environmental analysis. For example, many important accounting balances must be maintained in constructing an IO table (Polenske, 1989).

Third, an IO framework can help trace both the direct and indirect (i.e., total system) requirements of ecosystem services by the economy. By building on the inverse Leontief matrix, which quantifies direct and indirect flows, ecological multipliers which trace the direct and indirect requirements throughout the economy can be calculated.

Finally, the IO table is a flexible and accessible analytical tool. It can be made as detailed or as complex (for example, in sectoral disaggregation) as necessary for any given purpose (Miernyk, 1965: 16). An advantage of using IO tables is that results can be obtained quickly from published economic statistics without a detailed technical knowledge of the industrial processes involved (Wright, 1975: 38).

In conclusion, it seems there are a sufficient number of advantages of the ILM-based approach to warrant its use in estimating linkages related to employment–ecosystem service requirements. As with any empirical work, awareness of underlying assumptions and limitations is needed when interpreting results.

Results and discussion

The following results summarise information prepared for the Greater Christchurch UDS policy process. The data were collected as part of the preliminary phase of a New Zealand government funded research project. As such, the data will be subject to revision. We use the results here as an indication of the potential use of such an investigation into the employment–environment interface.

The discussion, below, presents information on the relative resource intensity (per FTE) of economic sectors (both directly and indirectly). These results are then analysed to identify those sectors where changes in employment are likely to have the greatest impact on land and energy use and waste production within Greater Christchurch. All results are calculated for the year ended March 2001.

Land use and employment

The total UDS land area is 143,366 hectares. Approximately 13 per cent of this is residential land. The remaining 87 per cent (124,985 hectares) is dominated by primary producing sectors (Figure 11.5).

A similar picture of land use is shown when considering land use per employee. Figure 11.6 shows the top 10 sectors on a land use per employee basis.

Not surprisingly, the land-based primary production sectors (livestock, cropping, dairy farming) are more intensive on a land per FTE basis. As counter-intuitive as it may seem, some sectors, such as water supply, are among the most intensive land users per FTE. The water supply sector employs relatively few people (12 FTEs) compared with the total land it uses (107 hectares for treatment plant facilities). The local government sector is also land-intensive per FTE because it includes all the public parks and gardens within Greater Christchurch (over 4,000 hectares). Finally, the fishing sector's inclusion in the list is also counter-intuitive. The reason for the relatively high land per FTE figure for the fishing sector is, it

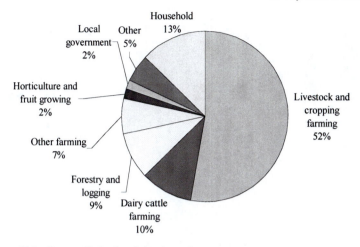

Figure 11.5 Greater Christchurch land area by sector.

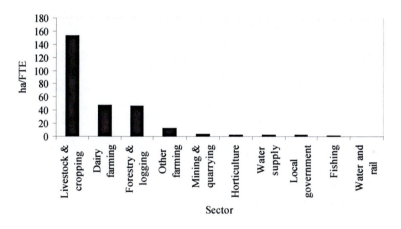

Figure 11.6 Land use per FTE (direct): top 10 sectors.

seems, the land occupied by associated office buildings and coastal port facilities within the Greater Christchurch boundary.

When one looks at indirect land use per indirect FTE, the list of top 10 sectors changes slightly (see Figure 11.7).

The sectors that have the highest indirect land-to-employee intensities tend to be those sectors that process land-based goods, including the meat and dairy processing sectors. Interestingly, some of the primary production sectors have relatively high indirect intensities (i.e., livestock and cropping, horticulture, etc.). The reason for this is that these sectors all purchase land-based goods themselves as inputs to their operations. For instance, the livestock sector purchases feed, hay, and grazing-related products directly from other primary production sectors.

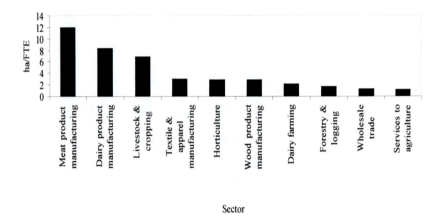

Figure 11.7   Land use per FTE (indirect): top 10 sectors.

The question, then, is what implication does this information provide for policy-makers responsible for designing the UDS? A key implication that needs to be considered is the impact on the land resources within the UDS system. For example, the UDS may project growth in employment in the UDS in the primary production processing sectors. In this case, Greater Christchurch planners would need to consider the direct and flow-on effects of this growth in the demand for land within the Greater Christchurch boundary. The finding of this chapter is that particular attention from a land perspective needs to be given to employment growth in the following sectors:

- land-based primary production sectors;
- water supply sector;
- fishing sector;
- primary-production processing sectors.

Energy

In 2001, Greater Christchurch used approximately 33,000 Gigajoules (GJ) of delivered energy. The major energy types in the UDS are electricity and diesel (Figure 11.8).

Energy use in the Greater Christchurch is dominated by the energy-intensive road transport, paper, and paper-product sectors. This is consistent with other regions in New Zealand. Compared with other regions in New Zealand, the Greater Christchurch sectors are consistently more energy intensive in terms of energy used per dollar of activity (see Figure 11.9). This is a surprising finding, and warrants further investigation.

Relating sectoral energy use to employment reveals a slightly different picture than that provided by Figure 11.9. In terms of direct energy use per employee,

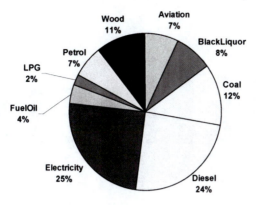

Figure 11.8 Energy use in the UDS by energy type, 2001.

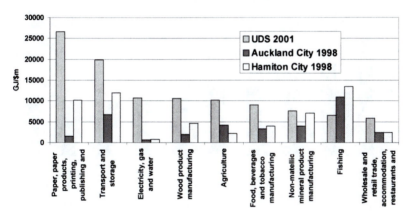

Figure 11.9 Regional comparison of selected sectors' energy intensities.

paper manufacturing, water supply, and dairy products manufacturing dominate, followed by wood product manufacturing and road transport (Figure 11.10).

The paper manufacturing and water supply sectors are both very energy intensive in their activities: paper, because of the energy-intensive nature of the processing method (high electrical motor demand); water supply, because of the huge pumping demands. Other sectors conform to expectations with regards to energy use per employee. Perhaps the only exception to this is the fishing sector. However, this sector uses large volumes of marine diesel oil in its fishing fleet (around 110,00 GJ in 2001) despite its relatively small workforce of 108 employees.

Indirect energy use per indirect employee reveals a similar sectoral list (Figure 11.11).

Notable sectors that stand out in Figure 11.11 are the printing sector, furniture manufacturing, and horticulture. The first two sectors are clearly linked to the

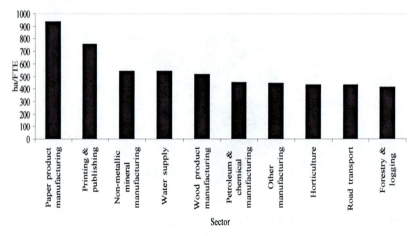

Figure 11.10   Energy use per FTE (direct): top 10 sectors.

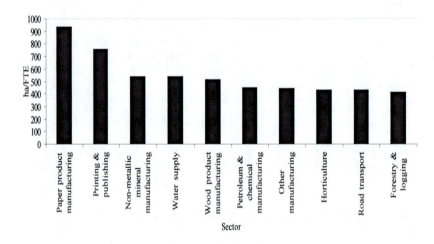

Figure 11.11   Energy use per FTE (indirect): top 10 sectors.

energy-intensive nature of the paper-manufacturing and wood product sectors. The horticultural sector's indirect intensity can be primarily explained by its use of energy-intensive petroleum-based chemicals (pesticides, fertilizers, etc.).

Figures 11.10 and 11.11 identify several sectors to which Greater Christchurch policy-makers should pay attention when considering changes in employment:

- paper product manufacturing;
- water supply;
- dairy product manufacturing;
- wood product manufacturing;
- road transport.

Of particular concern is the road transport sector. Several of the UDS scenarios project significant increases in road transport activity. This will result in greater energy use for transport. The energy intensity of this and other sectors should be of concern to planners for two reasons. First, as employment grows in these sectors, so too will energy demand. Moreover, the majority of the Greater Christchurch energy requirements are sourced from outside the area. Strategically, this means the Greater Christchurch area is vulnerable to other areas dictating how resources required by the UDS are used, which may not necessarily be in the interests of the Greater Christchurch community. A recent example of this was the Project Aqua case, where local opposition played a part in shelving a major hydro scheme that could have relieved some of New Zealand's forthcoming electricity constraints (*Newstalk ZB*, 2004). Interestingly, the Greater Christchurch area has the potential to provide much more of its own energy requirements through industrial cogeneration, distributed household generation, and wind and solar generation (Energy Efficiency and Conservation Authority, 1996).

Second, the Greater Christchurch area faces ongoing electricity transmission constraints. With electricity such a dominant energy carrier in the Greater Christchurch area, it would make sense for policy-makers to focus on improving the efficiency of electricity use. It is hoped that the findings of this research will add more impetus to the call for the UDS to encourage greater local renewable energy sources and energy efficiency.

Solid waste

Economic activity and households within the Greater Christchurch area generated around 241,000 tonnes of solid waste in 2001. Analysis of the solid waste accounts for the economic sectors (i.e., excluding households) reveals that much of the solid waste is wood, recyclable paper, and rubble (Figure 11.12).

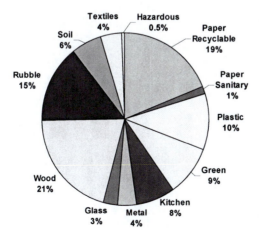

Figure 11.12 Solid waste type for the USD economic sectors, 2001.

The construction sector accounted for almost 41 per cent of total solid waste generation. Wholesale and retail trade accounted for another 18 per cent. Unfortunately, accurate data for other regions are not available for comparison. Analysis of the solid waste and employment data reveals that a further set of sectors also warrant attention in the UDS (see Figure 11.13).

The construction and accommodation sectors dominate the solid waste per FTE intensity in Greater Christchurch. The construction sector was the most intensive sector, generating over 4 tonnes of solid waste per employee in 2001. This waste intensity should be of concern to UDS policy-makers since all scenarios of Greater Christchurch project and increased rate of building activity.

Similarly, the high intensity for the accommodation sector is of potential concern. Along with many urban centres, Christchurch is attempting to attract an increasing share of the tourism market. As this sector grows, so too will the total quantity of solid waste generated. From the perspective of the indirect solid waste per FTE, the construction sector still dominates (see Figure 11.14).

Interestingly, the local government administration sector also has a relatively high solid waste output per employee. This does not augur well for local government officials as they try to persuade other sectors to reduce their waste intensity. The waste intensity of the Greater Christchurch sectors needs to be a focus of attention for the UDS process, for a number of reasons. First, existing landfill sites are nearing the end of their useful life. The pressure to develop new landfill sites highlights the tension between increasing quantities of solid waste generated by increased economic activity and employment and the finite space available for landfill waste disposal. The Greater Christchurch area does, however, encourage some recycling of waste; for example, in Christchurch City, 16 per cent of the total waste stream is diverted from landfill sites by council-provided recycling, composting, and other waste-minimisation schemes (Transwaste Canterbury, 2002). Nevertheless, landfills are expensive and the UDS must encourage further waste-minimisation policies.

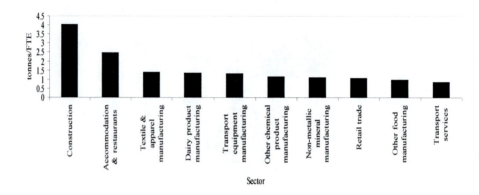

Figure 11.13 Solid waste per FTE (direct): top ten sectors.

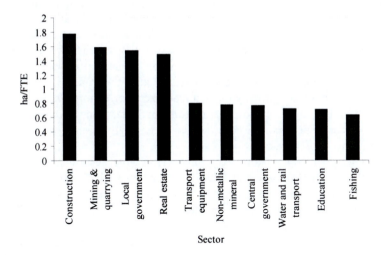

Figure 11.14 Solid waste per FTE (indirect): top ten sectors.

A second potential concern relates to waste security. The future landfill sites that the UDS will rely on are all located outside the Greater Christchurch area. Therefore, they lie within the jurisdiction of the individual councils. The Greater Christchurch residents and businesses are consequently vulnerable in two respects. First, they would have limited ability to ensure appropriate new landfill sites are developed (note: landfills take time to develop; the consent process alone for the Kate Valley Landfill site took almost two years to complete (Hurunui District Council, 2004)). Second, Greater Christchurch residents would have limited ability to affect the landfill fees charged for the waste they are disposing of. As a matter of priority, the UDS needs to support measures that encourage employees to minimise the waste they generate. The analysis conducted in this chapter provides information about which sectors need to be targeted for waste minimisation and recycling.

Conclusions

This chapter has made a case for considering the ecosystem service requirements of employment-related activities incorporated in many of New Zealand's Urban Development Strategies (UDS). The case for such a consideration is strong for two reasons. First, urban systems critically depend on ecosystem services. Therefore, information regarding ecosystem service appropriation – like that generated in this study – can provide an insight into the 'hidden' human requirements for ecosystem services. Second, understanding the ecosystem service appropriation of cities can improve policy development. This is particularly the case for infrastructure planning, environmental reporting, and proactive strategy making.

Unfortunately, few urban development strategies give adequate attention to ecosystem service appropriation issues. It is hoped that, via this research, the Greater Christchurch UDS will address these important ecosystem service appropriation issues. This research on the Greater Christchurch area highlights two key lessons for the UDS. To begin with, several sectors warrant attention from a land-use to employee-intensity perspective, including the primary production sectors, water supply, and primary product manufacturing sectors. From an energy-use perspective, the pulp and paper sectors dominate, along with several other energy-intensive sectors. The construction sector has the highest waste intensity (per employee) of all sectors.

A summary of the rankings of all the sectors' total land, energy, and waste intensities for 2001 is shown in Table 11.2. A rank of 1 indicates that the sector has the highest intensity of all sectors. Shaded cells reveal those sectors with the three highest intensities for that ecosystem service.

As Table 11.2 indicates, examining the ecosystem service intensities of various sectors will have important implications for Greater Christchurch Urban Development Strategy. Many of the sectors that the strategy highlights as potential employment growth areas rank poorly in terms of ecosystem service intensities and will thus place significant future demands on ecosystem services. The strategy has not, to date, considered these additional resource demands. Yet they must move centre-stage if Greater Christchurch is to remain a 'city that works'.

Note

1 In dynamic applications of IO matrices, four other assumptions are generally made:
   Linear production functions. The essence of the Leontief model is a technological relationship between the purchases (or inputs) of any sector and the output of that sector. This relationship is embodied in standard IO analysis as linear production functions, where inputs (purchases) are required in fixed proportions to output in each purchasing sector.
   Fixed input structure. That is, if output doubles, inputs are assumed to also double.
   No capacity constraints exist in any sector. The lack of capacity constraints means that the supply of each good is perfectly elastic.
   Constant direct-input coefficients (a_{ij}) over time. If the linear direct-input coefficients remain constant over time, they provide a nexus for linking final demand to gross output. Constant direct-input coefficients over time imply the assumption of static technology.

References

Bicknell, K., Ball, R., Cullen, R., and Bigsby, H. (1998), 'New methodology for the ecological footprint with an application to the New Zealand economy', *Ecological Economics*, 27, 149–160.

Billharz, S. and B. Moldan (1997), 'Elements of a research agenda', in B. Moldan, S. Billharz, and R. Matravers (eds), *Sustainability Indicators: A Report on the Project on Indicators of Sustainable Development*, New York: John Wiley & Sons on behalf of the Scientific Committee on Problems of the Environment (SCOPE), pp. 389–395.

Table 11.2 Rankings of all the sectors' total land, energy, and waste intensities for 2001 (1 = worst performance; 46 = best performance; three worst-performing sectors shaded)

Industry sector	Land intensity (Direct)	Land intensity (Indirect)	Energy intensity (Direct)	Energy intensity (Indirect)	Waste intensity (Direct)	Waste intensity (Indirect)
Horticulture	6	5	33	8	42	42
Livestock & cropping	1	3	14	18	42	42
Dairy farming	2	7	13	23	42	42
Other farming	4	11	22	31	42	42
Services to agriculture	35	10	40	30	24	21
Forestry & logging	3	8	18	10	40	28
Fishing	9	26	7	22	41	10
Mining & quarrying	5	21	44	11	34	2
Oil and gas exploration and extraction	45	46	44	45	42	42
Meat product manufacturing	15	1	16	16	11	38
Dairy product manufacturing	13	2	3	20	4	40
Other food manufacturing	14	13	15	15	9	22
Beverage manufacturing	16	15	12	24	14	33
Textile & apparel manufacturing	36	4	20	26	3	14
Wood product manufacturing	24	6	4	5	23	34
Paper product manufacturing	23	14	1	1	25	27
Printing & publishing	20	25	43	2	31	36
Petroleum & chemical manufacturing	19	28	6	6	21	23
Other chemical product manufacturing	21	22	25	12	6	25
Non-metallic mineral manufacturing	18	19	8	3	7	6
Basic metal manufacturing	31	24	9	21	17	31
Metal product manufacturing	29	27	24	25	16	17
Transport equipment manufacturing	32	32	17	27	5	5

continued overleaf

Table 11.2 Continued

Industry sector	Land intensity (Direct)	Land intensity (Indirect)	Energy intensity (Direct)	Energy intensity (Indirect)	Waste intensity (Direct)	Waste intensity (Indirect)
Machinery manufacturing	30	30	32	28	15	13
Other manufacturing	25	16	41	7	19	26
Electricity generation & supply	11	41	44	45	29	15
Water supply	7	20	2	4	32	32
Construction	27	23	29	13	1	1
Wholesale trade	39	9	26	17	12	35
Retail trade	38	17	30	33	8	29
Accommodation & restaurants	28	12	21	29	2	24
Road transport	34	39	5	9	20	18
Water and rail transport	10	18	10	14	22	8
Transport services	33	40	11	19	10	12
Communication services	37	43	28	39	30	30
Finance	42	42	38	43	35	41
Insurance	44	45	34	44	33	11
Financial services	43	44	42	41	36	39
Real estate	41	29	39	32	28	4
Business services	40	31	35	34	27	37
Central government services	17	36	37	40	39	7
Local government services	8	33	19	36	38	3
Education	22	35	31	37	26	9
Community services	26	37	36	42	18	19
Recreational services	45	34	27	38	13	16
Other community services	12	38	23	35	37	20

Bullard, C. and Herendeen, R. A. (1975), 'The energy cost of goods and services', *Energy Policy*, December, 3 (4), 268–278.

Burton, B. G. (1985), *A Multi-regional Modelling Framework for Policy Analysis in New Zealand*, Wellington: Ministry of Works and Development.

Costanza, R. and Hannon, B. (1989), 'Dealing with the mixed units problem in ecosystem network analysis', in F. Wulf, J. Field, and K. H. Mann (eds), *Network Analysis and Marine Ecology: Methods and Applications*, Berlin: Springer, pp. 90–115.

Daily, G. (1997), *Nature's Services: Societal Dependence on Natural Ecosystems*, Washington, DC: Island Press.

Di Pascoli, S., Femia, A., and Luzzati, T. (2001), 'Natural gas, cars and the environment: a (relatively) "clean" and cheap fuel looking for users', *Ecological Economics*, 38, 179–189.

Energy Efficiency and Conservation Authority (1996), *New and Emerging Renewable Energy Opportunities in New Zealand*, Wellington: Energy Efficiency and Conservation Authority and the Centre for Advanced Engineering.

Folke, C., Jansson, A., Larsson, J., and Costanza, R. (1997), 'Ecosystem appropriation by cities', *Ambio*, 26, 167–172.

Grimm, N., Grove, J. M., Pickett, S. T., and Redman, C. L. (2000), 'Integrated approaches to long-term studies of urban ecological systems', *BioScience*, 50, 571–584.

de Groot, R. S. (1987), 'Environmental functions as a unifying concept for ecology and economics', *The Environmentalist*, 7, 105–109.

de Groot, R. S., Wilson, M. A., and Boumans, R. M. J. (2002), 'A typology for the classification, description and valuation of ecosystem functions, goods and services', *Ecological Economics*, 41, 393–408.

Guo, Z., Xiao, X., Gan, Y., and Zheng, Y. (2001), 'Ecosystem functions, services and their values: a case study in Xingshan County of China', *Ecological Economics*, 38, 141–154.

Hannon, B. (1973), 'The structure of ecosystems', *Journal of Theoretical Biology*, 41 (3), 535–546.

Herendeen, R. (1998), *Ecological Numeracy: Quantitative Analysis of Environmental Issues*, New York: John Wiley & Sons.

Hite, J. and Laurent, E. A. (1971), 'Empirical study of economic–ecologic linkages in a coastal area', *Water Resources Research*, 7, 1070–1078.

Huang, S. (1998), 'Urban ecosystems, energetic hierarchies, and ecological economics of Taipei metropolis', *Journal of Environmental Management*, 52, 39–51.

Huang, S., and Hsu, W. (2003), 'Materials flow analysis and emergy evaluation of Taipei's urban construction', *Landscape and Urban Planning*, 63, 61–74.

Hurunui District Council (2004), *Canterbury Regional Landfill Project*: Hurunui District Council.

Jollands, N. (2003), 'An ecological economics of eco-efficiency: theory, interpretations and applications to New Zealand', PhD Thesis, Massey University.

Jollands, N. and Patterson, M. G. (2004), 'Four theoretical issues and a funeral: improving the policy-guiding value of eco-efficiency indicators', *International Journal of Environment and Sustainable Development*, 3, 235–261.

McDonald, G. and Patterson, M. G. (1999), *EcoLink Overview Report*, Auckland: McDermott Fairgray Group.

Miernyk, W. H. (1965), *The Elements of Input–Output Analysis*, New York: Random House.

Newcombe, K., Kalma, J. D., and Aston, A. R. (1978), 'The metabolism of a city: the case of Hong Kong, *Ambio*, 7, 3–15.

Newstalk ZB (2004), 'Meridian misjudged aqua opposition', 30 March

Patterson, M. G. and McDonald, G. (2004), *How Clean and Green is New Zealand Tourism? Lifecycle and Future Environmental Impacts*, Palmerston North: Manaaki Whenua Press.

Peet, N. J. (1987), *An Input–Output Energy Scenario Model*, Wellington: New Zealand Energy Research and Development Committee, Ministry of Energy.

Polenske, K. R. (1989), 'Historical international perspectives on input–output accounts', in R. Miller, K. R. Polenske, and A. Rose (eds), *Frontiers of Input–Output Analysis*, New York: Oxford University Press, pp. 37–50.

Regional Growth Forum (1999), *Auckland Regional Growth Strategy: 2050 – A Vision for Managing Growth in the Auckland Region*, Auckland: Auckland Regional Council.

Richardson, H. W. (1972), *Input–Output and Regional Economics*, London: Weidenfeld and Nicolson.

Sahely, H. R., Dudding, S., and Kennedy, C. A. (2003), 'Estimating the urban metabolism of Canadian cities: Greater Toronto area case study', *Canadian Journal of Civil Engineering*, 30, 468–483.

Statistics New Zealand (2004), *Census*, Statistics New Zealand, http://www.stats.govt.nz/census/default.htm.

Transwaste Canterbury (2002), *Background to the Canterbury Regional Landfill Project*, Christchurch: Transwaste Canterbury.

United Nations Population Division (1997), *Urban and Rural Areas, 1950–2030*, 1996 edn, New York: United Nations.

Urban Development Strategy Working Group (2004), *Proposed Brief for the Metropolitan Christchurch Urban Development Strategy – Scope, Structure and Process*, Christchurch: Banks Peninsula District Council, Christchurch City Council, Environment Canterbury, Selwyn District Council, Waimakariri District Council, Transit New Zealand.

Urban Development Strategy Working Group (2005), *Greater Christchurch Urban Development Strategy – Introduction to Issues*, Christchurch: Banks Peninsula District Council, Christchurch City Council, Environment Canterbury, Selwyn District Council, Waimakariri District Council, Transit New Zealand.

Victor, P. A. (1971), 'Input–output analysis and the study of economic and environmental interactions', PhD thesis, University of British Columbia.

Wolman, A. (1965), 'The metabolism of cities', *Scientific American*, 213, 179–190.

Wright, D. J. (1975), 'The natural resource requirements of commodities', *Applied Economics*, 7, 31–39.

12 Employment and environment in a sustainable Europe

Friedrich Hinterberger

Ines Omann

Andrea Stocker

Introduction: sustainable development – a European goal

European environmental policy is shaped by Article 6 of the EU Treaty, which reads as follows: 'Environmental protection requirements must be integrated into the definition and implementation of the Community policies and activities . . ., in particular with a view to promoting sustainable development.'

In line with this principle, environmental protection is considered to be not a sectoral policy, but a maxim involving all sectors. This means not that environmental ministries are not needed any more, but rather that interfaces are required in other sectors (see Görlach *et al.*, 1999; Schepelmann *et al.*, 2000).

Another important European process was triggered by the Lisbon Summit in June 2000 on economic reform, employment, and social cohesion, which agreed on what was called in European language a new strategic goal for the EU for the next decade: to become the most competitive and dynamic knowledge-based economy in the world, capable of sustainable economic growth with more and better jobs and greater social cohesion. The European Council acknowledged the need for an interlinked economic, employment, and social policy and triggered a mechanism of Council meetings each spring to examine economic and social questions and to ensure overall coherence and effective monitoring of progress.

In June 2001, the European Summit in Gothenburg launched a European strategy for sustainable development, in which it states what the integration of environmental, social, and economic concerns should look like. According to the EU Treaty (Article 2), sustainable development is to be characterised by a high degree of employment and social security, by continued economic growth, and by the strengthening of the competitiveness of European industry, as well as by environmental protection and improved environmental quality. The improvement of the quality of life is indicated as an overall objective.

There is wide agreement today, and it follows also from the legal requirements formulated above, that sustainable development – being a normative-integrative concept – has to pursue environmental, economic, and social objectives at the same time. The most important objectives of the environmental dimension include the long-term conservation of the ecosphere as a basis of human life, the sustainable utilisation of renewable resources, and minimised utilisation of non-renewable resources (Hinterberger *et al.*, 1996). The economic dimension mainly focuses on competitiveness as a prerequisite for the development of new eco-efficient technologies (Hinterberger and Luks, 2001). Other key elements are price stability and foreign-trade balance, as well as economic growth and the resulting potential increase in the quality of life. The central objective of sustainability's social dimension is the fair distribution of opportunities in both intra- and intergenerational terms. A high employment level combined with high-quality jobs is an important link between the economic and social dimensions.[1]

Indicators for the three dimensions of sustainable development

The aims of sustainable development are quite general and need further refinement. It is especially important to measure progress towards sustainability (or setbacks). The process of integration requires, therefore, the development of a political strategy to be evaluated by indicators in order to allow a transparent mechanism of reporting in order to see if goals are achieved within the determined timetables.

The European Council of Vienna (1998)[2] invited the Commission to present a report on the development of environmental and integration indicators in Helsinki. The so-called Helsinki Report on Environmental and Integration Indicators (European Commission, 1999) outlines the function of indicators, in particular with regard to transparency and accountability in the Union. According to the Commission, the following criteria to be met by the indicators are identified:

- limited in number;
- relevant;
- responsive;
- simple; and
- policy-relevant.

With regard to economic development and the social field, these objectives are relatively easy to operationalise; indicators exist in both areas (for example, the Gross Domestic Product and the unemployment rate). According to widely accepted norms in an economy, the values of these indicators are to be raised (GDP) or reduced (unemployment rate). These goals and indicators are of course not indisputable but widely used and can be taken as a general starting point.

On the basis of the indicators and the objectives defined, measures can be designed that could be conducive to reaching the objectives. The objectives in the environmental field, however, are much more difficult to operationalise. This is in part on account of the complexity of the matter because environmental burdens materialise and can be measured in many ways. Additionally, considerably less experience exists in this comparatively new policy area, which has been given high priority in EU's policy for only a relatively short period of time. In order to achieve an equal representation of economic, social, and environmental aspects of the sustainability vision, simple, well-known, and accepted indicators as well as comprehensible objectives that can be operationalised are also required for the environmental field (Hinterberger *et al.*, 1998).

From an environmental point of view, the main environmental problems result less from resource scarcity than from the ecological impacts of resource extraction, processing, and use in the economic process. Materials and energy flow through the socio-economic (sub-)system just as is the case with living organisms. To underline this parallelism, the term 'society's metabolism' has been introduced (Ayres and Simonis, 1994; Baccini and Brunner, 1991; Fischer-Kowalski, 1998).

To get a clear picture of the interrelations between the natural and the socio-economic (sub-)system, it is therefore of highest importance to develop a comprehensive system for physical accounting of resource flows (Schmidt-Bleek *et al.*, 1998). One of the methodological approaches for measuring material flows that chimed with the scientific community was developed at the Wuppertal Institute in Germany (e.g., Schmidt-Bleek *et al.*, 1996; Schmidt-Bleek, 1998).

This methodology focuses on the material inputs that form the material base for every human activity. In comparison with the traditional environmental policy, which focused on the regulation of the output side of the economy, this input-related approach guarantees a higher regulatory efficiency with much less effort in control (Spangenberg *et al.*, 1998).

In this approach, the total material input (TMI) comprises all materials that are required for the production, usage, and final deposit of a certain product. The TMI of a product includes the so-called 'ecological rucksack', which can be defined as the amount of material which has to be extracted from the environment in addition to the deadweight of the product itself (Hinterberger *et al.*, 1996). Relating this TMI to the service units, which are delivered by the analysed product, allows one to compare different products and production technologies with regard to their potential environmental burden.

Subtraction of domestic hidden flows and foreign hidden flows from TMI leads to a second concept of material input – the direct material input (DMI). The DMI comprises 'the flow of natural resource commodities that enter the industrial economy for further processing. Included in this category are grains used by a food processor, petroleum sent to a refinery, metals used by a manufacturer, and logs taken to a mill' (Adriaanse *et al.*, 1997: 8).

An important relationship is seen between 'stock' and 'flow' measures. The use of stock measurements (such as capital or habitat) is generally being recognised as a means to replace more conventional flow variables (e.g., savings or emissions) in the context of sustainable development. Although our focus is on the material flows, we emphasise that stocks are just as important, especially in those sectors where material flows depend on the capital used by households and industry (Kletzan *et al.*, 2001).

Whereas the size of stocks and their accessibility is an economic issue, from the ecological point of view, resource flows are the crucial parameters since they contribute to environmental impacts (see Spangenberg *et al.*, 1998). Thus, ecological economic discussion refers to natural capital as the stock of goods that enable the existence of flows, such as various ecosystem services and life-supporting functions (Hinterberger, *et al.*, 1997: 1–14). 'Ecosystem services consist of flows of materials, energy and information from natural capital stocks which combine with manufactured and human capital services to produce human welfare' (Costanza, 1991: 6). Total material flows are a way to operationalise this concept. The challenge for economists is therefore:

- to understand the role of material flows in modern economies (theory; see third major section of this chapter);
- to develop quantitative and qualitative scenarios for possible futures of the economy–environment relationship (data; fourth major section of this chapter);
- to make concrete suggestions for policies to reconcile the goals of dematerialisation and socio-economic development (policy; see chapter conclusions).

This chapter deals with the first two challenges. It has to be emphasised that the indicators mentioned above (TMI, GDP growth, unemployment rate) are possible indicators for the three dimensions, but are by no means exclusive. Concerning TMI, reasons for its choice have been given above. The unemployment rate in its usual form as a social indicator will be discussed below. The literature on the limitation of GDP growth as an indicator of economic performance is vast; general agreement seems to exist that it is not a useful indicator for societal well-being. Nevertheless, GDP growth is still an accepted goal within economic policy. It is also criticised by environmentalists who point out that economic growth is not compatible with environmental protection and, therefore, sustainable development. But taking GDP growth as one economic indicator allows us to show the trade-offs between and the links to different aims of sustainability.

Theoretical aspects of the economy–employment– environment relationship

The macroeconomic view

General and macro-related statements on the economy–employment–environment relationship from a theoretical point of view can be made by looking at productivities and key inequations. The indicators introduced in the preceding sections have the advantage of being applicable as variables in various concepts of economic theorising – just like employment and economic growth, which serve at the same time as economic variables and arguments in the political debate.

If we use the usual macroeconomic terminology, with Y being defined as an economy's income/production, K the (human-made) capital stock, L the labour force employed (employment measured in physical terms of persons employed), and h the total amount of working hours worked by employed persons, we can estimate the total material input (TMI) as defined in the last section. If we add the prices of the factors of production employed, we get *i* as the interest rate (i.e., the price for the use of capital), *w* as the wage rate (i.e., the price of an hour of average work), and PTMI as the price to be paid for the extraction of resources. This price usually equals zero because the cost of extraction matches the costs of labour and capital used in the extraction business, whereas the extraction companies usually receive some profit, all of which is accounted for in the usual economic income accounting and therefore is included in *Y*.

From this, we can derive a macroeconomic production function including material inputs. They play a twofold role. On the one hand, material inputs are a fundamental basis of any economic activity because it is impossible to produce something out of nothing. Therefore, the assumption that production is solely the result of the use of capital and labour is a shortcoming. Rather, TMI can be interpreted as a factor of production. On the other hand, as stated above, TMI is an indicator of the environmental pressure exerted by human activities.

One attempt to consider material input in a production function was made by Klingert (2000), who includes TMI in a neoclassical Cobb–Douglas production function and integrates it with a simple comparative static macroeconomic model. In integrating the concept of TMI into a macroeconomic model, not only the possible effects for production but also the consequences for demand must be considered.

Klingert also discusses the possibility of taxing TMI in this model, which leads to the expected result that 'all equilibrium quantities are affected by the imposing of an input tax (*t*), and all of them are non-linearly reduced compared to the original situation' (Klingert, 2000: 7).

The analytical deduction shows that the effect of this tax is not limited to the reduction of TMI. In addition, the output level decreases as does employment. But these undesirable accompanying effects could be avoided if a subsidy to reduce labour costs is introduced, as also shown in Klingert (2000).

From the presented results, it can be concluded that using resource-oriented instruments alone is not adequate for reaching sustainable development because the interdependencies of the factor markets are neglected. A dematerialisation strategy which combines a material input tax with a labour subsidy would be more promising because it raises the material costs and simultaneously reduces labour costs.

Within the research project 'Labour and Environment' (see fourth major section of this chapter), a scenario was developed in which a mix of policy instruments was suggested. One of the main measures is the implementation of a material input tax on the German TMI, rising from 0.50 to 30.70 euro per tonne of material input from 2000 to 2020. Labour costs were not reduced per se, but there are several instruments influencing labour costs, such as a negative income tax and a real wage orientation on labour productivity, whereby 50 per cent of the additional labour productivity is paid out in wages, while the remaining 50 per cent is transformed into the reduction of working hours.

In a dynamic and long-term view, it could be argued that the restriction in the input of labour due to the introduction of social policy more than 100 years ago, and the reduction of working hours per person employed, created an incentive for an increase in labour productivity which led to the unprecedented economic growth of the last 150 years. At the same time, the material flows involved increased for the longest time at a rate similar to the rate of economic growth. A similar argument could then be made for the present time, according to which an increase in resource productivity would not only be an imperative in ecological terms, but also strengthen the path towards an information-based economy.

Indicators for sustainable development, as defined earlier in the chapter – namely, GDP growth, the unemployment rate, TMI, and the productivities of labour and resource use – are not independent of each other but show interesting links, thus providing criteria for sustainability patterns, which are described in the following.

Inequations

In order to reach a dematerialisation or delinking of material use and economic growth (as described earlier), the material intensity (*TMI/Y*) must decrease or the material productivity (*Y/TMI*) must increase. This can happen on account of three factors:

1   change of demand for goods and services;
2   technological change (increasing efficiency);
3   substitution effects between resources.

A relative delinking (decreasing TMI) is not sufficient to ensure sustainability since an absolute decrease is necessary (i.e., the decrease of TMI must be stronger than the increase of GDP).

The resource productivity derived from the material input, labour productivity, and the rate of GDP growth can be related to each other by three inequations to show the minimum conditions for sustainable development (see, for example, Bockermann *et al.*, 2005).

If we accept that we are already close to the limits of nature's carrying capacity (on either side of the limit), adherence to the precautionary principle should result in industrial economies reducing the total throughput of resources. Consequently, with *Y* denoting the output of the economy, and *R* denoting the total volume of resources used, *Y/R* represents the *resource productivity* (frequently referred to as eco-efficiency), where *R* stands for TMI, CO_2, etc. *R* can be simply counted as material flows in tonnes (Adriaanse *et al.*, 1997).

Only if, in a given period of time, the resource productivity increases faster (declines slower) than the rate of change in output *Y* can an absolute reduction in TMI be achieved. This criterion is given by:

$$\frac{dY}{Y} < \frac{d(Y/R)}{(Y/R)} \tag{12.1}$$

where:

- dY/Y denotes the rate of change in output Y;
- $d(Y/R)/(Y/R)$ denotes the rate of change in resource productivity.

The criterion is a necessary condition for all environmentally sustainable strategies; it is not, however, a sufficient criterion since the rate and/or the speed at which R is delinked from Y can be too slow to resolve long-term environmental problems. Inequation (12.1) implies that GDP growth can lead to an environmentally sustainable path only if its rate of increase is exceeded by the rate of increase in resource productivity. In the long run, this relative limit to growth is quite strict in so far as the growth potential of resource productivity is limited by the laws of thermodynamics (see Georgescu-Roegen, 1971, 1976). We can thus assume that there are limits to the increase of the resource productivity – a factor of 10 may be possible, but a factor of 100 is unlikely. Hence economic growth has to be restrained to fulfil inequation (12.1).

The total output Y can be written as the total active labour force L multiplied by the average product per labour Y/L. The average product per labour is given as the average output per working hour or labour productivity Y/h multiplied by the average working hours per employed labour h/L. In other words:

$$Y/L = Y/h \times h/L \tag{12.2}$$

Given inequation (12.1) and equation (12.2), the number of people employed L increases only if, during a given period, the economy grows faster than the average product per labour. That is, if:

$$\frac{dY}{Y} > \frac{d(Y/L)}{(Y/L)} \tag{12.3}$$

If we regard the creation of additional jobs, at least in Europe, as an indisputable precondition of social sustainability, or alternatively, as one indicator for the social dimension of sustainable development, this relation describes a necessary, although not sufficient, precondition for social sustainability.

However, given equation (12.2), the average product of labour Y/L depends on the hourly productivity of labour Y/h as well as on average working hours per employed labour h/L. Clearly, the average product of labour will increase if either (a) labour productivity rises and h/L remains constant or (b) average working hours per employed labour rises and Y/h remains unchanged. Hence, the effect of weekly working time, early retirement, and part-time jobs on employment levels can be captured here through their effect on the average working time.

The growth of labour productivity, on the other hand, is boosted by technical innovations, training, and education. The impacts of these productivity-enhancing factors are subject to an upper limit not unlike the limit on increases in resource productivity. Once this limit has been reached, only a part of the labour force will be employed in traditional employee situations. The creation of additional jobs can potentially reduce unemployment.

On the positive side, flexibility of paid work regarding location, time, type of labour, and the content of labour is increasing in most nations. The differentiation of labour time (overtime, flexible working hours, time accounts, part-time employment, and early retirement) plus the organisation and the division of labour are also becoming increasingly important factors in dealing with unemployment issues. Informal labour, such as caring work, work in/for the community, etc., is also playing a critical role.

In the context of social sustainability, an extended definition of the term 'work' itself is necessary. Given the importance of formal and informal work, this extended definition of labour brings forth the concept of 'mixed work', which incorporates the following:

- the individual combination of different jobs at the same time (horizontal mixed work);
- different biographical combinations of jobs (vertical mixed work);
- and the transitions between the different combinations.

The concept of mixed work connects the dynamic development of employment with the requirements and potentials of social sustainability. It presupposes the revaluation of so-called informal work by focusing more on the equality of rights and participation through the reallocation of work to ensure that useful forms of employment are accessible to all people regardless of gender, race, and age. An emphasis on the quality of work is also an important feature of mixed work concept.

This aside, the reduction of the unemployment rate can be regarded as an adequate indicator of social sustainability because formal work (traditional jobs) plays the most important role in the concept of mixed work. In this sense, people should be encouraged to gain useful employment in the formal economy, but work fewer hours per year, if possible, and engage in work in the informal sectors of society.

We now turn to the condition for increasing employment:

$$\frac{dY}{Y} > \frac{d(Y/L)}{(Y/L)} = \frac{d\left[(Y/h)\times(h/L)\right]}{\left[(Y/h)\times(h/L)\right]} \tag{12.4}$$

where, *ceteris paribus*, the increase in labour productivity Y/h is limited to $d(Y/h)/(Y/h) < dY/Y$, otherwise the average working time h/L must decrease sufficiently to offset rises in labour productivity Y/h to keep the rate of increase in Y/L (i.e., the average product of labour) below the growth rate of Y.[3]

Combining the two relations in inequations (12.1) and (12.3), we can conclude that, as a necessary precondition, sustainable growth is possible only if:

$$\frac{d(Y/L)}{(Y/L)} < \frac{dY}{Y} < \frac{d(Y/R)}{(Y/R)} \tag{12.5}$$

We call this the *minimum condition of socio-environmental sustainability*. As a minimum condition, it helps to distinguish growth patterns that are definitely not sustainable from those that might be so. The key criterion to identify the genuinely sustainable conditions would then be quantitative in nature (i.e., whether the difference between the various terms is significant enough to signal a growth pattern distinctly different from the current unsustainable one). Guidance for assessing the quantitative necessities for sustainability can be drawn from targets derived from ecologically based research relating to the carrying capacity of natural systems on the right-hand side of inequation (12.5). These would be, for example, factor-of-four changes for energy consumption and factor-of-ten changes in material flows. As for the left-hand side of inequation (12.5), input can be gained from the social and political sciences and from societal debates regarding the accepted levels of unemployment and the preferred working times of workers in different countries.

We can now see that there is a trade-off between inequations (12.1) and (12.3). Inequation (12.1) requires slow economic growth to increase the chance of a sustainable path, whereas inequation (12.3) supports strong economic growth to reduce the unemployment rate. As said above, the growth of resource productivity is limited. Also limited, therefore, is the economic growth needed to fulfil inequation (12.1) and the growth in the average product of labour needed to fulfil inequation (12.3). Looking over the past 150 years, it is clear that labour productivity Y/h has been increasing and still continues to do so. From equation (12.2), we can see that, if labour productivity is rising, but output Y is steady at a sustainable level, rising unemployment can be averted if workers reduce their work time (i.e., if h/L falls). Hence part-time jobs, reduced yearly working time, and other forms of working time reduction can be seen as a potential solution to the environment–employment trade-off (Omann and Nordmann, 2000).

Empirical application

Experiences from a German case study

A German research project named 'Labour and Environment', which ran from 1998 to 1999, investigated possible future sustainability scenarios for Germany and fed them into a macroeconomic simulation model. The results show the relationships between the indicators, the various productivities, and how they can be influenced through policy measures.

The relationship represented in inequation (12.5), which has been at the heart of the so-called socio-environmental sustainability scenario (see Hans-Böckler-Stiftung, 2000: ch. 4.4), was used to evaluate the scenario assumptions based on dynamic model simulations. A highly disaggregated econometric model, 'Panta Rhei',[4] served to quantitatively illustrate the different possible issues and instruments proposed by the socio-environmental sustainability scenario. Panta Rhei is a dynamic input/output model based upon empirical data that has been expanded to include environmental data; namely, data related to energy use, emissions (e.g., CO_2, S_2, NO_x), and material flows.[5] It divides the economy into 58 sectors, and is thus able to provide information about inter- and intrasectoral structural change induced by a certain policy approach. The simulation was calibrated from 1980 to 1994 and will continue to run until 2020 (for more details, see Bockermann *et al.*, 2001; Meyer *et al.*, 1999). The results provide insights into possible trade-offs between macroeconomic, social, and environmental variables, such as economic growth, the unemployment rate, and material flows resulting from specific policy measures. The policy instruments that were suggested and tested in the scenario are detailed in Table 12.1. While searching for 'double dividend' opportunities, the scenario shows how policies for dematerialisation and the reduction of unemployment can be designed, and how macroeconomic, social, and environmental parameters are inter-related (see Spangenberg *et al.*, 1999).

Table 12.2 shows the development of the main quantitative indicators over the 20 years of simulation. They are measured either in monetary terms (e.g., GDP) or in physical terms (e.g., TMI, CO_2).

At a first glance, the results in Table 12.2 are satisfying. The GDP is growing at an annual rate of between 1.57 per cent and 1.97 per cent; the unemployment rate is decreasing significantly to what some would view as the full employment level; and both environmental indicators show negative growth rates. But these numbers must be seen in connection with the sustainability requirements developed earlier in the chapter.

Table 12.1 Selected policy strategies pursued in the scenario as inputs for simulations with Panta Rhei

Parameter	Comments
Real wage	Orientation on labour productivity per hour
Working week and overall lifetime work are shortened	About 50% of the increase in productivity is transformed into reduction of working hours
Transfers abroad	Foreign aid is increased to 0.7% of GDP until 2010; payments to the EU increase to 2% of GDP until 2010 and then remain constant
Material input tax	Quantitative tax on material flows, gradually increased to €30.70/tonne in 2020
CO_2 tax	Tax on emissions, gradually increased to €127.80/tonne in 2020
Subsidies	Restructuring and reduction between 2000 and 2020 following social and environmental criteria
Investment plan	One-third of the revenues gained by a cut in subsidies is used for various economic investments
Expenditures on research	Doubled between 2000 and 2020 from €7.7 billion to €15.3 billion
Value-added tax	Gradually raised to the EU average (20%); however, reduced VAT of 10% for certain products which are chosen using social, cultural, and environmental criteria

Source: Spangenberg *et al.* (1999).

Euro values are based on the conversion of Deutschmark (DM) to euro (€) at the exchange rate of €1 = DM1.95583.

Table 12.2 Results in absolute terms and the growth rates of selected indicators (simulations using the Panta Rhei): Germany

Indicator/absolute values	2000	2005	2010	2015	2020
GDP (billion euro in 1991 prices)	1743.5	1921.9	2091.1	2274.4	2458.8
TMI (million tonnes)	8667.0	7542.3	6817.3	6458.8	6257.8
CO_2 (million tonnes)	856.3	761.3	723.1	717.3	726.8
Unemployment rate	12.0	10.6	9.2	6.3	3.3

Indicator/growth rates	2000–2005	2005–2010	2010–2015	2015–2020	2000–2020
GDP (average annual % change)	1.97	1.70	1.69	1.57	1.74
TMI (average annual % change)	–2.74	–2.01	–1.07	–0.63	–1.61
CO_2 (average annual % change)	–2.32	–1.02	–0.11	0.26	–0.82
Resource productivity (average annual % change)	4.84	3.78	2.80	2.21	3.40
Average product of labour (average annual % change)	0.92	0.57	0.65	0.56	0.68

Sources: Hans-Böckler-Stiftung (2000); Hinterberger and Omann (2000).

Euro values are based on the conversion of Deutschmark (DM) to euro (€) at the exchange rate of €1 = DM1.95583.

The first criterion is deduced from the relationship depicted in inequation (12.1). In order to be environmentally sustainable, the resource productivity must increase faster (or decline slower) than the volume of output Y. The bottom half of Table 12.2 shows that the growth rates of the environmental indicators are negative, which is because the growth rate of resource productivity is higher than the growth rate of real GDP in each five-year period. This satisfies the condition set out in relation to inequation (12.1).

However, as can be seen easily from Table 12.2, the rate at which the material inputs (TMI) decline diminishes beyond 2005. This can also be seen in Figure 12.1, which reveals the growth rates of the various indicators. Both Table 12.2 and Figure 12.1 show that the growth rate of real GDP is positive over the 2000–2020 period; however, it decreases slightly from one five-year period to the next. Concerning CO_2 emissions, the relationship depicted by inequation (12.1) is satisfied from 2000–2015, but is not satisfied in the final five-year period (2015–2020) when CO_2 emissions increase.

The results revealed in Table 12.2 suggest that the positive effects of the tested policy measures weaken over time. It is therefore possible, in the long run, that the growth rate of real GDP will outstrip the growth rate of resource productivity and cause material inputs to rise (note the narrowing of the gap between the two growth rates in Figure 12.1). This would indicate an unsustainable development path as per inequation (12.1). To prevent this unsustainable dynamic, additional policy measures will need to be taken in the medium term (Bockermann *et al.*, 2005).

The relationship depicted by inequation (12.3) presents a minimum criterion for social sustainability. To recall, the number of people employed L increases

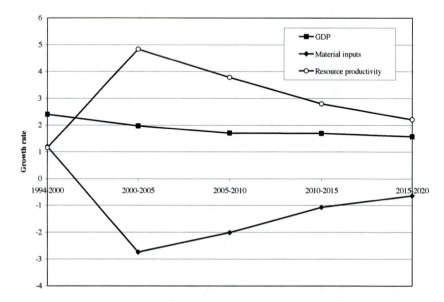

Figure 12.1 Growth rates of GDP, resource productivity, and TMI: Germany.

only if, during a particular period, the economy grows faster than the average product of labour. The relationship between the growth rates in real GDP, average product of labour, and employed persons is represented in Figure 12.2. The fulfilment of inequation (12.3) can also be verified from the data in Table 12.2. The table shows that, for each respective year, the growth rate of the average product of labour is less than the growth rate of real GDP. It is because of this that the unemployment rate decreases over the 2000–2020 period. As an indicator of social sustainability, the unemployment rate decreases from 12 per cent in 2000 to just over 3 per cent by 2020; this, in consequence, reduces the number of unemployed persons to 1.2 million. This fall in the unemployment rate reflects the reduction of working time (the average weekly working time in 2020 is around 27 hours per week) and the increase of gainful employment (number of employed persons increases at around 1 per cent per year from 2000 to 2020). Importantly, the available income rises by around 30 per cent over the study period (Spangenberg *et al.*, 1999). This may be assisting many employed people to reduce their working hours. Overall, in contrast to the environmental criterion, the social criterion appears to be achievable in the very long run.

Finally, we turn to the minimum condition to achieve socio-environmental sustainability as depicted by the relationship in inequation (12.5). Again, achieving such a condition requires the GDP growth rate to be greater than the growth rate of the average product of labour, but less than the growth rate in resource productivity. This, as Table 12.2 and Figure 12.3 show, is confirmed, since both the right-hand and the left-hand side of inequation (12.5) are fulfilled.

Despite these satisfying results, the impression that the trade-off between economy and environment may have been overcome does not hold in the long run. The strat-

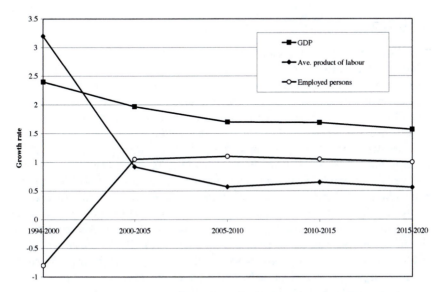

Figure 12.2 Growth rates of GDP, average product of labour, and employed persons: Germany. Source: Spangenberg et al. (1999).

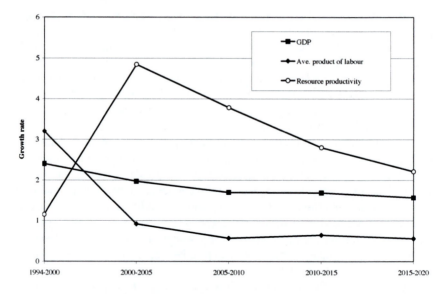

Figure 12.3 Growth rates of GDP, average product of labour, and resource productivity: Germany.

egies recommended in the scenario and which have been integrated into Panta Rhei lead to a momentary decoupling of economic growth and resource depletion (Luks, 1995). In the long run, however, additional policy measures will be necessary to cope with the scale effects of continued economic growth.

Austrian data

Based on data from Biffl (2000)[6] and Statistik Österreich/IFF – Social Ecology (Gerhold and Petrovic, 2000),[7] we also checked the minimum conditions for socio-environmental sustainability for Austria. Table 12.3 indicates that the condition for social sustainability (i.e., that the number of people employed L increases only if the economy grows faster than the average product of labour) is valid for Austria over the periods 1970–1980 and 1980–1990.

If we decompose the average product of labour by labour productivity and the average hours worked (as given by equation (12.2)), we obtain a more detailed picture. For example, using the data on labour volume (LV),[8] which is represented in terms of the number of labour hours, a measure of labour productivity (Y/h) can effectively be calculated by dividing real GDP (Y) by labour volume (i.e., Y/LV). Tables 12.3 and 12.4 can now be used to illustrate what happened to labour volume over the 1970–1980 and 1980–1990 periods. As can be seen from Table 12.4, the number of hours worked fell, implying that labour productivity (Y/LV) rose sharply in both periods. At the same time, the number of people employed increased (see Table 12.3). Given inequation (12.4), it is clear that the rise in labour productivity was sufficient to enable (a) more labour to be employed

Table 12.3 Relationship between GDP and labour during the periods 1970-1980 and 1980-1990: Austria

	Y (1960 = 100)	dY/Y	L (employees)	Y/L	d(Y/L)/(Y/L)
1970	158.7		3011028	0.5271	
1980	229.6	0.4468	3217339	0.7136	0.3540
1990	288.4	0.2561	3296526	0.8749	0.2259

Table 12.4 Relationship between GDP and labour volume (LV) during the periods 1970–1980 and 1980–1990: Austria

	Y (1960 = 100)	dY/Y	LV (000 hours)	Y/LV	d[(Y/LV)]/(Y/LV)
1970	158.7		7161547.62	0.2216	
1980	229.6	0.4468	6817625.34	0.3368	0.5197
1990	288.4	0.2561	6716415.61	0.4294	0.2750

in Austria (and for the unemployment rate to fall) and (b) workers to reduce the average number of hours they work – both of which are positive social outcomes.

Although the criterion for social sustainability is applicable only at the macroeconomic level, an analysis of the minimum condition for ecological sustainability is useful at both the macro and sectoral levels since a worthwhile environmental goal is to reduce the material inputs in all sectors of the economy. To evaluate the minimum condition for environmental sustainability at the sectoral level, we have employed the data arising from an environmentally extended input–output analysis of the Austrian economy by Luptacik and Stocker (2005). In their study, Luptacik and Stocker related the change in final demand between 1995 and 2000 to the change of the reciprocal values of the total intensities of material input between 1995 and 2000.

To recall, the environmental sustainability condition at the macro level (inequation (12.1)) requires the growth rate of GDP to be less than the growth rate of resource productivity for the entire economy. Similarly, to achieve sustainability at the sectoral level, the growth rate in sectoral output must be less than the sector's growth rate of resource productivity. Calculations for material inputs based on Luptacik and Stocker's input–output analysis (see Table 12.5) reveal that the minimum sustainability condition was satisfied neither at the macro level nor for the majority of the sectors within the Austrian economy.[8] Exceptions were those sectors that experienced a decrease in output over time, such as 'Food products and beverages' and 'Sale and repair of motor vehicles'.

More aggregated Austrian data for the periods 1970–1980 and 1980–1990 (see Table 12.6) confirm that in neither period was this minimum condition for sustainability satisfied at the macro level. That is, the growth rate of real GDP exceeded the growth rate of resource productivity in both periods. Having said this, the gap between the growth rate of real GDP and resource productivity, which was very high in the first decade (1970–1980), was much less during the second decade (1980–1990). This indicates that Austria is improving its environmental performance, although it remains to be seen whether the Austrian economy eventually satisfies the environmental sustainability condition.

Table 12.5 Relationship between sectoral output and direct material input (DMI) at the sectoral level during the period 1995–2000: Austria

NACE	Commodities	dY/Y (million euro)	(dY/MI)/(Y/MI) (million euro per million tonnes)	Ecologically sustainable dY < dY/ MI)
01	Agriculture, forestry, fishing	616	0.00	No
10	Mining of coal and lignite	7	−0.03	No
11	Crude petroleum, natural gas, metal gas ores	−8	0.01	Possible
14	Other mining and quarrying	34	0.00	No
15	Manufacture of food products and beverages	−289	0.11	Possible
16	Tobacco products	48	1.61	No
17	Textiles	444	3.86	No
18	Wearing apparel	65	2.06	No
19	Leather, leather products, footwear	133	0.37	No
20	Wood and products of wood	731	0.58	No
21	Paper and paper products	942	0.12	No
22	Publishing, printing and reproduction	921	3.62	No
23	Coke, refined petroleum products	4	2.66	No
24	Chemicals and chemical products	1,401	1.28	No
25	Rubber and plastic products	574	2.70	No
26	Other non-metallic mineral products	88	0.10	No
27	Basic metals	1,510	2.27	No
28	Fabricated metal products	1,071	2.60	No
29	Machinery and equipment n.e.c.	2,488	3.77	No
30	Office machinery and apparatus n.e.c.	457	8.40	No
31	Electrical machinery and apparatus n.e.c.	1,331	0.78	No
32	Radio, television equipment	920	1.78	No
33	Medical, precision, optical instruments, clocks	67	0.42	No
34	Motor vehicles and trailers	2,715	7.33	No
35	Other transport equipment	328	2.92	No

36	Furniture; manufacturing n.e.c.	873	2.38	No
37	Recycling	4	2.51	No
40	Electricity, gas, steam and hot water supply	695	-0.49	No
45	Construction	966	-0.07	No
50	Sale & repair of motor vehicles; retail sale of automotive fuel	-123	-2.96	Possible
51	Wholesale and commission trade	2,586	0.68	No
52	Retail trade, repair of household goods	1,738	0.12	No
55	Hotels and restaurants	739	0.24	No
60	Land transport; transport via pipelines	891	2.03	No
61	Water transport	587	2.51	No
62	Air transport	-8	-0.16	Possible
63	Supporting a. auxiliary transport activities; travel agencies	816	-0.71	No
64	Post and tele-communications	1,841	-19.04	No
65	Financial intermediation, except insur. a. pension funding	1,051	14.16	No
66	Insurance and pension funding, except social security	558	2.84	No
67	Activities auxiliary to financial intermediation	0	0.00	No
70	Real estate activities	1,400	-0.31	No
71	Renting of machinery and equipment without operator	158	1.27	No
72	Computer and related activities	920	2.35	No
73	Research and development	217	3.67	No
74	Other business activities	872	3.33	No
75	Public administration; compulsory social security	603	0.48	No
80	Education	454	-0.57	No
85	Health and social work	82	-1.65	No
90	Sewage and refuse disposal sanitation and similar act.	60	-0.64	No
91	Activities of membership organisations n.e.c.	178	-0.91	No
92	Recreational, cultural and sporting activities	594	-0.41	No
93	Other service activities	109	-0.38	No
	Total	35,461	0.28	No

Table 12.6 Relationship between GDP and direct material input (DMI) during the
periods 1970–1980 and 1980–1990: Austria

	Y (1960 = 100)	dY/Y	DMI (1960 = 100)	Y/DMI	d[(Y/DMI)]/(Y/DMI)
1970	158.7		130.8	1.21	
1980	229.6	0.4468	176.5	1.30	0.0722
1990	288.4	0.2561	186.3	1.55	0.1900

Conclusions

This chapter has showed how the relatively recent concept of total material flows
can be integrated in economic modelling as well as in empirical studies. Exploring this further will help with discussions concerning the effects and effectiveness
of measures and policies for dematerialisation on all relevant macroeconomic
variables. The whole range of instruments usually discussed in environmental
economics can also be used to achieve the more recent goal of dematerialisation:
from the provision of relevant information, fiscal reforms, and tradable permits
for the extraction of primary resources, to command and control measures. In
principle, the usual theoretical pros and cons that are discussed, for example, on
energy taxation, apply in relation to environmental goals. However, macroeconomic modelling, as this chapter has shown, can reveal in more detail the overall
possible outcomes of a specific mix of policy instruments. Further research is
needed to explore in more detail the structural, distributional, resource allocation,
and scale effects of such policies – especially for the Austrian and European
cases.

The German project on 'Labour and Environment', from which most of the
data presented in this chapter were derived, showed that, under the assumptions made, a policy towards sustainable development can lead to favourable
results in all relevant dimensions of sustainable development, as required by
the European Treaty and the sustainable development strategy. There are certainly
paths which lead to desirable results in one or two of the various dimensions but,
importantly, only relatively minor trade-offs between these dimensions exist,
and only then if adequate strategies are developed to follow economic, social,
and environmental policy goals.

Notes

1 Additionally, a fourth dimension (the institutional one) has increasingly been integrated
   into this concept (Spangenberg *et al.*, 1999). The inclusion of the institutional dimension takes account of the fact that each economic activity is performed within an institutional framework that decisively influences the result of the activity (Hinterberger
   and Luks, 2001). Therefore, socio-economic changes, such as the implementation of
   the sustainability concept, also require the further development of institutions.
2 See http://www.europa.eu.int/council/off/conclu/dec98.htm or the documentation in
   Schepelmann *et al.* (2000).
3 In this case, *h* is measured in hours.
4 Panta Rhei was developed by Professor Bernd Meyer at the University of Osnabruck,
   Germany. It is the environmental expansion of INFORGE, a dynamic input/output

model that belongs to the international INFORUM family (Meyer *et al.*, 1999). See also http://www.gws-os.de for more details.

5　The data for the material inputs in all 58 sectors of the German economy were provided by the Wuppertal Institute.

6　Biffl (2000) shows the development of labour volume and productivity from 1964 to 1999 for the Austrian economy.

7　To represent the material efficiency of the Austrian economy over time, Statistik Österreich/IFF – Social Ecology (Gerhold and Petrovic, 2000) have published an input time series of the material flows for the years 1960 to 1997. To operationalise the material input, the indicator direct material input (DMI) is used.

8　The term 'possible' in the right-hand column of Table 12.5 indicates that fulfilling the minimum condition does not mean that economic activity within the sector was actually sustainable.

References

Adriaanse, A., Bringezu, S., Hammond, A., Moriguchi, Y., Rodenburg, E., Rogich, D., and Schiitz, H. (1997), *Resource Flows: The Material Basis of Industrial Economies*, Washington, DC: World Resources Institute.

Ayres, R. U. and Simonis, U. E. (eds) (1994), *Industrial Metabolism – Restructuring for Sustainable Development*, Tokyo, New York, Paris: United Nations University Press.

Baccini, P. and Brunner, P. (1991), *The Metabolism of the Anthroposphere*, Berlin: Springer.

Biffl, G. (2000), *Die Entwicklung des Arbeitsvolumens und der Arbeitsproduktivität nach Branchen*, Vienna: WIFO.

Bockermann, A., Meyer, B., Omann, I., and Spangenberg, J. H. (2001), 'Modelling sustainability – European and German approaches', in M. Matthies, H. Malchow, and J. Kriz (eds), *Integrative Systems Approaches to Natural and Social Sciences – Systems Science 2000*, Berlin: Springer-Verlag.

Bockermann, A., Meyer, B., Omann, I., and Spangenberg, J. H. (2005), 'Modelling sustainability. Comparing an econometric (PANTA RHEI) and a systems dynamics model (SuE)', *Journal of Policy Modelling*, 27 (2), 189–210.

Costanza, R. (ed.) (1991), *Ecological Economics*, New York: Oxford University Press.

European Commission (1999), *Report on Environmental and Integration Indicators to Helsinki Summit*, European Commission Working Paper No. 1942, Brussels.

Fischer-Kowalski, M. (1998), 'Society's metabolism: the intellectual history of materials flow analysis, Part I, 1860–1970', *Journal of Industrial Ecology*, 2 (1), 61–78.

Gerhold, S. and Petrovic, B. (2000), *Materialflussrechnung: Bilanzen 1997 und abgeleitete Indikatoren 1960–1997*, Statistische Nachrichten 4/2000, Statistik Österreich, Vienna.

Georgescu-Roegen, N. (1971), *The Entropy Law and the Economic Process*, Cambridge, MA: Harvard University Press.

Georgescu-Roegen, N. (1976), *Energy and Economic Myths: Institutional and Analytical Economic Essays*, New York: Pergamon Press.

Görlach, B., Hinterberger, P., and Schepelmann, P. (1999), *Von Wien nach Helsinki. Umweltpolitische Anforderungen an den Prozess zur Integration von Umweltbelangen in andere Politikbereiche der Europäischen Union*, European Policy Paper No. 4, Wuppertal, Vienna.

Hans-Böckler-Stiftung (ed.) (2000), *Arbeit and Ökologie, Final Report*, Düsseldorf: Hans-Böckler-Stiftung.

Hinterberger, F. and Luks, R. (2001), 'Dematerialization, competitiveness, and employment in a globalized economy', in M. Munasinghe, O. Sunkel, and C. de Miguel (eds), *The Sustainability of Long-Term Growth*, Cheltenham, UK: Edward Elgar, pp. 107–135.

Hinterberger, F. and Omann, I (2000), 'Theoretische Grundlagen und empirische Ergebnisse eines ökologisch-sozialen Szenarios für Deutschland', in S. Hartard, C. Stahmer, and F. Hinterberger (eds), *Das magische Dreieck*, Marburg: Metropolis, pp. 13–41.

Hinterberger, P., Luks, R., and Stewen, M. (1996), *Ökologische Wirtschaftspolitik: Zwischen Ökodiktatur und Umweltkatastrophe*, Berlin, Basel, Boston: Birkhäuser.

Hinterberger, R., Luks, P., and Schmidt-Bleek, P. (1997), 'Material flows vs. "natural capital": what makes an economy sustainable?', *Ecological Economics*, 23, 1–14.

Hinterberger, R., Moll, S., and Femia, A. (1998), *Arbeitsproduktivität, Ressourcenproduktivität und Ressourcenintensität der Arbeit: makroökonomische und sektorale Analyse*, Graue Reihe des Instituts für Arbeit und Technik, Institut für Arbeit und Technik, Gelsenkirchen.

Kletzan, D., Koeppl, A., Kratena, K., Schleicher, S., and Wueger, M. (2001), 'Modelling sustainable consumption: from theoretical concepts to policy guidelines', paper presented at the Annual Conference of the Austrian Economic Association, NÖG 2001, Graz.

Klingert, S. (2000), *Material Flows in a Neoclassical Model*, n.p.: Hamilton.

Luks, F. (1995), 'Economic growth within a limited environmental space?', in J. H. Spangenberg (ed.), *Towards Sustainable Europe*, Luton: Friends of the Earth Publications, pp. 135–153.

Luptacik, M. and Stocker, A. (2005), 'Eco-efficiency and sustainability of the Austrian economy', project final report to the Österreichischen Jubiläumsfonds, Vienna.

Meyer, B., Bockermann, A., Ewerhart, G., and Lutz, C. (1999), *Marktkonforme Umweltpolitik*, Heidelberg: Physica.

Omann, I. and Nordmann, A. (2000), 'Gutes Leben statt Wachstum des Bruttosozialprodukts', in C. Boeser, C. T. Schemer, and D. Wolters (eds), *Kinder des Wohlstands – Auf der Suche nach neuer Lebensqualität*, Frankfurt/Main: VAS-Verlag, pp. 176–193.

Schepelmann P., Hinterberger, F., Görlach, B. and Moll, S. (2000), *Von Helsinki nach Göteborg*, Vienna: Studie im Auftrag des Bundesministeriums für Land- und Forstwirtschaft, Umwelt und Wasserwirtschaft.

Schmidt-Bleek, R., Bringezu, S., Hinterberger, R., Liedtke, C., Spangenberg, J. H., Stiller, H., and Welfens, M. J. (1998), *MAIA Einführung in die Material-Intensitäts-Analyse nach dem MIPS-Konzept*, Basel, Berlin, Boston: Birkhäuser.

Schmidt-Bleek, F. (1998), *Das MIPS-Konzept*, Munich: Droemer Knaur.

Schmidt-Bleek, F., Bringezu, S., Hinterberger, F., Liedtke, C., Malley, J., Schütz, H., Stiller, H., Tischner, U., Welfens, M. J., Behrenmeier, R., Brüggemann, U., Lehmann, H., Manstein, C., Merten, T., Richard-Elsner, C., and Zieschang, H. (1996), *MAIA. Einführung in die Materialintensitätsanalyse*, Berlin, Basel, Boston: Birkhäuser.

Spangenberg, J., Femia, A., Hinterberger, F., and Schutz, H. (1998), *Material Flow-Based Indicators in Environmental Reporting*, Environmental Issues Series, No. 14, European Environment Agency, Copenhagen.

Spangenberg, J. H., Omann, I., and Hinterberger, F. (1999), 'Sustainability, growth and employment in an alternative European economic policy. Theory, policy and scenarios for employment and the environment', paper presented at the Fifth Workshop on Alternative Economic Policy for Europe, Brussels, 1–3 October.

13 Managing without growth

Peter Victor
Gideon Rosenbluth

Introduction[1]

There are three main arguments why developed countries should consider managing without growth. First, continued economic growth worldwide is not an option, owing to environmental and resource constraints, and so developed countries should leave room for growth in developing countries where the benefits of growth are evident. Second, economic growth in developed countries is neither necessary nor sufficient to achieve full employment, the abolition of poverty, and protection of the environment. Third, in developed countries, there is evidence that growth has become uneconomic in the sense that it detracts more from well-being than it adds (Daly, 1996). There is an extensive literature exploring these arguments, much of which is summarised in Common and Stagl (2005: ch. 6 and 7). They are developed more fully in Victor (2008).

The purpose of this chapter is to explore no-growth and low-growth scenarios for Canada over the medium range to 2020 using LOWGROW, a dynamic simulation model. After describing LOWGROW, a scenario is presented that shows conditions under which the rate of unemployment in Canada could be reduced to historically low levels, poverty eliminated, fiscal balance maintained, and greenhouse gas emissions reduced to comply with Canada's commitment under the Kyoto Protocol, without relying on economic growth. This is not to say that zero growth should itself become a policy objective; rather that the dependence on and defence of economic growth should not be an obstacle to fulfilling the important welfare-enhancing objectives of full employment, eliminating poverty, and protecting the environment.

The chapter concludes with some policy implications for managing without growth, followed by an appendix which provides a technical description of LOW-GROW.

Simulating low/no growth in the Canadian economy

LOWGROW has been built using STELLA, a systems dynamics modelling language chosen for its flexibility (it can accommodate quantitative and qualitative variables), its facility for simulating change over time (STELLA is well suited for solving systems of difference equations), the ease with which it can handle 'what if' analysis for exploring policy options and different assumptions, the transparency of the models (all flow diagrams and equations are accessible), and its attractive user interface. Figure 13.1 shows the simplified structure of the simulation model. Key assumptions, equations, and data sources used in LOWGROW are detailed in the appendix. All monetary values in LOWGROW are in constant 1997 dollars, unless otherwise specified.

LOWGROW includes a Cobb–Douglas aggregate production function (macro supply in Figure 13.1) in which 'GDP Supplied' is a function of the employed stock of produced capital (i.e., the stock of produced capital multiplied by a capacity utilisation factor), the employed labour force (i.e., the labour force multiplied by the rate of employment), and time (to account for productivity gains in the use of capital and labour).[2]

LOWGROW also includes equations for consumption, business investment, government expenditure, exports, and imports that are the components of 'GDP Demanded' (macro demand in Figure 13.1). GDP Supplied is an independent variable in the equations for these components of aggregate demand. If aggregate demand exceeds aggregate supply, the rate of unemployment declines and the rate of capacity utilisation increases; and if aggregate supply exceeds aggregate demand, the rate of unemployment rises and the rate of capacity utilisation declines.

There is no explicit monetary sector in LOWGROW. The assumption is made that the Bank of Canada will continue to implement a monetary policy focused on maintaining the rate of inflation at about 2 per cent per year. The prime rate of interest is determined exogenously in LOWGROW.

Poverty is represented in LOWGROW as the number and percentage of Canadians with incomes below the Low Income Cutoff (LICO). LICO is a threshold below which a family is likely to spend significantly more of its income on food, shelter, and clothing than the average family (Giles, 2004: 10). In 1992, the average Canadian family spent 43.6 per cent of after-tax income on food, shelter, and clothing (*ibid.*). The LICO methodology adds 20 percentage points to this aver-

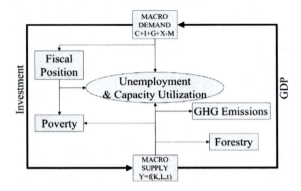

Figure 13.1 Simplified structure of LOWGROW.

age, representing the situation of a family that is spending a significantly higher proportion of income than the average on necessities. A family with an income below the cutoff is counted as being in poverty.

In LOWGROW the number of people living below LICO is affected by two factors. First, starting from an initial value of 3.55 million in 2003 (Statistics Canada, 2003: Table 8.1-1), LOWGROW allows income to be redistributed to bring people up to LICO as a result of a policy intervention. This amounts to $5,900 per individual and $7,000 per family below LICO in current dollars (*ibid*.: Table 8.3-3). LOWGROW computes the cost of raising any specified proportion of people living below LICO up to LICO. In practice, there are many forms of direct and indirect ways of providing income support. The 'additional transfers' computed in LOWGROW are a proxy for any and all of these.

Second, poverty is related to the prevalence of unemployment. In LOWGROW, the simplifying assumption is made that an unemployed person who becomes employed receives an income equal to or greater than LICO, and that an employed person who becomes unemployed experiences a reduction in income that takes them below LICO. This assumption is consistent with the close correlation between the unemployment and poverty rates in Canada between 1994 and 2003, the longest period for which consistent measures of both variables is available.

LOWGROW also calculates the UN's Human Poverty Index (HPI) (United Nations Development Programme, 2005.) The HPI defined for developed countries (HPI-2) is based on four variables: (a) the probability at birth of not surviving to age 60; (b) the percentage of adults lacking functional literacy skills; (c) the percentage of the population below the income poverty line (defined as 50 per cent of the median income, which is highly correlated with LICO, the variable used in LOWGROW); and (d) the long-term unemployment rate (lasting 12 months or more.) In 2005, the HPI-2 for Canada was the ninth lowest (i.e., ninth best) among 17 selected OECD countries (*ibid*.).

LOWGROW keeps track of the fiscal position (i.e., surplus/deficit and debt) of the three levels of government combined in Canada: federal, provincial, and municipal. According to data from Statistics Canada, the change in net debt of all three levels of government differs from the reported annual surplus or deficit, defined as outlays minus income (Statistics Canada, 2004; Department of Finance, 2004). This difference is not well explained in the relevant government documents. For the purposes of LOWGROW, a regression equation was estimated that relates the change in net debt to the annual surplus or deficit.

Finally, LOWGROW has an environmental dimension through the inclusion of greenhouse gas emissions (GHG), a Kyoto compliance module, and a sub-model of Canada's forestry sector.

LOWGROW runs from the start of 2000 to the start of 2020, a total of 20 years. For the years 2000–2003, LOWGROW reports values from Statistics Canada of the key economic variables. The model's equations take over at the start of 2004. The 'base case' scenario in which government policies regarding spending, taxes, and services delivered are unchanged from 2003 is shown in Figure 13.2.

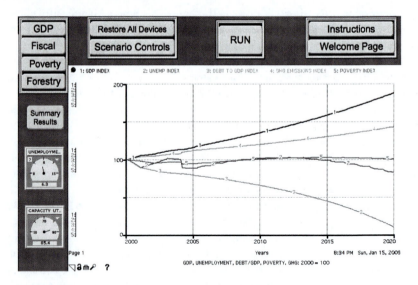

Figure 13.2 LOWGROW's dashboard and base case scenario.

Figure 13.2 shows the base case for real GDP (1), the rate of unemployment (2), the debt to GDP ratio (3), GHG emissions (4), and poverty (5). All of the variables in Figure 13.2 are converted to indexes with their actual values at the start of 2000 given as 100 for ease of comparison. A companion graph (not shown) gives the actual data for each variable. The model reports results from the start of 2000 to 2020.

In the base case scenario, shown in Figure 13.2, real Canadian GDP is projected to increase by 88 per cent from the start of 2000 to the start of 2020, with an average annual growth rate of 3.2 per cent. The average annual rate of growth from 1982 to 2003 was 3.1 per cent. The projected average annual rate of increase in per capita GDP is 2.4 per cent. In the absence of new initiatives to reduce Canadian GHG emissions, they are projected to rise by 43 per cent over the same period. Greenhouse gas emissions rise less than GDP on the assumption that GHG/GDP declines by the rate of productivity increase in the macro production function (nearly 1 per cent per year), which is consistent with the 13 per cent decline in emissions per unit of GDP from 1990 to 2003 (Environment Canada, 2004: ii).

The rate of unemployment is projected to fall to 6.7 per cent in 2005, to rise slowly to 7.8 per cent by 2011, and then to decline to 6.3 per cent by 2020, which is 80 per cent of its value in 2000. The debt to GDP index is projected to decline to 7 per cent as Canadian governments continue to pay off their debt over this period. Canadian governments, combined, have been running substantial budget surpluses for several years and using some of the surplus to redeem outstanding debt. In the base case, it is assumed that this pattern will continue until all the debt is redeemed.

The fifth index shown in Figure 13.2, the HPI for Canada, changes little over the period 2000 to 2020. It declines slightly until 2005 and then rises slowly back to 3 per cent above its initial value by 2014 before declining back to its value in 2000 by 2020. This is despite the projected increase in GDP and decline in unemployment. The reason for this is that, even though the rate of unemployment is projected to decline by the end of the period, the number of unemployed people is projected to increase and, with it, the number of people with incomes below the LICO as a proportion of the growing population. These factors largely balance out over the period 2000–2020 in the base case scenario. Since no changes are assumed in the other components of the HPI (i.e., the infant mortality rate, the literacy rate, and the rate of long-term unemployment), the HPI shows little change despite significant increases in GDP per capita.

To show how policy intervention can produce changes from the base case scenario, we first have to explain how our model determines certain key variables.

Net investment

Net investment is gross business investment plus gross government investment minus depreciation and demolition. Gross business investment is estimated as a linear function of the interest rate, GDP, and the average rate of corporation profits tax, all lagged one year. Government investment is taken as a constant proportion of business investment based on 2004 values. The depreciation and demolition rate of the capital stock is set at 4 per cent, the average rate from 1981 to 2003.

To simulate no-growth and low-growth scenarios, net investment is multiplied by a factor that can be set exogenously at any value from 0 to 1. For the 'no-growth' scenario, this factor is set to zero so that gross investment equals depreciation and net investment is zero.

Growth in productivity

The coefficient for time (t) in the production function is multiplied by a factor that varies from 0 to 1. If this factor is set at zero, there are no gains in productivity over time.

Growth in population and the labour force

The annual increase in population as projected by Statistics Canada is multiplied by a factor that varies from 0 to 1. If this factor is set at 0 there is no increase in population. This effect carries over to the labour force, which is estimated as a linear function of population and GDP.

Net trade balance

Imports are estimated as a linear function of GDP per capita and population, and exports as a linear function of US GDP and the Canada/US exchange rate. The model reduces the gap between exports and imports by reducing exports by the trade surplus multiplied by a factor that varies from 0 to 1. If this factor is set at 1, the trade surplus is zero.

Shorter work week

Increases in unemployment, other things equal, can be 'compensated' for by a reduction in the length of the work week so that more people are employed for any level of labour input. LOWGROW allows the user to reduce the average work week down to 97 per cent of its value in 2004.

Active labour management policies (ALMP)

ALMP refers to measures designed to assist re-employment. Such measures include improvements to the functioning of the Public Employment service (e.g., placement and counselling services), enhanced training programmes for the unemployed, targeted job creation measures for workers whose joblessness is particularly harmful to future prospects (e.g., long-term unemployed youth), employment subsidies, and employment programmes in the public sector.

LOWGROW provides the option of increasing government expenditures on ALMP and reducing the rate of unemployment.

Government expenditure

In the absence of policy intervention, the model assumes that government expend-iture will remain the same proportion of GDP as in 2003. As Figure 13.2 shows, in the base case the Canadian governments (all three levels combined) build very large budget surpluses over the projection period allowing elimination of the national debt.

Our model allows us to select several government expenditure strategies: a bal-anced budget, a counter-cyclical investment programme that is based on the rate of unemployment, and a stabilising expenditure programme that equates aggre-gate demand and aggregate supply. If a balanced budget is selected, the model sets total government expenditure equal to the endogenously determined government income (we can change the rates of corporation profits tax and the rate of personal tax and transfers, which affect government income). If the counter-cyclical in-vestment programme is selected, the model automatically increases government expenditure by $0.16 billion per percentage point by which the rate of unemploy-ment exceeds 4 per cent, and reduces government expenditure correspondingly when unemployment is less than 4 per cent (we can also vary the expenditure per percentage point). The default value is based on Okun's law for Canada in which 1.6 per cent of GDP is lost per 1 per cent increase in unemployment (Dornbusch, 1999). If the stabilisation option is selected, LOWGROW calculates the differ-ence between aggregate demand and aggregate supply and subtracts it from, or adds it, to total government expenditure in the following year. This strategy is a proxy for all of the possible fiscal and monetary measures that governments employ to maintain a balance between aggregate demand and aggregate supply.[3] We can also select the proportion of these stabilising expenditures spent by government on goods and services or investment. The default assumption is 50 per cent on each of these.

The final policy option is compliance with the Kyoto Protocol. The model estimates the generation of GHG by multiplying GDP by tonnes of GHG per million dollars of GDP based on values for 2002 (Environment Canada, 2004). This emission factor is then multiplied by the coefficient for time in the production function to reflect expected improvements in productivity throughout the economy. If the effective value of this coefficient is reduced to simulate the effects of a lower rate of increase in productivity, it has a similar effect on the expected reduction in GHG per million dollars GDP.

Compliance with the Kyoto Protocol is simulated in the model based upon the Canadian federal government's plan (Government of Canada, 2005).[4] Table 13.1 summarises the costs and total expected average annual GHG emissions reductions in 2008–2012 as interpreted from this report. All costs are assumed to be in 2005 dollars. No conversion to 1997 dollars is made in LOWGROW because the cost estimates in the plan (Government of Canada, 2005) are very approximate and difficult to decipher.

The expenditures in Table 13.1 are assumed to be incremental costs required to fulfil Canada's Kyoto plan (i.e., the costs over and above what would be spent anyway in Canada on activities that will reduce greenhouse gas emissions). LOW-GROW allows us to vary the government's share of these incremental costs from the value of 94 per cent implied in Table 13.1. In LOWGROW, the expenditures by government and business in Table 13.1 are treated not as additions to aggregate demand but as a reallocation from other expenditures. All expenditures by business are assumed to come from investment. Also, these expenditures are assumed not to add to productive assets in the economy. These are conservative assumptions in the sense that they are likely to overstate the negative macroeconomic impacts of these expenditures which, in any case, are projected to be minimal in LOWGROW.

Table 13.1 Summary of Canada's plan to meet its Kyoto commitments, 2008–2012

Sector	Expenditure
Federal government	$10.0 billion
Provincial government (partnership fund contribution)	$1.01 billion
Large emitters	$0.68 billion
Cost per year (all government)	$1.57 billion
Cost per year (business)	$0.10 billion
Reduction in GHG, 2008–2012	270 megatonnes
Cost per tonne reduction	$43

Source: Based on Annex 1 in Government of Canada (2005).

When the base case scenario is run in LOWGROW without the expenditures shown in Table 13.1 and the associated reduction in emissions, LOWGROW projects that Canadian GHG emissions will exceed the Canadian Kyoto target of 560 megatonnes (Mt) per year averaged over 2008 to 2012 by 269 Mt. Even with the expenditures and reductions set out in Table 13.1, LOWGROW projects Canada will miss its Kyoto target by an estimated 86 Mt. For the level of expenditure in Table 13.1 to generate a sufficient level of GHG reduction, the average cost per tonne of GHG reduction would have to be about $29, not the $43 implied by the federal government's plan.

LOWGROW also assumes that the federal government will purchase emission credits at $10 per tonne of GHG in 1997 dollars to cover any excess of Canadian GHG emissions during the first Kyoto compliance period 2008–2012 (Government of Canada, 2005). We can change this price. Any expenditure on GHG emission credits is added to Canadian imports, reducing the net trade balance. In the base case scenario, with the federal government's plan in place, the projected cost of emission credits that Canada will have to purchase to meet its Kyoto target is $853 million (i.e., the average annual emissions 2008–2012 minus Canada's Kyoto target multiplied by $10 per tonne.)

The forestry sub-model in LOWGROW simulates the change in Canadian timber assets over time. Starting in 2000, timber assets are reduced by harvesting (as a function of GDP), natural mortality (the average mortality rate from 1981 to 1997 is assumed), road building (a constant proportion of harvesting), and fire (a random function within the range experienced 1981 to 1997). In the base case, the annual harvest increases as does the amount of regeneration but not sufficiently to prevent a decline in the volume of standing timber.

Managing without growth: exploring no-/low-growth scenarios

LOWGROW can be used to generate a wide variety of low-growth and no-growth scenarios by altering the assumptions that are used in the base case scenario. Starting in 2007, and phased in over 10 years, a no-growth scenario in which net investment, productivity growth, population and labour force growth, and the positive trade balance all decline to zero yields very unpalatable results. Aggregate demand falls far short of aggregate supply and the economy enters a disastrous downward spiral. Even so, Canada's greenhouse gas emissions far exceed its Kyoto target. Clearly, no growth is not a panacea. Specific policy interventions are required to achieve desired objectives.

When the counter-cyclical government expenditure programme is activated as part of the no-growth scenario, GDP rises slightly (5 per cent from 2007 to 2020) because the capital stock is increased (assuming 50 per cent of the expenditures are spent on investment and 50 per cent on goods and services), which raises aggregate supply. Counter-cyclical expenditure also raises aggregate demand. The result is much improved but the unemployment rate is still above 10 per cent by the start of 2020. The HPI, which is related to unemployment, ends up 15 per cent higher than its value in 2000. The debt to GDP ratio declines not quite as much as in the base case scenario, but greenhouse gas emissions rise as there are no productivity gains in this scenario.

Overall, unemployment rises only to 9.1 per cent by 2020 when the stabilisation option for government expenditures is also activated to more effectively ensure a balance between aggregate demand and aggregate supply, the HPI stands 7 per cent above its value in 2000, and greenhouse gas emissions continue to exceed the Kyoto target. Something else is required to meet the employment, poverty alleviation, and environmental objectives.

The results of one illustrative low-growth then no-growth scenario is shown in Figure 13.3, in which the objectives of low unemployment, a declining debt-to-GDP ratio, the elimination of poverty, and compliance with Canada's Kyoto target for greenhouse gas emissions are achieved.

In this scenario, net investment, growth in population and the labour force, growth in productivity, and the net trade balance decline to zero over a 10-year phase-in period starting in 2007. The average working week also declines by 3 per cent.

The government adopts the stabilisation budget option, redistributes income so that by the end of the phase-in period no Canadian is living below the LICO poverty line, and implements the Kyoto plan set out in Table 13.1. Also, the government increases expenditures on Active Labour Management Policies by $2 billion per year and raises the average rate of personal taxes and transfers from 23 per cent to 33 per cent and the average rate of corporations profits tax from 27 per cent to 30 per cent, phased in over 10 years from 2007. Figure 13.3 shows the time path of GDP, unemployment, ratio of debt to GDP, poverty, and GHG emissions in this no-growth scenario.

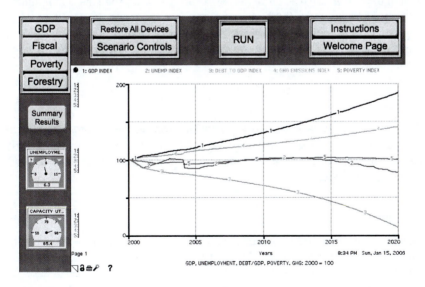

Figure 13.3 A no-growth scenario for Canada.

By 2012, GDP is about 36 per cent above its level in 2000 and remains stable through to 2020. GDP rises for a while because the no-growth measures are '] phased in. The debt-to-GDP ratio declines steadily to 11 per cent of its level in 2000 by 2020. The rate of unemployment declines to 5.5 per cent by 2020. The number of Canadians living below the Low Income Cutoff declines to zero while the Human Poverty Index stabilises at 86 per cent of the level in 2000. This is as low as the HPI can go with a decline in the number of poor people without changes in the other variables that enter the index, which are unchanged in this scenario. Greenhouse gas emissions decline and meet Canada's Kyoto target in the 2008–2012 compliance period (i.e., average annual GHG emissions of 560 Mt) but only on the assumption that these reductions can be achieved at an average cost of $30/tonne and not at $43/tonne as assumed in the federal government's plan (see Table 13.1 above).

A 20-year horizon is too short for a no-growth or low-growth scenario to have much impact on Canadian forests, in which the typical rotation is between 70 and 100 years depending on the species. Consequently, in this scenario Canada's timber assets continue to decline as losses from harvesting (now lower than in the base case scenario), road building, fire, and natural mortality continue to exceed regeneration.

Managing without growth: some policy implications

The previous section presented some results from LOWGROW suggesting that much can be accomplished without reliance on growth in a country, such as Canada, that has already achieved a very high material standard of living. Poverty can be eliminated, unemployment can be reduced to historically low levels, the government debt to GDP ratio can be reduced and international environmental commitments can be fulfilled with a zero rate of growth. However, to do so requires some significant departures from the policy status quo, the details and implications of which remain to be fully explored (see Victor, 2008). In brief, these departures include:

Poverty

Reliance on the gains from growth to trickle down to the poorest members of society should be replaced with programmes that redistribute income directly and provide support for the most important items of consumptions, such as food, clothing, and shelter.

Consumption

The disconnect between consumption and well-being has been documented in the literature (see Galbraith, 1958; Mishan, 1967; Leiss, 1976; Scitovsky, 1976; Hirsch, 1976; Daly, 1996; Douthwaite, 1999; Layard, 2005). It provides a basis for suggesting that welfare can be enhanced by redirecting consumption from private, positional goods, which confer lower benefits the greater is the number of people who have them, to public goods, including a less contaminated environment and fewer threatened species, which are of value to many simultaneously.

Investment

The construction of infrastructure and buildings, and the installation of new equipment, has long been recognised as an important engine of economic growth. Such investment should continue at least at a level required to replace physical capital that wears out. Replacement of worn-out capital provides opportunities for continual improvements in efficiency. However, to mirror the changes in consumption patterns just described, the mix of investment should change so that the production of public goods is enhanced and the production of positional goods is stabilised or reduced.

Productivity

Increases in the productivity of capital and labour can be realised as increases in production, increases in unemployment, or increases in leisure, or a combination of all three. There is much to be said for a greater proportion of any future gains in productivity being taken as an increase in leisure than in the past. It lowers the rate of unemployment, which alleviates poverty, and it places less stress on the environment and scarce natural resources.

Exports

Export-led growth has become the mercantilism of the twentieth and twenty-first centuries. Globally, net exports must be zero. Countries that can benefit the most from increasing exports – that is, those that have seen little of the gains from economic growth – should be permitted to pursue this goal more freely. Hence, countries such as Canada should moderate their efforts to export more than they import.

Population growth

Canada is one of many developed countries where the fertility rate has fallen below 2.1, the rate required to at least maintain a constant population. Without immigration in the range of 200,000–300,000 per year, the Canadian population would cease to grow. Moreover, there would be an increasing proportion of elderly people in the population, who would have to rely on a proportionately smaller labour force to support them after retirement (thereby reducing the rate of unemployment). The conventional response to this state of affairs is to encourage immigration, but not just any immigration. Usually countries, such as Canada, try to attract the most educated and wealthiest people from other countries. When these people come from developing countries, as has become more common (Centre for Canadian Studies at Mount Allison University, n.d.), it may help Canada but it weakens the capacity of the countries from which the immigrants come. A more satisfactory approach would be to come to terms with a stable population and address the income distribution implications of an aging population through pensions and other income support programmes. The low-growth scenario described earlier in this chapter suggests that this is a very real option.

Environment

Throughout this chapter, economic growth has been used synonymously with growth in GDP. However, GDP is a measure of value that is related to, but not identical with, growth in the physical inputs and outputs of the economy. Indeed, there are some encouraging signs that the value of economic output and the material and energy required to produce it have become somewhat decoupled. The picture is less clear when international trade is factored in since developed countries import material intensive products that they previously manufactured themselves. Yet it is these parameters – the physical inputs and outputs of the economy, and the impact by humans on the habitats required by other species – that put pressure on the environment and on scarce natural resources. Very gradually, these problems are being addressed by the explicit introduction of quantitative limits on inputs, outputs, and land use. The Montreal Protocol limiting the production and release of ozone-depleting substances and the Kyoto Protocol limiting the release of greenhouse gases are two examples of quantitative limits designed to protect the environment from the impacts of the economy. Other such limits in the Canadian context include fishing bans and quotas to protect what is left of the east coast fisheries, the provisions of the Canada–US Agreement on the Great Lakes requiring the virtual elimination of toxic substances, the prohibition of bulk water exports from the Great Lakes, the establishment of a green belt around the Greater Toronto Area to contain urban sprawl, and the establishment of a comprehensive system of national and provincial parks.

These types of quantitative, physical limits on throughput and land use offer the best way forward for ensuring that economies do not compromise the environment in which they are embedded and on which they depend.

Conclusion

This chapter began by noting three arguments why the possibility of developed countries, such as Canada, should entertain the possibility of managing without growth: (1) global economic growth is not an option because of environmental and resource constraints, so developed countries should leave room for those that benefit the most from growth; (2) in developed countries, growth is neither a necessary nor a sufficient condition for achieving such objectives as full employment, the elimination of poverty, and environmental protection; and (3) beyond a point that has been passed in developed countries, growth does not increase happiness.

The chapter then described LOWGROW, a simulation model designed to explore a wide range of low-growth scenarios in Canada. Results from LOWGROW comparing a base case scenario with a low/no-growth scenario were presented that suggest that much can be accomplished in developed countries without relying on economic growth. Many other low-growth or no-growth scenarios can be explored with LOWGROW (see www.managingwithoutgrowth.com). Finally, the chapter set out of the policy directions that would have to be adopted to steer the Canadian economy towards lower growth while, at the same time, achieving desirable employment, anti-poverty, and environmental objectives.

Appendix: LOWGROW – technical description

LOWGROW is an interactive dynamic model of the Canadian economy developed in STELLA, a systems dynamics modelling language. LOWGROW simulates the response of the Canadian economy to a wide range of policy interventions up to 2020. This description of LOWGROW is divided into two sections. The first section describes the macroeconomic model in LOWGROW. The second section describes the other components of LOWGROW: employment, fiscal, redistribution, Human Poverty Index, Kyoto, forestry.

The macroeconomic model

The macroeconomic model consists of a set of linear equations that determine GDP as aggregate demand and a Cobb–Douglas production function that determines GDP as aggregate supply. The model calculates GDP from the production function using initial values for produced assets, capacity utilisation rate, labour force, rate of unemployment, and time (which is a proxy for technical change). The value of GDP so derived is an independent variable in the demand equations, which is then used to compute aggregate demand. If aggregate demand exceeds aggregate supply, the rates of unemployment and capacity utilisation decrease in the next time period (i.e., a tenth of a year). If aggregate supply exceeds aggregate demand, the rates of unemployment and capacity utilisation increase in the next time period. All monetary values are in constant 1997 dollars.

The following equations were estimated using data for 1981–2003 from Statistics Canada. The estimation method was either ordinary least squares (OLS) or two-stage least squares (2SLS). The t-statistics for the coefficients are shown beneath in parentheses and the R-squared value is shown as well.

Consumption (2SLS)

$$c/p = 0.56731*g/p + 0.0038375*d/g - 0.0000516*i - 0.0014986*x \quad (13.1)$$

$$(73.8) \qquad\qquad (7.3) \qquad\qquad (-4.2) \qquad\qquad (-5.2)$$

R-squared = 0.995

where:

- c = consumption expenditure in millions of 1997 dollars;
- p = population in millions;
- g = GDP in millions of 1997 dollars;
- d = disposable income in millions of 1997 dollars;
- i = interest rate, prime three-month corporate paper;
- x = exchange rate, \$Canadian per \$US.

This equation was estimated with the added restriction that the estimated value of c/p for 2003 be at its actual value when the independent variables in the equation are at their 2003 values. The purpose of this constraint was to ensure that the simulation of future values in LOWGROW would start from their actual values in 2003. This approach did not work perfectly because the model simulations start from 2000 and, despite the incorporation of many actual values for variables between 2000 and 2003, not all variables in the model are predicted to be exactly at their 2003 values.

Equation (13.1) states that consumption per capita is a positive function of GDP per capita and disposable income per capita, and a negative function of the interest rate and the Canada/US exchange rate. Division of consumption by population in equation (13.1) is intended to eliminate common trend attributable to population.

Private investment (2SLS)

$$I = 72576 - 2552.5*li + 0.15881*lg - 0.12952*lc \tag{13.2}$$

(3.2)   (–3.5)   (10.0)   (–2.7)

R-squared = 0.926

where:

- I = business gross investment in structures, machinery, equipment, and net investment in inventories in millions of 1997 dollars;
- li = interest rate, lagged one year;
- lg = GDP lagged one year;
- lc = average rate of corporation profits tax, lagged one year.

Investment decisions are generally made on assumptions and expectations about the future. These assumptions and expectations are inevitably influenced by past experience, which is captured to some extent by the inclusion of lagged variables in the investment equation.

Imports (2SLS)

$$M = -804800 + 11099000*g/p + 26000*p \qquad (13.3)$$

$$(-14.3) \qquad (4.5) \qquad\qquad (6.0)$$

R-squared = 0.975

where:

- M = imports of goods and services in millions of 1997 dollars.

Equation (13.3) states that imports of goods and services are a function of per capita GDP and population. Imports seemed to be positively related to the Canada/US exchange rate, contrary to theory and assumed elasticities. Using 2SLS and imports per capita to eliminate common trends did not help and so the exchange rate was excluded from the equation.

Exports (OLS)

$$X = -417620 + 58.809*usgdp + 17880*x \qquad (13.4)$$

$$(-12.0) \qquad (42.8) \qquad\qquad (5.7)$$

R-squared = 0.986

where:

- X = exports of goods and services in millions of 1997 dollars;
- $usgdp$ = US GDP in millions of US$2000.

The predominance of the United States as a market for Canadian exports has risen steadily over the past 25 years, so that the US now accounts for over 80 per cent of Canada's exports. (Hessing *et al.*, 2005: table 2.4). This focus is captured in equation (13.4) in which Canadian exports are estimated as a positive function of US GDP and the Canada/US exchange rate.

Government expenditure

Government expenditure here consists of expenditure of goods and services and government investment in fixed capital and inventories. In LOWGROW, the expenditure and income of the federal, provincial, and municipal levels of government are combined. LOWGROW allows several user-controlled options for government expenditures:

1   Constant share – the default assumptions used in the base case scenario are that government expenditure on goods and services is maintained at the same share of GDP as in 2003 (i.e., 0.1883) and that government investment is maintained at the same proportion of private business investment as in 2003 (i.e., 0.15).

2   Balanced budget – if this option is selected, LOWGROW sets total government expenditure on investment and goods and services equal to total government income.

3   Counter-cyclical – if this option is selected, government investment is increased by 0.016 of GDP for each percentage point that the unemployment rate exceeds 4 per cent, based on Okun's Law for Canada (Dornbusch 1999: 43). It is reduced by the same amount for each percentage point that unemployment falls below 4 per cent. The amount of incremental investment expenditure can be varied by the user.

4   Stabilisation – under this option, the difference between aggregate demand and aggregate supply is calculated (under the constant share assumption or the counter-cyclical assumption) and the difference is subtracted from or added to government expenditure in the following year (50 per cent as government expenditure on goods and services and 50 per cent on government investment unless changed by the user). This pattern of government expenditure is a proxy for all of the possible fiscal and monetary measures that governments employ to maintain a balance between aggregate demand and aggregate supply and minimise fluctuations in the economy.

The equations for consumption, private investment, exports, and imports described above, combined with any one of the options for government expenditures, estimate aggregate demand in LOWGROW.

Production function (2SLS)

LOWGROW employs a conventional Cobb–Douglas production function. Output (GDP) is a positive function of capital employed, labour employed, and time.

$$\ln(g) = 1.2797 + 0.0099*T + 0.28281*\ln(cut) + 0.71812*\ln(emp) \qquad (13.5)$$

$$(1.1) \qquad (4.1) \qquad (1.7) \qquad (2.0)$$

R-squared = 0.996

where:

- $\ln(g)$ = natural log of GDP;
- T = time in years;
- $\ln(cut)$ = natural log of produced assets in millions of 1997 dollars plus the natural log of the capacity utilisation rate;
- $\ln(emp)$ = natural log of employment in thousands.

In its non-log form, the production function is:

$$g = 3.5956 * 1.00993^{t} * (K*CU)^{.2821} * LE^{.71821}$$ (13.6)

where:

- t = time in years;
- K = produced assets in millions of 1997 dollars;
- CU = the capacity utilisation rate of manufacturing assets as a percentage;
- LE = employed labour in thousands.

The exponents for capital and labour add up to unity, signifying constant returns to scale. This was not a constraint imposed in the estimation procedure. It is possible that some returns to scale have been captured in the coefficient that is raised to the power t. For the purposes of this study, this coefficient is interpreted as the effects of technical change over time (capturing all improvements in efficiency in capital and labour) and is estimated to raise GDP by almost 1 per cent per year.

LOWGROW allows the user to reduce the length of the average working week by up to 3 per cent so that a given amount of labour input corresponds to a lower rate of unemployment.

The capital stock in each time period increases as a result of business and government investment expenditures, net of depreciation, and demolition in the previous time period (set at 4 per cent of the stock of produced assets, the average rate from 1981 to 2003). Similarly, the labour force changes from one period to the next as shown in equation (13.7).

Labour force (OLS)

$$L = 1592.61 + 342.5*p + 0.00388*g$$ (13.7)

$$(1.6)   (5.7)   (4.2)$$

R-squared = 0.987

where:

- L = labour force in thousands.

Equation (13.8) models the labour force as a positive function of the population and of GDP. Population in LOWGROW is based on a projection by Statistics Canada for each year from 2000 to 2026 (Statistics Canada, 2001: Cansim Table 052-0001).

Capacity utilisation (OLS)

$$CU = 93.7 - 1.32*ur \qquad (13.8)$$

(32.7)   (-4.3)

R-squared = 0.46

where:

- ur = the rate of unemployment as a percentage.

In equation (13.7), the rate of capacity utilisation is a negative function of the rate of unemployment signifying that, when unemployment rises, the rate of capacity utilisation declines. This equation has a much lower R-squared than the other equations in the macroeconomic model. It is included in the model to recognise that both the employment of labour and the employment of capital can change in the economy in response to changes in aggregate demand.

Employment

Equation (13.7) above shows how the labour force is modelled in LOWGROW, as a function of population and GDP. The labour force is divided between employed and unemployed labour. Workers move between employment and unemployment depending on the rates of job finding and job separation. In LOWGROW, these rates are a function of the excess demand ratio; that is, the ratio of aggregate demand to aggregate supply. The rate of job finding is divided by the excess demand ratio and the rate of job separation is multiplied by the excess demand ratio. When this ratio is unity, the rates of job finding and job separation are unchanged (i.e., the economy is in a state of macro equilibrium) and the rates of unemployment and capacity utilisation are constant. When the excess demand ratio is above unity (i.e., when aggregate demand exceeds aggregate supply), the rate of job finding rises and the rate of job separation falls so that the unemployment and capacity utilisation rates decline. When the excess demand ratio is less than unity the opposite happens. New entrants to the labour force and those who exit are assumed to experience the same rate of unemployment as the rest of the labour force.

The number of employed persons is an independent variable in the production function so, when unemployment changes, aggregate supply changes in the opposite direction bringing the excess demand ratio back towards unity. Since GDP as aggregate supply is an independent variable in some of the aggregate demand equations, aggregate demand also increases if the rate of unemployment declines and declines if the rate of unemployment rises.

LOWGROW allows for employment to be affected by Active Labour Management Policies (ALMP). Expenditures by government on these policies reduce the time on average that a person is unemployed; this reduction is related directly to the rate of job finding. In 2002 and 2003, Canada spent US$3135.30 on ALMP per unemployed person (Brandt *et al.*, 2005: table A2.7). This is below average for OECD countries as a percentage of GDP per member of the labour force (Boone and van Ours, 2004: table 2). There is an extensive literature on the effectiveness of expenditures on ALMP for reducing the rate of unemployment. Analysing data for 20 OECD countries, Boone and van Ours estimate that an increase in expenditures on labour market training from 0.20 to 0.25 per cent of GDP reduces the rate of unemployment from 8 per cent to 7.7 per cent in the short run and 7.6 per cent in the long run (*ibid.*: 15.) This effect is captured in LOWGROW through an assumed graphical relationship between additional ALMP expenditures and the average time of unemployment that gives similar results.

Fiscal policies

LOWGROW keeps track of the consolidated accounts of the three levels of government. Government expenditures on goods, services, and investment were described above. In addition to these, LOWGROW calculates the interest paid by government on accumulated debt (using the prime interest rate), and transfers paid by the government to business and households. Transfers to business are kept at the level they were in 2004. Transfers to households are calculated using equation (13.9) which was estimated using OLS.

$$TH = -165472 + 21.53*UL + 0.008*p \qquad (13.9)$$

$$(-15.6) \quad (3.9) \qquad (23.9)$$

R-squared = 0.97

where:

* TH = transfers to households in millions of 1997 dollars;
* UL = number of unemployed in thousands.

One of the options available in LOWGROW is to increase transfer payments to people living below the poverty line (defined as the Low Income Cut-Off or LICO; Statistics Canada, 2003). LOWGROW calculates the required amount based on the number of families and individuals living in poverty and the average amount in constant 1997 dollars required to bring individuals and families up to the poverty line (*ibid.*: table 8-3-3.) The number of people living in poverty is calculated using the number for 2004 plus or minus any increase or decrease in the number of unemployed (based on the assumption that unemployment reduces incomes to a level below the poverty line.)

Total outlay by government is the sum of government expenditures on goods and services, government investment, interest paid on government debt, transfers to business, and transfers to households.

LOWGROW calculates government income as the sum of government investment income (held constant at the 2004 level), taxes on production and imports (the 2004 proportion of GDP), corporation profits tax (the 2003 proportion of GDP but can be changed), taxes and transfers from persons (the 2003 proportion of GDP but can be changed) and income taxes paid by non-residents (the 2003 proportion of GDP).

LOWGROW also calculates the combined net debt of the three levels of government. Starting from an initial value for 2003 the model calculates the change in net debt using equation (10) estimated with OLS.

$$CND = 11729.15 - 1.1253 *NI \qquad (13.10)$$

$$(2.7) \qquad (-9.0)$$

R-squared = 0.81

where:

- CND = change in net government debt (all three levels of government combined) in millions of 1997 dollars;
- NI = government net income defined as government income minus government outlay in millions of 1997 dollars.

Equation (13.10) suggests that government net debt rises on average by $11.7 billion when government outlay and income (as defined in Department of Finance Canada, 2004, and incorporated into LOWGROW) are equal, and that this amount is reduced on average by $1.125 for each dollar that government net income is positive. This estimation result implies that, under the accounting conventions used by our data source, some government income and outlays result in changes in government assets and liabilities that are not counted as net debt.

Human Poverty Index (HPI)

HPI-2 developed by the UNDP for developed countries (United Nations Development Programme, 2005) is defined by equation (13.11):

$$HPI = (0.25*DK^3 + 0.25*DL^3 + 0.25*DSL^3 + 0.25*EX^3)^{1/3} \qquad (13.11)$$

where:

- DK = deprivation of knowledge (measured as people lacking functional literacy skills, which are defined by the OECD as whether a person is able to understand and employ printed information in daily life, at home, at work, and in the community);

- *DL* = percentage of population not expected to survive to age 60;
- *DSL* = percentage of poor people in the population;
- *EX* = rate of long-term unemployment (greater than 12 months).

LOWGROW calculates the HPI for Canada. *DK* and *DL* are maintained at the values in the Human Development Report (UNDP, 2005). *DL* is calculated in LOWGROW using the number of people living below the poverty line. This is a different measure from that used by the UNDP (number of people living below half the median income) but, as Giles (2004) shows, the two measures in 2000 were very similar (10.9 per cent and 11.1 per cent respectively), so it may be assumed that any difference between the two measures of poverty in Canada is quite small.

In LOWGROW the rate of long-term unemployment is calculated as a constant share of the number of unemployed. The initial value used in LOWGROW is 11.84 per cent for 1999, calculated by dividing 0.9 per cent of the labour force in long-term unemployment (the value given in UNDP, 2005) by 7.6 per cent, the unemployment rate for Canada in 1999.

Greenhouse gases and Kyoto compliance

Canadian emissions of greenhouse gases (GHGs) are simulated in LOWGROW by multiplying GDP by a GHG emission coefficient expressed as tonnes of GHG per dollar of GDP (in 1997 dollars). This coefficient was calculated using data for 2002, the most recent year for which data were available (Environment Canada, 2004.)

To allow for productivity improvements as new capital equipment replaces old, and as the energy/GDP ratio declines, even without specific GHG reduction programmes, the GHG emission coefficient is reduced by an amount each year equal to the rate of productivity growth in the production function (i.e., about 1 per cent per year). If the rate of productivity growth in the economy in general is reduced, then the same lower rate of productivity growth is applied to the GHG emissions coefficient.

In the Kyoto compliance option, the total cost of Canada's Kyoto Plan and, the share of this cost incurred by the government, are specified. Default values for these variables are based on Government of Canada (2005). The average cost per tonne reduction in GHG emissions and the cost of any GHG allowances purchased by the Government of Canada to meet Canada's Kyoto target can also be specified. Default values for these variables are also provided in LOWGROW based, respectively, on information in Government of Canada (2005), including a provisional cost of $10/tonne for GHG allowances.

In LOWGROW, all expenditures by the government and business for compliance with Kyoto are assumed to be diverted from other expenditures that would otherwise have taken place. For business, the diversion is from investment, and for the government the proportions that come from investment and goods and services are variable. Hence, it is assumed that expenditures on Kyoto do not add to aggregate demand. This is a conservative assumption in the sense that it will understate the positive impact of such expenditures on GDP and employment. Furthermore, aggregate demand is reduced if the government buys GHG allowances from abroad to meet Canada's Kyoto target.

To the extent that investment expenditures decline because of the diversion of expenditure to assumed 'unproductive' measures to reduce GHG emissions, the capital stock is less than it would otherwise be in the absence of the Kyoto commitment. Again, this is a conservative assumption in that some capital expenditures to reduce GHG emissions might also add to the value of economic output. Overall, the assumptions made in this sub-model are likely to overstate the negative macroeconomic impacts and understate the positive macroeconomic impacts of expenditures required to fulfil Canada's Kyoto commitment.

LOWGROW takes all of this information, calculates average annual GHG emissions for 2008 to 2012, the first Kyoto compliance period, and calculates the cost of purchasing allowances to cover any excess emissions. LOWGROW assumes that the government buys allowances for only one year to cover any excess over the annual average from 2008 to 2012. Requirements for the 2012 period have yet to be negotiated among the signatory countries to the Kyoto Protocol.

Forestry

LOWGROW tracks changes to the stock of Canada's timber assets starting from an initial value for 2000. All data for estimating the forestry model come from Statistics Canada (2001). Deductions from the stock come from harvesting, natural mortality, fire, and road building. Additions to the stock come from regeneration.

The equations in the forestry sub-model are:

Harvest (OLS)

$$H = 76680 + 0.12505*g \qquad (13.12)$$

$$(2.9) \qquad (3.5)$$

R-squared = 0.44

where:

* H = annual harvest in thousand cubic metres;
* g = GDP.

Mortality

$$Mf = m*\mathrm{T} \qquad (13.13)$$

where:

- Mf = annual mortality in thousand cubic metres;
- m = the average annual mortality rate from 1981 to 1997 in cubic metres per cubic metre of timber assets (0.0030861);
- Tf = timber assets in thousand cubic metres.

Roads

$$R = r*H \qquad\qquad (13.14)$$

where:

- R = annual losses in timber assets due to road building;
- r = average annual loss from 1981 to 1997 in cubic metres per cubic metre of harvest (0.03).

Fire

LOWGROW simulates losses due to fire by using a random number to generate annual losses in the same range and with similar frequencies to those experienced from 1981 to 1997.

Notes

1 This chapter is based on Victor and Rosenbluth (2007). It includes some editorial changes and some minor corrections to the technical appendix. The results of the simulations have not been changed. A more complete account of managing without growth, based on an updated version of the simulation model, is provided in Victor (2008).
2 The Cobb–Douglas production function is a highly simplified representation of a complex and complicated national production system. Cobb–Douglas production functions have been criticised by ecological economists such as Georgescu-Roegen (1971) and Daly (1997) for inconsistency with the laws of thermodynamics. However, their main concern is with the use of a Cobb–Douglas production function for describing substitution possibilities among inputs over the long term. This important issue is outside the scope of this chapter, although it is addressed in Victor (1991).
3 This fiscal option arises because LOWGROW calculates aggregate demand and aggregate supply separately and relies on changes in the rates of unemployment and capacity utilisation to bring them into balance. These adjustment processes do not always completely eliminate differences between aggregate demand and supply. When the stabilisation option is activated, government expenditure is adjusted to make them equal. An alternative approach would have been to estimate aggregate demand from the equations for consumption, investment, and trade, to specify a level for government expenditure based on a particular fiscal policy, and then use the production function to estimate the associated levels of employment and capacity utilisation. This approach, which has been incorporated in subsequent versions of LOWGROW, ensures that aggregate demand and aggregate supply are always equal and eliminates the stabilisation option for government expenditure (Victor, 2008).

4 This was the plan of the Liberal government, which was defeated in the Canadian General Election in January 2006. The Conservative government, which won the election, abandoned the plan and has not developed an alternative one for meeting Canada's Kyoto commitment.

References

Boone, J. and van Ours, J. C. (2004), 'Effective labor market policies', http://www.cepr.org/pubs/dps/DP4707.asp.

Brandt, N., Buriniaux, J.-M., and Duval, R. (2005), *Assessing the OECD Jobs Strategy: Past Developments and Reforms*, Working Paper, volume 429, Economics Department, OECD.

Centre for Canadian Studies at Mount Allison University (n.d.), 'About Canada, multiculturalism in Canada', http://www.mta.ca/faculty/arts/Canadian_studies/English/about/multi#era.

Common, M. and Stagl, S. (2005), *Ecological Economics: An Introduction*, Cambridge: Cambridge University Press.

Daly, H. E. (1996), *Beyond Growth: The Economics of Sustainable Development*, Boston, MA: Beacon Press.

Daly, H. E. (1997), 'Georgescu-Roegen versus Solow/Stiglitz', *Ecological Economics*, 22 (3), 261–266.

Department of Finance Canada (2004) *Annual Financial Report of The Government of Canada, Fiscal Year 2003–2004*, Ottawa: Government of Canada.

Dornbusch, R. (1999), *Macroeconomics*, 5th Canadian edn, Toronto: McGraw-Hill.

Douthwaite, R. (1999), *The Growth Illusion: How Economic Growth has Enriched the Few, Impoverished the Many and Endangered the Planet*, Gabriola Island: New Society Publishers.

Environment Canada (2004), *Canada's Greenhouse Gas Inventory 1990–2002*, Ottawa: Greenhouse Gas Division.

Galbraith, J. K. (1958), *The Affluent Society*, Boston: Houghton Mifflin.

Georgescu-Roegen, N. (1971), *The Entropy Law and the Economic Process*, Cambridge, MA: Harvard University Press.

Giles P. (2004), *Low Income Measurement in Canada*, Statistics Canada Research Paper, Cat. no. 75F0002MIE-No. 011.

Government of Canada (2005), *Moving Forward on Climate Change: A Plan for Honouring our Kyoto Commitment*, Ottawa: Government of Canada.

Hessing, M., Howlett, M., and Summeville, T. (2005), *Canadian Natural Resource and Environmental Policy: Political Economy and Public Policy*, 2nd edition, Vancouver: UBC Press.

Hirsch, F. (1976), *Social Limits to Growth*, Cambridge, MA: Harvard University Press.

Layard, R. (2005), *Happiness: Lessons from a New Science*, London: Allen Lane, Penguin Books.

Leiss, W. (1976), *The Limits to Satisfaction: An Essay on the Problem of Needs and Commodities*, Toronto: University of Toronto Press.

Mishan, E. J. (1967), *The Costs of Economic Growth*, New York: F. A. Praeger.

Scitovsky, T. (1976), *The Joyless Economy: An Inquiry into Human Satisfaction and Consumer Dissatisfaction*, New York: Oxford University Press.

Statistics Canada (2001), *Econnections: Linking the Environment and Economy-Indicator and Detailed Statistics*, Report No. 16-200-XKE, Ottawa, Canada.

Statistics Canada (2003), *Incomes in Canada 2003*, Ottawa: Government of Canada.

Statistics Canada (2004), *Public Sector Accounts: Supplement*, Ottawa: Government of Canada.

United Nations Development Programme (UNDP) (2005), *Human Development Report 2005*, New York: UN.

Victor, P. A. (1991), 'Indicators of sustainable development: some lessons from capital theory', *Ecological Economics*, 4, 191–213.

Victor, P. A. (2008), *Slower by Design, Not by Disaster: Managing without Growth in Rich Countries*, Northampton, MA: Edward Elgar.

Victor, P. A. and Rosenbluth, G. (2007), 'Managing without growth', *Ecological Economics*, 61, 492–504.

Part VI
Conclusion

14 Final thoughts on reconciling the goals of ecological sustainability and full employment

Philip Lawn

Introduction

My task in this chapter is to draw upon and synthesise the views expressed so far to emerge with what I believe is a plausible means of reconciling the goals of ecological sustainability and full employment. What I ultimately emerge with will reflect my own thoughts on the matter and, as such, will occasionally diverge from the positions taken in some of the previous chapters. In order to achieve my task, I will focus most of my attention on Part III of the book. To recall, Part III centred on a debate concerning the most appropriate ways of ameliorating the social problems of poverty and unemployment. By taking account of what is required to achieve ecological sustainability, I plan to assess how well the various macroeconomic policy approaches put forward in Part III are likely to resolve the two policy goals of full employment and ecological sustainability.

Before doing this, it is worth summarising some of the general conclusions made throughout the book. In Chapter 1, it was argued that human development requires a balanced system of need satisfaction. Predicated on Maslow's needs hierarchy, it was stressed that, once an individual's lower-order needs have been satisfied, a healthy existential balance demands the fulfilment of emerging higher-order needs – the latter of which are largely psychological in nature. With this in mind, it was claimed that, in order to provide each citizen with the opportunities to fulfil their individual development potential, a society must uphold various universal rights and privileges. The most important of these was the right to an income beyond the absolute poverty level. The second was the right to paid employment given that unemployment often deprives individuals of their ability to satisfy safety and esteem needs and almost always starves those seeking paid employment of the ability to satisfy their self-actualisation needs. For this reason, it was argued that full employment must be viewed as a moral imperative and an obligatory macroeconomic objective for any nation serious about achieving a comprehensive form of sustainable development.

In Chapter 2, it was shown that there are an economic and an ecological limit to growth and that many countries – predominantly the rich – have surpassed them both. Because of the strong connection between employment levels and real

GDP growth, it was subsequently argued that: (a) the ability of nations to operate sustainably and achieve full employment is severely restricted; and (b) a conflict currently exists between environmental and employment goals as reflected by the fact that the wealthy countries impacting least on the ecosphere have a tendency to possess the highest unemployment rates. The general conclusion from Chapter 2 was that novel theoretical and policy approaches will be needed to achieve ecological sustainability as well as to enhance employment outcomes via improvements in labour market operations and a severing of the GDP–employment link.

Unfortunately, although Post-Keynesian economists have made valuable and innovative contributions towards the unemployment problem, they have tended to overlook environmental concerns in much the same way that ecological economists, in their quest to deal with the issue of ecological sustainability, have largely ignored employment considerations. Having said this, Part II revealed that there is enormous potential for Post-Keynesian economists to incorporate the holistic elements of ecological economics to develop the models and approaches required to better deal with the environment–employment dilemma. I also believe that a cross-fertilisation of ideas would be of great benefit to ecological economists given that, from my own experiences, many of them appear to lack an adequate understanding of macroeconomic fundamentals.

From a policy perspective, it was clear, from Part III, that there is considerable disagreement amongst Post-Keynesian economists and sympathisers about what can be done to alleviate acute levels of poverty through either universal income guarantees or employment guarantees. Exactly what might be implemented to achieve ecological sustainability and full employment I shall elaborate on soon. However, one irrefutable fact emerged from Part III that cannot be ignored – the solutions offered must be consistent with macroeconomic realities as well as ecological and biophysical principles. Indeed, they must also be consistent with the axiom recently highlighted by ecological economists that allocative efficiency is an insufficient condition to ensure ecological sustainability. This was no better exemplified than by the results revealed in Part IV – particularly Chapter 10 – which showed that, unless quantitative constraints are imposed on the rate at which resources pass through an economic system, efficiency gains will eventually be overwhelmed by the growing scale of economic activity (the so-called 'Jevons effect'). As a consequence, environmental stress levels will inevitably increase. Although not discussed in Chapter 12, I would argue that Hinterberger *et al.*'s claim that real output growth in Germany and Austria will soon outstrip the growth rate of resource productivity and cause material inputs in both countries to rise is also evidence of a Jevons effect that will inevitably transpire should policy-makers fail to impose the necessary constraints on the rate of resource throughput.

As explained in Chapter 2, there is no doubt that resource throughput restrictions, if introduced, would slow down the growth rate of real GDP and eventually bring forth a steady-state economy. However, in what must be considered a major breakthrough, Victor and Rosenbluth (Chapter 13) showed that the policy goals of full employment, poverty alleviation, and ecological sustainability are entirely feasible in a steady-state milieu. Without going into specific policy details, Victor and Rosenbluth also outlined the policy directions that need to be taken to steer an economy towards a lower rate of growth yet still achieve desirable employment, anti-poverty, and environmental objectives.

There were, however, a number of detailed policy initiatives outlined in Part III and Chapter 10 to potentially overcome the environment–employment dilemma. As I mentioned at the beginning of this introduction, it is to these policy initiatives that I will devote most of the remaining chapter. My assessment of them will begin with a reiteration of what is required to achieve full employment and ecological sustainability. Following this, I will assess the relative merits of the following four policy approaches: (1) the NAIRU or 'non-accelerating inflation rate of unemployment' approach to macroeconomic policy setting, which is essentially the dominant mainstream strategy; (2) the Basic Income approach (a guaranteed income for all); (3) the Job Guarantee approach (an employer of last resort programme); and (4) ecological tax reform.

What is necessary to achieve ecological sustainability and full employment?

Ecological sustainability

I need not go to any great lengths to explain what is required to achieve ecological sustainability. This was thoroughly discussed in Chapter 2 and led to the exposition of the following sustainability precepts:

- Sustainability precept no. 1: The rate of renewable resource extraction should not exceed the regeneration rate of renewable resource stocks.
- Sustainability precept no. 2: The depletion of non-renewable resources must be offset by using a portion of the depletion profits to cultivate renewable resource replacements.
- Sustainability precept no. 3: Where a substitute for a non-renewable resource does not exist, the availability of the resource should be spread across as many generations as possible. Any long-run reliance on the resource prior to its eventual depletion must be overcome.
- Sustainability precept no. 4: The quantity of waste generated by the economic process must not exceed the ecosphere's waste assimilative capacity.
- Sustainability precept no. 5: The generation of particular forms of hazardous waste should be limited and, in cases where they pose a major long-term threat to a healthy ecosphere, should be prohibited altogether.
- Sustainability precept no. 6: Native vegetation and critical ecosystems must be preserved, rehabilitated, and/or restored. In addition, the future exploitation of natural capital must be confined to areas already strongly modified by previous human activities.

Knowing what is necessary to achieve ecological sustainability is one thing. Introducing the policies needed to operate sustainably is something else entirely. One of the policy institutions briefly alluded to in Chapter 10 was a system of tradeable resource use permits – in effect, a 'cap-and-trade' system for each renewable resource type. The need for such a system arises because ecological economists have shown that a market-generated allocation of the incoming resource flow cannot ensure that the incoming resource flow is ecological sustainable. The explanation for this was given in Chapter 10 as was a brief account of how a cap-and-trade system can overcome the deficiency of market-generated outcomes without impeding the efficiency-facilitating role of market prices.

Cap-and-trade systems

Because the aim of this chapter is to outline ways to achieve both ecological sustainability and full employment, I shall now describe the features of a feasible cap-and-trade system in more detail.[1] This will assist in my later assessment of the sustainability merits of the macroeconomic policy approach being adopted in most countries and the three alternative approaches proposed in this book.

The first key aspect of a cap-and-trade system is the initial estimation of the maximum sustainable yield of all renewable resources.[2] This having been achieved, a purpose-designed government authority would auction off a limited number of resource use permits to the highest bidding resource buyers. For obvious reasons, the number of permits sold for each resource type would be restricted to the maximum sustainable yield of the particular resource in question. Importantly, the limit on the number of permits sold would impose an across-the-board restriction on the rate of renewable resource extraction that, at the very least, would ensure the existence of a policy instrument to satisfy sustainability precept no. 1.

Once bought, possession of a permit would grant an individual person or entity the right to purchase from resource-sellers a portion of the permissible resource flow. For example, a single permit might confer on its possessor the right to purchase one cubic metre of unprocessed timber. If so, a resource buyer would need to acquire 10 permits in order to obtain 10 cubic metres of raw timber. For each cubic metre of timber purchased, resource buyers would be required to forfeit one permit.

The auctioning process would be undertaken each year to allow the government authority to vary the number permits in line with novel changes in the ecosphere's regenerative and waste assimilative capacities. Given this, a permit would expire at the end of each year even if the permit was not used. To maintain competitive markets, there would be a limit on the number of permits that any single individual or firm could purchase. Any unwanted permits can be resold to other individuals or firms within the expiration period so long as the buyer is not already in possession of the maximum permissible quota of permits. Because the initial auctioning process is open to all, individuals and/or environmental groups have the opportunity to purchase some of the permits and opt not to use them should they would prefer an incoming resource flow less than the maximum sustainable rate.

By introducing a cap-and-trade system, a higher price is ultimately paid by resource buyers to secure each unit of the incoming resource flow. As per normal, resource buyers pay the amount charged by resource sellers to supply the resource. However, they now pay an additional amount to obtain the necessary resource use permits. This so-called 'premium' is equivalent to a throughput tax or, more accurately, an absolute scarcity rent that reflects the market internalisation of ecological limits, not simply ecological costs.

This last aspect of a cap-and-trade system is crucial for three reasons. To begin with, it ensures the existence of a policy instrument to: (a) facilitate the efficient allocation of the incoming resource flow; and (b) encourage the development and uptake of resource-saving technological progress. Secondly, it obviates the need for a government authority to calculate and impose a throughput tax since the tax rate is determined by the interaction of demand and artificially constrained supply forces in the resource use permit market. The benefit of this is quite obvious – if there is less need for bureaucratic calculations, there is less potential for bureaucratic error. Thirdly, the revenue raised from the sale of resource use permits can be redistributed to the poor and/or be used, where feasible, to rehabilitate the natural environment. This ensures the existence of a policy instrument to assist in achieving the goal of distributional equity. As we shall see, the revenue raised can also be used to part-finance a Job Guarantee programme.

In order to maximise the effectiveness of a cap-and-trade system, not only would a specific arrangement have to be designed to accommodate each renewable resource type but specific arrangements would need to be devised to cater for the different geographical and jurisdictional regions within which the particular resources are located.[3] The first reason for this is self-explanatory – different resource types have different regeneration rates. Although less obvious, the regional aspect is important because particular resource types (e.g., timber species) grow at different rates depending on their geographical location. In addition, a failure to consider regional effects can lead to an entire quota of a particular timber or fish species being sourced from one location, which has the potential to devastate a local fish population or timber reserve. Finally, since ecological sustainability requires all future exploitation of natural capital to be confined to locations already strongly modified by previous human activities (second part of sustainability precept no. 6), cap-and-trade systems designed with regional requirements in mind can help reduce or prohibit resource extraction from sensitive and hitherto low-impacted areas.

As useful as they are, cap-and-trade systems cannot, alone, ensure the satisfaction of all the six sustainability precepts listed above. This is because cap-and-trade systems are unable to deal adequately with sustainability precept no. 2 or the first part of sustainability precept no. 6. But they would play their role in satisfying sustainability precept no. 4 because the first law of thermodynamics ensures that the matter–energy entering the economy as low-entropy resources is inevitably equal to the amount of matter–energy exiting the economy as high-entropy waste. Thus, a limit on the incoming resource flow automatically imposes a quantitative limit on the amount of waste generated by the economic process. Having said this, it is possible, in some instances, for the paucity of sink capacity to be more of a binding constraint than the lack of resource availability. In such circumstances, the number of resource use permits auctioned each year would need to be determined in relation to waste absorption limits.

Cap-and-trade systems can also contribute towards the satisfaction of sustainability precept no. 3 by enabling a government authority to lengthen the intergenerational availability of non-renewable resources that have no known substitutes. In these circumstances, the number of permits auctioned each year would be determined on the basis of estimated stock levels, projected future discoveries, and the period over which their continued availability would be deemed to be intergenerationally just. Given the restrictions that a cap-and-trade system of this nature would place on the annual consumption of non-substitutable resources, it is reasonable to believe that the prices of these resources would rise relative to the prices of renewable and substitutable non-renewable resources. In doing so, cap-and-trade systems would encourage the wider use of the latter category of resources and greatly assist a nation to wean itself off non-substitutable resources.

Of course, cap-and-trade systems are not infallible. Whether they assist in achieving ecological sustainability depends largely on the accurate estimation of the maximum sustainable yield of all renewable resources or, where a paucity of sink capacity constitutes a binding constraint, the accurate estimation of waste absorption limits. If either or both are overestimated, too many permits will be auctioned and the incoming resource flow will exceed the maximum sustainable rate. To avoid any problems that might emerge from incorrectly estimating the maximum sustainable rate of throughput, it would be wise to adopt a 'precautionary' approach and limit the number of permits sold to, say, 75 per cent of the estimated maximum sustainable rate.

Operationalising the El Serafy Rule relating to non-renewable resource depletion

As alluded to above, cap-and-trade systems cannot ensure satisfaction of sustainability precept no. 2. This is because they do not compel the liquidators of non-renewable resources to cultivate the renewable resources necessary to keep the total stock of natural capital intact. To recall from Chapter 2, a variation of an ingenious formula was outlined as a means of determining the portion of depletion profits that needs to be set aside to ensure appropriate capital maintenance (equation 2.2). The formula is predicated on the Hicksian principle that sustainable income requires a non-renewable resource earmarked for depletion to be converted into a perpetual income stream (Hicks, 1946). This, in turn, requires a finite series of earnings from the sale of a non-renewable resource to be converted to an infinite series of true income such that the capitalised values of the two series are equal (El Serafy, 1989). To achieve this, an income and capital component of the finite series of earnings must first be calculated. Once obtained, the capital component constitutes the amount that needs to be set aside each year during the depletion phase of the non-renewable resource to ensure a perpetual income stream of constant value.

How might the so-called El Serafy Rule be operationalised to ensure the satisfaction of sustainability precept no. 2? One possible means is to compel re-source liquidators to establish 'capital replacement' accounts in the same way business owners in many countries are required to establish a superannuation fund for employees. This could be accomplished through changes in account-ing legislation. Ideally, the legislative changes would include a strict schedule of discount rates and average mine lives to apply when using the El Serafy Rule to calculate the set-aside component for each non-renewable resource type. The capital replacement accounts would be held by government-approved resource management companies whose task it would be to establish renewable replace-ment assets on behalf of the non-renewable resource liquidators.

Assurance bonds

I have mentioned a number of times that the first law of thermodynamics ensures that the matter–energy entering the economy as low-entropy resources is inevi-tably equal to the amount of matter–energy exiting the economy as high-entropy wastes. Thus, with cap-and-trade systems in place, there is no need to introduce a system of pollution permits to quantitatively limit the outgoing waste flow. How-ever, it is because of the second law of thermodynamics – the Entropy Law – that a quantitative restriction on the incoming resource flow has no influence on the *qualitative* nature of all outgoing waste. For this reason, cap-and-trade systems cannot ensure the satisfaction of sustainability precept no. 5.

It has been widely suggested that pollution taxes can be imposed to suitably control the qualitative nature of the outgoing waste flow (e.g., Pigou, 1932; Pearce and Turner, 1990; Field, 1998; Hussen, 2000; Kolstad, 2000). The weakness as-sociated with pollution taxes is that, although they render it more costly to pollute, the worse effects of pollution invariably take considerable time to emerge within the natural environment. This often means that polluters pay for the cost of their pollutive activities only at some stage after they have occurred. Because people have a tendency to discount future values, the prospect of having to pay much later for the cost of pollution is less of a disincentive to pollute than having to pay up front.

To overcome this problem, the concept of assurance bonds has been devised as a means of reducing the toxic and intractable nature of high-entropy wastes (Costanza and Perrings, 1990). With assurance bonds, a polluting firm pays a bond equal to the cost of the worst-case pollution scenario. Should the owners of a bond-paying firm demonstrate that the pollution they subsequently generate has had no deleterious impact of the natural environment, they receive the bond back in full plus any interest accrued over the period in which the bond has been held by a government authority. If the pollution has had an undesirable impact on the natural environment, the bond is confiscated either in full (when the pollution damage equals the worst-case scenario) or in part (when the pollution damage is something less than the worst-case scenario). If the worst-case scenario is unac-ceptably risky (i.e., involves highly toxic substances), the generation of the sub-stances in question will require prohibition or generation under strictly controlled conditions. Not unlike the premiums paid for resource use permits, confiscated bond money can be used for redistribution purposes and environmental rehabilitation projects.

It would not, however, be necessary for all firms to pay an assurance bond. Ideally, a government authority would identify 'low-risk' and 'high-risk' industries and confine bond payments to firms operating in the latter category. The high-risk category might also be divided into two sub-categories – for example, 'high-risk A' and 'high-risk B' – where the former sub-category would include industries generating highly dangerous substances. As just outlined, the waste generated by the firms operating in the 'high-risk A' sub-category would need to be rigorously controlled and monitored to avoid irrecoverable environmental damage.

Overall, by bringing the potential environmental cost of highly toxic and intractable wastes into the present decision-making domain, assurance bonds reduce the extent to which future environmental costs are discounted. This greatly increases the incentive for polluters to minimise their impact on the ecosphere. Barring illegal or corrupt activities, the introduction of both assurance bonds and strict controls on highly toxic substances would go a long way towards ensuring the satisfaction of sustainability precept no. 5.

Vegetation clearance controls

I explained earlier how regionally based cap-and-trade systems can assist in sparing low-impact areas from intensive resource exploitation. Unfortunately, cap-and-trade systems cannot ensure the preservation of native vegetation and critical ecosystems, particularly on privately owned land, which is necessary to satisfy the first part of sustainability precept no. 6. It has been conservatively estimated that around 20 per cent of a nation's land area should be preserved as habitat for wildlife conservation (Wilson, 2002).[4] To maximise the ecological values of protected areas, it has also been stressed that additional land needs to be set aside to serve as native vegetation refuges and vegetation corridors to connect critical ecosystems.

In order to satisfy the first part of sustainability precept no. 6, future land clearance needs to be kept to a minimum or be entirely prohibited altogether. To achieve this end, explicit and strict controls over native vegetation clearance must be imposed. A policy of this nature has already been introduced in the Australian state of South Australia in the form of the Native Vegetation Clearance Act (1990). Since its enactment, wholesale land clearance within the state has ceased. There are two major features of the Act. Firstly, land owners require permission to clear native vegetation, which is often denied. Secondly, unsuccessful applicants are provided with the funds required to fence off native vegetation and manage it effectively. As for public land, valuable parcels of remnant vegetation and critical ecosystems should be encompassed within newly established National Parks to meet the 20 per cent 'bottom line' recommended by ecologists.

One of the weaknesses of the Native Vegetation Clearance Act is its failure to compensate land owners for the potential loss of agricultural production or any other forgone mode of production. Compensation is clearly necessary to ensure equity considerations are adequately met. To help finance the compensation payments, governments should establish an 'environmental trust fund' from confiscated assurance bonds and the revenue raised from the sale of tradeable resource use permits.

The trust fund can also be put to two other useful purposes. Firstly, it can assist unviable farmers to exit the agricultural industry and resettle elsewhere or obtain new qualifications so that employment can be found locally. Secondly, where a marginal farming region is put at risk by vegetation clearance restrictions, the trust fund can be used to invest in a community level project to establish a suitable replacement industry. A similar approach can be applied to other industries potentially affected by land clearance controls (e.g., forestry, mining, and irrigation industries). Although many people would query the possible high cost of this restructuring process, it is likely to be considerably less than the eventual social and environmental costs of failing to adopt a proactive stance. In doing so, it would increase the political palatability of land clearance controls.

Full employment

As explained in Chapter 1, full employment is achieved when the economy generates enough work to eliminate all but frictional unemployment. To recall, this not only means that paid work must be available for everyone who seeks it, but underemployment must also be eradicated (i.e., no-one should work fewer hours than they desire at going real wage rates).

Because the throughput restrictions required to achieve ecological sustainability will eventually bring about a steady-state economy, one of the key questions raised throughout this book is how full employment can be achieved when, under the current institutional arrangements found in most countries, high rates of growth are required simply to prevent the unemployment rate from rising. As alluded to already, eliminating unemployment without increasing a nation's real GDP will require policies that sever the GDP–employment link. It will not, however, be possible to sever the link entirely. Some vestige of the strong connection between employment and real GDP will always remain if only because a nation's wage bill is principally financed out of the national product.

What, therefore, becomes a major task of policy-makers is to weaken the nexus between employment and real GDP sufficiently to ensure the full employment level of real GDP is ecologically sustainable. For many countries, this will require a significant reduction in the full employment level of real GDP.[5] As anyone familiar with standard macroeconomic policy-making will recognise, this strategy stands in direct contrast to the conventional unemployment-reducing approach of boosting real GDP in order to the narrow the gap between it and the full employment level of real GDP. For this reason, severing the GDP–employment link to the extent necessary to achieve full employment in a steady-state economy will require the implementation of a number of non-conventional policies.

Severing the GDP–employment link

The most plausible way to sever or at least weaken the nexus between employment and real GDP is to minimise the need for paid forms of employment. This can be achieved by increasing the productivity of labour, improving the quality of all newly produced goods (i.e., increasing the service efficiency of human-made capital), and reducing the rate at which the stock of human-made capital must be replaced (i.e., increasing the maintenance efficiency of human-made capital).[6] Whereas the former increases the real GDP per hour worked, the latter two advances boost profits and wages in so far as more durable goods with higher use values command higher selling prices.

Admittedly, a similar percentage rise in both wages and prices would not increase real wages. However, because the new goods available for purchase would be of better quality, workers would enjoy a higher level of consumption-related welfare per dollar of income earned or, equivalently, a higher level of consumption-related welfare per hour of work performed. This would allow workers to choose a new welfare-increasing combination of leisure and income involving fewer work hours, which would greatly facilitate job sharing and permit more paid workers to be engaged in the generation of a nation's real income.

Policy measures to increase the productivity of labour and improve the quality of newly produced goods include tax incentives to promote efficiency-increasing technological progress and an industrial relations system that promotes harmonious workplace relations, horizontal decision-making structures, and incentive-based means of remuneration (Weitzman, 1984; Estrin, 1986; Blandy and Brummitt, 1990).[7] Effective trade practices (anti-trust) legislation that limits the abuse of market power in oligopolistic industries can also promote efficiency and advances in labour productivity.

There are, unfortunately, three main obstacles preventing most people from reducing their hours of work. The first is the unequal distribution of wealth. The distribution of wealth is critical because wealth can provide its owner a flow of income without the need to engage in excessively laborious work. Because the majority of a nation's citizens possess little income-generating wealth, many are compelled to work long hours to obtain an income sufficient in magnitude to share equitably in the annual output of all newly produced goods. Policies therefore need to be introduced to bring about a more equitable distribution and ownership of wealth.[8] Incentive-based means of remuneration that include share ownership may assist greatly in this regard.

The second major obstacle is the degenerative influence that an unfettered global market with highly mobile capital flows has on wages and the conditions of employment (Daly, 1993; Røpke, 1994; Lawn, 2007). As long as the international trading environment continues to apply standards-lowering pressure on national economies, it will be difficult to bring about the increase in hourly wages required to reduce the need for work and to share the workload across the entire labour force. A so-called IMPEX system of exchange rate management is a pro-trade arrangement that has been posited as a way of internalising the cost of domestic environmental and social conditions of employment into the price of foreign-made goods without having to hinder exchange rate flexibility (Lawn, 2007). Provided the increases in wages and conditions of employment reflect rises in labour productivity, the IMPEX system allows domestic standards to be raised without reducing the international competitiveness of domestic producers.[9] It therefore promotes the domestic economic conditions conducive to job sharing.

The third major obstacle is the inflexibility of labour markets. Caused mainly by the existence of archaic industrial relations systems, labour market inflexibility makes it difficult for workers to negotiate a shorter working week with their employer. This results in many people having to work more hours than they would like at a time when others remain underemployed or unable to find work at all. Although labour market rigidities have been reduced over the past decade, the explosion of casual employment in most nations over the last 20 years cannot be regarded as evidence of increasingly flexible labour markets (Cowling *et al.*, 2006). Moreover, there have been many instances where modifications to industrial relations systems have led to the erosion of workers' wages and conditions of employment. Clearly, policy-makers need to install a form of labour market flexibility that protects workers' pay and conditions while extending their options beyond the current restrictive choice of having to work too many hours in a full-time occupation or a desired number of hours in a vulnerable casual job. Only then will the potential for job-sharing truly emerge.

Finally, the nexus between employment and real GDP can also be weakened by offering people a financial inducement to exit the labour force. Accomplishing this in a desirable manner is, nonetheless, a delicate exercise. The reason for this is that some of the measures that can induce a labour supply withdrawal have the potential to lower the existing level of real GDP, particularly if the inducement is financed out of national income and is not matched by an offsetting form of non-market production (Lawn, 2004). In such a situation, the withdrawal of labour is effectively 'artificial' rather than 'real' and efforts to equilibrate the full employment level of income with real GDP become a futile exercise akin to a cat chasing its own tail. The potential for a Basic Income Guarantee to induce an artificial withdrawal of labour forms the basis for some of the opposition towards it (Cowling *et al.*, 2006; Tcherneva, 2006). As we shall soon see, there are more viable ways to induce a real labour supply withdrawal to assist in achieving the goal of full employment.

Supply-side solutions

Supply-side solutions to the unemployment problem involve the implementation of incomes policies, labour market programmes, and initiatives designed to increase the flexibility of labour markets. I have already talked about the value of greater labour market flexibility as a means to increase productivity and facilitate job sharing. Labour market programmes entail training and skills development plus the introduction of incentives to encourage employers to take on more employees (Dawkins and Freebairn, 1997). Despite the success of a limited number of well-targeted labour market programmes in most countries, evidence suggests they are not very cost-effective. In addition, many labour market programmes do little more than shuffle existing unemployment queues. Few programmes have increased employment levels sufficiently to markedly reduce unemployment rates (Miller, 1994; Webster, 1997).

Incomes policies are designed to directly control aggregate wage outcomes as well as wage relativities between different occupations. Usually implemented at the national level, an incomes policy involves the adjustment of wages in response to price changes and advances in labour productivity. Ideally, wage adjustments are regulated to prevent the erosion of real wages and to ensure wage rises are commensurate with productivity gains. Although some would argue that the setting of a real wage floor can act as a stumbling block to unemployment reduction, others claim that the lowering of real wages at the bottom end of the wage scale encourages the adoption of low-skilled job-hiring strategies at the expense of capital investment, employee training, and research and development (Hancock, 1987; Harrison and Bluestone, 1990; Buchanan and Callus, 1993). Thus, by guarding against lower award rates, an incomes policy can promote the type of investment needed to increase labour productivity, boost real wages, and sustain employment growth.

On the down side of the ledger, an incomes policy reduces labour market flexibility and relies on bureaucrats rather than the market to alter wage relativities in response to productivity changes across different occupations. Apart from the negative impact of inflexible labour markets already outlined, this prevents labour markets from responding adequately to a nation's current and future labour requirements. An incomes policy can therefore lead to an undesirable imbalance between the demand and supply of certain forms of labour (i.e., skill shortages). Should an incomes policy be totally abandoned? Probably not. There will always be a good case for having real wages maintained by an independent government authority at the lower end of the relative wage scale to ensure a society's poorest workers are able to live decently.

In all, supply-side measures are important in so far as effective policies can boost labour productivity, increase real wages, and facilitate job sharing, all of which can lower unemployment. Having said this, any suggestion that all unemployment is supply-side related and/or the result of voluntary labour withdrawal is patently untrue. To some extent, persistent unemployment continues to be the manifestation of deficient aggregate demand (Modigliani, 2000; Mitchell, 2001). Unfortunately, the need to make a transition towards a steady-state economy places severe constraints on the use of expansionary demand-side policies to achieve full employment – as will now be discussed.

Demand-side solutions

Demand-side solutions involve the stimulation of aggregate demand to boost real output, which, in turn, generates more employment opportunities. Demand-side policies essentially take the form of a fiscal or monetary expansion. Expansionary fiscal policy entails an increase in government spending and/or a decrease in income taxes to augment the spending power of consumers.

For some time now, expansionary fiscal policy has been out of favour with governments and policy-makers alike. There are a couple of reasons for this. Firstly, it is feared that increased government spending can lead to higher interest rates that can crowd out private investment and consumer spending. Mitchell and Watts (2001) refute this assertion by arguing that the role of government debt is not to finance an increase in government spending but to maintain reserve balances in the short-term money market in order to defend the overnight cash rate. Lack of support by the central bank leads to a decline in the overnight cash rate, not a rise as conventionally understood. Thus, according to Mitchell and Watts, the notion of financial crowding out is meaningless.

Secondly, governments are increasingly concerned about the possibility of expansionary fiscal policies leading to high inflation and a long-run unemployment crisis. Mitchell and Watts (1997) again refute such a suggestion. They argue that inflationary pressure exists only when the economy is operating at the full employment level of national income or if the expansion in aggregate demand is indiscriminate in nature.[10] Should unemployment exist as a consequence of deficient demand, Mitchell and Watts believe the economy can safely respond to nominal impulses via a well-targeted expansion of real output – for example, a Job Guarantee scheme whereby the payment of a minimum award wage to Job Guarantee employees ensures price stability by averting any competition for labour with the private sector (see Chapter 8 of this volume).

Doubts surrounding the use of expansionary fiscal policies have led many governments to rely on expansionary monetary policies to stimulate investment and consumer spending. Nevertheless, loose monetary policy has been used only to stimulate the economy when in recession and never to the extent needed to achieve full employment. The failure to do this is again related to fears that the magnitude of the expansion would lead to an unacceptable level of inflation that would eventually result in a higher unemployment rate than the one that existed prior to the policy's implementation.

Let's assume, for the moment, that the standard fears concerning the long-term inflationary and crowding out effects of expansionary fiscal and monetary policies are unfounded. Since both involve the stimulation of the economy, to what extent can they be used to reduce unemployment if a steady-state economy necessitates the cessation of a high-growth policy?

To formally analyse the possibilities, the standard IS–LM framework used by most macroeconomists has been extended to include an 'environmental equilibrium' or EE curve (Heyes, 2000; Lawn, 2007). The EE curve represents the locus of real output/real interest rate combinations that ensures natural capital maintenance. As explained previously, natural capital maintenance is the minimum condition necessary to ensure ecological sustainability. Provided the policies outlined earlier in the chapter have been instituted – in particular, cap-and-trade systems – it is possible to ensure that an economy operates on the EE curve.

Should a central government implement an expansionary fiscal or monetary policy to reduce the unemployment rate and should, beforehand, the economy be teetering on an ecological precipice, the IS–LM–EE framework indicates that the emerging macroeconomic equilibrium will be ecologically unsustainable (i.e., the equilibrium point will lie to the right of the EE curve) (Lawn, 2007). With cap-and-trade systems in place to limit the incoming resource flow, an unsustainable equilibrium is averted. Instead, an excess demand for low entropy resources ensues. This forces resource buyers to bid up the price of the limited number of resource use permits, which raises resource prices. In turn, this increases the resource input cost of production. Exactly how much the higher resource costs translate into inflated goods prices depends on the extent of any resource-saving technological progress induced by the higher resource prices themselves.

Irrespective of the rate of technological progress, the increase in goods prices reduces the supply of real money balances.[11] This leads to a deficit in the short-term money market, which places upward pressure on the overnight cash rate, thus reducing private sector investment. In the end, real GDP is likely to be less than it was prior to the implementation of the expansionary fiscal or monetary policy. Hence, rather than lowering unemployment, an expansionary policy in the presence of cap-and-trade systems is just as likely to increase the unemployment rate. It will almost certainly fail to reduce the unemployment rate by the amount originally envisaged. It is therefore clear that demand-side policies cannot be relied upon in a steady-state setting to achieve the full employment objective.

An assessment of four major policy approaches

We are now in a position to assess the NAIRU, Basic Income, Job Guarantee, and ecological tax reform approaches in terms of how well they resolve the ecological sustainability and full employment objectives. Following a brief description of each approach, I shall outline their positives and shortcomings. This will subsequently form the basis for a tentative reform agenda to simultaneously achieve the goals of full employment and ecological sustainability.

The NAIRU approach to macroeconomic policy-making

The non-accelerating inflation rate of unemployment (NAIRU) is an unemployment rate that, when achieved, is accompanied by a constant inflation rate.[12] An increase in real GDP that reduces the unemployment rate below the NAIRU leads to non-productivity-related wage rises and an accelerated rate of price inflation (Dornbusch and Fischer, 1990).

The general consensus since the 1970s is that a nation's macroeconomic performance depends largely on the central government's ability to keep the rate of price inflation low. The reason for the emphasis on inflation control is the belief that any attempt to reduce the unemployment rate below the NAIRU leads to a buildup of inflationary pressure within the economy. As mentioned earlier in the chapter, this requires a counteractive response on the part of the central government that has the potential to bring about an unemployment rate higher than what existed prior to the demand stimulus. There is, therefore, some considerable truth in the importance of controlling inflation and the need to wisely undertake demand-side policies. But many question whether the possible emergence of inflation, rather than its high probability, warrants a macroeconomic obsession with inflation control (Blinder, 1987; Modigliani, 2000).

This issue aside, the overwhelming fear of inflation has resulted in the NAIRU approach to macroeconomic policy becoming the preferred policy stance in most countries. To this end, most central governments will use demand-side policies to reduce the unemployment rate only if the unemployment rate is above the NAIRU (Mitchell and Mosler, 2001; Mitchell and Muysken, 2008). Should the NAIRU be attained, governments will generally rein in public expenditure to prevent the unemployment rate from falling below the prevailing NAIRU. In support, central banks will normally raise interest rates to discourage excessive private sector spending.

At present, many governments are content to remain at the NAIRU. Indeed, for some governments, just reducing the unemployment rate to somewhere near the NAIRU is a remarkable achievement. As for the governments wanting to reduce the unemployment rate further, the most popular strategy involves the complex task of lowering the NAIRU and allowing the unemployment rate to fall in unison with it. By adopting this approach, it is argued that the unemployment rate can be gradually reduced without leading to an undesirable acceleration of the inflation rate. As difficult as it is to attain the NAIRU through conventional macroeconomic policy setting, it appears more difficult, if not impossible, for governments to substantially lower the NAIRU below an unemployment rate of 3–4 per cent.

From a full employment perspective, the most damning feature of the NAIRU policy is obvious – its success relies upon the existence of an unemployed pool of labour. In a very real sense, the health of a nation's economy depends upon the misfortune of a minority yet substantial number of 'sacrificed' citizens (Blinder, 1987; Modigliani, 2000; Mitchell and Mosler, 2001). NAIRU advocates respond by arguing that productivity increases, supply-side initiatives, and the lowering of inflationary expectations can reduce the NAIRU over time and lessen the number of disadvantaged citizens. Although there is evidence indicating that the NAIRU has fallen in many countries over the past decade, there is one piece of evidence that cannot be refuted – the NAIRU approach has been unsuccessful in bringing about full employment as defined in this chapter. Moreover, the NAIRU approach is unlikely to do so unless full employment itself becomes an explicit macroeconomic policy objective. The NAIRU approach simply does not result in the level of aggregate demand needed to eliminate all but frictional unemployment. Nor does it deal directly with critical issues regarding the severing of the GDP–employment link, labour market flexibility, and job sharing.

In terms of ecological sustainability, the NAIRU approach fails on two counts. Firstly, there is nothing inherent in the NAIRU policy that amounts to a separate institutional mechanism to quantitatively restrict the incoming resource flow to the maximum sustainable rate. The NAIRU approach to sustainability relies entirely upon the use of the market or tax-adjusted market prices to ensure that the physical scale of the economy remains ecologically sustainable. As already explained, this helps to facilitate increases in the efficiency of resource use but does not ensure that the aggregate level of economic activity and the resource flow required to fuel it remain within the regenerative and waste assimilative capacities of the natural environment.

Secondly, the NAIRU approach relies upon the growth of the economy to maintain or lower the NAIRU/unemployment rate. Thus, apart from failing to impose the necessary throughput constraints to achieve ecological sustainability outright, the NAIRU approach encourages the rates of growth that result in resource efficiency gains being overwhelmed by the scale of increased economic activity. In other words, the NAIRU approach openly invites the Jevons effect that has been partly responsible for the continued rise in environmental stress levels throughout the world (see Chapters 10, 13, and 14).

In response, one might suggest that ecological sustainability can be guaranteed provided the NAIRU approach is adopted alongside the environmental policy measures outlined in this chapter. Notwithstanding the fact that nothing can be categorically guaranteed, there is little doubt that the introduction of the environmental policies would go a long way towards ensuring ecological sustainability. However, without the implementation of some of the unemployment-reducing measures outlined in this chapter, the introduction of the environmental policies would almost certainly lead to a widening disparity between the NAIRU and the actual unemployment rate. Given this, it would be virtually impossible to maintain the unemployment rate at the NAIRU. One can therefore conclude that a NAIRU policy, by itself, is incapable of satisfying the full employment and ecological sustainability objectives.

A Basic Income Guarantee

As Part III revealed, the Basic Income Guarantee has been advocated as a means of overcoming the income insecurity associated with unemployment (Baetz, 1972; Van Parijs, 1991, 2000; Atkinson, 1995; Clark and Kavanagh, 1996). The Basic Income Guarantee is usually proposed in the form of an unconditional and universal transfer payment financed by increased tax rates or a widening of the tax base. Set above the absolute poverty line, the Basic Income Guarantee is designed to replace existing forms of public assistance (e.g., unemployment benefits, disability allowances, and old-age pensions) (Clark and Kavanagh, 1996).

The aims of the Basic Income Guarantee are many, but the primary objective is to ensure that each and every citizen is provided with a basic living wage irrespective of their contribution to society. Advocates claim that, by avoiding the link between the transfer payment and work, the Basic Income Guarantee affords individuals a 'real' sense of freedom in so far as it provides the basic means by which individuals can realise their genuine aims and desires (Gintis, 1997). One of the other potential benefits of the Basic Income Guarantee is that it reduces a person's need and/or incentive to work and can thus precipitate a labour supply withdrawal. This, in turn, can reduce the full employment level of income, thereby limiting the need to undertake expansionary demand-side measures to reduce the unemployment rate.

Critics of the Basic Income Guarantee claim, first and foremost, that it does not guarantee full employment (Saunders, 2002; Cowling *et al.*, 2006). Indeed, many critics argue that high unemployment rates are likely to persist in the presence of a Basic Income Guarantee because it cannot, without the discipline of unemployment, attenuate emerging wage–price or price–price pressures (Cowling *et al.*, 2006). Thus, like the NAIRU approach to inflation control, the inflationary impact of a Basic Income Guarantee can be averted only if there is a sufficiently large pool of unemployed labour. Clearly, although the Basic Income Guarantee provides a liveable wage for those who choose not to work, it will not guarantee work for those who still seek it. Given the important role that work plays towards the satisfaction of the full spectrum of human needs (Chapter 1), the failure of the Basic Income Guarantee to ensure full employment cannot be readily dismissed.

Secondly, critics point out that the level of national output needed to support a Basic Income Guarantee requires an adequate number of people to remain in paid forms of employment. Even if a sufficient number of people continue working, those engaged in paid employment effectively 'pay' for the non-work of those who exit the labour market. Thus, the freedom from work exigency that the Basic Income Guarantee affords one person becomes the source of another worker's alienation (Cowling *et al.*, 2006).

Thirdly, the Basic Income Guarantee constitutes an indiscriminate form of Keynesian pump-priming. Like any indiscriminate demand-side expansion, the Basic Income Guarantee has the potential to trigger periodic phases of demand–pull and cost–push inflation at low rates of unemployment, which must be countered with contractionary fiscal measures. This leads to high rates of unemployment (Cowling *et al.*, 2006). As will be soon explained, a Job Guarantee avoids this dilemma by providing the minimum demand expansion necessary to achieve full employment – no more, no less.

Finally, critics argue that the capacity of the Basic Income Guarantee to reduce unemployment is flawed because, apart from the potential problems outlined above, it encourages an artificial labour supply withdrawal (Cowling *et al.*, 2006: 8). Of course, the legitimacy of this criticism depends very much on what is meant by 'artificial'. One can identify three main sources of a genuine or 'real' withdrawal of labour. The first two have already been outlined but are worth repeating. They include:

1   Increased labour productivity. Improvements in labour productivity lead to higher real wages that allow people to reduce the number of hours they work.
2   Increased labour market flexibility. Flexible labour markets enable more people who are not presently free to modify their working arrangements to reduce their work hours.
3   Government cash payments to reflect the contribution that non-paid work makes to the social product (e.g., unpaid household work, child rearing, and volunteer work).

Why is the last an example of a real labour supply withdrawal? Because the cash payment not only reflects the contribution that one makes to a nation's real income, thereby ensuring that the value of any withdrawn labour is precisely matched by a real demand-side outcome, but ensures that those who continue to work are not, in effect, subsidising the non-work of those who exit the labour market.

Of these three sources of genuine labour supply withdrawal, it is the last which is most relevant to the Basic Income Guarantee. To what extent the Basic Income Guarantee induces a real or artificial labour supply withdrawal depends on how much the transfer payment involved exceeds a level of remuneration approximating the unpaid work contribution made by the average citizen towards the social product.[13] I refer to the average citizen because it would be too complex to determine the exact unpaid work contribution of each person and remunerate them accordingly. It would also be administratively simpler to provide the Basic Income Guarantee on a universal basis.

Clearly, a Basic Income Guarantee set at the basic living wage – as most of its proponents advocate – would far exceed the average person's unpaid work contribution and precipitate a large artificial withdrawal of labour. However, a Basic Income Guarantee set at a value equivalent to the unemployment benefit paid in most wealthy countries (approximately 40 per cent of the minimum wage) would be much closer to the mark.[14] It would, as a consequence, induce little in the way of an artificial withdrawal of labour. Should the potential for an artificial labour supply withdrawal still exist, it could be minimised by having the public sector provide a range of fractional job positions since this would allow people to supply the portion of their labour not covered by the Basic Income Guarantee. Nonetheless, such an arrangement would be insufficient to bring about full employment.

Given the important role that inducing people to leave the labour force can play towards weakening the GDP–employment nexus and the contribution that a Basic Income Guarantee can make towards this process, there are two further reasons why the Basic Income should be provided at less than the basic living wage. Firstly, and if only for socio-political reasons, it has been stressed by many observers that any policy initiative aimed at reducing poverty must not violate social attitudes towards work, non-work, and welfare payments to the poor. If the dominant social view is that no-one should receive 'something for nothing' (such as a Basic Income at the living wage), it is utterly inconsistent for people to receive 'nothing for something' (such as no Basic Income at all). The Basic Income Guarantee, in the form proposed above, would go along way towards ensuring the rightful receipt of 'something for something', even if it were, as I have recommended, administered in a very blunt and universal manner.

Secondly, the failure of most governments to remunerate unpaid work has significantly distorted worker incentives. In stark contrast to the fears that a Basic Income Guarantee would induce an artificial withdrawal of labour, non-payment for household and volunteer work has long induced an artificial influx of reluctant workers into conventional labour markets. Apart from placing enormous pressure on families and other social institutions, this has increased the real GDP that a nation must generate to achieve full employment (i.e., has increased the full employment level of real GDP). The Basic Income Guarantee proposed here would correct this socially destructive labour market distortion.

It is true that one would prefer to see traditional unpaid work remain unpaid on the basis that it constitutes an integral part of a nation's social capital – in other words, people undertake this form of work because they feel morally obligated to perform it. However, if market forces have the propensity to deplete social capital (see Hirsch, 1976; Daly and Cobb, 1989), the preservation and replenishment of social capital may require non-pecuniary assets to be valued in the same way as other assets. If so, the case for a modified Basic Income Guarantee is further enhanced.

In terms of achieving ecological sustainability, many would argue that a Basic Income Guarantee can reduce environmental pressure by lessening the need for work and consequently the need to produce the same quantity of real output over time. Although the Basic Income Guarantee can reduce the environmental impact per unit of economic activity by weakening the nexus between real GDP and employment, it suffers the same fate as the NAIRU approach to macroeconomic policy. By this I mean that it does not involve the explicit imposition of quantitative restrictions on the rate of resource throughput. The Basic Income Guarantee cannot, therefore, prevent the economy from physically growing beyond its maximum sustainable scale – that is, it cannot ensure that the incoming resource flow required to sustain the economy at its prevailing or growing physical scale is consistent with the regenerative and waste assimilative capacities of the natural environment. In all, the Basic Income Guarantee is incapable of achieving both full employment and ecological sustainability.

The Job Guarantee

To recall from Part III, the Job Guarantee is a demand-side policy whereby the government acts as an employer of last resort to absorb all labour displaced by the private sector (Mitchell and Watts, 2001). With a Job Guarantee programme in place, any person unable to secure employment in the private sector or conventional public sector is automatically offered a Job Guarantee occupation. In keeping with business cycle fluctuations, government spending on the Job Guarantee increases as the number of private sector jobs decline, but decreases in line with a private sector recovery.

An important feature of the scheme is the payment of a minimum hourly award wage to Job Guarantee employees. This would ensure that the basic needs of full-time Job Guarantee employees and their dependents are met. It would also prevent the government from competing up the wage scale against the private sector for labour. Hence, with a minimum award wage in place, there would be no disturbance of the private wage structure. As an added bonus, the minimum hourly wage would establish a wage floor for the entire economy in the sense that the possibility of losing employees to the Job Guarantee scheme would deter private sector employers from paying an hourly wage less than the minimum.[15]

Although a Job Guarantee, by its very nature, can ensure full employment, two major concerns continue to be expressed about the scheme. They are: (a) would the Job Guarantee ensure price stability?; and (b) is it possible that the Job Guarantee could be sufficiently destructive of the economy to result in an absurdly large number of Job Guarantee employees?

As to price stability, because Job Guarantee employees are paid a minimum award wage, the scheme is able to stifle the emergence of wage-related inflation (Tcherneva, 2003; Mitchell and Muysken, 2008). However, there are two alternative sources of inflationary pressure to consider – one being demand–pull in nature; the other being of the cost–push variety. The former, which can arise as real GDP nears the potential output level, can be dealt with by employing a similar inflation-control mechanism to the NAIRU. Mitchell and Watts (2001) refer to this mechanism as the NAIBER – a 'non-accelerating inflation buffer employment ratio'. It works in the following manner. Firstly, assume that a NAIRU policy is being employed and exists at a 6 per cent unemployment rate.[16] The Job Guarantee scheme is introduced to eliminate all but frictional unemployment. Because the scheme necessitates an increase in government spending, it boosts aggregate demand and real GDP. Let's assume that demand–pull inflationary pressures begin to emerge within the economy. Fearing the impact of inflation, the government dampens private sector activity by employing monetary policy instruments to raise interest rates.[17] As a consequence, the percentage of the labour force employed in the private sector declines while the percentage employed at the minimum wage under the Job Guarantee scheme increases. Provided the interest rate is appropriately manipulated, the ratio of Job Guarantee workers to private sector employees rises until the inflation rate is again stabilised. Inflation control and full employment are simultaneously accomplished and the NAIBER is attained.

Given the above, the NAIBER is likely to be higher than the NAIRU in the short run. For critics of the Job Guarantee, this is an undesirable outcome since it means that those displaced by the private sector will be on the much lower floor wage. This is true; however, the outcome is undoubtedly more equitable than having a permanent pool of unemployed labour under a NAIRU policy.

There are a number of other positive aspects associated with the Job Guarantee scheme worth considering. Firstly, unlike unemployed labour, Job Guarantee workers retain and acquire new and existing skills. This increases the combined productivity of the entire labour force, which can help boost the floor wage. Secondly, since Job Guarantee workers maintain their employability, they represent a more credible threat to disaffected private sector employees than the unemployed. Presumably the NAIBER would serve as a more effective inflation control mechanism than the NAIRU (Mitchell, 2000). Thirdly, because the combined labour force is more productive under a Job Guarantee scheme, the NAIBER is likely to decline over time and fall below the NAIRU in the long run. Thus, apart from achieving full employment, the Job Guarantee would eventually increase the percentage of the labour force being paid a wage above the minimum level. Thus, any increase in the number of people living on the floor wage is likely to be short-lived and would constitute a small price to pay to ensure the availability of paid employment for anyone who desires it.

A second source of inflationary pressure would emerge if cap-and-trade systems were operating to limit the incoming resource flow to the maximum sustainable rate. This is because the increase in aggregate demand brought about by an introduction of the Job Guarantee scheme would force resource buyers to pay a higher price for the limited number of resource use permits. As previously explained, this would raise resource prices, increase the real interest rate, dampen private investment, and result in a lower equilibrium output level. With a Job Guarantee in place together with cap-and-trade systems we might expect private sector employment to fall even further and the number of Job Guarantee employees to initially be greater than it would under a typical NAIBER scenario. Consequently, what I would call an 'ecologically sustainable' NAIBER, or an ESNAIBER, would presumably be higher than the standard NAIBER in the short run.

What about the long run? The much higher price for low-entropy resources brought about by the introduction of tradeable resource use permits would almost certainly induce a much greater rate of resource-saving technological progress. This would allow higher levels of real GDP to be obtained from the maximum sustainable rate of resource throughput and dramatically reduce the inflationary pressure generated by the Job Guarantee. This, in turn, would keep interest rates low and encourage producers to adopt the best available 'green' technologies.[18] It is therefore highly probable, that in the long run, the ESNAIBER would be lower than the NAIBER, which, as already explained, would be lower than the NAIRU. As a consequence, there are likely to be fewer people employed by the Job Guarantee scheme under an ESNAIBER policy than there would be unemployed people under a NAIRU policy scenario. Above all, it is clear that concerns regarding the possibility of a large number of people ending up as Job Guarantee employees are unfounded.

Although the Job Guarantee has the potential to deal adequately with the full employment objective, one must question whether it can achieve ecological sustainability. Advocates of the Job Guarantee believe it can facilitate the movement towards ecological sustainability provided a sufficient number of Job Guarantee activities are low in resource use intensity and/or devoted to environmental rehabilitation activities (Cowling *et al.*, 2006). Indeed, Job Guarantee advocates believe the scheme is ideally suited to environmental causes given that, firstly, one of its central aims is to ensure it does not compete with private sector activities, and secondly, environmental systems and services have public goods characteristics which require government involvement to ensure their preservation.

There is no doubt that Job Guarantee programmes can be designed to generate long-term environmental benefits. For example, programmes devoted to reafforestation, erosion control, and the establishment of renewable resource assets to replace non-renewable resources can assist in maintaining the stock of natural capital and augmenting its productivity. This can go along way towards raising the growth and exploitative efficiencies of natural capital (Ratios 3 and 4 from Chapter 2). Job Guarantee workers can also be involved in the management of National Parks and other vegetation refuges aimed at connecting critical ecosystems.

Unfortunately, the Job Guarantee scheme cannot, either by itself or in conjunction with mainstream environmental policy solutions, ensure ecological sustainability. There are two main reasons for this. Firstly, the Job Guarantee is essentially an expansionary demand-side policy that relies heavily upon physically growing the economy to achieve the goal of full employment. As much as Job Guarantee programmes can be designed to be low in resource use intensity, there is no denying that the scheme, as a whole, will immediately consume additional resources.[19] Should the economy be teetering on an ecological precipice, the introduction of a Job Guarantee will almost certainly push the economy beyond its maximum sustainable scale.

Secondly, even though environmentally targeted Job Guarantee programmes have the potential to increase the growth and exploitative efficiencies of natural capital, an increase in efficiency is not enough to ensure ecological sustainability because, as explained, a failure to have in place cap-and-trade systems means it is impossible to prevent efficiency advances from being overwhelmed by the increasing scale of economic activity (the Jevons effect). Quite simply, a Job Guarantee, alone, cannot ensure that the rate of resource throughput required to fuel the economic process remains within the ecosphere's regenerative and waste assimilative capacities. Only if the Job Guarantee is accompanied by the full range of environmental policies outlined earlier in this chapter can there be both full employment and ecological sustainability (i.e., an ESNAIBER scenario).

Importantly, should a nation's economy already be operating at or beyond its maximum sustainable scale, the resolution of the two policy goals would not be achieved, following the introduction of a Job Guarantee, by a consequent increase in aggregate demand.[20] It would be achieved as a result of the Job Guarantee serving as a rationing device to equitably ration paid work to the extent required to ensure that: (a) everyone wanting paid work is employed and at least in receipt of a minimum living wage; and (b) there is price stability (no runaway inflation). This, of course, is not what Job Guarantee advocates had in mind when they first conceived of the Job Guarantee. But in a 'full' world where the economies of most countries already appear to have exceeded their maximum sustainable scale, and where numerous more are about to do likewise, this may prove to be the Job Guarantee's most important practical function.

Ecological tax reform

As described in Chapter 10, ecological tax reform (ETR) involves a combination of tax cuts on 'goods' such as labour, income, and wages, and tax impositions on such 'bads' as resource depletion and pollution. ETR advocates argue, firstly, that the former encourages value adding in production, which boosts, among other things, real wages. Provided labour markets are suitably flexible, this allows workers located on the backward-bending section of their labour supply curve to reduce their working hours and increase their welfare. Hence, ETR goes a long way towards severing the GDP–employment link.

Another key element of the ETR package promoted by its advocates is its capacity to alter the cost structure of commercial operations. Because ETR increases the cost of resource use but reduces the cost of hiring labour, it is argued that employers will, as much as possible, substitute the latter for the former. Consequently, more people and fewer resources will be employed to produce a given level of real output.

Finally, ETR advocates argue that tax increases on depletion and pollution can encourage the resource-saving technological progress that is needed to significantly reduce the resource intensity of economic activity. In doing so, it is argued that ETR can limit the throughput of resources to the rate required to ensure ecological sustainability. Overall, ETR advocates believe that a well-targeted ETR package can promote the transition towards a steady-state economy whilst simultaneously alleviating the unemployment problem.

Although tax cuts on labour, income, and wages can increase the attractiveness of employing labour and promote job-sharing by encouraging people to reduce their hours of work, it is difficult to imagine ETR achieving full employment. In the unlikely event that it does, it would not be sustained over time. The main reason for this is that the employment elements of an ETR package are incapable of ensuring a level of aggregate demand sufficient to continuously absorb the entire labour force.

In view of the above discussion on the Job Guarantee, it is clear that an increase in aggregate demand is not required to achieve full employment. However, the advantage of the Job Guarantee over ETR is that it provides paid work for anybody who desires it while allowing a central government to manipulate the economy until such time as an inflation-controlling ratio of Job Guarantee workers to conventional workers is reached. ETR offers no such guarantee of paid employment and relies entirely upon the clearance of the labour market to eliminate all unemployment and underemployment. Unfortunately, a natural clearance of the labour market is only likely to be a remote and short-term possibility. This is because: (a) for the full employment level of real GDP to be achieved, there will almost certainly be an unacceptable level of price inflation (which, in order to sedate, requires a reduction in aggregate demand *below the full employment level*); (b) central governments generally run budget surpluses in the modern age, which, by necessity, generates an unemployment gap (see Chapters 7 and 8); and (c) where central governments run budget deficits, the spending is indiscriminately and inappropriately targeted, thus triggering inflationary pressure before the full employment level of real GDP is reached.

The other employment-related weakness of ETR is its heavy reliance upon the substitution of labour for resource inputs in production. It was explained at length in Chapter 2 that human-made capital/labour and low-entropy resource inputs are effectively complements – a consequence of low-entropy resources being the only material cause of all production, including that of all human-made capital and labour. Although there is some scope to substitute labour for resources, it is largely confined to X-efficiency gains arising from the use of a more appropriate combination of factor inputs. However, room for this form of substitution is minutely small and rapidly exhausted once exploited.

In purely physical terms, the greatest scope for substitution lies in the switching of labour for human-made capital (producer goods). For many decades now, economic forces have brought about a rise in the capital intensity of production. Although tax reform has the potential to alter the relative preference for using labour and human-made capital in production, ETR as it is currently proposed would be unable to induce a widespread shift towards labour – certainly not enough to guarantee full employment.

The inability of conventional ETR measures to achieve ecological sustainability was thoroughly explained and empirically analysed in Chapter 10. Without wanting to repeat myself too much, conventional ETR measures rely on the use of tax-adjusted resource prices to bring the rate of resource throughput into line with ecosphere's regenerative and waste assimilative capacities. As evidenced in Chapter 10, tax-adjusted resource prices can facilitate a more efficient allocation of the incoming resource flow, which can subsequently reduce the environmental impact per unit of economic activity.[21] However, because a conventional ETR package does not include policy measures aimed at quantitatively restricting the rate of resource throughput (e.g., cap-and-trade systems), it cannot limit the physical growth of the economy or the rate at which the economy expands. It cannot, therefore, prevent the scale effect of a growing economy from overwhelming the efficiency gains induced by the introduction of depletion and pollution taxes. This ultimately means that conventional ETR measures are unable to prevent the rate of resource throughput from exceeding the ecosphere's long-run carrying capacity.

In fact, as Daly (2008) argues, the 'efficiency first' principle embodied in the conventional ETR approach may encourage a greater rate of resource use. How? Daly suggests that the efficiency induced by depletion and pollution taxes makes the frugality required to achieve ecological sustainability appear less necessary – for example, the development of more fuel-efficient cars can foster the perception that there is less need to travel fewer kilometres. Whether the additional fuel consumed from the extra travel is likely to exceed the fuel saved by travelling more efficiently is a moot point. In an economic climate where the physical expansion of the economy is openly welcomed and facilitated by governments, there is a high probability that it would. A similar scenario would presumably pertain to all resource types.

Conventional ETR advocates might counter this argument by suggesting that governments could cease to encourage excessive rates of growth by employing contractionary macroeconomic policies to quash any growth-inducing forces emerging within the economy. This is a possible option, albeit a difficult and clumsy means of operating sustainably with potentially dire economic consequences (see Lawn, 2008). But the inescapable point is that an 'efficiency first' strategy does not ensure the level of frugality required to prevent the rate of resource throughput from exceeding the regenerative and waste assimilative capacities of the natural environment. Conversely, a 'frugality first' strategy – which is a characteristic feature of cap-and-trade systems – is able to guarantee a sustainable rate of resource use up front. Moreover, by reflecting ecological limits and not just ecological costs, the prices paid for the permits associated with cap-and-trade systems are more likely to stimulate efficiency advances than conventional ETR measures. As the saying goes, 'necessity is the mother of invention', and cap-and-trade systems institutionalise the 'necessity' factor in a way that depletion and pollution taxes do not. To make matters worse, a conventional ETR package does not include the remaining array of policy measures listed earlier in the chapter to achieve ecological sustainability. In all, ETR in its conventional form fails to go far enough to achieve both ecological sustainability and full employment.

A strategy to deal with the full employment/ sustainability dilemma

A potential solution to the full employment/sustainability dilemma can be obtained by extracting the desirable aspects from three of the four macro policy approaches assessed in this chapter. I say three out of four approaches because there is little to recommend the NAIRU approach as a means to achieving the ecological sustainability and full employment objectives. It can therefore be rejected as a legitimate policy strategy.

Despite its many weaknesses, I believe ETR should constitute the centrepiece of any policy strategy to achieve the twin goals of ecological sustainability and full employment. My reason for this is that ETR stands as the only policy agenda that explicitly aims to resolve both policy objectives. It can therefore serve as an ideal policy platform that can be easily modified to incorporate the sustainability policies outlined earlier in this chapter as well as the desirable aspects of the Job Guarantee and Basic Income.

With the aforementioned in mind, the overall policy strategy should begin with a reduction in taxes on labour, income, and wages to encourage value-adding in production and to induce employers to exploit whatever potential exists to employ more labour. Because the employment aspect of an ETR package cannot reduce the unemployment rate sufficiently to achieve full employment, the strategy should include a Job Guarantee. However, to maximise the flexibility of labour markets, boost labour productivity, and successfully achieve full employment, the Job Guarantee must satisfy the work preferences of the labour force. Indeed, to guarantee full employment as defined in this chapter, people must be neither overworked nor underemployed. The former often eventuates if the only option available is a full-time occupation when only part-time work is desired. The latter usually occurs if a person unable to take on a full-time occupation is forced to accept a casual job that offers fewer than the desired number of working hours.[22]

To satisfy labour market preferences as well as possible, the Job Guarantee programme must include a range of fractional jobs, all with the benefits and privileges normally associated with full-time employment (e.g., annual leave and sick-leave entitlements). Given that the average full-time job in most countries involves approximately 37.5 hours of work per week, or 7.5 hours daily, fractional positions should be established alongside 37.5-hour full-time positions to allow individuals to work 7.5 hours (one day), 15.0 hours (two days), 22.5 hours (three days), or 30.0 hours (four days) per week. To further increase flexibility, a Job Guarantee programme should also provide the opportunity for people to work half-days (3.75 hours per day) for, say, a minimum of two half-days per week. Not unlike the disciplining effect of a minimum or floor wage, the creation of fractional positions would force the hand of the private sector to offer similar working arrangements, thus facilitating a 'standards-guaranteeing' form of labour market flexibility.[23]

It was indicated earlier that Job Guarantee employees should be paid a minimum award wage. From an equity perspective, the actual source of one's income is not important.[24] What ultimately matters is that all citizens receive, at the very least, a liveable income. I therefore propose that the after-tax income received from a full-time Job Guarantee occupation should be less than the minimum liveable income. My reasoning for this is as follows. Firstly, I believe a universal Basic Income Guarantee should be introduced to reflect the non-paid work contribution made by the average citizen towards the social product. The Basic Income Guarantee should be set at around 40 per cent of the minimum liveable income and be paid in the form of a demogrant (negative income tax) or non-transferable vouchers and food stamps.[25] Should a system of vouchers and food stamps be the chosen option, it ought to be designed to provide individuals with basic health and dental care, staple food items, essential accommodation, limited use of public transport facilities, and access to post-secondary education services.[26] A Basic Income Guarantee set at 40 per cent of the minimum liveable income would induce a real albeit partial withdrawal of labour that would reduce the real GDP required to achieve full employment. In doing so, the Basic Income Guarantee would ease any pressure associated with the imposition of quantitative throughput restrictions as well as limit the number of people employed on the Job Guarantee scheme.

Clearly, if a Basic Income Guarantee is providing 40 per cent of the minimum liveable income, the Job Guarantee need only cover the unmet 60 per cent. Determination of the hourly Job Guarantee wage would then depend on: (a) the estimated minimum liveable income; (b) the Basic Income Guarantee paid to each adult citizen; (c) the marginal income tax rate applicable to low-income earners; and (d) the number of work hours required of a full-time Job Guarantee employee. As a means of illustration, assume that the minimum liveable income is estimated at $500 per week, the Basic Income Guarantee is set at $200 per week ($500 × 0.4), and a full-time Job Guarantee employee is required to work 37.5 hours per week. Table 14.1 reveals the various before-tax Job Guarantee incomes and hourly wages corresponding to different marginal tax rates (columns *e* and *f*). As Table 14.1 shows, the greater the marginal tax rate, the larger is the before-tax income and hourly wage that must be paid to Job Guarantee employees to ensure receipt of a minimum liveable income.

Because JG employees are low-income earners, it makes little sense to subject them to the higher marginal tax rates presented in Table 14.1. A 20 per cent tax rate would seem both fair and appropriate. At this tax rate, all Job Guarantee

Table 14.1 Tax and income schedule of a Job Guarantee with a Basic Income Guarantee set at 40% of the minimum liveable income (MLI) and the MLI estimated at $500.00 per week

Minimum liveable income	Basic Income Guarantee $(a \times 0.4)$	After-tax JG income $(a - b)$	Marginal tax rate	Before-tax JG income $(c/(1 - d))$	JG hourly wage $(e/37.5)$
a	b	c	d	e	f
$500.00	$200.00	$300.00	0.10	$333.33	$8.89
$500.00	$200.00	$300.00	0.15	$352.94	$9.41
$500.00	$200.00	$300.00	0.20	$375.00	$10.00
$500.00	$200.00	$300.00	0.25	$400.00	$10.67
$500.00	$200.00	$300.00	0.30	$428.57	$11.43
$500.00	$200.00	$300.00	0.35	$461.54	$12.31
$500.00	$200.00	$300.00	0.40	$500.00	$13.33
$500.00	$200.00	$300.00	0.45	$545.45	$14.55
$500.00	$200.00	$300.00	0.50	$600.00	$16.00

employees – whether full-time or part-time – would be remunerated at a wage rate of $10 per hour. As such, full-time Job Guarantee workers would be paid a before-tax income of $375 per week but receive an after-tax income of $300 per week. Of course, this exercise merely serves as an illustrative example. In the end, the hourly Job Guarantee wage rate would be best determined following an intensive study to ascertain what constitutes an appropriate liveable income as well as a nation's economic capacity to support such a wage.[27]

What about private sector employees? Would they also be guaranteed a minimum liveable income? Most private sector employees would be earning considerably more than the Job Guarantee wage. Hence, the issue of a liveable income would not be directly relevant to them. As for people employed in low-paid jobs, the government can essentially rely upon the market-disciplining role of the Job Guarantee to ensure low-paid workers receive at least 60 per cent of a minimum liveable income from their full-time employment.[28] This, in turn, would guarantee that all citizens receive a minimum liveable income.

Finally, there are likely to be private sector concerns about the incentive effects of a Basic Income Guarantee. These concerns would be greatly alleviated by combining the Basic Income and Job Guarantee wage in the manner suggested above (i.e., 40 per cent and 60 per cent of a liveable income respectively). This is because the minimum hourly wage of a full-time Job Guarantee occupation would be 40 per cent lower than it would be if the Job Guarantee existed as one's sole means to a liveable income.[29] Assuming that the private sector can attract low-skilled labour by paying an hourly wage equal to that of a Job Guarantee occupation, the minimum hourly private sector wage would also be 40 per cent lower under the above-suggested arrangement. In this sense, the modified Basic Income would serve as a private sector wage subsidy that would not only strengthen the employment-related ETR element of the overall policy strategy (i.e., increase the attractiveness of employing labour), but reduce the increase in production costs resulting from measures designed to internalise the cost of resource depletion and pollution generation.

It has been explained many times that tax increases on resource depletion and pollution can facilitate a more efficient allocation of the incoming resource flow and encourage the development and uptake of resource-saving and pollution-reducing technology. Because depletion and pollution taxes cannot ensure an eco-logically sustainable rate of resource throughput, the overall policy strategy must eventually incorporate the full array of environmental policy measures outlined earlier in the chapter. These include:

- cap-and-trade systems to prevent the over-harvesting of individual renewable resource types;
- operationalisation of the El Serafy rule to ensure, where possible, that renewable resources are cultivated to replace depleted non-renewable resource stocks;
- cap-and-trade systems to lengthen the intergenerational availability of non-renewable resources that have no known substitutes;
- assurance bonds to limit the generation of hazardous wastes;
- vegetation clearance controls to maintain critical ecosystems and the important vegetation corridors connecting them;
- a sufficient number of National Parks and other conservation zones to ensure that at least 20 per cent of a nation's land area is preserved as wildlife habitat;
- an environmental trust fund to finance soil conservation measures, to assist landowners in the management of remnant vegetation, to compensate people affected by environmental measures, and to finance any ensuing restructuring process.

It will, however, be difficult if not irresponsible to introduce all of these envi-ronmental policies upfront. Like any system in a coevolutionary world, economic systems exhibit path-dependent features (Capra, 1982; David, 1985; Arthur, 1989). By this I mean that the immediate integrity of an economic system depends very much upon the maintenance of the institutions and modes of production that have evolved within them over time – even if they are growth-centred and there-fore unsustainable in the long run. Radical and sudden changes can be highly destructive. For this reason, and given that tax increases on resource depletion and pollution constitute a major advance over the present policy approach, it would be efficacious to begin with the adoption of a more conventional ETR approach and gradually phase in the above-listed environmental measures over time. Apart from promoting greater efficiency, the more conventional ETR approach would serve as an ideal means of preparing a nation's economy, and its citizens, for the more radical measures needed to fully resolve the goal of ecological sustainability in an efficient and progressive manner.

Before I conclude, I would just like to make mention of two larger benefits that would emerge as a consequence of implementing the strategy outlined above

– in particular, from combining the Job Guarantee scheme with cap-and-trade systems. I explained earlier that, if a Job Guarantee was introduced, it would be possible for inflationary pressure to build up within the economy that, in order to dampen, would require contractionary measures such as an increase in tax rates or interest rates to quell private sector spending. It was also explained that the contractionary measures need to be carefully implemented and monitored to bring about an inflation-stabilising ratio of Job Guarantee workers to private sector employees (i.e., the NAIBER).

There is little doubt that achieving the NAIBER would be a complex task similar in difficulty to achieving the NAIRU under the current arrangements in most countries. However, in the case where the Job Guarantee scheme exists together with cap-and-trade systems (i.e., an ESNAIBER scenario), this fine-tuning exercise is rendered redundant. This is because the premium paid for the limited resource use permits is able to deflate the economy by the precise amount needed to bring about the ESNAIBER. There would, as a consequence, be no need for a bureaucratic department to adjust interest rates or tax rates. The resource use permit market would automatically fulfil this important fine-tuning role as the premium paid for permits – equivalent to an absolute scarcity tax – fluctuates in accordance with the changes in the demand for resource use permits relative to their limited supply.

Finally, it was shown in Chapter 2 (Figure 2.5) that an economy need not be exceeding ecological limits for its physical expansion to reduce a nation's sustainable economic welfare. It was also explained how the implementation of various components of the above-proposed strategy would, apart from ensuring ecological sustainability and an inflation-stabilising form of full employment, improve the distribution of income and wealth, increase value-adding in production, boost labour productivity, and facilitate the development and uptake of resource-saving and pollution-reducing technology. All of these advances would undoubtedly increase the four eco-efficiency ratios outlined and discussed at length in Chapter 2 (equation 2.7). As such, they would bring about desirable shifts of the uncancelled benefit (UB) and uncancelled cost (UC) curves and, in doing so, go a long way towards ensuring that the goals of ecological sustainability and full employment are achieved in a manner consistent with the broader goal of sustainable development.

In conclusion, not for one moment do I believe that the above policy measures would unequivocally achieve ecological sustainability and full employment in a glitch-free manner. What I have done is tentatively provide a strategy that includes the policies that I believe are necessary to reconcile the conflict between employment and environmental considerations – a conflict that has arisen largely as a consequence of humankind's addiction to GDP growth. In the fullness of time, a more appropriate set of policies may surface, as also might a better way of combining them to achieve the twin goals of ecological sustainability and full employment. I am also acutely aware that some of the policies I have recommended would be politically unpalatable and involve considerable adjustment costs.

Indeed, the manner and pace in which the proposed policies are implemented may be as much a key to their eventual success as is their intrinsic worthiness.

In the end, if all this book manages to do is stimulate a broader debate on how to reconcile the twin goals of ecological sustainability and full employment, I believe it will have served a valuable purpose. After all, debates on the environment–employment dilemma have been conspicuous by their relative absence. Should, however, this book lead to the emergence of a more desirable short-term and long-term strategy than the one I have outlined in this chapter, it will have served an even more valuable purpose. But, no matter what form the eventual strategy may take, it will need to be consistent with biophysical and macroeconomic realities to in any way generate a sustainable full-employment outcome. I have no doubt that it is possible to develop a workable and saleable solution to the environment–employment dilemma. I just hope, given the gravity of the situation humankind confronts, that an appropriate strategy emerges sooner rather than later.

Notes

1 A feasible resource use permit system (cap-and-trade system) is also explained at length in Lawn (2007).

2 The estimation of the maximum sustainable yield of a renewable resource is more difficult and more complex than that described by a typical logistic growth curve found in most textbooks (Bell and Morse, 2008). This is because, as Pitcher and Hart (1982) have stressed, the concept of maximum sustainable yield often excludes the effects of competition, symbiotic and coevolutionary relationships with other species and ecosystems, and changes in ecological carrying capacity brought about by human influences. As best as possible, these factors need to be taken into account to ensure the permissible harvest rate of the renewable resource in question is in no way unsustainable in both the short and the long term.

3 In an ideal world, the boundaries of legal and political jurisdictions within nations would closely resemble geographical or biophysical regions, such as a river basin. Unfortunately, many environmental problems are accentuated by the legal and political complexities arising from multiple jurisdictions existing within a well-defined geographical or biophysical region. The Murray–Darling Basin in Australia involving the states of Queensland, New South Wales, Victoria, and South Australia is a case in point.

4 Indeed, as outlined in Chapter 2, Wilson believes it should be more in the region of 50 per cent.

5 The full employment level of real GDP is the lowest level of real GDP required to achieve full employment given society's labour-supplying preferences.

6 The service efficiency and maintenance efficiency of human-made capital were discussed in Chapter 2. Both are respectively measured by Ratios 1 and 2 from equation (2.7).

7 Interestingly, most studies indicate that productivity benefits are greatest when employment conditions are based on collective enterprise arrangements rather than individually negotiated contracts. Regrettably, the latter are becoming part and parcel of the industrial relations landscape of most countries.

8 Although one would not want to downplay the significance of relative income shares across the total population, not enough attention is given to the distribution of wealth,

which, in most nations, is far more unequal than the distribution of income (ABS, 1995; EPAC, 1995; Davy, 1996; ABS, various).

9 The IMPEX system of exchange rate management is 'protectionist' in the sense that it protects hard-won social and environmental standards. However, it does not protect inefficient industries. The question that is often posed when measures are taken by wealthy nations to protect social and environmental standards is: would it not allow rich countries to stay rich and keep the Third World poor? Consider what Daly has said about the internalisation of social and environmental standards into the prices of foreign goods: to wit, 'Granted this makes it harder for poor countries to export – so does a minimum wage and the existence of free labour unions and the outlawing of child labour within the poor country. In my view it is not all bad to make it harder for poor countries to export to countries like the USA. That means that instead of planting all their land in bananas or fancy fruits and lowers for export, the poor country might have to plant more rice and beans for its own citizens. And to sell the rice and beans to its own citizens, it will have to worry about their purchasing power – about domestic jobs and decent wages, and the distribution of income within their country. And they might worry a bit less about cutting wages and social benefits in order to be more competitive in the global market, as they must do in the export-led model of development to which the IMF and WTO are so totally committed. Admittedly, less export revenue will be available to buy expensive toys for elite, but even that might not be all that bad. Maybe they will begin to invest some of their surplus in their own country.' Taken from an internet seminar on Daly's (1996) book entitled *Beyond Growth*. See http://csf.colorado.edu/seminars/daly97/proceedings.

10 It has been shown that an indiscriminate fiscal policy stance can lead to an undesirable dynamic characterised by periodic phases of demand–pull inflation and induced cost–push inflation at low rates of unemployment. To bring the dynamic under control, a contractionary policy must be instituted that can increase the unemployment rate beyond its original level (Cowling *et al.*, 2006).

11 Real money balances, or the real money supply, are measured by the nominal money supply (M) divided by the general price level (P). That is, the real money supply equals M/P. The higher the rise in the general price level, the greater the decline in the real money supply.

12 The NAIRU differs from the natural rate of unemployment referred to in Chapter 1. The natural rate arises as a consequence of people moving between jobs or because of an imbalance between the location and skills of the unemployed and those of the jobs on offer. It is a rate of unemployment independent of the rate of price inflation. The NAIRU, on the other hand, exists entirely in the context of a non-accelerating rate of price inflation. It is therefore possible for the NAIRU to exist at an unemployment rate at which structural unemployment is quite prevalent. In most cases, the NAIRU is slightly higher than the natural rate of unemployment.

13 Virtually all people contribute to the social product by way of some form of unpaid work. Even 'dropouts' and people who exit the labour market in the presence of a Basic Income Guarantee must engage in the generation of some surplus value to survive or live comfortably. Note, also, that in so-called primitive societies everyone had a crucial role to play and was not 'paid' for their work. They contributed to the social product and were subsequently distributed their entitlement. Although modern societies differ greatly, there remains some requirement on the part of each citizen to generate some surplus value.

14 This would not apply to old-age pensioners and people on disability support payments. These people would still receive the full payment.

15 Although it is not the aim of the Job Guarantee scheme to compete against the private sector for labour, workers are free to quit their private sector job, if dissatisfied with it, and accept a Job Guarantee occupation. This allows the government to indirectly

impose on the private sector a minimum hourly wage and minimum conditions of employment.

16 The NAIRU is typically around 6 per cent of the labour force in most countries.

17 In actual fact, the use of monetary instruments in most countries is conducted by central banks acting independently of the central government. Having said this, central banks invariably perform their monetary policy role with the aim of achieving a desired inflationary target band that is legislatively inscribed in the central bank's charter by the central government. Hence, as much as monetary policy is conducted by central banks, it is merely undertaken by central banks on behalf of central governments.

18 The higher the interest rate, the greater is the opportunity cost of employing cleaner production techniques. See Lawn (2007: ch. 13).

19 Even an emphasis on the delivery of services will not, as Chapter 2 revealed, prevent a rise in the required level of resource use.

20 An increase in aggregate demand is still permissible, even with cap-and-trade systems in place, if a nation's current rate of resource use is well within ecologically sustainable limits.

21 In Chapter 10, it was revealed that CO_2 and energy taxes can induce substantial increases in the real GDP/CO_2 ratio. Overall, however, conventional ETR measures can increase the maintenance efficiency of human-made capital and the growth and exploitative efficiencies of natural capital (Ratios 2–4 from Chapter 2). Any one of these advances can reduce the uncancelled cost of economic activity and, in doing so, shift the UC curve in Figure 2.7 downwards and to the right.

22 A *part-time* job is a job involving fewer hours than the standard working week but with most of the entitlements associated with full-time employment intact, including job permanency. In almost all instances, a *casual* job involves fewer hours than the standard working week but does not involve the permanency or the usual entitlements associated with full-time employment. To offset some of the lost privileges, the hourly wage for a casual job is often slightly higher than for a similar part-time job.

23 One of the other benefits of a Job Guarantee scheme is that allows a government to indirectly implement a progressive industrial relations policy. For example, a government could introduce post-industrial workplace practices (e.g., greater participatory democracy through the devolution of power in the workplace) that would give people the choice between a potentially demeaning but higher-paid job in the private sector and a self-actualising but lower-paid Job Guarantee job. In the same way as the Job Guarantee wage acts as a disincentive for the private sector to pay very low wages, the Job Guarantee scheme can act as a disincentive for the private sector to generate demeaning jobs or introduce draconian workplace practices.

24 When I say that the source of one's income is not important, I am ruling out income from illegal sources or activities involving exploitative workplace practices. Income obtained from rent-seeking behaviour is also of concern given that it constitutes 'unearned' income. Many of the policies recommended in this chapter would significantly limit this last form of income.

25 For more on demogrants and what constitutes a negative income tax and how it might operate, see Fischer *et al.* (1988), Daly and Cobb (1989), and Lawn (2000). During paternity leave, which should also be accessible to anyone with a new-born child, the Basic Income Guarantee would be paid at 100 per cent of the minimum liveable income.

26 The vouchers and food stamps should be non-transferable to prevent people from using them irresponsibly.

27 For example, in poor nations, a minimum liveable income may provide only a few basic necessities of life, whereas, in wealthier nations, it may extend well beyond

this to include some luxury items (non-necessities). In addition, since relative income (relative poverty) is a key welfare issue (Easterlin, 1995), the minimum liveable income could be set in relation to a nation's per capita income or in terms of an order-of-magnitude difference between the eventual minimum income and the average income of people in the highest income quintile.

28 Given that it is still possible for workers in the private sector to be exploited, a government employee-advocate could exist to ensure that the pay and conditions of all private sector workers is at least on a par with the Job Guarantee.

29 Irrespective of the marginal tax rate, the percentage difference in the hourly wage will always be equal to the percentage of the minimum liveable income that the Basic Income Guarantee constitutes.

References

Arthur, W. (1989), 'Competing technologies, increasing returns, and lock-in by historical events', *Economic Journal*, 99, 116–131.

Atkinson, A. (1995), *Public Economics in Action: The Basic Income/Flat Tax Proposal*, Oxford: Clarendon Press.

Australian Bureau of Statistics (ABS) (1995), *National Balance Sheets for Australia: Issues and Experimental Estimates, 1989–1992*, Occasional Paper, AGPS, Canberra.

Australian Bureau of Statistics (ABS) (various), *Income Distribution in Australia*, AGPS, Canberra, Catalogue No. 6523.0.

Baetz, R. (1972), 'The Nuffield Canadian Seminar and after: a personal view', in *Guaranteed Annual Income: An Integrated Approach*, Background papers and proceedings of the Nuffield Canadian Seminar held at Ste-Adele, Quebec, April 12–14, 1972, organized by the Canadian Council on Social Development, Ottawa: Canadian Council on Social Development, pp. 13–39.

Bell, S. and Morse, S. (2008), *Sustainability Indicators: Measuring the Immeasurable?*, 2nd edn, London: Earthscan.

Blandy, R. and Brummitt, W. (1990), *Labour Productivity and Living Standards*, Sydney: Allen & Unwin.

Blinder, A. (1987), *Hard Heads, Soft Hearts*, New York: Addison-Wesley.

Buchanan, J. and Callus, R. (1993), 'Efficiency and equity at work: the need for labour market regulation in Australia', *Journal of Industrial Relations*, 35, 515–527.

Capra, F. (1982), *The Turning Point*, London: Fontana.

Clark, C. and Kavanagh, C. (1996), 'Basic income, inequality, and unemployment: rethinking the linkage between work and welfare', *Journal of Economic Literature*, 30 (2), 399–407.

Costanza, R. and Perrings, C. (1990), 'A flexible assurance bonding system for improved environmental management', *Ecological Economics*, 2, 57–76.

Cowling, S., Mitchell, W., and Watts, M. (2006), 'The right to work versus the right to income', *International Journal of Environment, Workplace and Employment*, 2 (1), 89–113.

Daly, H. (1993), 'The perils of free trade', *Scientific American*, 269, 24–29.

Daly, H. (1996), *Beyond Growth: The Economics of Sustainable Development*, Boston: Beacon Press.

Daly, H. (2008), *Ecological Economics and Sustainable Development: Selected Essays of Herman Daly*, Cheltenham: Edward Elgar.

Daly, H. and Cobb, J. (1989), *For the Common Good: Redirecting the Economy Toward Community, the Environment, and a Sustainable Future*, Boston: Beacon Press.

378   *Lawn*

David, P. (1985), 'Clio and the economics of QWERTY', *American Economic Review*, 75 (2), 332–337.

Davy, G. (1996), 'Some notes on personal share ownership in Australia', Griffith University Mimeo.

Dawkins, P. and Freebairn, J. (1997), 'Towards full employment', *Australian Economic Review*, 30, 405–417.

Dornbusch, R. and Fischer, S. (1990), *Macroeconomics*, 5th edn, New York: McGraw-Hill.

Easterlin, R. (1995), 'Will raising the incomes of all increase the happiness of all?', *Journal of Economic Behavior and Organization*, 27, 35–47.

Economic Planning Advisory Council (EPAC) (1995), 'Income distribution in Australia: recent trends and research', *Commission Paper*, 7, 46–64.

El Serafy, S. (1989), 'The proper calculation of income from depletable natural resources', in Y. Ahmad, S. El Serafy, and E. Lutz (eds), *Environmental Accounting for Sustainable Development*, Washington, DC: World Bank, pp. 10–18.

Estrin, S. (1986), *Profit-Sharing, Motivation and Company Performance: A Survey*, Department of Economics Pamphlet, London School of Economics.

Field, B. (1998), *Environmental Economics: An Introduction*, 2nd edn, New York: McGraw-Hill.

Fischer, S., Dornbusch, R., and Schmalensee, R. (1988), *Economics*, 2nd edn, New York: McGraw-Hill.

Gintis, H. (1997), 'Review of *Real Freedom for All* by Philippe Van Parijs', *Journal of Economic Literature*, 35, 181–182.

Hancock, K. (1987), 'Regulation and deregulation in the Australian labour market', *Australian Bulletin of Labour*, 13, 94–107.

Harrison, B. and Bluestone, B. (1990), 'Wage polarisation in the US and the flexibility debate', *Cambridge Journal of Economics*, 14, 351–373.

Heyes, A. (2000), 'A proposal for the greening of the textbook macro: IS–LM–EE', *Ecological Economics*, 32, 1–7.

Hicks, J. (1946), *Value and Capital*, 2nd edn, London: Clarendon.

Hirsch, F. (1976), *The Social Limits to Growth*, London: Routledge & Kegan Paul.

Hussen, A. (2000), *The Principles of Environmental Economics: Economics, Ecology and Public Policy*, London: Routledge.

Kolstad, C. (2000), *Environmental Economics*, New York: Oxford University Press.

Lawn, P. (2000), *Toward Sustainable Development: An Ecological Economics Approach*, Boca Raton, FL: CRC Press.

Lawn, P. (2004), 'Reconciling the policy goals of full employment and ecological sustainability', *International Journal of Environment, Workplace and Employment*, 1 (1), 62–81.

Lawn, P. (2007), *Frontier Issues in Ecological Economics*, Cheltenham: Edward Elgar.

Lawn, P. (2008), 'Macroeconomic policy, growth, and biodiversity conservation', *Conservation Biology*, 22 (6), 1418–1423.

Miller, P. (1994), 'Wage subsidies', *Economic and Labour Relations Review*, 5, 1–10.

Mitchell, W. (2000), *The Job Guarantee and Inflation Control*, Centre of Full Employment and Equity Working Paper 00-01, January.

Mitchell, W. (2001), *The Unemployed Cannot Search for Jobs that Are Not There!*, Centre of Full Employment and Equity Working Paper 01-07, August.

Mitchell, W. and Mosler, W. (2001), *Fiscal Policy and the Job Guarantee*, Centre of Full Employment and Equity Working Paper 01-09, August.

Mitchell, W. and Muysken, J. (2008), *Full Employment Abandoned: Shifting Sands and Policy Failures*, Cheltenham, UK: Edward Elgar.

Mitchell, W. and Watts, M. (1997), 'The path to full employment', *Australian Economic Review*, 30, 436–444.

Mitchell, W. and Watts, M. (2001), *Addressing Demand Deficient Unemployment: The Job Guarantee*, Centre of Full Employment and Equity Working Paper 01-05, June.

Modigliani, F. (2000), 'Europe's economic problems', *Carpe Oeconomiam Papers in Economics*, Third Monetary and Finance Lecture, Freiburg, 6 April.

Pearce, D. and Turner, R. (1990), *Economics of Natural Resources and the Environment*, London: Harvester Wheatsheaf.

Pigou, A. (1932), *The Economics of Welfare*, London: Macmillan & Co.

Pitcher, T. and Hart, P. (1982), *Fisheries Biology*, London: Chapman & Hall.

Røpke, I. (1994), 'Trade, development, and sustainability – a critical assessment of the free trade dogma', *Ecological Economics*, 9, 13–22.

Saunders, P. (2002), 'The impact of unemployment on poverty, inequality, and social exclusion', in P. Saunders and R. Taylor (eds), *The Price of Prosperity – the Economic and Social Costs of Unemployment*, Sydney: UNSW Press, pp. 175–193.

Tcherneva, P. (2003), *Job or Income Guarantee?*, Center for Full Employment and Price Stability Working Paper, No. 29, August, University of Missouri–Kansas City.

Tcherneva, P. (2006), 'Universal assurances in the public interest: evaluating the economic viability of Basic Income and Job Guarantees', *International Journal of Environment, Workplace and Employment*, 2 (1), 69–88.

Van Parijs, P. (1991), 'Why surfers should be fed: the liberal case for an unconditional Basic Income', *Philosophy and Public Affairs*, 20, 101–131.

Van Parijs, P. (2000), 'A Basic Income for all', *Boston Review*, October–November, 4–8.

Webster, E. (1997), *Labour Market Programmes: A Review of the Literature*, Melbourne Institute of Applied Economic and Social Research Working Paper 23 (97), University of Melbourne.

Weitzman, M. (1984), *The Share Economy*, Cambridge, MA: Harvard University Press.

Wilson, E. O. (2002), *The Future of Life*, New York: Alfred A. Knopf.

Index